US Warships of World War II

U.S.S. Franklin (CVI3), 21st February 1944, as completed. Note outboard elevator on port side

FRONT COVER

The U.S.S. Franklin (CVI3). She was badly damaged and 724 of her crew were killed in a spectacular fire caused by enemy bombing off the Japanese coast on 19th February, 1945.

US Warships
of
World War II

PAUL H. SILVERSTONE

**Naval
Institute
Press**

Grateful acknowledgments are made to the United States
Navy Department for all official photographs used in this
book, excepting those in the U.S. Coastguard section,
which are official United States Coastguard photographs.

First published 1965
Reprinted 1989

Published and distributed in the United States
of America by the Naval Institute Press,
Annapolis, Maryland 21402

Library of Congress Catalog Card No. 88-64139

ISBN 0-87021-773-9

Manufactured in Great Britain

CONTENTS

U.S.S. Maryland (BB46) following U.S.S. Tennessee (BB43) in mid-Pacific, November 1943. Originally near sisters, note difference in beam and silhouette.

INTRODUCTION

TWENTY years ago, in 1945, the United States Navy was at the greatest strength of its history. The Navy List contained over 3,600 named vessels of a bewildering variety of types from battleships to tugs, plus thousands of unnamed craft, bearing numbers only, such as landing ships and subchasers. In addition there were the ships of the Coast Guard which were under Navy control.

This vast armada had grown from the pre-war navy whose ships of varying age formed the nucleus of the victorious fleets of World War II. By 1945, many of the older ships had been replaced on the front line by modern craft, of greater speed and more versatile, with heavy anti-aircraft protection; ships which operated to new concepts, carrier task forces and amphibious fleets replacing the old line of battleships which symbolized the more limited uses of the old navy. The vast distances of the Pacific Ocean in which the fleets operated caused an enormous expansion of the auxiliary fleet, freeing the fighting ships from their bases and then bringing the bases along with the advance.

This book lists and describes the Navy and Coast Guard ships of the Second World War. All named ships on the navy list in 1941 are included, together with those ordered or acquired during the war, even though some of these were not eventually built. Vessels built under lend-lease for foreign navies have been noted but not included by name.

The details given for the various classes are for the year 1941 or as completed, for later ships. Changes occurring during the war are given in the notes below. Insofar as possible, all questions have been resolved by reference to official publications.

Displacement given is standard light tonnage.

Dimensions are waterline and overall length, maximum beam, and mean draft at standard displacement.

Machinery includes the number of propellor shafts and type of engines, horsepower and speed as designed.

Armor shows maximum thicknesses only.

Armament includes guns, torpedo tubes, mines and aircraft carried. The notation (4 × 3) indicates four triple turrets or mounts. Armament given is that authorized; ships were not always up to full strength. Except for smaller craft, guns of a caliber less than 40 mm. are not given.

Complement figures are approximate war strength.

The tabular lists show in successive columns the official naval number (as explained on p. 391); name and names prior to launching or acquisition; builder of hull and machinery, if different; and fate, including changes of name and flag. The former names given are generally navy names except for acquired vessels in which case only the most recent former merchant name is given. The term " discarded " indicates the ship was removed from the navy list and further disposition is unavailable (such ships were often laid up in reserve merchant fleets for years). " Returned " indicates the ship was returned to its original owners and resumed its former merchant name. Because of space limitations, ships' histories have not usually been followed after the first postwar merchant name.

Wartime alterations and details of major ships' war histories are given in the Notes. The " campaigns " noted are terms for overall operations, brief details of which are given in the Chronology (p. 9). In this connection, the term Marianas indicates service at all three operations: landings on Saipan and Guam and the Battle of the Philippine Sea. The term " Pacific Raids " indicates service during that year as a unit of carrier task forces which carried out major raids on enemy bases. Details of war losses are to be found in a separate section.

The pictures have been selected with care, using as much as possible wartime pictures which have not previously appeared in a popular work.

All pictures, except where noted, are Official U.S. Navy Photographs.
The author acknowledges with appreciation the use of the following works:
U.S. Navy, *Ships' Data, U.S. Naval Vessels* (various editions).
Jane's Fighting Ships (various editions).
Fahey, James C., *Ships and Aircraft of the U.S. Fleet* (various editions).
Morison, Samuel Eliot, *History of U.S. Naval Operations in World War II* (volumes 1-15).
Roscoe, Theodore, *U.S. Destroyer Operations in World War II* (1953); *U.S. Submarine Operations in World War II* (1949).
Willoughby, Malcolm F., *U.S. Coast Guard in World War II* (1957).
U.S. Navy, *U.S. Naval Chronology, World War II* (1955); *U.S. Navy and Marine Corps Awards Manual* (Revised ed., 1953); *Dictionary of American Naval Fighting Ships* (volumes I-II, A-F, 1959-63).

Last, but certainly not least, the author wishes to extend his thanks to Lieutenant-Commander F. A. Prehn, U.S.N. and Lieutenant-Commander D. M. Cooney, U.S.N., of the Office of Information, Department of the Navy, and Lieutenant-Commander Adrian L. Lonsdale, U.S.C.G., for their kind and most useful assistance in obtaining information and photographs; Water Barbash lately of the photographic division of the National Archives in Washington; Andrew D. Heineman for all his needed and most helpful comments and corrections, Robert S. Weinberg, William H. Davis, H. T. Lenton and J. J. Colledge, and the World Ship Society and the Belgian Nautical Research Association.

New York, 1965.   PAUL H. SILVERSTONE

CHRONOLOGY OF WORLD WAR II

(With emphasis on the events of the Pacific War)

September 1, 1939. **START OF WORLD WAR II:** Germany invaded Poland. On *September 6* U.S. Navy commenced its Neutrality Patrol to guard Atlantic coast.

May 20, 1940. "Two-Ocean Navy." 1,325,000 tons of new construction in major combatant vessels ordered.

September 2, 1940. Fifty destroyers to be transferred to R.N. in exchange for bases in 6 British American colonies.

September 22, 1940. Japanese troops occupied French Indo-China. The war in China, which commenced in 1937, continued, as Japanese military preparations increased alarmingly.

April 10, 1941. First action against German forces by U.S.N.: unsuccessful attack on U-boat by destroyer NIBLACK. On *July 7*, U.S. troops landed in Iceland. Attitude of war increased with attack by U-boat on destroyer GREER on *September 4*, and damaging of KEARNY by U-568 on *October 17*. On *October 31*, U-562 sank destroyer REUBEN JAMES, first U.S. warship lost.

December 7, 1941. **OUTBREAK OF WAR IN THE PACIFIC.** Japanese carrier planes attacked Pearl Harbor causing heavy damage to U.S. battle fleet. This was followed up the next day by landings in the Philippines, Guam and Malaya. The U.S. garrison on tiny Wake Island surrendered on *December 23* after a heroic defense. On *December 10* Japanese aircraft sank the H.M.S. PRINCE OF WALES and REPULSE. Japanese successes continued with the fall of Hong Kong on *December 25*, Manila on *January 2, 1942* and culminating in the capture of Singapore on *February 15*.

February 27, 1942. Mixed Allied fleet routed by Japanese force in **Battle of the Java Sea;** two cruisers and three destroyers sunk. Remaining ships fled for Australia during the following week, but many were sunk south of Java. On *February 19* the Japanese fleet made its most southerly incursion with a carrier attack on Port Darwin, Australia.

The remaining U.S. forces in the Philippines fought a desperate rear-guard action after the departure of General MacArthur on *March 11*. On *April 9* forces on the Bataan Peninsula, Luzon, surrendered, and on *May 6* Corregidor Island in Malila Bay was captured.

March 18, 1942. U.S. Naval task force joined the British Home Fleet. During *April*, carrier WASP made two trips ferrying R.A.F. fighter aircraft to Malta.

April 5, 1942. Japanese carrier force in Indian Ocean attacked Ceylon, British carrier and two cruisers sunk.

April 18, 1942. Tokyo bombed by U.S. Army bombers launched from carrier HORNET.

May 4-8, 1942. Japanese thrust to the South halted in the **Battle of the Coral Sea,** the first naval battle to be fought entirely in the air. Japanese lost carrier SHOHO; U.S. carriers LEXINGTON sunk and YORKTOWN badly damaged.

June 4-6, 1942. Japanese landing on Midway thwarted in the **Battle of Midway,** the turning point of the Pacific War. Japan crippled by loss of carriers AKAGI, KAGA, HIRYU and SORYU and many experienced carrier pilots. U.S. carrier YORKTOWN, hurriedly repaired after the Coral Sea, lost, but

Japan remained on the defensive from this time. Simultaneous attack on Dutch Harbor, Alaska, was also repelled, but Attu and Kiska in the Aleutians were captured.

August 7, 1942. First American offensive began with landings in the Solomon Islands on Guadalcanal and Tulagi. These landings set off a series of surface actions fought at night in the waters around Guadalcanal as the Japanese attempted to repel the Americans. The success of the Japanese 24 in. torpedo was noteworthy in these actions. The most important follow: **Battle of Savo Island** *August 9*, three U.S. and an Australian cruiser sunk in surprise Japanese attack on the landing force. Aerial **Battle of the Eastern Solomons,** second major attempt by Japanese resulting in loss of carrier RYUJO, *August 24.* On *September 15*, U.S. carrier WASP sunk and battleship NORTH CAROLINA damaged by Japanese submarines. *October 26*, aerial **Battle of Santa Cruz.** U.S. carrier HORNET sunk, leaving ENTERPRISE the only U.S. carrier in service in the Pacific. *November 12-15*, **Battle of Guadalcanal,** a succession of night battles constituting one of the decisive battles of the Pacific war. Japanese lost battleships HIYEI and KIRISHIMA, a cruiser and three destroyers in their last major attempt to repel U.S. forces on Guadalcanal. U.S. losses were two cruisers and eight destroyers. *November 30*, **Battle of Tassafaronga,** an American cruiser sunk and three seriously damaged in the last major battle of the Campaign. Japanese resistance on Guadalcanal continued until *February 9, 1943.*

November 8, 1942. Allied landings in Morocco and Algeria.

March 2, 1943. U.S. and Australian aircraft destroyed large Japanese convoy carrying reinforcements to New Guinea in the **Battle of the Bismarck Sea.**

March 5, 1943. Entry of escort groups into the Atlantic War.

March 26, 1943. **Battle of the Komandorski Islands,** cruiser action in the North Pacific. In *May*, Attu was recaptured.

June 8, 1943. Japanese battleship MUTSU destroyed by magazine explosion.

June 30, 1943. Moving up the Solomon Islands chain, Americans landed on Rendova and New Georgia. Japanese counter-attack repelled at the **Battle of Kula Gulf,** *July 6*, with loss of one U.S. cruiser. Japanese again repelled, *July 13*, but three Allied cruisers were damaged in **Battle of Kloombangara.** On *August 6*, three Japanese destroyers were sunk in **Battle of Vella Gulf.**

July 10, 1943. Allied landings in Sicily, followed by landings at Salerno, *September 9*. Surrender of Italy, *September 3*.

November 1, 1943. Landings on Bougainville, northernmost of Solomons. Japanese defeated in night attempt to repel landings in **Battle of Empress Augusta Bay.**

November 20, 1943. Action moved from the Solomons with landings in the Gilbert Islands on Makin and Tarawa.

January 31, 1944. Landings in Marshall Islands on Kwajalein, Roi and Namure, and on Eniwetok on *February 17*.

February 17-18, 1944. First major carrier attack on Truk, Japanese bastion in Caroline Islands.

April 22, 1944. The " island-hopping " campaign began in earnest as American forces broke out of the Solomons with landings at Hollandia, New Guinea.

June 6, 1944. Allied landings in France.

June 15, 1944. Advancing into the Central Pacific, American forces landed on Saipan in the Marianas. Japanese made a major attempt to destroy the American fleet, but were defeated in the **Battle of the Philippine Sea,** losing carriers TAIHO, SHOKAKU and HIYO and 92% of their carrier planes. On *July 21,* American forces returned to Guam.

August 15, 1944. Allied landings in Southern France.

September 15, 1944. Landings in Palau Islands, on Peleliu and Angaur.

October 20, 1944. American forces returned to the Philippines, landing on Leyte. A three-pronged attack by main Japanese fleet was repelled in the **Battle of Leyte Gulf,** spelling the end of the Japanese fleet as an effective fighting force. Battleships MUSASHI, FUSO, YAMASHIRO, carriers ZUIKAKU, CHITOSE, CHIYODA, ZUIHO, ten cruisers and nine destroyers were sunk. The battle in Surigao Strait proved to be the last surface action fought between battleships, although most enemy losses were caused by air attack. U.S. lost carrier PRINCETON, two escort carriers and three destroyer types. During *November-December 1944,* many air and surface actions were fought around Ormoc Bay on the west coast of Leyte, as Japanese made desperate efforts to retain control of the island.

November 21, 1944. Japanese battleship KONGO sunk by U.S. submarine SEALION. On *November 29,* ARCHERFISH sank carrier SHINANO, largest in the world, while on her trials. On *December 19,* REDFISH sank the carrier UNRYU.

January 9, 1945. American forces landed on Luzon in Lingayen Gulf. Start of attacks by suicide planes (*Kamikaze*).

January-March 1945. Fast carrier task forces roam the Pacific, bombarding at will Japanese forces on the Asiatic mainland from Indo-China to China, and finally, on *February 16,* Tokyo and other Japanese cities.

February 19, 1945. Landings on Iwo Jima. Sustained *Kamikaze* attacks on U.S. fleet.

April 1, 1945. Landings on Okinawa. During April and May, *Kamikaze* attacks caused the U.S. Navy's heaviest losses in any campaign, 28 ships sunk and 131 damaged, 4,900 men killed and missing. On *April 7,* Japanese force led by battleship YAMATO, without sufficient fuel to return to Japan, was destroyed by air attack before reaching the invasion fleet.

May 1, 1945. Australians landed on Borneo at Balikpapan. On *June 10,* further landings were made at Brunei.

July 1945. Heavy carrier attacks, almost daily, made on Japan by U.S. and British task forces. Battleships and cruisers bombarded towns on Honshu. Remainder of Japanese fleet was destroyed, including battleships ISE, HYUGA, HARUNA and carrier AMAGI.

August 6, 1945. First atomic bomb exploded over Hiroshima.

August 15, 1945. **Hostilities ended.** Cease fire signed aboard battleship MISSOURI in Tokyo Bay, *September 2.*

11

DISTRIBUTION OF THE FLEET
7 December 1941

PACIFIC FLEET

Pearl Harbor, Hawaii: BB WEST VIRGINIA, PENNSYLVANIA, CALIFORNIA, TENNESSEE, MARYLAND, NEVADA, ARIZONA, OKLAHOMA; CA NEW ORLEANS, SAN FRANCISCO; CL PHOENIX, HELENA, HONOLULU, ST. LOUIS, RALEIGH, DETROIT.

En route to Midway Island: CV LEXINGTON; CA CHICAGO, PORTLAND, ASTORIA.

Returning to Pearl Harbor: CV ENTERPRISE; CA NORTHAMPTON, CHESTER, SALT LAKE CITY.

At sea, south of Oahu: CA MINNEAPOLIS.

Johnston Island: CA INDIANAPOLIS.

escort duty: CA PENSACOLA, LOUISVILLE.

Philippine & Borneo Area: CA HOUSTON; CL BOISE, MARBLEHEAD.

San Diego, Cal.: CV SARATOGA; CL CONCORD.

Off coast of South America: CL TRENTON (Panama), RICHMOND (Peru).

Bremerton, Wash.: BB COLORADO (Overhaul).

ATLANTIC FLEET

BB *NEW MEXICO, *IDAHO, *MISSISSIPPI, NEW YORK, TEXAS, ARKANSAS, *NORTH CAROLINA, WASHINGTON.

CV *WASP, *YORKTOWN, RANGER, *HORNET, CVE LONG ISLAND.

CA WICHITA, AUGUSTA, TUSCALOOSA, *VINCENNES, *QUINCY.

CL BROOKLYN, SAVANNAH, NASHVILLE, PHILADELPHIA.

South Atlantic: CL MILWAUKEE, OMAHA, CINCINNATI, MEMPHIS.

* transferred to Pacific, Jan-June 1942.

NEW CONSTRUCTION, 1925-1945

Program	Battleships and Carriers	Cruisers	Destroyers	Submarines	Misc.
1925		CA.24–25		SS.167–8	PR.3–8
1927		CA.26–31			
1929		CA.32–36		SS.169	
1930	CV.4	CA.38			
1931		CA.37	DD.348–55	SS.170–1	
1933	CV.5–6	CA.39, 44 CL.40–43	DD.356–379	SS.172–175	PG.50–51
1934		CA.45 CL.46–48	DD.380–393	SS.176–181	
1935	CV.7	CL.49–50	DD.394–408	SS.182–187	
1936			DD.409–420	SS.188–193	
1937	BB.55–56		DD.421–428	SS.194–197	AD.14 AV.4
1938	BB.57–60	CL.51–54	DD.429–436	SS.198–203	CM.5 AM.55–56 AV.5 AVP.10–13 AR.5, AD. 15 AS.11
1939	BB.61–62 CV.8		DD.437–444	SS.204–211	
1940	BB.63–71 CV.9–19 CB.1–6	CL.55–67 CL76–100 CA.68–75	DD.453–648	SS.212–284	CM.6–7 AM.57–65 AV.7, 11–13 AVP 21–32 AR.6–8 AS.12, 15–19 AN.1–4
1941	CV.20–21	CL.101–102	DD.649–664 DE.1–50	SS.285–307	AM.82–131 AD.17–19
1942	CV.22–41 CVE.55–104	CA.122–143 CL.103–118	DD.665–808 DE.51–800	SS.308–434	AM.132–350 PF.1–98

Program	Battleships and Carriers	Cruisers	Destroyers	Submarines	Misc.
1943	CV.42–49 CVE.105–119	CA.148–149 CL.119–121 CL.144–147	DD.809–890 DE.801–1005	SS.435–544	AM.351–390 PF.99–102
1944	CV.50–55 CVE.120–127				
1945	CV.56–57 CVE.128–139	CA.150–153	DD.891–926	SS.545–550	AM.391–420

BATTLESHIPS

In 1941, the United States Navy included 17 battleships, of which only two were of a post-World War I design. Three (ARKANSAS, TEXAS and NEW YORK) were veterans of service with the Grand Fleet in 1917-18. All the older ships had been built with the distinctive cage masts, but by 1941 only five still retained them. Extensive rebuilding had been carried out on the older vessels between 1925 and 1934.

In the late thirties, new battleships were planned with specific attention being given to anti-aircraft protection. Thicker armored decks and modern anti-aircraft guns were included, although the latter proved to be completely inadequate and were greatly increased in number and effectiveness during the war. The new ships, compact in appearance with their control towers and funnels grouped in pyramidal style, contrasted strongly with the scattered silhouettes presented by the older ships.

During the war, the pre-war ships all had their masts cut down or removed, and were otherwise greatly changed by the addition of radar and A.A. guns. Many of them had been fitted, by 1945, with standard 5 in. dual-purpose guns in twin turrets in place of their old secondary armament amidships. Twin and quadruple 20 mm. and 40 mm. A.A. guns were placed wherever space could be found. The use of scouting aircraft by battleships became more and more unnecessary as greater use was made of radar and carrier planes. Nevertheless, aircraft and catapults were still carried at the end of the war.

Of the nine battleships with the Pacific Fleet, eight were at Pearl Harbor when the Japanese attacked the base on December 7, 1941. ARIZONA, OKLAHOMA,

WEST VIRGINIA, and CALIFORNIA were sunk, NEVADA beached, and PENNSYLVANIA, MARYLAND, and TENNESSEE less seriously damaged. All except the first two eventually rejoined the fleet, three having been completely rebuilt.

In the Atlantic were the new NORTH CAROLINA and WASHINGTON, the three NEW MEXICO'S and the three oldest ships. In 1942, WASHINGTON joined the British Home Fleet before being transferred to the Pacific, where she and SOUTH DAKOTA showed the worth of the new battleships in the hard-fought Battle of Guadalcanal, sinking the Japanese battleship KIRISHIMA.

As the war progressed, the role of the battleship became one principally of pre-invasion bombardments and protection of the carriers. ARKANSAS, NEW YORK, TEXAS and NEVADA were at Normandy for the former task. In the Pacific, the new battleships teamed up with the fast carrier task forces, while their older sisters supported the landings on Saipan, Leyte, Iwo Jima, Okinawa and others. It was at Leyte that the old battleships had the honor of fighting the last battleship-to-battleship combat in a night battle in Surigao Strait, turning back the Japanese fleet which attempted to attack the landing force.

In 1945, the older battleships were decommissioned, four of them later being used in the target fleet at Bikini for the nuclear tests. At the time of writing, four of the wartime battleships still exist, albeit laid up, the last of their line.

Battleships are named after the states of the United States and are designated by the symbol BB.

BATTLESHIPS

Arkansas

Displacement:	26,100 tons.
Dimensions:	555½ (wl) 562 (oa) × 106¼ × 26 ft.
Machinery:	4-shaft geared turbines, S.H.P. 28,000 = 21 knots.
Armor:	belt 11 in., turrets 12 in.
Armament:	12—12 in. (6 × 2), 16—5 in. (16 × 1), 8—3 in. (8 × 1) A.A. guns; 3 aircraft (1 catapult).
Complement:	1,650.

P. No	Name	Builder	Launched	Fate
BB.33	ARKANSAS	New York Sbdg.	14. 1.11	Expended Bikini atom test 25/7/46.

Notes:—Originally built with two funnels and two cagemasts, she was rebuilt in 1925-27, being converted to oil fuel, losing one funnel and cage mainmast being replaced by tripod aft of " Q " turret. In 1942, the remaining forward cagemast was replaced by a lower tripod. Her original secondary armament of 21—5 in./51 guns had been reduced after **W.W.I**; by 1945 it consisted of 6—5 in./51 10—3 in./50 DP, 36—40 mm. A.A. guns. Sister WYOMING (BB.32) was converted in 1932 to gunnery training ship (AG.17). **W.W.II**: Atlantic 1941, Normandy, S. France, Iwo, Okinawa.

Texas class

Displacement:	27,000 tons.		
Dimensions:	565 (wl) 573 (oa) × 106 × 26 ft.		
Machinery:	2-shaft reciprocating (V.T.E.), S.H.P. 28,100 = 21 knots.		
Armor:	belt 12 in., turrets 14 in.		
Armament:	10—14 in. (5 × 2), 16—5 in. (16 × 1), 8—3 in. (8 × 1) A.A. guns; 3 aircraft (1 catapult).		
Complement:	1,530.		

BB.34	NEW YORK	New York N.Yd.	30.10.12	Bikini target ship (7/46). Sunk 8/7/48.
BB.35	TEXAS	Newport News	18. 5.12	Preserved as relic in Texas (1948).

Notes:—Improved **Arkansas** class with 14 in. guns, they were the last flush-deck battleships until 1941. Rebuilt in 1925–27, they were converted to oil fuel, lost one funnel and both cagemasts were replaced by tripods, the mainmast being moved to aft of " P " turret. Following refit they were slower, bad sea boats and hard to handle in rough weather. Original secondary armament of 21—5 in / 51 guns was reduced after **W.W.I** and again in 1941, when elevation of 14 in. guns was increased. Final secondary armament was 6—5 in./51, 10—3 in./50 DP, 40—40 mm. A.A. guns. **W.W.II:** NEW YORK: Atlantic 1941, N. Africa, Iwo, Okinawa. TEXAS: Atlantic 1941, N. Africa, Normandy, S. France, Iwo, Okinawa.

Oklahoma class

Displacement:	29,000 tons.		
Dimensions:	575 (wl) 583 (oa) × 108 × 27½ ft.		
Machinery:	2-shaft geared turbines except OKLAHOMA reciprocating (V.T.E.), S.H.P. 26,500 = 20½ knots.		
Armor:	belt 13½ in., turrets 18 in.		
Armament:	10—14 in. (2 × 3 & 2 × 2), 12—5 in. (12 × 1), 12—5 in. A.A. guns; 3 aircraft (2 catapults).		
Complement:	2,100.		

BB.36	NEVADA	Bethlehem (Quincy)	11. 7.14	Bikini target ship (7/46). Sunk 31/7/48.
BB.37	OKLAHOMA	New York Sbdg.	23. 3.14	Lost 7/12/41. Sunk en route to shipbreakers, 17/5/47.

Notes:—The first dreadnoughts in the world with " all-or-nothing " protection; also had (2) triple turrets and oil-fired boilers. Extensively rebuilt in 1927–29 when tall tripods replaced cagemasts, secondary armament raised one deck. Bulges were added making these ships unwieldy at low speeds. Originally mounted 21—5 in./51 guns as secondary armament but this was reduced after **W.W.I**; A.A. protection increased 1941. NEVADA was torpedoed and beached at Pearl Harbor, 7/12/41, recommissioned in 12/42 after rebuilding. Old masts removed, lighter foremast installed and prominent funnel cap added; superstructure was rearranged to favor increased arcs of fire for A.A. guns. New secondary armament in twin turrets: 16—5 in./38 DP, 32—40 mm. A.A. guns. **W.W.II:** NEVADA: Pearl Harbor, Attu, Normandy (flag), S. France, Iwo, Okinawa (hit by *Kamikaze* 26/3/45). OKLAHOMA, capsized at Pearl Harbor, was raised in 1944 but not repaired.

Left: U.S.S. Arkansas (BB33), 1943. Note bulges amidships and fire control director on No. 5 turret.

Right: U.S.S. New York (BB34), 15th May 1944.

17

Above: U.S.S. Nevada (BB36), 2nd September 1945. Small tripod mainmast has been replaced.

Below: U.S.S. Pennsylvania (BB38), 28th June 1945. Final appearance showing small tower and pole which replaced large tripod mainmast. Note secondary armament is on one level.

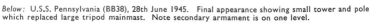

Left: U.S.S. Mississippi (BB41) in North Atlantic grey at Iceland, October, 1941. (I.W.M.

Right: U.S.S. Mississippi (BB41) in dazzle camouflage, 1944. Catapult has been removed from No. 3 turret; funnel cap added.

19

Pennsylvania class

Displacement:	33,100 tons except ARIZONA, 32,600 tons.
Dimensions:	600 (wl) 612¼ (oa) × 106¼ × 29½ ft.
Machinery:	4-shaft geared turbines, S.H.P. 33,375 = 21 knots.
Armor:	belt 14 in., turrets, 18 in.
Armament:	12–14 in. (4 × 3), 12–5 in. (12 × 1), 12–5 in. A.A. guns; 3 aircraft (2 catapults).
Complement:	2,290.

BB.38	PENNSYLVANIA	Newport News: Westing-house	16. 3.15	Bikini target ship 7/46 sunk 10/2/48.
BB.39	ARIZONA	New York N.Yd.	19. 6.15	Lost 7/12/41.

Notes:—Enlarged NEVADA class with two additional 14 in. guns. Were excellent sea boats and very economical. Rebuilt in 1928–31 when tall tripods replaced cagemasts. Original secondary armament of 22—5 in./51 guns reduced after **W.W.I**; A.A. guns increased and radar fitted in 1941. PENNSYLVANIA, for many years flagship of U.S. Fleet, was lightly damaged at Pearl Harbor 7/12/41. During 1942, mainmast was replaced by low mast and pole topmast; old 5 in. guns were replaced by new twin turrets mounted entirely on superstructure deck, and catapult was removed from " X " turret. By 1945, secondary armament was 16 5in./38 DP (8 x 2), 40—40 mm. A.A. guns. 14 in. guns from OKLAHOMA were installed in 1945. **W.W.II**: PENNSYLVANIA: Pearl Harbor, Attu, Gilbert Is., Kwajalein, Eniwetok, Saipan, Guam, Palau, Leyte, Surigao Strait, Lingayen. Damaged by aircraft torpedo 12/8/45.

New Mexico class

Displacement:	33,400 tons except MISSISSIPPI, 33,000 tons.
Dimensions:	600 (wl) 624 except MISSISSIPPI, 625¾ (oa) × 106¼ × 29½ ft.
Machinery:	4-shaft geared turbines, S.H.P. 40,000 = 21¾ knots.
Armor:	belt 14 in., turrets 18 in.
Armament:	12—14 in. (4 × 3), 12—5 in. (12 × 1), 12—5 in. A.A. guns; 3 aircraft (2 catapults).
Complement:	1,930.

BB.40	NEW MEXICO (ex-California)	New York N.Yd.	23. 4.17	Scrapped Newark 11/47.
BB.41	MISSISSIPPI	Newport News	25. 1.17	Experimental gunnery ship (AG.128) 12/45. Scrapped Baltimore 12/56.
BB.42	IDAHO	New York Sbdg.	30. 6.17	Scrapped Newark 12/47. All engined Westinghouse.

Notes:—New type hull form for U.S. battleships with clipper bow, improved compartmentation. Turrets composed entirely of flat plate armor. Completely rebuilt in 1930–34 when all were re-engined with new geared turbines, effecting an increase in speed. NEW MEXICO originally built with electric machinery. Armor was increased, both cagemasts were removed and replaced by increased super-structure, secondary battery raised one deck. Remained the most modern U.S. battleships until completion of NORTH CAROLINA. A.A. batteries increased in 1941. Secondary armament in 1945 included 8—5 in./38 DP (10 in IDAHO) (8 x 1), 40—40 mm. A.A. guns. Proposed installation of 16—5 in. in twin turrets abandoned at end of war. **W.W.II**: all Neutrality Patrol Atlantic 1941. NEW MEXICO: Attu, Gilbert Is., Kwajalein, Saipan, Guam, Lingayen (hit on bridge by *Kamikaze* 6/1/45), Okinawa. MISSISSIPPI: Attu, Gilbert Is., Kwajalein, Palau, Leyte, Surigao Strait, Lingayen, Okinawa. IDAHO: Attu, Gilbert Is., Kwajalein, Saipan, Guam, Palau, Iwo, Okinawa.

California class

| Displacement: | 32,600 tons. |
| Dimensions: | 600 (wl) 624 (oa) × 108 × 30½ ft. |

Left: U.S.S. Idaho (BB42), 3rd January 1944, with single 5 in. turrets amidships. Only Idaho was so armed.

Right: U.S.S. Tennessee (BB43). March 1942, as modified after Pearl Harbor with cage mainmast replaced by small tower. Note catapult atop No. 3 turret; radar on foremast.

Above: U.S.S. Tennessee (BB43), 11th January 1945, as rebuilt.

Below: U.S.S. Colorado (BB45), firing main battery 5th November 1943. She carried light A.A. guns atop stump cage mast.

Above: U.S.S. Colorado (BB45), 9th February 1942. Early appearance before any modernization had taken place, showing both cage masts and catapult atop No. 3 turret.

Below: U.S.S. Maryland (BB46), 26th April 1944, cage mainmast replaced by small tower. She still retains her pre-war secondary armament.

Machinery:	4-shaft turbo-electric drive, S.H.P. 30,000 = 21 knots.
Armor:	belt 14 in., turrets 18 in.
Armament:	12—14 in. (4 × 3), 12—5 in. (12 × 1), 12—5 in. A.A. guns 3 aircraft (2 catapults).
Complement:	2,200.

| BB.43 | TENNESSEE | New York N.Yd.: Westing-house | 30. 4.19 | Scrapped Baltimore 7/59 |
| BB.44 | CALIFORNIA | Mare Is. N.Yd.: G.E. | 20.11.19 | Scrapped Baltimore 1959. |

Notes:—Repeat NEW MEXICO class but distinguished by larger bridge, two smaller funnels and omission of secondary battery recesses in hull. Were not modernised before **W.W.II**. TENNESSEE, slightly damaged at Pearl Harbor, had cage mainmast replaced by small controls in early 1942, was completely rebuilt 1943. Blisters forming almost an additional hull around the original provided greater beam (114 ft.), stability and underwater protection. Cagemasts and funnels were removed and new superstructure similar to SOUTH DAKOTA was built. Modern secondary battery installed. CALIFORNIA, sunk at Pearl Harbor, was similarly rebuilt, recommissioning May 1944. Displacement increased to 37,000 tons; secondary armament: 16—5 in./38 DP (8 x 2), 56—40 mm. A.A. (40 in TENNESSEE) guns. Both ships decommissioned in 1946. **W.W.II:** TENNESSEE: Pearl Harbor, Gilbert Is., Kwajalein, Eniwetok, Saipan, Guam, Palau, Leyte, Surigao Strait, Iwo, Okinawa. CALIFORNIA: Pearl Harbor, Saipan, Guam, Leyte, Surigao Strait, Iwo, Okinawa.

Maryland class

Displacement:	31,500 tons except COLORADO 32,500 tons; WEST VIRGINIA 31,800 tons.
Dimensions:	600 (wl) 624 (oa) × 108 × 30 ft.
Machinery:	4-shaft turbo-electric drive, S.H.P. 31,000 = 21 knots.
Armor:	belt 16 in., turrets 18 in.
Armament:	8—16 in. (4 × 2), 10—5 in. (10 × 1), 8—5 in. A.A. (8 × 1) guns; 3 aircraft (2 catapults).
Complement:	2,100.

BB.45	COLORADO	New York Sbdg.: Westing-house	22. 3.21	Scrapped Seattle 7/59.
BB.46	MARYLAND	Newport News: G.E.	20. 3.20	Scrapped Oakland 8/59.
BB.47	WASHINGTON	New York Sbdg.	1. 9.21	Sunk incomplete as target 25/11/24.
BB.48	WEST VIRGINIA	Newport News G.E.	19.11.21	Scrapped Seattle 1/61.

Notes:—Identical to **Tennessee** class except for main battery. The fourth ship of the class, WASHINGTON was destroyed under the terms of the Naval Washington Treaty, when only 75% complete. These ships were not modernised before **W.W.II** except for increased A.A. protection in 1941. COLORADO and MARYLAND had the cage mainmast cut down in early 1942 and entirely replaced by a small control tower in 1943. Forward cagemast was retained. Secondary armament varied but by 1945 MARYLAND mounted 16—5 in./38 DP (8 x 2), 48—40 mm. A.A. guns; COLORADO, 8—5 in./51, 38—40 mm. A.A. guns. WEST VIRGINIA was torpedoed and sunk at Pearl Harbor, 7/12/41, but was refloated and rebuilt in similar fashion to TENNESSEE and recommissioned in 9/44. Blisters were added to hull enlarging beam to 114 ft.; modern secondary armament was installed, 16—5 in./38 DP (8 x 2), 40—40 mm. A.A. guns. Armor was

U.S.S. West Virginia, burning furiously and listing, and U.S.S. Tennessee (behind), at the height of the attack on Pearl Harbor, 7th December 1941. Particularly note early type radar atop West Virginia's foremast.

Left: U.S.S. Washington (BB56), April 1942, operating with the Home Fleet. (*I.W.M.*)

Right: U.S.S. West Virginia (BB48). October 1944, as rebuilt, rejoining the fleet off the Philippines.

26

Above: U.S.S. North Carolina (BB55), 29th November 1942. Note arrangement of secondary armament on two levels.

Left: U.S.S. South Dakota (BB57) 9th August 1943. Note ridge in hull amidships; only four twin 5in. turrets a side.

27

improved and new fire control added. Displacement increased to 37,800 tons. All three decommissioned in 1946. **W.W.II:** COLORADO: Gilbert Is., Kwajalein, Eniwetok, Saipan, Guam, Leyte, Lingayen, Okinawa. MARYLAND: Pearl Harbor, Gilbert Is., Kwajalein, Saipan (torpedoed 22/6/44), Palau, Leyte (extensive damage by *Kamikaze* 29/11/44), Surigao Strait, Okinawa. WEST VIRGINIA: Pearl Harbor, Leyte, Surigao Strait, Lingayen, Iwo, Okinawa. BB49-54, Scrapped prior to launching in 1922, were to displace 43,200 tons, mount 12-16 in. guns.

North Carolina class

Displacement: 35,000 tons.
Dimensions: 714 (wl) 729 (oa) $\times$ 108$\frac{1}{4}$ $\times$ 26$\frac{3}{4}$ ft.
Machinery: 4-shaft geared turbines, S.H.P. 121,000 = 28 knots.
Armor: belt 16 in., turrets 18 in.
Armament: 9—16 in. (3 $\times$ 3), 20—5 in. DP (10 $\times$ 2), 16—1.1 in. (4 $\times$ 4), A.A. guns; 3 aircraft (2 catapults). *Complement:* 2,500.

BB.55	NORTH CAROLINA	New York N.Yd.: G.E.	13. 6.40	Preserved as relic in North Carolina (1961).
BB.56	WASHINGTON	Philadelphia N.Yd.: G.E.	1. 6.40	Scrapped Newark 10/61.

Notes:—The first U.S. fast battleships with new design features representing a radical departure from the older ships. This class introduced the tower foremast, secondary armament in twin turrets. Main battery featured a new type of 16 in. gun. A.A. armament changed to 60—40 mm. guns (NORTH CAROLINA increased to 96). Both decommissioned in 1947. **W.W.II:** NORTH CAROLINA: N. Atlantic 1941, Guadalcanal landings, Eastern Solomons, Torpedoed by *I-15* 15/9/42. Gilbert Is., Kwajalein, Truk raid, Saipan, Philippine sea, Iwo, Pacific raids 1944-45. WASHINGTON: N. Atlantic 1942 (British Home Fleet), Battle of Guadalcanal, Gilbert Is., Kwajalein, Saipan, Marianas, Palau, Surigao Strait, Iwo, Okinawa, Pacific raids 1943-45.

South Dakota class

Displacement: 35,000 tons.
Dimensions: 666 (wl) 680 (oa) $\times$ 108$\frac{1}{4}$ $\times$ 29$\frac{1}{4}$ ft.
Machinery: 4-shaft geared turbines, S.H.P. 130,000 = 28 knots.
Armor: belt 18 in., turrets 18 in.
Armament: 9—16 in. (3 $\times$ 3), 20—5 in. DP (10 $\times$ 2), 48—40 mm. A.A. guns, except SOUTH DAKOTA, 16—5 in. DP (8 $\times$ 2) 56—40 mm. A.A. guns; 3 aircraft (2 catapults).
Complement: 2,500.

BB.57	SOUTH DAKOTA	New York Sbdg.: G.E.	7. 6.41	Scrapped Kearny 11/62.
BB.58	INDIANA	Newport News: Westinghouse	21.11.41	Scrapped Richmond Cal. 12/63.
BB.59	MASSACHU-SETTS	Bethlehem (Quincy): G.E.	23. 9.41	For Disposal 1962.

28

U.S.S. Massachusetts (BB59) 11th July 1944, with heightened mainmast.

U.S.S. Alabama (BB60) 1st December 1942, as completed.

U.S.S. Iowa (BB61) 12th April 1943, as completed.

Left: U.S.S. New Jersey (BB62), at Ulithi 8th December 1944.

Below: U.S.S. Missouri (BB63). 28th September 1944

U.S.S. Missouri (BB63, right), transferring men to U.S.S. Iowa (BB61) while en route to the landings in Japan, August 1945.

BB.60	ALABAMA	Norfolk N.Yd.: Westinghouse	16. 2.42	Preserved as relic in Alabama, 1964

Notes:—A very effective class for their displacement. Short length made them extremely maneuverable. Secondary battery mounted one deck higher than in NORTH CAROLINA. Pyramidal superstructure, with funnel faired into tower, rendered visual estimation of the ship as a target difficult. Recess in hull amidships provided for bunker intakes. SOUTH DAKOTA fitted as force flagship; A.A. armament increased to 68—40 mm., MASSACHUSETTS, to 72—40 mm. All decommissioned in 1947. **W.W.II:** SOUTH DAKOTA: Santa Cruz (damaged), Battle of Guadalcanal (damaged), British Home Fleet 1943, Gilbert Is., Kwajalein, Truk raid, Hollandia, Saipan, Philippine Sea, Leyte Gulf, Iwo, Okinawa, Pacific raids 1944–45. INDIANA: Gilbert Is., Kwajalein, Marianas, Palau, Iwo, Okinawa, Pacific raids 1943–45. MASSACHUSETTS: N. Africa, Gilbert Is., Kwajalein, Truk raid, Hollandia, Palau, Leyte Gulf, Iwo, Okinawa, Pacific raids 1944–45. ALABAMA: British Home Fleet 1943, Gilbert Is., Kwajalein, Truk raid, Marianas, Palau, Leyte Gulf, Okinawa, Pacific raids 1944–45.

Iowa class

Displacement: 45,000 tons.
Dimensions: 861¼ (wl) 887¼ (oa) × 108¼ × 29 ft.
Machinery: 4-shaft geared turbines, S.H.P. 212,000 = 33 knots.
Armor: belt 19 in., turrets 18 in.
Armament: 9—16 in. (3 × 3), 20—5 in. DP (10 × 2), 80—40 mm. A.A. guns; 3 aircraft (2 catapults).
Complement: 2,700.

BB.61	IOWA	New York N.Yd.: G.E.	27. 8.42	
BB.62	NEW JERSEY	Philadelphia N.Yd.: Westinghouse	7.12.42	
BB.63	MISSOURI	New York N.Yd.: G.E.	29. 1.44	
BB.64	WISCONSIN	Philadelphia N.Yd.: Westinghouse	7.12.43	
BB.65	ILLINOIS	Philadelphia N.Yd.		Cancelled 12/8/45 22% complete.
BB.66	KENTUCKY	Norfolk N.Yd.	20. 1.50	Construction suspended 17/2/47 69.2% complete and scrapped Baltimore 11/58.

Notes:—Largest battleships built by U.S.N. Distinguished by shape of hull lines, long main deck, clipper bow. Reported to be excellent sea boats. **W.W.II:** IOWA: Kwajalein, Truk raid, Hollandia Marianas, Palau, Leyte Gulf, Okinawa, Pacific raids 1944–45. Carried President Roosevelt to Casablanca 1943. NEW JERSEY: Kwajalein, Truk raid, Marianas, Leyte Gulf (flag), Iwo, Okinawa, Pacific raids 1944–45. MISSOURI: Iwo, Okinawa, Pacific raids 1945. Japanese surrender signed aboard in Tokyo Bay 2/9/45. WISCONSIN: Leyte, Iwo, Okinawa, Pacific raids 1944–45. Conversion of KENTUCKY to missile ship cancelled. All except MISSOURI decommissioned 1948–50, but recommissioned during Korean War MISSOURI decommissioned 1954, NEW JERSEY 1957, IOWA and WISCONSIN 1958.

Left: U.S.S. Wisconsin (BB64). September 1944.

Below: Model of a Montana class battleship.

Montana class

Displacement: 60,500 tons.
Dimensions: 890 (wl) 921¼ (oa) × 121¼ × 36 ft.
Machinery: 4-shaft geared turbines, S.H.P. 172,000 = 28 knots.
Armament: 12—16 in. (4 × 3), 20—5 in. (10 × 2), 32—40 mm. (8 × 4)
A.A. guns.

BB.67	MONTANA*	Philadelphia N.Yd.		
BB.68	OHIO*	Philadelphia N.Yd.		
BB.69	MAINE*	New York N.Yd.		All cancelled 21/7/43.
BB.70	NEW* HAMPSHIRE	New York N.Yd.		
BB.71	LOUISIANA*	Norfolk N.Yd.		*These ships were never laid down.

BATTLECRUISERS

In the late nineteen-thirties, observing the German **Scharnhorst** class and the reports that Japan planned similar ships, the U.S. Navy designed a vessel between the battleship and cruiser in size and armament. The result was the **Alaska** class of large cruisers. Completion of these ships was deferred to permit building of more needed escort vessels; only two were finally commissioned, joining the Pacific Fleet for the final push against Japan in late 1944.

Alaska class

Displacement: 27,500 tons.
Dimensions: 791 (wl) 808½ (oa) × 91 × 31½ ft.
Machinery: 4-shaft geared turbines, S.H.P. 150,000 = 33 knots.
Armor: belt 9 in., turrets 12¾ in.
Armament: 9—12 in. (3 × 3), 12—5 in. (6 × 2), 56—40 mm. A.A. guns;
4 aircraft (2 catapults). *Complement:* 2,200.

CB.1	ALASKA	New York Sbdg.: G.E.	15. 8.43	Scrapped Newark 7/61.
CB.2	GUAM	,,	21.11.43	Scrapped Baltimore 8/61.
CB.3	HAWAII	,,	3.11.45	Construction suspended 17/2/47 when 82.4% complete. Scrapped Baltimore 1/60.
CB.4	PHILIPPINES	,,		Cancelled 24/6/43.
CB.5	PUERTO RICO	,,		Cancelled 24/6/43.
CB.6	SAMOA	,,		Cancelled 24/6/43.

Notes:—Officially described as *large cruisers*, they follow standard U.S. cruiser design with a battleship's tower foremast and capital ship armament. Very well suited for carrier task force operations but completed relatively late in the war. **W.W.II:** (both) Okinawa, Pacific raids 1945. Both decommissioned in 1946. Conversion of HAWAII to missileship cancelled. CB4—6 were never laid down.

Above: U.S.S. Alaska (CB1), 5th July 1944, as completed. Note catapult below funnel; superfiring 5in. guns above No. 2 turret. [*Robert S. Weinberg*

Below: U.S.S. Guam (CB2) 21st February 1945 at a Pacific anchorage. Observe port catapult swung out below crane.

AIRCRAFT CARRIERS

American carrier-based aviation had its birth with the conversion of the collier JUPITER to an aircraft carrier in 1922. Renamed LANGLEY, she was the laboratory which eventually led to the development of the carrier task force. She remained in service until 1937 when she was converted to a seaplane tender. With her flight deck cut down, the old veteran was lost in 1942 during the evacuation of Java.

With the appearance of the LEXINGTON and SARATOGA in 1927, the fleet was able to develop rapidly the new strategy and tactics made possible by aircraft based at sea. During the 1930's, concepts in offense and defense were tested in the vast Pacific, developing the functions of the carrier which were put to use with the outbreak of war in 1941.

It was fortunate that no carriers were in Pearl Harbor at the time of the Japanese attack; the four carriers of the Pacific Fleet were thus available for immediate action, but losses came more quickly than reinforcements from the Atlantic. During 1942, LEXINGTON, YORKTOWN, WASP, and HORNET were lost, while SARATOGA and ENTERPRISE were out of action for varying periods. For the first time naval battles were fought in the air—there were four such battles during the year. For several weeks in late 1942, ENTERPRISE was the only Allied carrier in the Pacific, although she was joined for a short period by H.M.S. VICTORIOUS.

The arrival of the first units of the converted **Independence** and the larger **Essex** classes heralded the coming of the fast carrier task force, the World War II equivalent of the battle fleet of World War I. The carrier was the new capital ship around which the fleet was formed, with anti-aircraft protection provided by battleships, cruisers and destroyers. These magnificent armadas were able to remain at sea for long periods, being supplied by mobile logistics units consisting of oilers, ammunition ships and escort carriers with replacement planes.

In the fall of 1943, ESSEX, with new YORKTOWN and LEXINGTON, and light carriers BELLEAU WOOD, INDEPENDENCE and COWPENS, delivered the first carrier task force attack against major land targets. In November, SARATOGA, ESSEX, BUNKER HILL, INDEPENDENCE and PRINCETON attacked Rabaul and emerged from an all-out attack by defending planes without damage for the first time in the war.

Using improved planes, new anti-aircraft protection and radar, the carriers soon wiped out enemy sea and air forces in the South Pacific and passed on to the next area of operations. Probing more deeply into enemy waters, they moved from the Carolines and Marianas to the Philippines and Ryukyus, then Indo-China, the China coast, Formosa and finally the main islands of Japan itself. Japanese counter-attack was fierce, yet American damage control had improved so greatly that only PRINCETON was lost after 1943, although many carriers were hit and some very extensively damaged. Among the latter should be noted INTREPID, BUNKER HILL and FRANKLIN (which suffered 724 killed in a spectacular fire caused by enemy bombs).

Vast damage was often caused by suicide planes (*Kamikaze*) crashing through the wooden flight decks into the hangar below. Although British carriers could carry fewer planes because of their armor, the steel flight decks showed their worth against *Kamikaze* attack.

The number of aircraft carried aboard a carrier varied according to the types of squadrons making up the air group. **Essex** class ships might have attached as few as 65 or as many as 102 planes at any one time.

U.S. carriers are named after battles or after famous ships of the past, and are designated by the symbol CV (CVL for light carriers).

Island and flight deck of U.S.S. Enterprise (CV6).

Saratoga class

Displacement: 33,000 tons.
Dimensions: 850 (wl) 888 (oa) × 105½ × 24¼ ft.
Machinery: 4-shaft turbo-electric drive, S.H.P. 180,000 = 34 knots.
Armament: 8—8 in. (4 × 2), 12—5 in. A.A. (12 × 1) guns; 90 aircraft.
Complement: 3,300.

CV.2	LEXINGTON	Bethlehem, (Quincy): G.E.	3.10.25	Lost 8/5/42.
CV.3	SARATOGA	New York Sbdg.: G.E.	7. 4.25	Expended, Bikini atom tests, 25/7/46.

Notes:—Laid down as battle cruisers but converted while building following the Washington Naval Treaty. When completed were the largest aircraft carriers in the world, remaining such until **W.W.II**, with high sustained speed and large aircraft capacity. During 1942 SARATOGA'S 8 in. guns were replaced by 5 in. DP. Final armament in 1945 was 16—5 in./38 DP (8 × 2), 96—40 mm. A.A. guns. Flight deck was enlarged giving new dimensions, 901¼ (oa) x 130 ft. (extreme beam). Foremast and funnel cut down, bulge added to port side to complement weight of island. LANGLEY was CVI. **W.W.II:** LEXINGTON: Raids 1942, Coral Sea. SARATOGA: Torpedoed off Hawaii, 11/1/42. Guadalcanal. Torpedoed by *I-26* in Solomons 31/8/42. Eastern Solomons, Bougainville, Gilbert Is., Kwajalein, Eniwetok, Iwo (severely damaged by *Kamikaze* 21/2/45), Pacific raids 1944. British Eastern Fleet 1944.

Ranger

Displacement: 14,500 tons.
Dimensions: 728 (wl) 769 (oa) × 80 × 19¾ ft. (109½ ft. extreme beam.)
Machinery: 2-shaft geared turbines, S.H.P. 53,500 = 29.5 knots.
Armament: 8—5 in. (8 × 1) guns; 86 aircraft.
Complement: 2,000.

CV.4	RANGER	Newport News	25. 2.33	Scrapped Chester, Pa. 2/47.

Notes:—First U.S. carrier built as such from the keel up. Three folding funnels on each side were not satisfactory. Speed was sacrificed for other essentials under treaty limitations, reducing her efficiency as a first-line unit. Flight deck and island built as superstructure and not as part of hull, setting the standard for U.S. carriers. 24—40 mm. A.A. guns added during war. **W.W.II:** Atlantic 1941–44, N. Africa, raid on Norway 10/43. Training 1944–45.

Yorktown class

Displacement: 19,900 tons, except HORNET 20,000 tons.
Dimensions: 761 (wl) 809½ (oa) × 83¼ × 21¾ ft.
Machinery: 4-shaft geared turbines, S.H.P. 120,000 = 34 knots.
Armament: 8—5 in. (8 × 1) guns; 100 aircraft.
Complement: 2,200.

CV.5	YORKTOWN	Newport News	4. 4.36	Lost 7/6/42.
CV.6	ENTERPRISE	Newport News	3.10.36	Scrapped Kearny ⊂
CV.8	HORNET	Newport News	14.12.40	Lost 27/10/42.

Notes:—Enlarged RANGERS with reversion to vented boiler uptakes. Three elevators enclosed by flight deck; mounted only defensive A.A. guns. HORNET was of a slightly di⬤ During the war ENTERPRISE flight deck was enlarged to 827 (oa) x 114ft. (extreme beam) replaced former A.A. guns. As she had participated in nearly every major action in the hoped to preserve ENTERPRISE but this proved impossible. **W.W.II:** YORKTOWN Coral Sea (damaged), Midway. ENTERPRISE: Pearl Harbor (aircraft only), Midwa landings, Eastern Solomons (damaged), Santa Cruz (damaged), Battle of Guadalca Kwajalein, Truk raid, Hollandia, Saipan, Philippine Sea, Palau, Leyte, Iwo, Okinawa (⬤ and 13/4/45), Pacific raids 1942–45 HORNET: Midway, Santa Cruz. Launched A raid on Tokyo 18/4/42.

38

U.S.S. **Lexington** (CV2) October 1941, in war grey. U.S.S. Saratoga had same appearance prior to modification.

U.S.S. Saratoga (CV3) May 1945, showing final appearance. Note new radar mast and sleek cruiser lines.

U.S.S. Ranger (CV4) 1943 with forward elevator lowered and smokepipes in vertical position.

Left: U.S.S. Enterprise (CV6) 11th December 1943.

Right: U.S.S. Hornet (CV8) at Pearl Harbor, May 1942.

40

Left: U.S.S. Wasp (CV7), 1942.

Below: A *Kamikaze* exploding aboard U.S.S. Essex (CV9), 25th November 1944.

Wasp

Displacement:	14,700 tons.
Dimensions:	688 (wl) 741¼ (oa) × 80¾ × 20 ft.
Machinery:	2-shaft geared turbines, S.H.P. 75,000 = 29·5 knots.
Armament:	8—5 in. (8 × 1) guns; 84 aircraft.
Complement:	1,800.

CV.7	WASP	Bethlehem (Quincy)	4. 4.39	Lost 15/9/42.

Notes:—A reversion to a smaller type, this ship was similar to RANGER in hull design but with island as in YORKTOWN. **W.W.II:** Relief of Malta 4/42, Guadalcanal landings.

Essex class

Displacement:	27,100 tons.
Dimensions:	820 (wl) 872 (oa) × 93 × 28½ ft. (147½ ft. extreme beam.)
Machinery:	4-shaft geared turbines, S.H.P. 150,000 = 33 knots.
Armament:	12—5 in. (4 × 2 & 4 × 1), 44/68—40 mm. A.A. guns; 100 aircraft.
Complement:	3,500.

CV.9	ESSEX	⎫	31. 7.42	
CV.10	YORKTOWN (ex-Bon Homme Richard)	⎬ Newport News	21. 1.43	
CV.11	INTREPID	⎰	26. 4.43	
CV.12	HORNET (ex-Kearsarge)	⎱	30. 8.43	
CV.13	FRANKLIN	⎭	14.10.43	AVT 8 (5/59) Discarded 10/64.
CV.16	LEXINGTON (ex-Cabot)	⎫	26. 9.42	
CV.17	BUNKER HILL	⎬ Bethlehem (Quincy)	7.12.42	AVT 9 (5/59).
CV.18	WASP (ex-Oriskany)	⎭	17. 8.43	
CV.20	BENNINGTON	⎫ New York N.Yd.	26. 2.44	
CV.31	BON HOMME RICHARD	⎬	29. 4.44	

All engined Westinghouse.

Notes:—Improved and enlarged version of YORKTOWN, this class became the standard U.S. fleet carrier of the war and made up the core of the fast carrier task forces. Introduced outboard elevator and overhanging flight deck on port side. These ships showed a remarkable ability to survive severe damage and although many were hit none were sunk. Four were renamed for lost carriers prior to launching. **W.W.II:** ESSEX: Bougainville, Gilbert Is., Kwajalein, Truk raid, Marianas, Palau, Leyte Gulf, Iwo, Pacific raids 1943—45. Hit by *Kamikaze* 25/11/44. YORKTOWN: Gilbert Is., Kwajalein, Truk raid, Hollandia, Marianas, Iwo, Pacific raids 1943—45. INTREPID: Kwajalein, Truk raid (torpedoed), Palau, Leyte Gulf, Pacific raids 1944—45. Severely damaged by *Kamikaze* off Luzon 25/11/44 and Okinawa 16/4/45. HORNET: Marianas, Palau, Leyte Gulf, Iwo, Pacific raids 1944—45. FRANKLIN: Guam, Palau, Leyte, Pacific raids 1944—45. Damaged by *Kamikaze* off Luzon 15 and 30/10/44. Severely damaged by bombs off Kyushu 19/3/45. LEXINGTON: Gilbert Is., Hollandia, Marianas, Palau, Leyte Gulf (flag), Iwo, Pacific raids 1943—45. Torpedoed off Kwajalein 4/12/43. Damaged by *Kamikaze* off Luzon 5/11/44. BUNKER HILL: Bougainville, Gilbert Is., Kwajalein, Truk raid, Hollandia, Marianas, Palau, Leyte, Iwo, Pacific raids 1943—45. Severely damaged by *Kamikaze* off Okinawa 11/4/45. WASP: New Guinea, Marianas, Palau, Leyte, Iwo, Pacific raids 1944—45. Damaged by bomb off Kyushu 19/3/45. BENNINGTON: Iwo, Pacific raids 1945. BON HOMME RICHARD: Raids on Japan 1945.

Above: U.S.S. Franklin (CV13) listing and afire off the coast of Japan following enemy bombing attack 19th February 1945. Notice buckled elevator forward, flight deck amidships obscured by smoke.

Left: U.S.S. Bunker Hill (CV17) 28th March 1945, at sea in Okinawa area.

43

U.S.S. Wasp (CVl8) 11th December 1944.

44

U.S.S. Ticonderoga (CV14) 8th December 1944, at Ulithi.

As above, except length 888 (oa) ft., have rounded bows. Flight deck terminated short of bow and stern.

CV.14	TICONDEROGA (ex-Hancock)	Newport News	7. 2.44	
CV.15	RANDOLPH		29. 6.44	
CV.19	HANCOCK (ex-Ticonderoga)	Bethlehem (Quincy)	24. 1.44	
CV.21	BOXER	Newport News	14.12.44	LPH 4 (1/59).
CV.32	LEYTE (ex-Crown Point)		23. 8.45	AVT 10 (5/59).
CV.33	KEARSARGE	New York N.Yd.	5. 5.45	
CV.34	ORISKANY		13.10.45	
CV.35	REPRISAL			Cancelled 11/8/45 when 52.3% complete. Hull sunk as target.
CV.36	ANTIETAM	Philadel- phia N.Yd.	20. 8.44	
CV.37	PRINCETON (ex-Valley Forge)		8. 7.45	LPH 5 (3/59).
CV.38	SHANGRI-LA	Norfolk N.Yd.	24. 2.44	
CV.39	LAKE CHAMPLAIN		2.11.44	
CV.40	TARAWA		12. 5.45	AVT 12 (1961).
CV.45	VALLEY FORGE	Philadelphia N.Yd.	18.11.45	LPH 8 (7/61).
CV.46	IWO JIMA	Newport News		Cancelled 11/8/45.
CV.47	PHILIPPINE SEA (ex-Wright)	Bethlehem (Quincy)	5. 9.45	AVT 11 (5/59).
CV.50	Unnamed.			Cancelled 27/3/45.
CV.51	Unnamed.			Cancelled ,,
CV.52	Unnamed.			Cancelled ,,
CV.53	Unnamed.			Cancelled ,,
CV.54	Unnamed.			Cancelled ,,
CV.55	Unnamed.			Cancelled ,,

All engined Westinghouse.

Notes:—W.W.II: TICONDEROGA: Palau, Leyte, Pacific raids 1944. Severely damaged by *Kamikaze* off Formosa 21/1/45. RANDOLPH: Iwo, Pacific raids 1945. HANCOCK: Philippines, Iwo, Pacific raids 1944–45. Damaged by explosion 21/1/45 and by *Kamikaze* 7/4/45. SHANGRI-LA: Pacific raids 1945. ANTIETAM was present in Tokyo Bay 9/45.

Independence class

Displacement:	11,000 tons.	
Dimensions:	600 (wl) 622½ (oa) × 71½ × 26 ft. (109¼ ft. extreme beam.)	
Machinery:	4-shaft geared turbines, S.H.P. 100.000 = 31.6 knots.	
Armament:	26—40 mm. A.A. guns; 45 aircraft.	
Complement:	1,560.	

CVL.22	INDEPEN- DENCE (ex-Amsterdam, CL.59)	New York Sbdg.: G.E.	22. 8.42	Bikini target ship (7/46) Sunk 30/1/51.
CVL.23	PRINCETON (ex-Tallahassee, CL.61)		18.10.42	Lost 24/10/44.

U.S.S. Independence (CVL22) 1943. Observe cruiser hull.

CVL.24	BELLEAU WOOD (ex-New Haven, CL.76)		6.12.42	French BOIS BELLEAU (9/53); scrapped Chester 1962.
CVL.25	COWPENS (ex-Huntington, CL.77)		17. 1.43	AVT 1 (5/59) scrapped Portland, 1962
CVL.26	MONTEREY (ex-Dayton, CL.78)		28. 2.43	AVT 2 (5/59).
CVL.27	LANGLEY (ex-Crown Point, ex-Fargo, CL.85)	New York Sbdg.: G.E.	22. 5.43	French LA FAYETTE (6/51); scrapped Baltimore, 1964.
CVL.28	CABOT (ex-Wilmington, CL.79)		4. 4.43	AVT 3 (5/59).
CVL.29	BATAAN (ex-Buffalo, CL.99)		1. 8.43	AVT 4 (5/59) Discarded 1959.
CVL.30	SAN JACINTO (ex-Reprisal, ex-Newark, CL.100)		26. 9.43	AVT 5 (5/59).

Notes:—Laid down as CLEVELAND class light cruisers and re-ordered in 3/42 as carriers under the war emergency program. Construction was rushed, the first ship being completed within a year. Highly successful as a conversion, they had the speed of fleet carriers but the deficiencies of escort carriers. Boiler uptakes vented through four funnels angled out on starboard side; small island. Early ships mounted 1—5 in./38 guns; armament later was limited to A.A. Hulls widened during construction. **W.W.II:** INDEPENDENCE: Bougainville, Gilbert Is. (severely damaged by torpedo 20/11/43), Palau, Leyte Gulf, Pacific raids 1943–45. PRINCETON: Bougainville, Gilbert Is., Kwajalein, Eniwetok, Hollandia, Marianas, Palau, Leyte. BELLEAU WOOD: Gilbert Is., Kwajalein, Truk raid, New Guinea, Marianas, Palau, Leyte Gulf. Severely damaged by *Kamikaze* 30/10/44. Iwo, Pacific raids 1943–45. COWPENS: Gilbert Is., Kwajalein, Truk raid, New Guinea, Marianas, Palau, Leyte Gulf, Philippines, Iwo, Pacific raids 1943–45. MONTEREY: Gilbert Is., Kwajalein, Truk raid, New Guinea, Marianas, Palau, Leyte Gulf, Pacific raids 1943–45. LANGLEY: Kwajalein, Eniwetok, Marianas, Palau, Leyte Gulf, Philippines, Iwo, Pacific raids 1944–45. CABOT: Kwajalein, Truk raid, Philippine Sea, Guam, Palau, Leyte Gulf, Philippines, Iwo, Pacific raids 1944–45. Damaged by *Kamikaze* off Luzon 25/11/44. BATAAN: Hollandia, Marianas, Pacific raids 1944–45. SAN JACINTO: Marianas, Palau, Leyte Gulf, Philippines, Iwo, Pacific raids 1944–45.

Midway class

Displacement:	45,000 tons.
Dimensions:	900 (wl) 986 (oa) × 113 × $32\frac{3}{4}$ ft. (136 ft. extreme beam.)
Machinery:	4-shaft geared turbines, S.H.P. 212,000 = 33 knots.
Armament:	18—5 in. A.A. (18 × 1), 84—40 mm. A.A. (21 × 4) guns; 137 aircraft.
Complement:	4,085.

CVB.41	MIDWAY	Newport News: Westinghouse	20. 3.45	
CVB.42	FRANKLIN D. ROOSEVELT (ex-Coral Sea)	New York N.Yd.: G.E.	29. 4.45	

Above: U.S.S. Belleau Wood (CVL24) 22nd December 1943. Note break in hull below forward gun sponsons.

Below: U.S.S. Midway (CVB41) 2nd June 1949, showing 5in. guns ranged along edge of flight deck.

49

CVB.43	CORAL SEA	Newport News: Westing-house	2. 4.46	
CV.44	Unnamed			Cancelled, 11/1/43.
CVB.56	Unnamed			Cancelled, 27/3/45.
CVB.57	Unnamed			Cancelled, 27/3/45.

Notes:—Largest aircraft carriers of their time and first U.S. carriers with armored flight decks. A.A. guns mounted on sponsons below flight deck. Commissioned just too late to see action in W.W.II.

Saipan class

Displacement: 14,500 tons.
Dimensions: 664 (wl) $683\frac{1}{2}$ (oa) $\times 76\frac{3}{4} \times 25$ ft. (115 ft. extreme beam).
Machinery: 4-shaft geared turbines, S.H.P. 120,000 = 33 knots.
Armament: 40—40 mm. A.A. guns; 48 aircraft.
Complement: 1,700.

CVL.48	SAIPAN	New York	8. 7.45	AGMR 2 (1965).
CVL.49	WRIGHT	Sbdg.: G.E.	1. 9.45	CC2 (5/63).

Notes:— WRIGHT converted to command ship 1963; conversion of SAIPAN cancelled and changed to major communications relay ship.

ESCORT CARRIERS

The vast distances of the ocean and the short range of anti-submarine aircraft led to the development of the escort carrier. These ships were converted from merchant hulls by altering interior arrangements and adding a flight deck. Despite their ungainly appearance, their effectiveness in combating U-boats was evident with the entrance of H.M.S. AUDACITY into the convoy war as early as 1941.

With their own aviation, convoys were able to cross the Atlantic with small losses while inflicting heavy losses on the attacking U-boats, a reversal of the previous situation. From the spring of 1943, the result of the Atlantic convoy war was increasingly favorable to the Allies.

The escort carriers, cheaply built and mass-produced, were used for a variety of purposes in the Pacific, supporting landings, supplying the fast carriers and island bases with aircraft as well as anti-submarine warfare. Perhaps one of the most epic sea-fights of the war took place at Leyte Gulf when the lightly-armed escort carrier groups supporting the Philippine invasion fought off the main Japanese battle fleet in a surface action.

Escort carriers were originally designated by the symbol AVG, changed in 8/42 to ACV, changed again in 7/43 to CVE. They are named after bays or World War II battles.

ESCORT AIRCRAFT CARRIERS
Long Island

Displacement: 11,300 tons.
Dimensions: 465 (wl) 492 (oa) $\times 69\frac{1}{2} \times 25\frac{3}{4}$ ft. (102 ft. extreme beam).
Machinery: 1-shaft diesel motors, S.H.P. 8,500 = 18 knots.
Armament: 1—5 in., 2—3 in. (2 $\times$ 1) guns; 21 aircraft.
Complement: 950.

U.S.S. Saipan (CVL48), 2nd November 1946 as completed.

51

P. No.	Name	Builder	Completed	Fate
CVE.1	LONG ISLAND (ex-mercantile Mormacmail)	Sun: Busch-Sulzer	2. 6.41	Mercantile NELLY (1949), SEVEN SEAS (1953).

Notes:—First U.S escort carrier. Conversion carried out similarly to that of LANGLEY in 1920 with flight deck built up on hull. Original flight deck extended only two-thirds of length and was lengthened after completion. No island. Sister to R.N. ARCHER.

Charger

As above, except 11,000 tons, 1—5 in., 4—3 in. (4 × 1), 16—40 mm. A.A. guns.

P. No.	Name	Builder	Completed	Fate
CVE.30	CHARGER (ex-BAVG 4, ex-mercantile Rio de la Plata)	Sun	3. 3.42	Mercantile FAIRSEA (1949).

Notes:—Similar to LONG ISLAND but with small island. Used mainly for training. Three sister ships transferred to R.N.

Bogue class

Displacement: 9,800 tons.
Dimensions: 465 (wl) 495¾ (oa) × 69½ × 23¼ ft. (111½ ft. extreme beam).
Machinery: 1-shaft geared turbines, S.H.P. 8,500 = 18 knots.
Armament: 2—5 in. (2 × 1), 20—40 mm. A.A. guns; 21 aircraft.
Complement: 890.

P. No.	Name	Builder	Launched	Fate
CVE.9	BOGUE (ex-mercantile Steel Advocate)		15. 1.42	Scrapped Japan 11/60.
CVE.11	CARD		21. 2.42	AKV 40 (59/5).
CVE.12	COPAHEE (ex-mercantile Steel Architect)	Seattle-Tacoma (Tacoma): Allis-Chalmers	21.10.41	Scrapped Japan 5/61.
CVE.13	CORE		15. 5.42	AKV 41 (59/5).
CVE.16	NASSAU		4. 4.42	Scrapped Japan 6/61.
CVE.18	ALTAMAHA		22. 5.42	Scrapped Japan 1961.
CVE.20	BARNES		22. 5.42	Scrapped Japan 2/60.
CVE.21	BLOCK ISLAND		6. 6.42	Lost 29/5/44.
CVE.23	BRETON		27. 6.42	AKV 42 (5/59).
CVE.25	CROATAN		3. 8.42	AKV 43 (5/59).
CVE.31	PRINCE WILLIAM		23. 8.42	Scrapped Japan 3/61.

Notes:—Converted from merchant hulls of C–3 type in similar fashion to LONG ISLAND. 26 sister ships transferred to R.N. BLOCK ISLAND, BOGUE, CARD, CORE, and CROATAN were in the Atlantic; remainder in the Pacific.

Left: U.S.S. Long Island (CVE1) 27th April 1944, with cargo and planes stowed on flight deck.

Below: U.S.S. Charger (CVE30).

53

Left: U.S.S. Block Island (CVE21) 12th October 1943.

Right: U.S.S. Sangamon (CVE26), September 1942, as converted. Note paucity of A.A. gun platforms as compared with U.S.S. Suwanee later in the war.

54

Sangamon class

Displacement: 11,400 tons.
Dimensions: 525 (wl) 553 (oa) × 75 × 30½ ft. (114¼ ft. extreme beam).
Machinery: 2-shaft geared turbines, S.H.P. 13,500 = 18.3 knots.
Armament: 2—5 in. 28—40 mm. A.A. guns; 34 aircraft.
Complement: 1,100.

P. No.	Name	Builder	Completed	Fate
CVE.26	SANGAMON (ex-AO.28, ex-mercantile Esso Trenton)—	Federal (Kearny): G.E.	25. 8.42	Mercantile SANGA-MON (1947); scrapped 1960.
CVE.27	SUWANEE (ex-AO.33, ex-mercantile Markay)—		24. 9.42	Scrapped Bilbao 6/62.
CVE.28	CHENANGO (ex-AO.31, ex-mercantile Esso New Orleans)—	Sun: Westing-house	19. 9.42	Scrapped Bilbao 7/62.
CVE.29	SANTEE (ex-AO.29, ex-mercantile Seakay)—		24. 8.42	Scrapped Hamburg 5/60.

Notes:—Converted fleet oilers built in 1939 and acquired in 1940. Had low freeboard amidships, tapered flight deck forward, two elevators. Were used operationally with regular fleet units in 1943 during the shortage of carriers in the Pacific. **W.W.II:** CHENANGO: N. Africa, Gilbert Is., Kwaja-lein, Eniwetok, Saipan, Guam, Leyte, Okinawa. SANGAMON: N. Africa, Gilbert Is., Kwajalein, Eniwetok, Marianas, Leyte, Leyte Gulf, (damaged 25/10/44), Okinawa, (damaged by *Kamikaze* 4/5/45), Pacific raids 1943. SANTEE: N. Africa, Guam, Leyte, (severely damaged 25/10/44), Okinawa. SUWANEE: N. Africa, Gilbert Is., Kwajalein, Eniwetok, New Guinea, Saipan, Leyte (damaged 26/10/44), Okinawa.

Casablanca class

Displacement: 7,800 tons.
Dimensions: 490 (wl) 512¼ (oa) × 65¼ × 19¾ ft. (108 ft. extreme beam).
Machinery: 1-shaft reciprocating, S.H.P. 9,000 = 19¼ knots.
Armament: 1—5 in., 16—40 mm. A.A. guns; 28 aircraft.
Complement: 860.

P. No.	Name	Builder	Launched	Fate
CVE.55	CASABLANCA (ex-Alazon Bay, ex-Ameer)	Kaiser (Van-couver, Wash.): Nordberg	5. 4.43	Scrapped Chester 1947.
CVE.56	LISCOME BAY		19. 4.43	Lost 24/11/43.
CVE.57	CORAL SEA (ex-Alikula Bay)		1. 5.43	Renamed ANZIO (9/44). Scrapped Hamburg 3/60.
CVE.58	CORREGIDOR (ex-Anguilla Bay)		12. 5.43	Scrapped New Orleans 1960.

Above: U.S.S. Suwanee (CVE27 22nd April 1943, anchored at Espiritu Santo, with both elevators lowered.

Below: U.S.S. Guadalcanal (CVE60), with captured German submarine U-505 alongside off the coast of Africa 4th June 1944.

U.S.S. Midway (CVE63) 10th April 1944. Later renamed St. Lo.

57

CVE.59	MISSION BAY (ex-Atheling)		26. 5.43	Scrapped Japan 1/60.
CVE.60	GUADAL-CANAL (ex-Astrolabe Bay)		5. 6.43	Scrapped Japan 1/60.
CVE.61	MANILA BAY (ex-Bucareli Bay)		10. 7.43	Scrapped Japan 2/60.
CVE.62	NATOMA BAY (ex-Begum)		20. 7.43	Scrapped Japan 2/60.
CVE.63	MIDWAY (ex-Chapin Bay)		17. 8.43	Renamed ST. LO (10/44). Lost 25/10/44.
CVE.64	TRIPOLI (ex-Didrickson Bay)	Kaiser (Vancouver, Wash.): Nordberg	2. 9.43	Scrapped Japan 1/60.
CVE.65	WAKE ISLAND (ex-Dolomi Bay)		15. 9.43	Scrapped Baltimore 1947.
CVE.66	WHITE PLAINS (ex-Elbour Bay)		27. 9.43	Scrapped Boston 8/59.
CVE.67	SOLOMONS (ex-Nassuk Bay, ex-Emperor)		6.10.43	Scrapped 1947.
CVE.68	KALININ BAY		15.10.43	Scrapped 1947.
CVE.69	KASAAN BAY		24.10.43	Scrapped Hamburg 3/60.
CVE.70	FANSHAW BAY		1.11.43	Scrapped Portland 1959.
CVE.71	KITKUN BAY		8.11.43	Scrapped 1947.
CVE.72	TULAGI (ex-Fortaleza Bay)		15.11.43	Scrapped 1947.
CVE.73	GAMBIER BAY		22.11.43	Lost 25/10/44.
CVE.74	NEHENTA BAY (ex-Khedive)		28.11.43	Scrapped Hong Kong 6/60.
CVE.75	HOGGATT BAY		4.12.43	Scrapped Bilbao 5/60.
CVE.76	KADASHAN BAY		11.12.43	Scrapped Hong Kong 6/60.
CVE.77	MARCUS ISLAND (ex-Kanalku Bay)		16.12.43	Scrapped Japan 6/60.
CVE.78	SAVO ISLAND (ex-Kaita Bay)		22.12.43	Scrapped Hong Kong 6/60.
CVE.79	OMMANEY BAY		29.12.43	Lost 4/1/45.
CVE.80	PETROF BAY		5. 1.44	Scrapped Antwerp 9/59.
CVE.81	RUDYERD BAY		12. 1.44	Scrapped Genoa 1960.
CVE.82	SAGINAW BAY		19. 1.44	Scrapped Rotterdam 4/60.
CVE.83	SARGENT BAY		31. 1.44	Scrapped Antwerp 9/59.
CVE.84	SHAMROCK BAY		4. 2.44	Scrapped Hong Kong 11/59.

Above: The destruction of U.S.S. St. Lo (CVE63) at Leyte Gulf, 25th October 1944.

Below: U.S.S. Wake Island (CVE65) 9th November 1944.

CVE.85	SHIPLEY BAY	12. 2.44	Scrapped Japan 1/61.
CVE.86	SITKOH BAY	19. 2.44	Scrapped Japan 1961.
CVE.87	STEAMER BAY	26. 2.44	Scrapped Portland 1959.
CVE.88	CAPE ESPERANCE (ex-Tananek Bay)	3. 3.44	Scrapped Japan 1/61.
CVE.89	TAKANIS BAY	10. 3.44	Scrapped Japan 11/60.
CVE.90	THETIS BAY	16. 3.44	Amphibious Assault Ship LPH.6 (2/55). Sold 1965.
CVE.91	MAKASSAR STRAIT (ex-Ulitaka Bay)	22. 3.44	Discarded 1959.
CVE.92	WINDHAM BAY	29. 3.44	Scrapped Japan 2/61.
CVE.93	MAKIN ISLAND (ex-Woodcliff Bay)	5. 4.44	Scrapped 1947.
CVE.94	LUNGA POINT (ex-Alazon Bay)	11. 4.44	Scrapped Japan 11/60.
CVE.95	BISMARCK SEA (ex-Alikula Bay)	17. 4.44	Lost 21/2/45.
CVE.96	SALAMAUA (ex-Anguilla Bay)	22. 4.44	Scrapped 1947.
CVE.97	HOLLANDIA (ex-Astrolabe Bay)	28. 4.44	Scrapped Japan 11/60.
CVE.98	KWAJALEIN (ex-Bucareli Bay)	4. 5.44	Scrapped Japan 1/61.
CVE.99	ADMIRALTY ISLANDS (ex-Chapin Bay)	10. 5.44	Scrapped 1947.
CVE.100	BOUGAIN-VILLE (ex-Didrickson Bay)	16. 5.44	Scrapped Japan 1960.
CVE.101	MATANIKAU (ex-Dolomi Bay)	22. 5.44	Scrapped Japan 11/60.
CVE.102	ATTU (ex-Elbour Bay)	27. 5.44	Merc. GAY (1947); scrapped Baltimore 1949.
CVE.103	ROI (ex-Alava Bay)	2.6.44	Scrapped 1947.
CVE.104	MUNDA (ex-Tonowek Bay)	8. 6.44	Scrapped Japan 10/60.

The bracket spanning CVE.85–CVE.104 is labelled: Kaiser (Vancouver, Wash.): Nordberg

Notes:—First escort carriers built as such from the keel up. Had greater streamlining, squared off stern, two boiler uptakes on either side of flight deck. Construction proceeded very rapidly, the fiftieth unit being completed exactly one year after the first. All served in the Pacific except GUADALCANAL and KASAAN BAY which remained in the Atlantic. FANSHAW BAY, GAMBIER BAY, KALININ BAY, KITKUN BAY, ST. LO, and WHITE PLAINS were engaged by the main Japanese fleet off Samar, Leyte Gulf, 25/10/44. KADASHAN BAY, KITKUN BAY and SALAMAUA were all severely damaged by Kamikaze at Lingayen 8–13/1/45. GUADALCANAL led force which captured U–505 off the Azores, 4/6/44.

U.S.S. Hollandia (CVE97).

61

Commencement Bay class

Displacement: 10,900 tons.
Dimensions: 525 (wl) 557 (oa) × 75 × 30½ ft. (105¼ ft. extreme beam).
Machinery: 2-shaft geared turbines, S.H.P. 16,000 = 19 knots.
Armament: 2—5 in. (2 × 1), 36—40 mm. A.A. guns; 34 aircraft.
Complement: 1,066.

P. No.	Name	Builder	Launched	Fate
CVE.105	COMMENCE-MENT BAY (ex-St. Joseph Bay)	⎫	9. 5.44	
CVE.106	BLOCK ISLAND (ex-Sunset Bay)*		10. 6.44	Scrapped Japan 6/60.
CVE.107	GILBERT ISLANDS (ex-St. Andrews Bay)		20. 7.44	ANNAPOLIS (AGMR1) 1963.
CVE.108	KULA GULF (ex-Vermillion Bay)†		15. 8.44	
CVE.109	CAPE GLOUCESTER (ex-Willapa Bay)		12. 9.44	
CVE.110	SALERNO BAY (ex-Winjah Bay)	Todd-Pacific (Tacoma): Allis-Chalmers	26. 9.44	Scrapped Bilbao 1962.
CVE.111	VELLA GULF (ex-Totem Bay)		19.10.44	
CVE.112	SIBONEY (ex-Frosty Bay)		9.11.44	
CVE.113	PUGET SOUND (ex-Hobart Bay)		30.11.44	Scrapped Hong Kong 1962.
CVE.114	RENDOVA (ex-Mosser Bay)†		28.12.44	
CVE.115	BAIROKO (ex-Portage Bay)		25. 1.45	Scrapped Hong Kong 1/61.
CVE.116	BADOENG STRAIT (ex-San Alberto Bay)*		15. 2.45	
CVE.117	SAIDOR (ex-Saltery Bay)		17. 3.45	
CVE.118	SICILY (ex-Sandy Bay)	⎭	14. 4.45	Scrapped Hong Kong 3/61

Left: U.S.S. Gilbert Islands (CVE107) 18th July 1945.

Below: U.S.S. Sable (IX81) 10th August 1943. Used for training carrier pilots on the Great Lakes.

CVE.119	POINT CRUZ (ex-Trocadero Bay)		18. 5.45	
CVE.120	MINDORO		27. 6.45	Scrapped Hong Kong 9/60.
CVE.121	RABAUL	Todd-Pacific (Tacoma): Allis-Chalmers	14. 7.45	
CVE.122	PALAU		6. 8.45	Scrapped Bilbao, 1960.
CVE.123	TINIAN		5. 9.45	
CVE.124	BASTOGNE			
CVE.125	ENIWETOK			
CVE.126	LINGAYEN			
CVE.127	OKINAWA			
CVE.128	Unnamed			
CVE.129	Unnamed			
CVE.130	Unnamed			
CVE.131	Unnamed			
CVE.132	Unnamed			Cancelled, 11/8/45.
CVE.133	Unnamed			
CVE.134	Unnamed	Kaiser Vancouver		
CVE.135	Unnamed			
CVE.136	Unnamed			
CVE.137	Unnamed			
CVE.138	Unnamed			
CVE.139	Unnamed			

* Completed Commercial I.W.   † *Completed Willamette.*

Notes:—Modified **Sangamon** class. BLOCK ISLAND, CAPE GLOUCESTER and GILBERT ISLANDS participated in the closing actions of the Pacific War. RABAUL and TINIAN were never commissioned.

TRAINING AIRCRAFT CARRIERS

In 1942, two paddle steamers were hurriedly converted into aircraft carriers by stripping the funnels and superstructure and installing large flight decks. They were used exclusively for training on the Great Lakes, the planes being flown to and from shore bases each day.

7,200 tons; 484½ (wl) 500 (oa) × 58¼ × 15½ ft.; paddle reciprocating (3 cyl. VC), H.P. 11,000 = 18 knots.

IX.64	WOLVERINE (ex-mercantile Seeandbee)	Detroit Sbdg.	1912	Scrapped Cleveland 1947.

8,000 tons; 519 (wl) 535 (oa) × 58 × 15½ ft.; paddle reciprocating (3 cyl. VC) H.P. 12,000 = 18 knots.

IX.81	SABLE (ex-mercantile Greater Buffalo)	American Sbdg. (Lorain): American Sbdg. (Detroit)	27.10.23	Scrapped 1948.

Above: U.S.S. Tennessee (BB44), May 1943—showing her enormous beam.

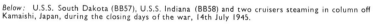

Below: U.S.S. South Dakota (BB57), U.S.S. Indiana (BB58) and two cruisers steaming in column off Kamaishi, Japan, during the closing days of the war, 14th July 1945.

CRUISERS

At the start of the war in December 1941, 18 heavy cruisers and 19 light cruisers were in service.

The oldest heavy cruisers were the **Pensacola** class, notable for the combination of two and three gun turrets. A tendency to roll was eliminated by modifications to the hull and superstructure. The slightly larger **Northampton** class of 1927 set the pattern for all succeeding heavy cruisers with main armament reduced to nine 8-inch guns in three triple turrets. The **Astoria** class of 1929 appeared with a new silhouette but retained the same armament and machinery. The older heavy cruisers had been modified before the war by the removal of torpedo tubes and addition of greater A.A. protection.

Two distinct types of light cruisers were in service, of which half were of the older **Omaha** class. These distinctive ships, with four tall funnels, had been designed during World War I as scout cruisers; during World War II they were relegated to subsidiary war zones (e.g., North Pacific, South Atlantic). No other light cruisers were ordered until the mid-thirties when the **Brooklyn** class was begun. This class featured a new hull design with the aircraft handling arrangements moved to the stern, and mounted fifteen 6-inch guns in five triple turrets. The heavy cruiser WICHITA was identical except in armament and armor. Her superfiring 5-inch A.A. guns fore and aft were an innovation which was retained in all World War II-built cruisers.

Of the ships completed following the outbreak of war, the small but fast **Atlanta** class of anti-aircraft cruisers was most singular. Similar in design and concept to the British **Dido** class, they were the only U.S. cruisers with 5-inch guns as main armament. In 1940, the fleet expansion program produced the eight original **Baltimore** class heavy cruisers and the thirty-four original **Cleveland** class light cruisers. Of the latter class, twenty-seven were finally completed (including war programs), nine having been built as aircraft carriers. They were the largest class of cruisers ever built to a single design.

Following Pearl Harbor, with the remaining battleships withdrawn for protection of troop convoys, cruisers became the principal surface combat ship in the Pacific. All but a few* were withdrawn from the Atlantic and sent to the Pacific combat zones. Only once were the battleships brought directly into contact with enemy surface forces. During the long Solomons campaign, every pre-war cruiser involved was either sunk or damaged. Following 1943, cruisers served principally as escort for carrier task forces and invasion fire support vessels, and were no longer used as scouts or raiders operating apart from the fleet.

As the older ships went in for repairs or refit, many modifications were made. These generally included rearrangement of masts, installation of new radar and increased A.A. protection, and narrowing of flying bridge and superstructures. Addition of so much equipment topside tended to decrease stability in some cases. This was particularly noticeable in the sinking of the INDIANAPOLIS in 1945.

The new ships were outstanding in ability to withstand severe damage. RENO, CANBERRA and HOUSTON (ii) were all brought to port despite major torpedo damage. Survival of HOUSTON (ii) was especially noteworthy, the ship being torpedoed a second time while under tow. Defects of sometimes hasty

*AUGUSTA, BROOKLYN, SAVANNAH, PHILADELPHIA and 4 **Omaha** class remained in the Atlantic throughout the war.

66

war construction were also evident, most spectacularly when PITTSBURGH, of welded construction, lost 90 feet of her bow in a typhoon.

The pre-war cruisers were all retired after the war, although a number were not scrapped until many years later. Six of the light cruisers were sold to South American countries where they still survive. After 1953, various of the war-built cruisers were rebuilt as guided missile cruisers. A few of the older war-built ships remain on the navy list, together with the newer **Des Moines** and **Worcester** classes.

Cruisers are named after cities, and are designated by CA (heavy cruiser) and CL (light cruiser).

HEAVY CRUISERS

Pensacola class

Displacement: 9,100 tons.
Dimensions: 570 (wl) 585¾ (oa) × 65¼ × 16¼ ft.
Machinery: 4-shaft geared turbines, S.H.P. 107,000 = 32.7 knots.
Armament: 10—8 in. (2 × 3 & 2 × 2), 8—5 in. (8 × 1) guns; 2 aircraft.
Complement: 1,200.

P. No.	Name	Builder	Launched	Fate
CA.24	PENSACOLA	New York N.Yd.	25. 4.29	Bikini target ship (7/46). Sunk 10/11/48.
CA.25	SALT LAKE CITY	New York Sbdg.	23. 1.29	Bikini target ship (7/46). Sunk 25/5/48.

Notes:—First U.S. cruisers built under the Washington Treaty. Flush deck with very low freeboard. Tripod mainmast cut down to control tower in 1941; light pole stepped abaft second funnel. In 1945 they mounted 24—40 mm. A.A. guns. **W.W.II:** PENSACOLA: Midway, Santa Cruz, Guadalcanal battle, Tassafaronga (severely damaged), Gilbert Is., Kwajalein, Iwo, Okinawa, Pacific raids 1942-44. SALT LAKE CITY: Guadalcanal-Tulagi, Cape Esperance (damaged), Komandorski Is. (damaged), Attu, Gilbert Is., Kwajalein, Leyte, Iwo, Okinawa, Pacific raids 1942-45.

Northampton class

Displacement: 9,050 tons, except CHESTER 9,200 tons, CHICAGO 9,300 tons.
Dimensions: 582 (wl) 600¼ (oa) × 66¼ × 16½ ft.
Machinery: 4-shaft geared turbines, S.H.P. 107,000 = 32.7 knots.
Armament: 9—8 in. (3 × 3), 8—5 in. (8 × 1) A.A. guns; 3 aircraft.
Complement: 1,100.

CA.26	NORTH-AMPTON	Bethlehem (Quincy)	5. 9.29	Lost 1/12/42.
CA.27	CHESTER	New York Sbdg.	3. 7.29	Scrapped Panama City 11/59.
CA.28	LOUISVILLE	Puget Sd.N.Yd.	1. 9.30	Scrapped Panama City 1960.
CA.29	CHICAGO	Mare I.N.Yd.	10. 4.30	Lost 30/1/43.
CA.30	HOUSTON	⎱ Newport	7. 9.29	Lost 1/3/42.
CA.31	AUGUSTA	⎰ News	1. 2.30	Scrapped Kearny 4/60.

U.S.S. Pensacola (CA24) 20th May 1944, after modifications, showing tripod mainmast replaced by small tower.

U.S.S. Pensacola (CA 24) May 1942, at Pearl Harbor. Notice old radar on foremast, small tripod aft.

68

U.S.S. Salt Lake City (CA25) 1944. Notice low freeboard, high foremast.

U.S.S. Houston (CA30) October 1935, flying pennant of the Commander-in-Chief (President Roosevelt) from mainmast.

U.S.S. Augusta (CA31) late in the war with tripod mainmast around second funnel.

Indianapolis class

Displacement: 9,800 and 9,950 tons respectively.
Dimensions: 592 (wl) 610¼ (oa) × 66¼ × 17¼ ft.
Machinery: 4-shaft geared turbines, S.H.P. 107,000 = 32.7 knots.
Armament: 9—8 in. (3 × 3), 8—5 in. (8 × 1) A.A. guns; 3 aircraft
Complement: 1,150.

| CA.33 | PORTLAND | Bethlehem (Quincy) | 21. 5.32 | Scrapped Panama City Fla. 12/59. |
| CA.35 | INDIANAPOLIS | New York Sbdg. | 7.11.31 | Lost 29/7/45. |

Astoria class

Displacement: 9,950 tons except TUSCALOOSA 9,975 tons, QUINCY 9,375 tons, VINCENNES 9,400 tons.
Dimensions: 578 (wl) 588 (oa) × 61¾ × 19½ ft.
Machinery: 4-shaft geared turbines, S.H.P. 107,000 = 32.7 knots.
Armament: 9—8 in. (3 × 3), 8—5 in. (8 × 1) A.A. guns; 4 aircraft.
Complement: 1,050.

CA.32	NEW ORLEANS	New York N.Yd.	12. 4.33	Scrapped Baltimore 10/59.
CA.34	ASTORIA	Puget Sd.N.Yd.	16.12.33	Lost 9/8/42.
CA.36	MINNEAPOLIS	Philadelphia N.Yd.	6. 9.33	Scrapped Chester 7/60.
CA.37	TUSCALOOSA	New York Sbdg.	15.11.33	Scrapped Baltimore 7/59.
CA.38	SAN FRANCISCO	Mare Is.N.Yd.	9. 3.33	Scrapped Panama City, 5/61.
CA.39	QUINCY	⎱ Bethlehem	19. 6.35	Lost 9/8/42.
CA.44	VINCENNES	⎰ (Quincy)	21. 5.36	Lost 9/8/42.

Engines by Westinghouse except CA.37, 39, 44, by builders.

U.S.S. Indianapolis (CA35) 14th December 1944.

U.S.S. Helena (CL50) June 1940. Modified Brooklyn. Observe superstructure aft and mainmast close to second funnel, secondary armament in turrets.

U.S.S. Indianapolis
(CA35) 10th May
1943.

U.S.S. Portland
(CA33) 22nd April
1943.

73

U.S.S. San Francisco (CA38) 13th October 1944, after refit.

U.S.S. San Francisco (CA38) 10th October 1943, camouflaged as a destroyer. Flush deck is disguised by paint. Searchlight platform between funnels has been removed.

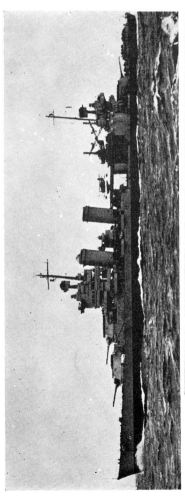

U.S.S. Tuscaloosa
(CA37) 1943.

[I.W.M.

U.S.S. Wichita
(CA45) 1942.

[I.W.M.

75

U.S.S. Vincennes (CA44), at Pearl Harbor, May 1942. Scout plane on water in foreground.

U.S.S. Canberra (CA70) October 1944.

76

U.S.S. New Orleans
(CA32) 1942. Notice
wide bridge, search-
light platform.

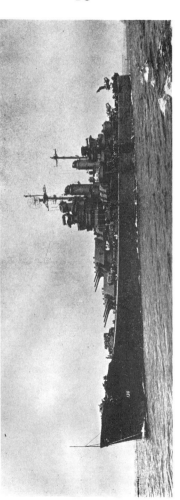

U.S.S. Chicago
(CA136) 1945.

77

U.S.S. Des Moines (CA134) 15th November 1948, as completed

78

others. 24—40 mm. A.A. guns added during the war. **W.W.II:** NEW ORLEANS: Pearl Harbor, Coral Sea, Midway, Guadalcanal-Tulgi, Eastern Solomons, Tassaforonga (torpedoed, lost bow), Gilbert Is., Kwajalein, Truk raid, Hollandia, Marianas, Palau, Leyte Gulf, Okinawa, Pacific raids 1942-44. ASTORIA: Coral Sea, Midway, Guadalcanal-Tulapi. MINNEAPOLIS: Coral Sea, Midway, Guadalcanal-Tulagi, Eastern Solomons, Tassafaronga (torpedoed, lost bow), Gilbert Is., Kwajalein, Truk raid, Hollandia. Marianas, Palau, Leyte, Lingayen. Okinawa. Pacific raids 1942-44. TUSCALOOSA: N. Africa, Normandy, S. France, Iwo, Okinawa. SAN FRANCISCO: Pearl Harbor, Guadalcanal-Tulagi, Cape Esperance, Guadalcanal battle (damaged), Attu, Gilbert Is., Kwajalein, Truk raid, Hollandia, Marianas, Leyte, Iwo, Okinawa, Pacific raids 1942-44. QUINCY: Guadalcanal-Tulagi. VINCENNES: Midway, Guadalcanal-Tulagi. Survivors laid up 1946.

Wichita

Displacement: 10,000 tons.
Dimensions: 600 (wl) 608¼ (oa) × 61¾ × 19½ ft.
Machinery: 4-shaft geared turbines, S.H.P. 100,000 = 34 knots.
Armament: 9—8 in. (3 × 3), 8—5 in. (8 × 1) D.P. guns; 4 aircraft.
Complement: 1,100.

CA.45	WICHITA	Philadelphia N.Yd. New York Sbdg.	16.11.37	Scrapped Panama City, 11/59

Notes:—Brooklyn class with 8 in. guns. 4—5 in. guns are in enclosed mounts. 24—40 mm. A.A. guns added. **W.W.II:** N. Africa, Attu, Kwajalein, Truk raid, Hollandia, Marianas, Palau, Leyte Gulf, Okinawa, Pacific raids 1944-45. Laid up 1946.

Baltimore class

Displacement: 13,600 tons except CA.122-129, 137-138, 13,700 tons.
Dimensions: 664 (wl) 675 (oa) × 71 × 20½ ft.
Machinery: 4-shaft geared turbines, S.H.P. 120,000 = 33 knots.
Armament: 9—8 in. (3 × 3), 12—5 in. (6 × 2) D.P., 48—40 mm. A.A. guns; 4 aircraft.
Complement: 1,700.

CA.68	BALTIMORE		28. 7.42	
CA.69	BOSTON		26. 8.42	CAG 1 (11/56).
CA.70	CANBERRA (ex-Pittsburgh)		19. 4.43	CAG 2 (6/56).
CA.71	QUINCY (ex-St. Paul)		23. 6.43	
CA.72	PITTSBURGH (ex-Albany)		22. 2.44	
CA.73	ST. PAUL (ex-Rochester)	Bethlehem (Quincy)	16. 9.44	
CA.74	COLUMBUS		30.11.44	CG 12 (12/62).
CA.75	HELENA (ex-Des Moines)		28. 4.45	
CA.122	OREGON CITY		9. 6.45	
CA.123	ALBANY		30. 6.45	CG 10 (11/62).
CA.124	ROCHESTER		28. 8.45	
CA.125	NORTHAMP-TON		27. 1.51	Completed as CLC1 (1953).
CA.126	CAMBRIDGE			Cancelled 12/8/45.

U.S.S. Baltimore (CA68) 1st July 1943, showing catapults and twin cranes.

U.S.S. Pittsburgh (CA72) 10th June 1945, returning to base after losing her bow in a typhoon.

U.S.S. Pittsburgh (CA72) 9th October 1944, in dazzle camouflage, as commissioned.

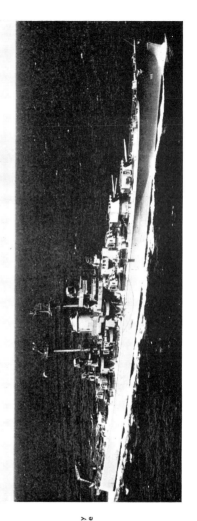

U.S.S. Oregon City (CA122) 17th June 946.

81

CA.127	BRIDGEPORT	⎫ Bethlehem		Cancelled 12/8/45.
CA.128	KANSAS CITY	⎬(Quincy)		Cancelled 12/8/45.
CA.129	TULSA	⎭		Cancelled 12/8/45.
CA.130	BREMERTON	⎫	2. 7.44	
CA.131	FALL RIVER	⎱ New York	13. 8.44	
CA.132	MACON	⎰ Sbdg.	15.10.44	
CA.133	TOLEDO	⎭	6. 5.45	
CA.135	LOS ANGELES	⎫ Philadel-	20. 8.44	
CA.136	CHICAGO	⎬ phia	20. 8.44	CG 11 (5/64).
CA.137	NORFOLK	⎰ N.Yd.		Cancelled 12/8/45.
CA.138	SCRANTON	⎭		Cancelled 12/8/45.

All Engined by G.E.   CAG, CG: Guided Missile Cruiser.

Notes:—CA.122-129, 137-138: one funnel and more compact superstructure. CA.68-71 have two cranes at stern over aircraft hangars. **W.W.II:** BALTIMORE: Gilbert Is., Kwajalein, Truk raid, Eniwetok, Hollandia, Marianas, Iwo, Okinawa, Pacific raids 1944-45. BOSTON: Kwajalein, Eniwetok, Hollandia, Marianas, Palau, Leyte Gulf, Iwo, Pacific raids 1944-45. CANBERRA: Eniwetok, Hollandia, Marianas, Palau, Leyte. Severely damaged by a/c torpedo, Formosa, 13/10/44. QUINCY: Normandy, S. France, Pacific raids 1945. PITTSBURGH: Iwo, Pacific raids 1945. Lost bow in typhoon 5/6/45. ST. PAUL and CHICAGO: Pacific raids 1945.

Des Moines class

Displacement: 17,000 tons.
Dimensions: 700 (wl) 716½ (oa) × 76½ × 22 ft.
Machinery: 4-shaft geared turbines, S.H.P. 120,000 = 33 knots.
Armament: 9—8 in. (3 × 3), 12—5 in. (6 × 2), 20—3 in. A.A. guns; 4 aircraft.
Complement: 1,860.

CA.134	DES MOINES	⎫ Bethlehem	27. 9.46	
CA.139	SALEM	⎬(Quincy)	25. 3.47	
CA.140	DALLAS	⎭		Cancelled 6/6/46.
CA.148	NEWPORT NEWS	Newport News	6. 3.47	

All Engined by G.E.

Notes:—8 unnamed sisters cancelled (CA.141-143, 149-153). 8 in. guns are in automatic mounts. Rounded stern, high director tower. Planned secondary armament was 16—5 in. DP, 48—40 mm. A.A. guns.

LIGHT CRUISERS

Omaha class

Displacement: 7,050 tons.
Dimensions: 550 (wl) 555½ (oa) × 55½ × 13½ ft.
Machinery: 4-shaft geared turbines, S.H.P. 90,000 = 34 knots.
Armament: 10—6 in. (except OMAHA, CONCORD, TRENTON, MEMPHIS 12—6 in.) (2 × 2 & 6/8 × 1), 8—3 in. guns; 6—21 in. (2 × 3) T.T.; 2 aircraft.
Complement: 800.

U.S.S. Rochester (CA124) 19th December 1946.

U.S.S. Marblehead (CL12) 10th May 1944. Notice small structure amidships, searchlight platform removed, radar on mainmast.

83

U.S.S. Detroit (CL8) 14th April 1944. Radar is on foremast.

U.S.S. Raleigh (CL7) struggling to stay afloat following torpedo damage during attack on Pearl Harbor, 7th December 1941.

CL.4	OMAHA	⎫ Todd	14.12.20	Scrapped 1946.
CL.5	MILWAUKEE	⎪ (Tacoma)	24. 3.21	Russian MURMANSK (4/44) returned and scrapped Wilmington 1949.
		⎬ Westing-house		
CL.6	CINCINNATI	⎪	23. 5.21	Scrapped 1946.
CL.7	RALEIGH	⎨ Bethlehem	25.10.22	Scrapped 1946.
CL.8	DETROIT	⎧ (Quincy)	29. 6.22	Scrapped Baltimore 1946.
CL.9	RICHMOND	⎩	29. 9.21	Scrapped Baltimore 1946.
CL.10	CONCORD		15.12.21	Scrapped Baltimore 1946.
CL.11	TRENTON	⎬ Cramp	16. 4.23	Scrapped Baltimore 1946.
CL.12	MARBLEHEAD		9.10.23	Scrapped 1946.
CL.13	MEMPHIS	⎭	17. 4.24	Scrapped Baltimore 1946.

Notes:—Originally designed with 8—6 in. guns but 4—6 in. in two turrets added prior to completion. At end of war armament varied considerably: Only DETROIT retained 12—6 in. guns; MEMPHIS was reduced to 7—3 in. and OMAHA, MILWAUKEE and MARBLEHEAD to 6—3 in. secondary armament; all had added 6—40 mm. A.A. guns, but MEMPHIS had only 4, CINCINNATI had 8 and DETROIT 10—40 mm. A.A. Position of masts and radar varied in these ships. **W.W.II:** OMAHA: S. Atlantic patrol, S. France, MILWAUKEE: S. Atlantic patrol, CINCINNATI: S. Atlantic patrol, S. France. RALEIGH: Pearl Harbor (damaged), Attu, Kurile Is. DETROIT: Pearl Harbor, Attu, Iwo, Okinawa. RICHMOND: Komandorski Is., Attu, Kurile Is. CONCORD and TRENTON: Kurile Is. MARBLEHEAD: Far East 1942 (damaged by aircraft, 4/2/42), S. France. MEMPHIS: S. Atlantic patrol.

Brooklyn class

Displacement: 10,000 tons except BROOKLYN and PHILADELPHIA 9,700 tons, SAVANNAH and NASHVILLE 9,475 tons, HONOLULU 9,650 tons.
Dimensions: 600 (wl) 608½ (oa) × 61¾ × 19½ ft.
Machinery: 4-shaft geared turbines, S.H.P. 100,000 = 34 knots.
Armament: 15—6 in. (5 × 3), 8—5 in. (8 × 1) guns; 4 aircraft.
Complement: 1,300.

CL.40	BROOKLYN	New York N.Yd.	30.11.36	Chilean O'HIGGINS (/51).
CL.41	PHILADELPHIA	Philadelphia N.Yd.	17.11.36	Brazilian BARROSO (1/51).
CL.42	SAVANNAH	New York Sbdg.	8. 5.37	Scrapped Baltimore 2/60.
CL.43	NASHVILLE	New York Sbdg.	2.10.37	Chilean PRAT (/51).
CL.46	PHOENIX	New York Sbdg.	12. 3.38	Argentine 17 DE OCTUBRE (4/51) GENERAL BELGRANO (1956)
CL.47	BOISE	Newport News	3.12.36	Argentine 9 DE JULIO (4/51).
CL.48	HONOLULU	New York N.Yd.	26. 8.37	Scrapped Baltimore 1/60.
CL.49	ST. LOUIS	Newport News	15. 4.38	Brazilian TAMANDARÉ (1/51).
CL.50	HELENA	New York N.Yd.	27. 8.38	Lost 6/7/43.

U.S.S. Trenton (CLII) IIth May 1943, in the Gulf of Panama.

U.S.S. Honolulu (CL48) 30th January 1942, showing search-light platform and wide bridge.

U.S.S. Brooklyn (CL40) 11th June 1943, before modifications.

U.S.S. Philadelphia (CL41) 21st November 1943.

U.S.S. Atlanta (CL51) 25th October 1942, shown shortly before her loss off Guadalcanal. Notice extra turret alongside aft superstructure, fitted only on early ships of this class.

Notes:—New type flush-deck hull with high transom stern; built in hangar aft. ST. LOUIS and HELENA have mainmast stepped immediately abaft funnels; new type 5 in. guns. During the war bridge structure was narrowed and simplified; 24—40 mm. A.A. guns (28 in. CL.42, 43 and 20 in. CL.40, 41) added. In 1945, bridge and after superstructure in SAVANNAH and HONOLULU were rebuilt, 8—5 in. (2 x 4) guns installed and bulges added. **W.W.II:** BROOKLYN: N. Africa, Sicily, Anzio, S. France PHILADELPHIA: N. Africa, Sicily, Salerno, Anzio, S. France. SAVANNAH: N. Africa, Sicily, Salerno (damaged). NASHVILLE: New Guinea, Leyte (severely damaged by *Kamikaze* 13/12/44), Mindoro, Borneo, Pacific raids 1943-44. PHOENIX: Pearl Harbor, Hollandia, Leyte, Mindoro, Lingayen, Borneo. BOISE: Far East 1941, Cape Esperance (damaged), Sicily, Salerno, Hollandia, Leyte, Mindoro, Lingayen, Borneo. HONOLULU: Pearl Harbor, Tassafaronga, New Georgia, Kula Gulf (damaged), Saipan, Guam, Palau, Leyte (torpedoed). ST. LOUIS: Pearl Harbor, New Georgia, Kula Gulf (damaged), Bougainville, Saipan, Guam, Leyte, Pacific raids 1942-45. HELENA: Pearl Harbor (torpedoed), Cape Esperance, Guadalcanal battle, New Georgia, Kula Gulf.

Atlanta class

Displacement:	6,000 tons.			
Dimensions:	530 (wl) 541½ (oa) × 53¼ × 16½ ft.			
Machinery:	2-shaft geared turbines, S.H.P. 75,000 = 32 knots.			
Armament:	CL.51-54: 16—5 in. D.P., 10—40 mm. A.A. guns, 8—21 in. T.T.			
	CL.95-98: 12—5 in. D.P., 16—40 mm. A.A. guns, 8—21 in. T.T.			
	CL.119-121: 12—5 in. D.P., 24—40 mm. A.A guns.			
Complement:	800.			

CL.51	ATLANTA	} Federal	6. 9.41	Lost 13/11/42.
CL.52	JUNEAU (i)		25.10.41	Lost 13/11/42.
CL.53	SAN DIEGO	{ Bethlehem	26. 7.41	Scrapped Seattle 12/60.
CL.54	SAN JUAN	ʃ (Quincy)	6. 9.41	Scrapped Terminal I. 1962.
CL.95	OAKLAND		23.10.42	Scrapped Oakland 1962.
CL.96	RENO	Bethlehem	23.12.42	Scrapped 1962.
CL.97	FLINT (ex-Spokane)	} (San Francisco)	25. 1.44	
CL.98	TUCSON		3. 9.44	
CL.119	JUNEAU (ii)		15. 7.45	Scrapped Kearny 3/61.
CL.120	SPOKANE	} Federal	22. 9.45	
CL.121	FRESNO		5. 3.46	

All engined Westinghouse.

Notes:—Anti-Aircraft Cruisers. Flush-decked with no aircraft hangar or catapults. ATLANTA made 40 knots on trials. 4—5 in. guns (wing turrets) were to be removed from CL.53-54 but this was not carried out. **W.W.II:** ATLANTA: Midway, Guadalcanal-Tulagi, Eastern Solomons, Guadalcanal battle. JUNEAU (i): Santa Cruz, Guadalcanal battle. SAN DIEGO: Santa Cruz, Guadalcanal battle, Bougainville, Gilbert Is., Kwajalein, Truk raid, Marianas, Palau, Leyte Gulf, Iwo, Pacific raids 1944-45. SAN JUAN: Guadalcanal-Tulagi, Santa Cruz, Bougainville, Gilbert Is., Kwajalein, Eniwetok, Hollandia, Marianas, Iwo, Pacific raids 1944-45. OAKLAND: Gilbert Is., Kwajalein, Truk raid, Hollandia, Marianas, Palau, Leyte Gulf, Pacific raids 1944-45. RENO: Marianas, Palau, Leyte Gulf. Torpedoed by *I-41* off Leyte, 4/11/44. FLINT: Iwo, Pacific raids 1944-45. TUCSON: Pacific raids 1945.

Cleveland-Fargo class

Displacement:	10,000 tons.
Dimensions:	600 (wl) 610¼ (oa) × 66½ × 20 ft.
Machinery:	4-shaft geared turbines, S.H.P. 100,000 = 33 knots.
Armament:	12—6 in. (4 × 3), 12—5 in. (6 × 2), 28—40 mm. A.A. guns, except CL.81-92, 101-105 24—40 mm. A.A. guns; 4 aircraft.
Complement:	1,200.

U.S.S. San Juan (CL54) June 1944.

U.S.S. Atlanta (CL51) 1942, shown fueling at sea. Notice mottled camouflage on upper works.

U.S.S. Savannah (CL42) April 1945, showing modified bridge structure, new twin 5" secondary armament.

U.S.S. Wilkes-Barre (CL103) 10th July 1944.

U.S.S. Montpelier (CL57) 11th June 1944, with curved bridge, typical of early units of this class.

U.S.S. Houston (CL81) 1st May 1944, showing square bridge of later units of the class.

92

U.S.S. Cleveland (CL55) 27th March 1946.

U.S.S. Oklahoma City (CL91).

93

CL.55	CLEVELAND	⎫	1.11.41	Scrapped Baltimore 2/60.
CL.56	COLUMBIA	⎪	17.12.41	Scrapped Chester 1960.
CL.57	MONTPELIER	⎪	12. 2.42	Scrapped Baltimore 1960.
CL.58	DENVER	⎬New York	4. 4.42	Scrapped Kearney 11/60.
CL.59	AMSTERDAM	Sbdg.		CVL22 (1942).
CL.60	SANTA FE	⎪	10. 6.42	Scrapped Portland, Ore. 1960.
CL.61	TALLAHASSEE	⎭		CVL23 (1942).
CL.62	BIRMINGHAM	⎫	20. 3.42	Scrapped Long Bch. 12/59.
		⎬Newport News		
CL.63	MOBILE	⎭	15. 5.42	Scrapped Portland, Ore 1960.
CL.64	VINCENNES (ex-Flint)	⎫ Bethlehem	17. 7.43	
CL.65	PASADENA	⎬(Quincy)	28.12.43	
CL.66	SPRINGFIELD	⎪	9. 3.44	CLG7 (7/60).
CL.67	TOPEKA	⎭	19. 8.44	CLG8 (3/60).
CL.76	NEW HAVEN	⎫		CVL 24 (1942).
CL.77	HUNTINGTON	⎪		CVL 25 (1942).
CL.78	DAYTON	⎬New York		CVL 26 (1942).
CL.79	WILMING-TON	Sbdg.		CVL 28 (1942).
CL.80	BILOXI	⎫	23. 2.43	Scrapped Portland, Ore. 1962.
		⎬Newport News		
CL.81	HOUSTON (ex-Vicksburg)	⎭	19. 6.43	Scrapped Baltimore 1960.
CL.82	PROVIDENCE	⎱ Bethlehem	28.12.44	CLG 6 (9/59).
CL.83	MANCHESTER	⎰(Quincy)	5. 3.46	Scrapped Richmond Cal. 1961.
CL.84	BUFFALO (i)	Federal (Kearny)		Cancelled 16/12/40.
CL.85	FARGO	New York Sbdg.		CVL 27 (1942).
CL.86	VICKSBURG (ex-Cheyenne)	⎱ Newport ⎰News	14.12.43	Test hull 1962. Scrapped Terminal I., 9/64.
CL.87	DULUTH		13. 1.44	Scrapped 1961.
CL.88	(Unnamed)	Federal (Kearny)		Cancelled 16/12/40.
CL.89	MIAMI	⎫	12. 8.42	Scrapped Richmond Cal. 1962.
CL.90	ASTORIA (ex-Wilkes-Barre)	⎪	6. 3.43	
CL.91	OKLAHOMA CITY	⎬Cramp	20. 2.44	CLG 5 (9/60).
CL.92	LITTLE ROCK	⎪	27. 8.44	CLG 4 (6/60).
CL.93	GALVESTON	⎪	22. 4.45	CLG 3 (5/58).
CL.94	YOUNGS-TOWN	⎭		Cancelled 12/8/45, 54% complete.
CL.99	BUFFALO (ii)	⎱ New York		CVL 29 (1942).
CL.100	NEWARK	⎰ Sbdg.		CVL 30 (1942).
CL.101	AMSTERDAM	⎱ Newport	25. 4.44	
CL.102	PORTSMOUTH	⎰ News	20. 9.44	

94

U.S.S. Oakland (CL95) July 1945. Notice square bridge, absence of wing turrets aft.

U.S.S. Biloxi (CL80) 15th September 1943.

U.S.S. Dayton (CL105) 23rd April 1945.

U.S.S. Columbia (CL56) in Surigao Strait, 3rd January 1945.

U.S.S. Huntington (CL107) 27th March 1946.

U.S.S. Miami (CL89) 3rd July 1944.

CL.103	WILKES-BARRE		24.12.43	
CL.104	ATLANTA	New York Sbdg.	6. 2.44	IX 304 (5/64). (test hull).
CL.105	DAYTON		19. 3.44	Scrapped Baltimore 1962.
CL.106	FARGO		25. 2.45	
CL.107	HUNTINGTON		8. 4.45	Scrapped Baltimore 6/62.
CL.108	NEWARK	New York Sbdg.		Cancelled 12/8/45; 67.8% complete, test hull; scrapped 1949.
CL.109	NEW HAVEN			Cancelled 12/8/45.
CL.110	BUFFALO			Cancelled 12/8/45.
CL.111	WILMINGTON	Cramp		Cancelled 12/8/45.
CL.112	VALLEJO	New York Sbdg.		Cancelled 5/10/44.
CL.113	HELENA			Cancelled 5/10/44.
CL.114	(Unnamed)			Cancelled 5/10/44.
CL.115	ROANOKE			Cancelled 5/10/44.
CL.116	TALLAHAS-SEE			Cancelled 12/8/45.
CL.117	CHEYENNE	Newport News		Cancelled 12/8/45.
CL.118	CHATTA-NOOGA			Cancelled 12/8/45.

All Engined G.E.   CLG: Guided Missile Cruiser.

Notes:—Improved **Brooklyn** class with one less 6 in. turret. Early units have rounded bridge structure. Nine more sisters converted to light carriers while under construction (for names, see **Independence** class, p.46). CL.106-118: one funnel and more compact superstructure. **W.W.II:** CLEVELAND: N. Africa, New Georgia, Kula Gulf, Bougainville, Marianas, Palau, Lingayen, Borneo. COLUMBIA: New Georgia, Kula Gulf, Bougainville, Palau, Leyte, Lingayen (severely damaged by *Kamikaze* 5 and 9/1/45), Borneo. MONTPELIER: New Georgia, Bougainville, Marianas, Leyte, Lingayen, Borneo. DENVER: New Georgia, Bougainville (torpedoed 13/11/43), Guam, Palau, Leyte Gulf, Lingayen, Borneo. SANTA FE: Attu, Bougainville, Gilbert Is., Kwajalein, Truk raid, Hollandia, Marianas, Palau, Leyte Gulf, Iwo. BIRMINGHAM: Sicily, Bougainville (torpedoed 8/11/43), marianas, Leyte (damaged by explosion of carrier PRINCETON), Iwo, Okinawa (*Kamikaze* 3/5/45) MOBILE: Bougainville, Gilbert Is., Kwajalein, Truk raid, Hollandia, Marianas, Leyte Gulf, Okinawa. VINCENNES: Marianas, Palau, Leyte Gulf, Iwo, Okinawa. PASADENA: Palau, Philippines, Iwo. BILOXI: Eniwetok, Truk raid, Hollandia, Marianas, Palau, Leyte Gulf, Iwo, Okinawa (*Kamikaze* 26/3/45). HOUSTON: Marianas, Palau, Leyte. Severe damage by aircraft torpedoes, 14 and 16/10/44. MIAMI: Marianas, Palau, Leyte Gulf, Iwo. ASTORIA: Iwo, Okinawa. OKLAHOMA CITY: Okinawa. All of above plus SPRINGFIELD, TOPEKA, VICKSBURG, DULUTH, AMSTERDAM, WILKES-BARRE, ATLANTA, DAYTON: Pacific raids

Worcester class

Displacement:	14,700 tons.
Dimensions:	664 (wl) $679\frac{1}{2}$ (oa) $\times$ $70\frac{3}{4}$ $\times$ $21\frac{1}{2}$ ft.
Machinery:	4-shaft geared turbines, S.H.P. 120,000 = 32 knots.
Armament:	12—6 in. (6 $\times$ 2), 20—3 in. (10 $\times$ 2) D.P., 12—40 mm. A.A. guns; 3 aircraft.
Complement:	1,300.

CL.144	WORCESTER	New York Sbdg.: G.E.	4. 2.47	
CL.145	ROANOKE		16. 6.47	
CL.146	VALLEJO			Cancelled 12/8/45.
CL.147	GARY			Cancelled 12/8/45.

Notes:—6 in. guns in new automatic mounts. Planned secondary armament was 12-3 in. DP, 48-40 mm. AA guns. CL154-159 (unnamed) cancelled.

U.S.S. Worcester (CL144) 24th June 1948, just prior to commissioning.

99

DESTROYERS

On December 7, 1941, there were 171 destroyers in commission.

Over one-third of these were of World War I vintage: the famous " flush-deck " class, of which 272 had been built. Between the wars 12* had been lost and 93 had been scrapped under the London Naval Disarmament Treaty of 1930. An additional 46 were serving in subsidiary duties, and deducting the 50 transferred to the United Kingdom in 1940, 71 remained in service at the outbreak of war.

The remaining ships had all been built after 1932. The **Farragut, Mahan**, and **Craven** classes were successive modifications of a basic design with an armament of 5-inch guns and torpedo tubes. The **Porter** and **Somers** classes, built during the same period, were designed as destroyer leaders and mounted eight 5-inch guns in twin mounts with all T.T. on the centre line. Increased armament in the **Sims** and early **Benson** classes made them topheavy, necessitating the removal of one 5-inch gun and one bank of T.T. Later **Benson** class ships were completed with the reduced armament. Construction proceeded early in the war on two basic types, the **Benson** and larger **Fletcher** classes. An attempt to include scouting aircraft and catapult in the latter class proved futile. Nevertheless, the 175 ships of this highly successful class which were completed proved to be the mainstay of Pacific Fleet destroyers after 1943. The more heavily armed **Sumner** class joined the fleet starting in 1944. They were followed by the **Gearing** class, ships of similar armament on a longer hull, some of which saw service in combat zones before V-J Day.

During the 1930's, U.S. Navy officers became convinced the next war would be fought in the Pacific. Faced with the vast distances in that ocean and a scarcity of land bases, means were undertaken to enable the fleet to operate despite these difficulties. One of these means was the development of the fleet train which was built up to a huge number of ships during the war and is treated in a later section. Another was the building of ships with an extended range of action superior to that of other, land-based, navies. Early **Craven** class destroyers were credited with a range of 9,000 miles at 15 knots; contemporary British " F " class destroyers only 6,000 miles at the same speed. All U.S. destroyers were equipped to refuel from oilers at sea, which practice became a matter of routine. Enabled to remain at sea continuously for long periods, combat ships of all types were formed into the fleet which swept the enemy from the sea and maintained position off landing beaches and enemy coasts for weeks on end.

During 1941, the new **Benson** class served with the Atlantic Fleet, participating in the " Neutrality Patrol " and pre-hostilities convoy duty, KEARNY being torpedoed, and NIBLACK carrying out the first attack as early as April 1941. One result of this disposition was that the destroyer force of the Asiatic Fleet in the Philippines had only flush-deckers, which, however, bore up well in the several surface actions fought against newer and superior Japanese ships.

The destroyers built in the 1930's and after were used almost from the start as fleet units, escorting heavier units and patrol duty, and not as convoy escorts, a job left to the older flush-deckers, Coast Guard cutters, and later, destroyer escorts. During 1942-43, the Solomons campaign provided many opportunities for destroyer actions during which 23 destroyers were lost. As the new **Fletcher** class joined the fleet in increasing numbers, the older ships were withdrawn from the front line to pre-invasion bombardment, anti-submarine and escort duties. Ships of the **Craven, Somers** and **Benson** classes were used to advantage in Europe and the Mediterranean.

Including REUBEN JAMES.

100

U.S.S. Allen (DD66) May 1944. Torpedo tubes amidships next to funnels.

U.S.S. Selfridge (DD357) 10th April 1944, with single 5" mount replacing No. 3 turret, and No. 2 turret removed. (See also page 117.)

U.S.S. Lea (DD118) 4th January 1945, with small mainmast, three funnels.

It was upon the **Fletcher** and **Sumner** classes that the main weight of the Kamikaze (suicide plane) attacks at Okinawa was thrown. A new development at this time as a result of these attacks was the radar picket ship. Destroyers were stationed 15 to 100 miles beyond the invasion force to give early warning of approaching enemy aircraft and direct friendly fighters. Ships on this duty suffered great losses. No fewer than 64 destroyers* were sunk or severely damaged during the Okinawa campaign.

After the war all destroyers built prior to 1940 were discarded. Destroyers are designated by the symbol DD and are named after deceased distinguished officers and men of the Navy and Marine Corps and civilians who have been of service to the Navy.

*Including DM and DMS types.

Allen

Displacement: 920 tons.
Dimensions: 310 (wl) 315¼ (oa) × 30½ × 9¼ ft.
Machinery: 2-shaft geared turbines, S.H.P. 17,500 = 29.5 knots.
Armament: 4—4 in. guns, 6—21 in. T.T.
Complement: 145.

DD.66	ALLEN	Bath Iron Works	5.12.16	Scrapped 1946.

Notes:—Sole survivor of the pre-flush-deck destroyers. Stationed at Pearl Harbor during entire war; used for training.

"Flush-Deck" classes

Displacement: DD.103-164: 1,090 tons. DD.186-343: 1,190 tons.
Dimensions: 310 (wl) 314½ (oa) × 31¾ × 8¾ ft.
Machinery: 2-shaft geared turbines, S.H.P. 26,000 = 35 knots.
Armament: 4—4 in., 1—3 in. guns, 12—21 in. T.T.
Complement: 150.

DD.103	SCHLEY	Union Iron Works: Bethlehem	28. 3.18	APD 14 (1/43). Scrapped 1946.
DD.106	CHEW		26. 5.18	Scrapped 1946.
DD.109	CRANE		4. 7.18	Scrapped 1947.
DD.113	RATHBURNE		27.12.17	APD 25 (5/44). Scrapped 1947.
DD.114	TALBOT		20. 2.18	APD 7 (10/42). Scrapped 1946.
DD.115	WATERS	Cramp	9. 3.18	APD 8 (10/42). Scrapped 1947.
DD.116	DENT		23. 3.18	APD 9 (10/42). Scrapped 1946.
DD.118	LEA		29. 4.18	Scrapped 1945.

U.S.S. Barney (DD149) March 1945.

U.S.S. Dallas (DD199), early 1942, arriving in Northern Ireland. [*I.W.M.*

U.S.S. Bernadou (DD153) November 1943, shown during landings in Morocco, with masts removed. Structure forward of aft guns is for landing of troops.

U.S.S. Roper (DD147) 5th January 1943. Retains original four funnels.

DD.125	TATTNALL		5. 9.18	APD 19 (7/43). Scrapped 1947.
DD.126	BADGER	New York	24. 8.18	Scrapped 1945.
DD.128	BABBITT	Sbdg.	30. 9.18	AG 102 (6/45). Scrapped 1946.
DD.130	JACOB JONES		20.11.18	Lost 28/2/42.
DD.137	KILTY (ex-AG 20)	Mare	25. 4.18	APD 15 (1/43). Scrapped 1946.
DD.138	KENNISON	Island N.Yd.	8. 6.18	AG 83 (10/44). Scrapped 1947.
DD.139	WARD (ex-Cowell)		1. 6.18	APD 16 (1/43). Lost 7/12/44.
DD.142	TARBELL		28. 5.18	Scrapped 1945.
DD.144	UPSHUR		4. 7.18	AG 103 (6/45). Scrapped 1947.
DD.145	GREER		1. 8.18	Scrapped 1945.
DD.147	ROPER		17. 8.18	APD 20 (10/43). Scrapped 1946.
DD.148	BRECKIN- RIDGE		17. 8.18	AG 112 (6/45). Scrapped 1946.
DD.149	BARNEY	Cramp	5. 9.18	AG 113 (6/45). Scrapped 1946.
DD.150	BLAKELEY		19. 9.18	Scrapped 1945.
DD.151	BIDDLE		3.10.18	AG 114 (6/45). Scrapped 1947.
DD.152	DU PONT		22.10.18	AG 80 (9/44). Scrapped 1947.
DD.153	BERNADOU		7.11.18	Scrapped 1945.
DD.154	ELLIS		30.11.18	AG 115 (6/45). Scrapped 1947.
DD.155	COLE		11. 1.19	AG 116 (6/45). Scrapped 1947.
DD.156	J. FRED TALBOTT		14.12.18	AG 81 (9/44). Scrapped 1947.
DD.157	DICKERSON		12. 3.19	APD 21 (8/43). Lost 4/4/45.
DD.158	LEARY	New York	18.12.18	Lost 24/12/43.
DD.159	SCHENCK	Sbdg.	23. 4.19	AG 82 (9/44). Scrapped 1947.
DD.160	HERBERT		8. 5.19	APD 22 (12/43). Scrapped 1946.
DD.164	CROSBY	Bethlehem (Quincy)	28. 9.18	APD 17 (1/43). Scrapped 1947.
DD.186	CLEMSON (ex-AVD 4)		5. 9.18	APD 31 (3/44). Scrapped 1946.
DD.187	DAHLGREN		20.11.18	AG. 91 (3/45). Scrapped 1946.
DD.188	GOLDS- BOROUGH (ex-AVD 5)	Newport News: Westing-	20.11.18	APD 32 (3/44). Scrapped 1946.
DD.196	GEORGE E. BADGER (ex-AVD 3)	house	6. 3.20	APD 33 (4/44). Scrapped 6/46.
DD.199	DALLAS		31. 5.19	ALEXANDER DALLAS (3/45). Scrapped 1945.

U.S.S. McCormick (DD223) 1944, refueling at sea.

U.S.S. Whipple (DD217) 15th January 1944.

U.S.S. Jouett (DD396) 16th February 1942, close-up amidships.

U.S.S. Alden (DD211) 15th January 1944.

		Builder	Date	Fate
DD.210	BROOME		14. 5.19	AG 96 (5/45). Scrapped 1946.
DD.211	ALDEN		7. 6.19	Scrapped 1945.
DD.213	BARKER		11. 9.19	Scrapped 1945.
DD.215	BORIE		4.10.19	Lost 2/11/43.
DD.216	JOHN D. EDWARDS (ex-Stewart)		18.10.19	Scrapped 1945.
DD.217	WHIPPLE		6.11.19	AG 117 (6/45). Scrapped 1946.
DD.218	PARROTT		25.11.19	Lost 2/5/44.
DD.219	EDSALL		29. 7.20	Lost 1/3/42.
DD.220	MacLEISH		18.12.19	AG 87 (1/45). Scrapped 1947.
DD.221	SIMPSON	Cramp	28. 4.20	AG 97 (5/45). Scrapped 1946.
DD.222	BULMER		22. 1.20	AG 86 (11/44). Scrapped 1947.
DD.223	McCORMICK		14. 2.20	AG 118 (6/45). Scrapped 1947.
DD.224	STEWART		4. 3.20	Lost 2/3/42. Salved by Japan, recovered 8/45 sunk as target 24/5/46.
DD.225	POPE		23. 3.20	Lost 1/3/42.
DD.226	PEARY		6. 4.20	Lost 19/2/42.
DD.227	PILLSBURY		3. 8.20	Lost 1/3/42.
DD.228	JOHN D. FORD (ex-Ford)		2. 9.20	AG 119 (6/45). Scrapped 1947.
DD.229	TRUXTUN		28. 9.20	Lost 18/2/42.
DD.230	PAUL JONES		30. 9.20	AG 120 (6/45). Scrapped 1947.
DD.231	HATFIELD		17. 3.19	AG 84 (10/44). Scrapped 1947.
DD.232	BROOKS		24. 4.19	APD 10 (10/42). Lost 6/1/45.
DD.233	GILMER		24. 5.19	APD 11 (10/42). Scrapped 1947.
DD.234	FOX		12. 6.19	AG 85 (10/44). Scrapped 1947.
DD.235	KANE	New York Sbdg.: Westinghouse	12. 8.19	APD 18 (1/43). Scrapped 1946.
DD.236	HUMPHREYS		28. 7.19	APD 12 (10/42). Scrapped 1946.
DD.237	McFARLAND (ex-AVD 14)		30. 3.20	Scrapped 1946.
DD.239	OVERTON		10. 7.19	APD 23 (8/43). Scrapped 1945.
DD.240	STURTEVANT		29. 7.20	Lost 26/4/42.
DD.242	KING		14.10.20	Scrapped 1946.
DD.243	SANDS		28.10.19	APD 13 (12/42). Scrapped 1946.
DD.244	WILLIAMSON (ex-AVD 2)		16.10.19	Scrapped 1946.

U.S.S. Hatfield (DD231) May 1942.

U.S.S. Davis (DD395) March 1945, showing final modifications with single 5" mount aft, and No. 2 mount removed.

110

U.S.S. Cummings (DD365) September 1944. Notice light gun shields forward, no shields aft.

U.S.S. Overton (DD239) 29th June 1943, alongside for refueling during North Atlantic convoy operations.

DD.245	REUBEN JAMES	New York	4.10.19	Lost 31/10/41.
DD.246	BAINBRIDGE	York	12. 6.20	Scrapped 1945.
DD.247	GOFF	Sbdg:	2. 6.20	Scrapped 1945.
DD.248	BARRY	Westing-house	28.10.20	APD 29 (1/44). Lost 25/5/45.
DD.250	LAWRENCE		10. 7.20	Scrapped 1946.
DD.251	BELKNAP (ex-AVD 8)	Bethlehem	14. 1.19	APD 34 (6/44). Lost 11/1/45.
DD.255	OSMOND INGRAM (ex-AVD 9)	(Fore River)	28. 2.19	APD 35 (6/44). Scrapped 1946.
DD.266	GREENE (ex-AVD 13) (ex-Anthony)	Bethlehem (Squantum)	2.11.18	APD 36 (6/44). Lost 9/10/45.
DD.336	LITCHFIELD	Mare Island	12. 8.19	AG 95 (3/45). Scrapped 1946.
DD.341	DECATUR	N.Yd.	29.10.21	Scrapped 1945.
DD.342	HULBERT (ex-AVD 6)		28. 6.19	Scrapped 1946.
DD.343	NOA	Norfolk N.Yd.	28. 6.19	APD 24 (8/43). Lost 14/9/44.

Notes:—50 of these classes were transferred to R.N. in 1940. Many ships of these classes were converted prior to the war to Light Minelayers (DM), High Speed Minesweepers (DMS), and Seaplane Tenders (AVD). A number of the latter were reclassified as destroyers in 11/43; they were armed with 2—3 in. guns, no T.T. Further ships were adapted as High Speed Transports (APD) or relegated to training (AG), as noted above. They were little modified prior to the war, but DAHLGREN was re-engined in 1938 and had 3rd and 4th funnels combined. During the war, mainmast and fourth funnel were removed, remaining funnels cut down. Armament of most changed to 6—3 in., 2—20 mm. A.A. guns, 6—21 in. T.T., except DD.106, 148-151, 211, 213, 216, 217, 228, 230, 245, 247, 250 and possibly others, which retained 4—4 in. guns, and DD.109 which kept only 2—4 in. guns, no T.T. These ships, good sea boats and of rugged construction, served as Atlantic convoy escorts until late in the war, even though of short range and required refuelling from tankers while on passage. Twelve (DD.211, 213, 216-19, 222, 224-27, 230) were the only U.S. destroyers in the Far East at the outbreak of war and bore the brunt of the early fighting in that theatre. When recovered from the Japanese, STEWART was not given her old name back as a new ship (DE.238) had received the name. Others still existing were SEMMES (AG24, ex-DD 189), DCH-1 (1x44, ex-Walker, DD 163), MOOSEHEAD (1x98, ex-Turner, DD 259) and TAYLOR (ex-DD 94), whose bow was used to repair torpedoed BLAKELEY.

Farragut class

Displacement: 1,395 tons except FARRAGUT, 1,365 tons, DEWEY 1,345 tons, AYLWIN 1,375 tons.
Dimensions: 334 (wl) 341½ (oa) × 34¼ × 9 ft.
Machinery: 2-shaft geared turbines, S.H.P. 42,800 = 36.5 knots.
Armament: 5—5 in. (5 × 1) guns, 8—21 in. (2 × 4) T.T.
Complement: 250.

| DD.348 | FARRAGUT (ex-Smith, ex-Farragut) | Bethlehem (Quincy) | 15. 3.34 | Scrapped 1947. |

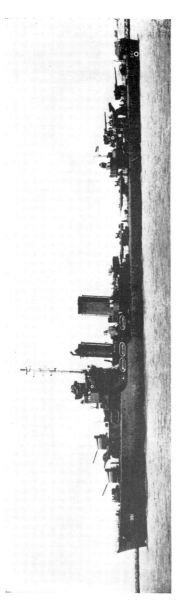

U.S.S. MacDonough (DD351) 20th April 1942. Notice that aft guns are not shielded; original No. 3 mount abaft funnel removed.

U.S.S. Conyngham (DD371) February 1943.

DD.349	DEWEY (ex-Phelps, ex-Dewey)	Bath Iron Works	28. 7.34	Scrapped 1947.
DD.350	HULL	New York N.Yd.	31. 1.34	Lost 18/12/44.
DD.351	Mac-DONOUGH	Boston N.Yd.	22. 8.34	Scrapped 1947.
DD.352	WORDEN	Puget Sound N.Yd.	27.10.34	Lost 12/1/43.
DD.353	DALE	New York N.Yd.	23. 1.35	Scrapped 1947.
DD.354	MONAGHAN	Boston N.Yd.	9. 1.35	Lost 18/12/44.
DD.355	AYLWIN	Philadel-phia N.Yd.	10. 7.34	Scrapped 1947.

Notes:—First post-war destroyer; enlarged versions of contemporary British destroyers. Introduced quadruple T.T. and 5 in. D.P. guns. After guns not protected by gun shields. During the war mainmast was removed, armament modified to 4—5 in., 4—40 mm. A.A. guns.

Porter class

Displacement: 1,850 tons (first 4); 1,805 tons (last 4).
Dimensions: 372 (wl) $381\frac{1}{4}$ (oa) $\times$ 37 $\times$ $10\frac{1}{2}$ ft.
Machinery: 2-shaft geared turbines, S.H.P. 50,000 = 37 knots.
Armament: 8—5 in. (4 $\times$ 2) guns, 8—21 in. (2 $\times$ 4) T.T.
Complement: 290.

DD.356	PORTER		12.12.35	Lost 26/10/42.
DD.357	SELFRIDGE		18. 4.36	Scrapped 1947.
DD.358	McDOUGAL	New York Sbdg.	17. 7.36	Training Ship, AG 126 (9/45). Discarded 1949.
DD.359	WINSLOW		21. 9.36	Training Ship, AG 127 (9/45). Discarded 1957.
DD.360	PHELPS		18. 7.35	Scrapped 1947.
DD.361	CLARK	Bethlehem	15.10.35	Scrapped 1946.
DD.362	MOFFETT	(Quincy)	11.12.35	Scrapped 1947.
DD.363	BALCH		24. 3.36	Scrapped 1946.

Notes:—Designed as squadron leaders; introduced the twin 5 in. mount. The heavy tripod masts were replaced early in the war with a pole foremast; " X " turret removed, 12—40 mm. A.A. guns added. In 1944, " B " turret was removed, single 5 in. turret added at " X " position. Final armament: 5—5 in. (2 x 2, 1 x 1), 8—40 mm. A.A. guns, 8—21 in. T.T. SELFRIDGE lost bow at Vella Lavella, 6/10/43.

Mahan class

Displacement: 1,500 tons, except MAHAN 1,450 tons; CUMMINGS, CUSH-ING, PERKINS, 1,465 tons; DRAYTON, LAMSON, SMITH, PRESTON, FLUSSER, REID, 1,480 tons; DUNLAP, FAN-NING, 1,490 tons.
Dimensions: 334 (wl) $341\frac{1}{2}$ (oa) $\times$ $35\frac{1}{2}$ $\times$ 10 ft.
Machinery: 2-shaft geared turbines, S.H.P. 49,000 = 36.5 knots.
Armament: 5—5 in. (5 $\times$ 1) guns; 12—21 in. (3 $\times$ 4) T.T.
Complement: 172.

U.S.S. Jarvis (DD393) 8th May 1942. Notice huge boiler uptakes to funnel.

U.S.S. Warrington (DD383) 1942, with original armament, no radar.

115

U.S.S. Ralph Talbot (DD390) February 1945.

U.S.S. Aylwin (DD355) December 1944, little changed in appearance during the war.

116

U.S.S. Selfridge (DD357) 19th April 1945. (See also page 102).

DD.364	MAHAN	⎞ Bethlehem	15.10.35	Lost 7/12/44.
DD.365	CUMMINGS	⎟ (Staten Is)	11.12.35	Scrapped 1947.
DD.366	DRAYTON	⎰ Bath	26. 3.36	Scrapped 1947.
DD.367	LAMSON	⎱ Iron	17. 6.36	Expended atom tests.
		Works		Bikini 2/7/46.
DD.368	FLUSSER	⎱	28. 9.35	Scrapped 1948.
DD.369	REID	⎰ Federal	11. 1.36	Lost 11/12/44.
DD.370	CASE	⎱	14. 9.35	Scrapped 1948.
DD.371	CONYNG-HAM	⎰ Boston	14. 9.35	Sunk as target 2/7/48.
		N.Yd.		
DD.372	CASSIN	⎱ Philadel-	28.10.35	Scrapped 1948.
DD.373	SHAW	⎰ phia N.Yd.	28.10.35	Scrapped 1946.
DD.374	TUCKER	⎱ Norfolk	26. 2.36	Lost 4/8/42.
DD.375	DOWNES	⎰ N.Yd.	22. 4.36	Scrapped 1948.
DD.376	CUSHING	⎱ Puget	31.12.35	Lost 13/11/42.
DD.377	PERKINS	⎰ Sound	31.12.35	Lost 29/11/43.
		N.Yd.		
DD.378	SMITH	⎱ Mare Is.	20. 2.36	Scrapped 1947.
DD.379	PRESTON	⎰ N.Yd.	22. 4.36	Lost 14/11/42.
DD.384	DUNLAP	⎱ Bethlehem	18. 4.36	Scrapped 1948.
DD.385	FANNING	⎰ (Staten Is.)	18. 9.36	Scrapped 1948.

Engined by G.E.

Notes:—During 1941, pole foremast replaced tripod and pole mainmast removed; 1—5 in. guns removed. SHAW lost bow and CASSIN and DOWNES were destroyed at Pearl Harbor; machinery and armament fitted in new hulls launched at Mare Island 25/6/43 (CASSIN), 22/5/43 (DOWNES). DUNLAP and FANNING were slightly different with forward guns in turrets and being built with pole foremast. Armament changed to 4—5 in., 8—40 mm. A.A. guns, 4—21 in. T.T. except DD.372 and 375, 8—21 in. T.T.

Somers class

Displacement:	1,850 tons.
Dimensions:	371 (wl) 381¼ (oa) × 37 × 10¼ ft., except DD.394-396, 391 (oa) ft.
Machinery:	2-shaft geared turbines, S.H.P. 52,000 = 37.5 knots.
Armament:	8—5 in. (4 × 2) guns; 12—21 in. (3 × 4) T.T.
Complement:	270.

DD.381	SOMERS	⎱ Federal	13. 3.37	Scrapped 1947.
DD.383	WARRING-TON	⎰	15. 5.37	Lost 13/9/44.
DD.394	SAMPSON	⎱ Bath	16. 4.37	Scrapped 1946.
DD.395	DAVIS	⎰ Iron	30. 7.38	Scrapped 1947.
DD.396	JOUETT	⎱ Works	24. 9.38	Scrapped 1946.

All engined G.E.

Notes:—Improved **Porter** class. Armament changed in stages as in **Porter** class. Final armament: 5 except SOMERS and SAMPSON 6—5 in. guns, 6—40 mm. A.A. guns, 8—21 in. T.T.

U.S.S. Trippe (DD403), 24th July 1944, in dazzle camouflage, leaving Boston.

U.S.S. Phelps (DD360), February 1943, with No. 3 mount replaced by AA guns; pole foremast in place of original tripod.

U.S.S. Dunlap (DD384) May 1942.

U.S.S. Wainwright (DD419) February 1945.

U.S.S. Stack (DD406) 1942.   [I.W.M.

U.S.S. Rhind (DD404) 1942.   [I.W.M.

U.S.S. Maury (DD401) November 1943.

U.S.S. Sterett (DD407) 1942.   [I.W.M.

123

Craven class

Displacement: 1,500 tons.
Dimensions: 334 (wl) 341½ (oa) × 36 × 10 ft.
Machinery: 2-shaft geared turbines, S.H.P. 49,000 = 36.5 knots.
Armament: 4—5 in., 4—1.1 in. A.A. guns; 16—21 in. T.T.
Complement: 250.

DD.380	GRIDLEY	} Bethlehem	1.12.36	Scrapped 1947.
DD.382	CRAVEN	} (Quincy)	25. 2.37	Scrapped 1947.
DD.386	BAGLEY	Norfolk	3. 9.36	Scrapped 1947.
DD.387	BLUE	} N.Yd.:	27. 5.37	Lost 22/8/42.
DD.388	HELM		27. 5.37	Scrapped 1947.
DD.389	MUGFORD		31.10.36	Bikini target ship (7/46).
		Boston		Sunk 22/3/48.
DD.390	RALPH TALBOT	} N.Yd.:	31.10.36	Bikini target ship (7/46). Sunk 8/3/48.
DD.391	HENLEY	Mare Is. N.Yd.	12. 1.37	Lost 3/10/43.
DD.392	PATTERSON	} Puget Sound N.Yd.	6. 5.37	Scrapped 1947.
DD.393	JARVIS		6. 5.37	Lost 9/8/42.
DD.397	BENHAM		16. 4.38	Lost 15/11/42.
DD.398	ELLET	} Federal	11. 6.38	Scrapped 1947.
DD.399	LANG		27. 8.38	Scrapped 1947.
DD.400	McCALL	} Bethlehem (San Fran-	20.11.37	Scrapped 1948.
DD.401	MAURY	cisco)	14. 2.38	Scrapped 1946.
DD.402	MAYRANT		14. 5.38	Bikini target ship (7/46). Sunk 4/4/48.
		Boston		
DD.403	TRIPPE	} N.Yd.	14. 5.38	Bikini target ship (7/46). Sunk 3/2/48.
DD.404	RHIND	Philadel- phia N.Yd.	28. 7.38	Bikini target ship (7/46). Sunk 22/3/48.
DD.405	ROWAN	Norfolk	5. 5.38	Lost 10/9/43.
DD.406	STACK	} N.Yd.	5. 5.38	Bikini target ship (7/46). Sunk 24/4/48.
DD.407	STERETT	Charleston N.Yd.	27.10.38	Scrapped 1947.
DD.408	WILSON	Puget Sound N.Yd.	12. 4.39	Bikini target ship (7/46). Sunk 8/3/48.

DD.386-93 engined G.E.; 397-99, 402-08 Westinghouse; others builders.

Notes:—DD.386-393 differ in having very prominent boiler trunks; DD.397-408 after-guns enclosed by shields. This class mounted the heaviest T.T. battery. Were little changed during the war; final armament of remaining ships: 4—5 in., 4—40 mm. A.A. guns, 8—21 in. T.T. (except DD.386, 388-90, 392, 393).

U.S.S. Morris (DD417) and a sister during the Battle of Coral Sea, 8th May 1942.

U.S.S. Morris (DD417) December 1943. Notice there is no gunhouse on No. 3 mount.

125

Sims class

Displacement:	1,570 tons.			
Dimensions:	341 (wl) 348 (oa) × 36 × 10 ft.			
Machinery:	2-shaft geared turbines, S.H.P. 49,000 = 38 knots.			
Armament:	5—5 in. (5 × 1), 4—1.1 in. A.A. guns; 12—21 in. (3 × 4) T.T.			
Complement:	250.			

DD.409	SIMS	⎫ Bath	8. 4.38	Lost 7/5/42.
DD.410	HUGHES	⎬ Iron	17. 6.39	Bikini target ship (7/46).
		Works		Sunk 16/10/48.
DD.411	ANDERSON	⎫	4. 2.39	Expended Bikini atom
		⎬ Federal		tests, 1/7/46.
DD.412	HAMMANN	⎭	4. 2.39	Lost 6/6/42.
DD.413	MUSTIN	⎱ Newport	8.12.38	Bikini target ship (7/46).
		⎰ News		Sunk 18/4/48.
DD.414	RUSSELL		8.12.38	Scrapped 1947.
DD.415	O'BRIEN	⎱ Boston	20.10.39	Lost 19/10/42.
DD.416	WALKE	⎰ N.Yd.	20.10.39	Lost 14/11/42.
DD.417	MORRIS	Norfolk	1. 6.39	Scrapped 1947.
		N.Yd.		
DD.418	ROE	Charleston	21. 6.39	Scrapped 1947.
		N.Yd.		
DD.419	WAIN-	Norfolk	1. 6.39	Bikini target ship (7/46).
	WRIGHT	N.Yd.		Sunk 2/7/48.
DD.420	BUCK	Philadel-	22. 5.39	Lost 9/10/43
		phia N.Yd.		

All engined Westinghouse.

Notes:—Improved **Benham** class. Some ships completed with only two T.T. mounts, and 1—5 in. gun was removed in 1941. Final armament: 4—5 in., 4—40 mm. A.A. guns, 8—21 in. T.T.

Benson-Livermore class

Displacement:	1,620 tons, except DD.423-424 and Group 2, 1,630 tons.			
Dimensions:	341 (wl) 347¾ (oa) × 36¼ × 10¼ ft. (except Group 2, 348¼ ft. (oa)).			
Machinery:	2-shaft geared turbines, S.H.P. 50,000 = 37 knots.			
Armament:	4—5 in., 4 to 10—.50 cal. A.A. guns; 5—21 in. T.T., except			
	DD.421-444, 5—5 in. guns; 10—21 in. T.T.			
Complement:	250.			

(Group 1)

DD.421	BENSON	⎱ Bethlehem	15.11.39	Chinese LO YANG
		⎰ (Quincy)		(2/54).
DD.422	MAYO		26. 3.40	
DD.423	GLEAVES	⎱ Bath Iron	9.12.39	
DD.424	NIBLACK	⎰ Works	18. 5.40	
DD.425	MADISON	⎱ Boston	20.10.39	
DD.426	LANSDALE	⎰ N.Yd.	20.10.39	Lost 20/4/44.
DD.427	HILARY P.	Charleston	14.12.39	Chinese HAN YANG
	JONES	N.Yd.		(2/54).
DD.428	CHARLES F.	Puget Sound	16. 5.40	
	HUGHES	N.Yd.		

U.S.S. Champlin (DD601) 16th October 1944.

U.S.S. Harding (DD625) 13th October 1943.

127

U.S.S. Sampson (DD394) 27th September 1944, with No. 3 turret removed.

U.S.S. Barton (DD599) 29th May 1942, as completed.

128

DD.459	LAFFEY	Bethlehem	30.10.41	Lost 13/11/42.
DD.460	WOOD-WORTH	(San Francisco)	29.11.41	Italian ARTIGLIERE (6/51).
DD.491	FARENHOLT	Bethlehem	19.11.41	
DD.492	BAILEY	(Staten Is.)	19.12.41	
DD.598	BANCROFT		31.12.41	
DD.599	BARTON	Bethlehem	31. 1.42	Lost 13/11/42.
DD.600	BOYLE	(Quincy)	15. 6.42	
DD.601	CHAMPLIN		25. 6.42	
DD.602	MEADE	Bethlehem	15. 2.42	
DD.603	MURPHY	(Staten	29. 4.42	
DD.604	PARKER	Island)	12. 5.42	
DD.605	CALDWELL		15. 1.42	
DD.606	COGHLAN		12. 2.42	
DD.607	FRAZIER	Bethlehem	17. 3.42	
DD.608	GANSE-VOORT	(San Francisco)	11. 4.42	
DD.609	GILLESPIE		8. 5.42	
DD.610	HOBBY		4. 6.42	
DD.611	KALK		18. 7.42	
DD.612	KENDRICK		2. 4.42	
DD.613	LAUB	Bethlehem	28. 4.42	
DD.614	MACKENZIE	(San	27. 6.42	
DD.615	McLANAHAN	Pedro)	7. 9.42	
DD.616	NIELDS	Bethlehem	1.10.42	
DD.617	ORDRONAUX	(Quincy)	9.11.42	

All engined by Bethlehem, except DD.423-4, Westinghouse; 426 builder.

(Group 2)

DD.429	LIVERMORE (ex-Grayson)	Bath Iron Works: Westinghouse	3. 8.40	Expended in tests 1950
DD.430	EBERLE	house	14. 9.40	Greek NIKI (4/51).
DD.431	PLUNKETT	Federal: Westinghouse	9. 3.40	Chinese NAN YANG (2/59).
DD.432	KEARNY	house	9. 3.40	
DD.433	GWIN	Boston	25. 5.40	Lost 13/7/43.
DD.434	MEREDITH	N.Yd.	24. 4.40	Lost 15/10/42.
DD.435	GRAYSON (ex-Livermore)	Charleston N.Yd.: Westinghouse	7. 8.40	
DD.436	MONSSEN	Puget Sound N.Yd.	16. 5.40	Lost 13/11/42.
DD.437	WOOLSEY	Bath Iron Works: Westinghouse	12. 2.41	
DD.438	LUDLOW	house	11.11.40	Greek DOXA (4/51).
DD.439	EDISON	Federal: Westinghouse	23.11.40	
DD.440	ERICSSON	house	23.11.40	

U.S.S. Bristol (DD453) as completed 21st October 1941, in pre-war colors without gun-shields.

U.S.S. Endicott (DD495) 4th August 1943. Notice flat funnels.

U.S.S. Swanson (DD443) 1942, with tender alongside.

U.S.S. Emmons (DD457) November 1943, showing round funnels, single torpedo tubes mounted between funnels.

131

DD.441	WILKES	Boston	31. 5.40	
DD.442	NICHOLSON	N.Yd.:	31. 5.40	Italian AVIERE
		G.E.		(6/51).
DD.443	SWANSON	Charleston	2.11.40	
		N.Yd.:		
DD.444	INGRAHAM	G.E.	15. 2.41	Lost 22/8/42.
DD.453	BRISTOL		25. 7.41	Lost 12/10/43.
DD.454	ELLYSON		25. 7.41	DMS 19 (11/44). Japanese ASAKAZE (10/54).
DD.455	HAMBLETON	Federal: G.E.	26. 9.41	DMS 20 (11/44).
DD.456	RODMAN		26. 9.41	DMS 21 (11/44). Chinese HSUEN YANG (7/55).
DD.457	EMMONS	Bath Iron Works:	23. 8.41	DMS 22 (11/44). Lost 6/4/45.
DD.458	MACOMB	Westing-house	23. 9.41	DMS 23 (11/44). Japanese HATAKAZE (10/54).
DD.461	FORREST	Boston N.Yd.	14. 6.41	DMS 24 (11/44). Scrapped 1946.
DD.462	FITCH		14. 6.41	DMS 25 (11/44).
DD.463	CORRY	Charleston N.Yd.	28. 7.41	Lost 6/6/44.
DD.464	HOBSON		8. 9.41	DMS 26 (11/44). Lost 27/4/52.
DD.483	AARON WARD		22.11.41	Lost 7/4/43.
DD.484	BUCHANAN		22.11.41	Turkish GELIBOLU (4/49).
DD.485	DUNCAN	Federal:	20. 2.42	Lost 12/10/42.
DD.486	LANSDOWNE	Westing-house	20. 2.42	Turkish GAZIANTEP (/50).
DD.487	LARDNER		20. 3.42	Turkish GEMLIK (/50).
DD.488	McCALLA		20. 3.42	Turkish GIRESUN (4/49).
DD.489	MERVINE		3. 5.42	DMS 31 (5/45).
DD.490	QUICK		3. 5.42	DMS 32 (6/45).
DD.493	CARMICK	Seattle-Tacoma	8. 3.42	DMS 33 (6/45).
DD.494	DOYLE	(Seattle):	17. 3.42	DMS 34 (6/45).
DD.495	ENDICOTT	Allis-Chalmers*	5. 4.42	DMS 35 (5/45).
DD.496	McCOOK		30. 4.42	DMS 36 (5/45).
DD.497	FRANKFORD		17. 5.42	
DD.618	DAVISON		19. 7.42	DMS 37 (6/45).
DD.619	EDWARDS	Federal:	19. 7.42	
DD.620	GLENNON	Westing-house	26. 8.42	Lost 10/6/44.
DD.621	JEFFERS		26. 8.42	DMS 27 (11/44).
DD.622	MADDOX		15. 9.42	Lost 10/7/43.
DD.623	NELSON		15. 9.42	
DD.624	BALDWIN		14. 6.42	Destroyed after going aground, 16/4/61.
DD.625	HARDING	Seattle-Tacoma (Seattle):	28. 6.42	DMS 28 (11/44). Scrapped 1947.
DD.626	SATTERLEE	Westing-house	17. 7.42	
DD.627	THOMPSON		10. 8.42	DMS 38 (5/45).
DD.628	WELLES		7. 9.42	

U.S.S. Pringle (DD477) December 1942, with catapult replacing after tubes and No. 3 gun. Dots above forward turrets are open hatches.

U.S.S. LaVallette
(DD448) 1944.

U.S.S. Killen (DD593)
8th June 1944.

DD.632	COWIE		27. 9.41	DMS 39 (5/45).
DD.633	KNIGHT	Boston	27. 9.41	DMS 40 (5/45).
DD.634	DORAN	N.Yd.	10.12.41	DMS 41 (5/45).
DD.635	EARLE		10.12.41	DMS 42 (5/45).
DD.636	BUTLER	Philadel-	12. 2.42	DMS 29 (11/44).
		phia N.Yd:		Scrapped 1948.
DD.637	GHERARDI	G.E.	12. 2.42	DMS 30 (11/44)
DD.638	HERNDON	Norfolk	5. 2.42	
		N.Yd.:		
DD.639	SHUBRICK	G.E.	18. 4.42	Scrapped 1947.
DD.640	BEATTY	Charleston	20.12.41	Lost 6/11/43.
DD.641	TILLMAN	N.Yd.	20.12.41	
DD.645	STEVENSON	Federal	11.11.41	
DD.646	STOCKTON	Westing-	11.11.41	
DD.647	THORN	house*	28. 2.43	
DD.648	TURNER		28. 2.43	Lost 3/1/44.

* DD.493, 496 engined G.E.; DD.645 Allis-Chalmers.

Notes:—Group 1 has square funnels; Group 2 round. 24 of Group 2 were converted to High Speed Minesweepers (DMS) by removal of " Y " turret and T.T. and addition of sweeping gear. Final war armament: 4—5 in., 4—40 mm. A.A. guns, 5—21 in. T.T. (except DD.421-443: 10—21 in.). Installation of additional 4—40 mm. A.A. guns abandoned in 1945.

Fletcher class

Displacement: 2,050 tons.
Dimensions: 369¼ (wl) 376½ (oa) × 39½ × 17¾ ft.
Machinery: 2-shaft geared turbines, S.H.P. 60,000 = 37 knots.
Armament: 5—5 in., 6 to 10—40 or 20 mm. A.A. guns; 10—21 in. T.T.
Complement: 300.

DD.445	FLETCHER		3. 5.42	DDE (1949).
DD.446	RADFORD	Federal:	3. 5.42	DDE (1949).
DD.447	JENKINS	G.E.	21. 6.42	DDE (1951).
DD.448	LA VALLETTE		21. 6.42	
DD.449	NICHOLAS	Bath	19. 2.42	DDE (1949).
		Iron		
DD.450	O'BANNON	Works:	14. 3.42	DDE (1949).
		Westing-		
DD.451	CHEVALIER	house*	11. 4.42	Lost 7/10/43.
DD.465	SAUFLEY	Federal:	19. 7.42	DDE (1949).
DD.466	WALLER	G.E.	15. 8.42	DDE (1950).
DD.467	STRONG	Bath Iron	17. 5.42	Lost 5/7/43.
DD.468	TAYLOR	Works:	7. 6.42	DDE (1951).
DD.469	DE HAVEN	G.E.*	28. 6.42	Lost 1/2/43.
DD.470	BACHE	Bethlehem	27. 7.42	DDE (1951).
		(Staten Is.):		
DD.471	BEALE	G.E.	24. 8.42	DDE (1951).
DD.472	GUEST		20. 2.42	Brazilian PARA (6/59).
DD.473	BENNETT	Boston	16. 4.42	Brazilian PARAIBA
		N.Yd.:		(12/59).
DD.474	FULLAM	Allis-	16. 4.42	Sunk as target 7/7/62.
DD.475	HUDSON	Chalmers	3. 6.42	
DD.476	HUTCHINS		20. 2.42	
DD.477	PRINGLE	Charleston	2. 5.42	Scrapped 1948.
DD.478	STANLY	N.Yd.*	2. 5.42	Lost 16/4/45.
DD.479	STEVENS		24. 6.42	

U.S.S. McCord (DD534) August 1943, aerial view showing arrangement of turrets, torpedo tubes.

U.S.S. Phelps (DD360) May 1942, showing original armament.

U.S.S. Heerman (DD532) laying a smokescreen off Samar during the Battle of Leyte Gulf, 25th October 1944.

DD.480	HALFORD	Puget Sound N.Yd.*	29.10.42	
DD.481	LEUTZE		29.10.42	Scrapped 1947.
DD.498	PHILIP		13.10.42	DDE (1950).
DD.499	RENSHAW	Federal:	13.10.42	DDE (1950).
DD.500	RINGGOLD	G.E.	11.11.42	W. German Z-2 (7/59).
DD.501	SCHROEDER		11.11.42	
DD.502	SIGSBEE		7.12.42	
DD.503	STEVENSON			Cancelled 10/2/64.
DD.504	STOCKTON			Cancelled 10/2/64.
DD.505	THORN			Cancelled 10/2/63.
DD.509	TURNER			Cancelled 10/2/64.
DD.507	CONWAY		16. 8.42	DDE (1949).
DD.508	CONY		16. 8.42	DDE (1949).
DD.509	CONVERSE	Bath Iron Works:	30. 8.42	Spanish ALMIRANTE VALDES (7/59).
DD.510	EATON	G.E.*	20. 9.42	DDE (1951).
DD.511	FOOTE		11.10.42	
DD.512	SPENCE		27.10.42	Lost 18/12/44.
DD.513	TERRY		22.11.42	
DD.514	THATCHER	Bath Iron Works:	6.12.42	Scrapped 1948.
DD.515	ANTHONY		20.12.42	W. German Z-1 (1/58).
DD.516	WADSWORTH	G.E.	10. 1.43	W. German Z-3 (10/59).
DD.517	WALKER		31. 1.43	DDE (1949).
DD.518	BROWNSON		24. 9.42	Lost 26/12/43.
DD.519	DALY	Bethlehem (Staten Is.):	24.10.42	
DD.520	ISHERWOOD		24.10.42	Peruvian GUISE (10/61).
DD.521	KIMBERLY	G.E.	4. 2.43	
DD.522	LUCE		6. 3.43	Lost 3/5/45.
DD.526	ABNER READ		18. 8.42	Lost 1/11/44.
DD.527	AMMEN		17. 9.42	Scrapped 1961.
DD.528	MULLANY (ex-Beatty)		10.10.42	
DD.529	BUSH		27.10.42	Lost 6/4/45.
DD.530	TRATHEN		22.10.42	
DD.531	HAZELWOOD		20.11.42	
DD.532	HEERMANN	Bethlehem (San Francisco):	5.12.42	Argentine BROWN (8/61).
DD.533	HOEL		19.12.42	Lost 25/10/44.
DD.534	McCORD	Westinghouse*	10. 1.43	
DD.535	MILLER		7. 3.43	
DD.536	OWEN		21. 3.43	
DD.537	THE SULLI-VANS (ex-Putnam)		4. 4.43	
DD.538	STEPHEN POTTER		28. 4.43	
DD.539	TINGEY		28. 5.43	
DD.540	TWINING		11. 7.43	
DD.541	YARNALL		25. 7.43	
DD.544	BOYD	Bethlehem (San Pedro):	29.10.42	
DD.545	BRADFORD		12.12.42	Greek THYELLA (10/62).
DD.546	BROWN	G.E.*	21. 2.43	Greek NAVARINO (10/62).

U.S.S. Drexler (DD741) 6th December 1944.

U.S.S. Stoddard (DD566) April 1944.

DD.547	COWELL	Bethlehem (SP)G.E.*	18. 3.43	
DD.550	CAPPS		31. 5.42	Spanish LEPANTO (5/57).
DD.551	DAVID W. TAYLOR	Gulf Sbdg.: Westing-house*	4. 7.42	Spanish ALMIRANTE FERRANDIZ (5/57).
DD.552	EVANS		4.10.42	Scrapped 1947.
DD.553	JOHN D. HENLEY		15.11.42	
DD.554	FRANKS		7.12.42	
DD.555	HAGGARD		9. 2.43	Scrapped 1946.
DD.556	HAILEY		9. 3.43	Brazilian PERNAM-BUCO (7/61).
DD.557	JOHNSTON		25. 3.43	Lost 25/10/44.
DD.558	LAWS		22. 4.43	
DD.559	LONGSHAW	Seattle-Tacoma (Seattle): G.E.*	4. 6.43	Lost 18/5/45.
DD.560	MORRISON		4. 7.43	Lost 3/5/45.
DD.561	PRICHETT		31. 7.43	
DD.562	ROBINSON		28. 8.43	
DD.563	ROSS		10. 9.43	
DD.564	ROWE		30. 9.43	
DD.565	SMALLEY		27.10.43	
DD.566	STODDARD		19.11.43	
DD.567	WATTS		31.12.43	
DD.568	WREN		29. 1.44	
DD.569	AULICK		2.3. 42	Greek SFENDONI (8/59).
DD.570	CHARLES AUSBURNE		16. 3.42	W. German Z-6 (4/60).
DD.571	CLAXTON		1. 4.42	W. German Z-4 (12/59).
DD.572	DYSON		15. 4.42	W. German Z-5 (2/60).
DD.573	HARRISON		7. 5.42	
DD.574	JOHN RODGERS	Consoli-dated (Orange, Tex). G.E.	7. 5.42	
DD.575	McKEE		2. 8.42	
DD.576	MURRAY		16. 8.42	DDE (1951).
DD.577	SPROSTON		31. 8.42	DDE (1949).
DD.578	WICKES		13. 9.42	
DD.579	WILLIAM D. PORTER		27. 9.42	Lost 10/6/45.
DD.580	YOUNG		11.10.42	
DD.581	CHARRETTE		3. 6.42	Greek VELOS (6/59).
DD.582	CONNER		18. 7.42	Greek ASPIS (9/59).
DD.583	HALL	Boston N.Yd.: G.E.*	18. 7.42	Greek LONKHI (2/60).
DD.584	HALLIGAN		19. 3.43	Lost 26/3/45.
DD.585	HARADEN		19. 3.43	
DD.586	NEWCOMB		4. 7.43	Scrapped 1947.
DD.587	BELL		24. 6.42	
DD.588	BURNS	Charleston N.Yd.: Allis-Chalmers	8. 8.42	
DD.589	IZARD		8. 8.42	
DD.590	PAUL HAMILTON		7. 4.43	
DD.591	TWIGGS		7. 4.43	Lost 16/6/45.

DD.592	HOWORTH	⎤	10. 1.43	Sunk as target 8/3/62.
DD.593	KILLEN		10. 1.43	Discarded 1963.
DD.594	HART (ex-Mansfield)	Puget Sound N.Yd.:	25. 9.44	
DD.595	METCALFE	Westing-	25. 9.44	
DD.596	SHIELDS	house*	25. 9.44	
DD.597	WILEY	⎦	25. 9.44	
DD.629	ABBOT	⎤	17. 2.43	
DD.630	BRAINE		7. 3.43	
DD.631	ERBEN		21. 3.43	Korean CHUNG MU (5/63).
DD.642	HALE	Bath Iron Works: G.E.	4. 4.43	Colombian ANTIO-QUIA (12/60).
DD.643	SIGOURNEY		24. 4.43	
DD.644	STEMBEL	⎦	8. 5.43	Argentine ROSALES (8/61).
DD.649	ALBERT W. GRANT	Charleston N.Yd. Allis-Chalmers	29. 5.43	
DD.650	CAPERTON	⎤ Bath	22. 5.43	
DD.651	COGSWELL	Iron	5. 6.43	
DD.652	INGERSOLL	Works:	28. 6.43	
DD.653	KNAPP	G.E.	10. 7.43	
DD.654	BEARSS	Gulf	25. 7.43	
DD.655	JOHN HOOD	Sbdg.:	25.10.43	
DD.656	VAN VAL-KENBURGH	Allis-Chalmers	19.12.43	
DD.657	CHARLES J. BADGER	⎤ Bethlehem (Staten Is.):	3. 4.43	
DD.658	COLAHAN	G.E.	3. 5.43	
DD.659	DASHIELL	⎤ Federal:	6. 2.43	
DD.660	BULLARD	G.E.	28. 2.43	
DD.661	KIDD	⎦	28. 2.43	
DD.662	BENNION	⎤	4. 7.43	
DD.663	HEYWOOD L. EDWARDS	Boston N.Yd.*	6.10.43	Japanese ARIAKE (3/59).
DD.664	RICHARD P. LEARY	⎦	6.10.43	Japanese YUGURE (3/59).
DD.665	BRYANT	Charleston N.Yd.: Allis-Chalmers	29. 5.43	
DD.666	BLACK	⎤	28. 3.43	
DD.667	CHAUNCEY		28. 3.43	
DD.668	CLARENCE K. BRONSON		18. 4.43	
DD.669	COTTEN	Federal	12. 6.43	
DD.670	DORTCH	G.E.	20. 6.43	Argentine ESPORA (8/61).
DD.671	GATLING		20. 6.43	
DD.672	HEALY		4. 7.43	
DD.673	HICKOX	⎦	4. 7.43	

U.S.S. Halford (DD480) July 1943, with scout plane and catapult in place of after tubes and No. 3 turret.

U.S.S. Cassin Young (DD793) 13th January 1944.

U.S.S. Massey (DD778) 22nd December 1944.

DD.674	HUNT	⎫	1. 8.43	
DD.675	LEWIS		1. 8.43	
	HANCOCK			
DD.676	MARSHALL	Federal	29. 8.43	
DD.677	McDERMUT	⎬ G.E.	17.10.43	
DD.678	McGOWAN		14.11.43	Spanish JORGE JUAN (12/60).
DD.679	McNAIR		14.11.43	
DD.680	MELVIN	⎭	17.10.43	
DD.681	HOPEWELL	⎫ Bethlehem (San	2. 5.43	
DD.682	PORTER- FIELD	⎬ Pedro): Westing- house	13. 6.43	
DD.683	STOCKHAM	⎫ Bethlehem (San Fran- cisco):	25. 6.43	
DD.684	WEDDER- BURN	⎬ Westing- house	1. 8.43	
DD.685	PICKING	⎫ Bethlehem	1. 6.43	
DD.686	HALSEY POWELL	⎬ (Staten Island):	30. 6.43	
DD.687	UHLMANN	G.E.	30. 7.43	
DD.688	REMEY	⎫ Bath	25. 7.43	
DD.689	WADLEIGH	Iron	7. 8.43	Chilean BLANCO ENCALADA (7/62).
DD.690	NORMAN SCOTT	⎬ Works: G.E.*	28. 8.43	
DD.691	MERTZ	⎭	11. 9.43	
DD.792	CALLAGHAN	⎫ Bethlehem	1. 8.43	Lost 28/7/45.
DD.793	CASSIN YOUNG	(San Pedro):	12. 9.43	
DD.794	IRWIN	⎬ Westing-	31.10.43	
DD.795	PRESTON	⎭ house*	12.12.43	
DD.796	BENHAM	⎫ Bethlehem (Staten	30. 8.43	Peruvian VILLAR (12/60).
DD.797	CUSHING	⎬ Island): G.E.	30. 9.43	Brazilian PARANA (7/61).
DD.798	MONSSEN		30.10.43	Scrapped 1964.
DD.799	JARVIS	⎫	14. 2.44	Spanish ALCALA GALIANO (11/60).
DD.800	PORTER	Seattle-	13. 3.44	
DD.801	COLHOUN	Tacoma	10. 4.44	Lost 6/4/45.
DD.802	GREGORY	(Seattle):	8. 5.44	
DD.803	LITTLE	G.E.	22. 5.44	Lost 3/5/45.
DD.804	ROOKS	⎭	6. 6.44	Chilean COCHRANE (7/62).

DDE: Escort Destroyer.

* DD.451, 480, 794 engined G.E.; 468, 478, 507, 557, 560, 563, 688-9 Westing-house; 479, 481, 508-9, 532, 541, 546-7, 550-1, 581-2, 586, 592-3, 597, 662 Allis-Chalmers.

U.S.S. Laffey (DD724)
8th August 1944.

U.S.S. Maddox
(DD731) August
1944.

144

U.S.S. Soley (DD707) 22nd December 1944.

U.S.S. Cooper (DD695) with Task Force 38 in the Western Pacific, 7th November 1944. In rear is carrier Yorktown (CV10).

Notes:—New basic destroyer designed with increased beam and flush-deck hull. DD.476-481 were designed with a catapult in place of after T.T. mount and " Q " turret; only DD.477, 479 and 480 were so completed, but proving impracticable, it was removed. The following unnamed vessels were also cancelled in 1941: DD.523-525, 542-543, 548-549. A highly successful design, this class provided the backbone of the Pacific Fleet. In addition to those ships sunk or scrapped as a result of damage, the following were severely damaged at Okinawa: BACHE, BRYANT, BRAINE, CASSIN YOUNG, HAZELWOOD, ISHERWOOD, KIDD, MULLANY, SIGSBEE. Two additional ships with similar specifications were planned as experimental types. PERCIVAL (DD.452) was to have ultra-high pressure boilers; WATSON (DD.482) diesel engines. Both were ordered from Federal but cancelled in 1946.

Allen M. Sumner class

Displacement:	2,200 tons.	
Dimensions:	369 (wl) 376½ (oa) × 41 × 19 ft.	
Machinery:	2-shaft geared turbines, S.H.P. 60,000 = 36.5 knots.	
Armament:	6—5 in. (3 × 2), 12—40 mm. A.A. guns; 10—21 in. T.T.	
Complement:	350.	

DD.692	ALLEN M. SUMNER		15.12.43	
DD.693	MOALE		16. 1.44	
DD.694	INGRAHAM		16. 1.44	
DD.695	COOPER		9. 2.44	Lost 3/12/44.
DD.696	ENGLISH		27. 2.44	
DD.697	CHARLES S. SPERRY		13. 3.44	
DD.698	AULT		26. 3.44	
DD.699	WALDRON		26. 3.44	
DD.700	HAYNS-WORTH		15. 4.44	
DD.701	JOHN W. WEEKS	Federal: G.E.	21. 5.44	
DD.702	HANK		21. 5.44	
DD.703	WALLACE L. LIND		14. 6.44	
DD.704	BORIE		4. 7.44	
DD.705	COMPTON		17. 9.44	
DD.706	GAINARD		17. 9.44	
DD.707	SOLEY		8. 9.44	
DD.708	HARLAN R. DICKSON		17.12.44	
DD.709	HUGH PURVIS		17.12.44	
DD.722	BARTON		10.10.43	
DD.723	WALKE		27.10.43	
DD.724	LAFFEY		21.11.43	
DD.725	O'BRIEN		8.12.43	
DD.726	MEREDITH	Bath Iron Works: G.E.	21.12.43	Lost 9/6/44.
DD.727	DE HAVEN		9. 1.44	
DD.728	MANSFIELD		29. 1.44	
DD.729	LYMAN K. SWENSON		12. 2.44	
DD.730	COLLETT		5. 3.44	
DD.731	MADDOX		19. 3.44	

DD.732	HYMAN	Bath	8. 4.44	
DD.733	MANNERT L. ABELE	Iron Works:	23. 4.44	Lost 12/4/45.
DD.734	PURDY	G.E.	7. 5.44	
DD.741	DREXLER		3. 9.44	Lost 28/5/45.
DD.744	BLUE		28.11.43	
DD.745	BRUSH		28.12.43	
DD.746	TAUSSIG		25. 1.44	
DD.747	SAMUEL N. MOORE		23. 2.44	
DD.748	HARRY E. HUBBARD	Bethlehem (Staten	24. 3.44	
DD.752	ALFRED A. CUNNING-HAM	Island): G.E.*	3. 8.44	
DD.753	JOHN R. PIERCE		1. 9.44	
DD.754	FRANK E. EVANS		3.10.44	
DD.755	JOHN A. BOLE		1.11.44	
DD.756	BEATTY		30.11.44	
DD.757	PUTNAM		26. 3.44	
DD.758	STRONG	Bethlehem	23. 4.44	
DD.759	LOFBERG	(San Fran-	12. 8.44	
DD.760	JOHN W THOMASON	cisco): G.E.*	30. 9.44	
DD.761	BUCK		11. 3.45	
DD.762	HENLEY		8. 4.45	
DD.770	LOWRY		6. 2.44	
DD.774	HUGH W. HADLEY	Bethlehem	16. 7.44	Scrapped 1947.
DD.775	WILLARD KEITH	(San Pedro):	29. 8.44	
DD.776	JAMES C. OWENS	G.E.	1.10.44	
DD.777	ZELLARS		19. 7.44	
DD.778	MASSEY	Todd-	19. 8.44	
DD.779	DOUGLAS H. FOX	Pacific (Seattle):	30. 9.44	
DD.780	STORMES	Allis-	4.11.44	
DD.781	ROBERT K. HUNTING-TON	Chalmers	5.12.44	
DD.857	BRISTOL	Bethlehem (San Pedro): G.E.	29.10.44	

* DD.748, 752-54, 759 engined Westinghouse.

Notes:—Improved **Fletcher** class with new twin 5 in. turrets and quadruple 40 mm. A.A. guns. 12 (DD.735-40, 749-51, 771-73) completed as Light Minelayers without T.T. (see page 212). Aft T.T. mount replaced by 4-40 mm. guns in 1945. LAFFEY survived attack by twenty-two *Kamikaze* planes (being hit by six) off Okinawa, 16/4/45. Others severely damaged at Okinawa included DOUGLAS H. FOX, INGRAHAM, HYMAN, O'BRIEN, PURDY, STORMES and ZELLARS. Although some of this class were at Normandy, the majority went to the Pacific.

Gearing class

Displacement: 2,425 tons.
Dimensions: 383 (wl) 390½ (oa) × 40¾ × 19 ft.
Machinery: 2-shaft geared turbines, S.H.P. 60,000 = 35 knots.
Armament: 6—5 in. (3 × 2), 12—40 mm. A.A. guns, 10—21 in. T.T., except DD.742-743, 805-808, 829-835, 873-883: 6—5 in., 16—40 mm. A.A. guns, no T.T.
Complement: 350.

DD.710	GEARING		18. 2.45	
DD.711	EUGENE A. GREENE		18. 3.45	
DD.712	GYATT		15. 4.45	Guided Missile Destroyer, DDG.1 (4/57).
DD.713	KENNETH D. BAILEY		17. 6.45	
DD.714	WILLIAM R. RUSH		8. 7.45	
DD.715	WILLIAM M. WOOD	Federal: Westinghouse*	29. 7.45	
DD.716	WILTSIE		31. 8.45	
DD.717	THEODORE E. CHANDLER		20.10.45	
DD.718	HAMNER		24.11.45	
DD.719	EPPERSON		22.12.45	Completed as DDE (3/49).
DD.720	CASTLE		.46	Sold 8/55 (incomplete).
DD.721	WOODROW R. THOMPSON		.46	Sold 8/55 (incomplete).
DD.742	FRANK KNOX	Bath Iron Works: Westinghouse	17. 9.44	
DD.743	SOUTHERLAND		5.10.44	
DD.763	WILLIAM C. LAWE		21. 5.45	
DD.764	LLOYD THOMAS	Bethlehem (San Francisco): G.E.*	5.10.45	DDE (1949).
DD.765	KEPPLER		24. 6.46	DDE (1949).
DD.766	LANSDALE		20.12.46	Scrapped incomplete 1959.
DD.767	SEYMOUR D. OWENS		24. 2.47	Scrapped incomplete 1959.
DD.768	HOEL			Cancelled 9/46.
DD.769	ABNER READ			Cancelled 9/46.
DD.782	ROWAN		29.12.44	
DD.783	GURKE	Todd-Pacific (Seattle): G.E.*	15. 2.45	
DD.784	McKEAN		31. 3.45	
DD.785	HENDERSON		28. 5.45	
DD.786	RICHARD B. ANDERSON		7. 7.45	
DD.787	JAMES E. KYES		4. 8.45	

U.S.S. Higbee (DD806) 18th March 1945. as completed with tripod mainmast replacing forward tubes.

U.S.S. Southerland (DD743) 6th January 1945. Early unit of Gearing Class as completed with two torpedo tube mounts.

149

DD.788	HOLLISTER	Todd-	9.10.45	
DD.789	EVERSOLE	Pacific	8. 1.46	
DD.790	SHELTON	(Seattle)	8. 3.46	
DD.791	SEAMAN	G.E.*	20. 5.46	Scrapped 1962 (not commissioned).
DD.805	CHEVALIER		29.10.44	
DD.806	HIGBEE	Bath Iron	12.11.44	
DD.807	BENNER	Works:	30.11.44	
DD.808	DENNIS J. BUCKLEY	G.E.	20.12.44	
DD.817	CORRY		28. 7.45	
DD.818	NEW		18. 8.45	
DD.819	HOLDER		25. 8.45	
DD.820	RICH	Consoli-	5.10.45	
DD.821	JOHNSTON	dated	19.10.45	
DD.822	ROBERT H. McCARD	(Orange, Tex.):	9.11.45	
DD.823	SAMUEL B. ROBERTS	G.E.*	30.11.45	
DD.824	BASILONE	Consoli- dated	22.12.45	Completed as DDE (7/49).
DD.825	CARPENTER	(Orange, Tex.):	28.12.45	Completed as DDE (12/49).
DD.826	AGERHOLM	G.E.	30. 3.46	
DD.827	ROBERT A. OWENS		15. 7.46	Completed as DDE (11/49).
DD.828	TIMMERMAN		19. 5.51	Completed as experimental ship, AG.152 (9/52). Scrapped 1959.
DD.829	MYLES C. FOX		13. 1.45	
DD.830	EVERETT F. LARSON		28. 1.45	
DD.831	GOODRICH		25. 2.45	
DD.832	HANSON		11. 3.45	
DD.833	HERBERT J. THOMAS		25. 3.45	
DD.834	TURNER		8. 4.45	
DD.835	CHARLES P. CECIL		22. 4.45	
DD.836	GEORGE K. MACKENZIE		13. 5.45	
DD.837	SARSFIELD	Bath Iron	27. 5.45	
DD.838	ERNEST G. SMALL	Works: G.E.	14. 6.45	
DD.839	POWER		30. 6.45	
DD.840	GLENNON		14. 7.45	
DD.841	NOA		30. 7.45	
DD.842	FISKE		8. 9.45	
DD.843	WARRINGTON		27. 9.45	
DD.844	PERRY		25.10.45	
DD.845	BAUSSELL		19.11.45	
DD.846	OZBOURN		22.12.45	
DD.847	ROBERT L. WILSON		5. 1.46	

U.S.S. Madison (DD425) at sea, 1942. Notice 5in. mount aft of second funnel, later removed.

U.S.S. Steinaker (DD863) 13th June 1945, as completed with quadruple 40 mm. A.A. guns replacing after set of tubes.

DD.848	WITEK	Bath Iron	2. 2.46	DDE (1950).
DD.849	RICHARD E. KRAUS	Works G.E.	2. 3.46	
DD.850	JOSEPH P. KENNEDY JR.		26. 7.45	
DD.851	RUPERTUS	Bethlehem	21. 9.45	
DD.852	LEONARD F. MASON	(Quincy): Westing-	4. 1.46	
DD.853	CHARLES H. ROAN	house	15. 3.4ᶜ	
DD.858	FRED T. BERRY	Bethlehem	28. 1.45	DDE (1950).
DD.859	NORRIS	(San	25. 2.45	DDE (1950).
DD.860	McCAFFERY	Pedro):	12. 4.45	DDE (1950).
DD.861	HARWOOD	G.E.*	22. 5.45	DDE (1950).
DD.862	VOGEL-GESANG		15. 1.45	
DD.863	STEINAKER		13. 2.45	
DD.864	HAROLD J. ELLISON		14. 3.45	
DD.865	CHARLES R. WARE		12. 4.45	
DD.866	CONE	Bethlehem	10. 5.45	
DD.867	STRIBLING	(Staten	8. 6.45	
DD.868	BROWNSON	Island):	7. 7.45	
DD.869	ARNOLD J. ISBELL	G.E.*	6. 8.45	
DD.870	FECHTELER		19. 9.45	
DD.871	DAMATO		21.11.45	DDE (1950).
DD.872	FORREST ROYAL		17. 1.46	
DD.873	HAWKINS (ex-Beatty)		7.10.44	
DD.874	DUNCAN		27.10.44	
DD.875	HENRY W. TUCKER		8.11.44	
DD.876	ROGERS		20.11.44	
DD.877	PERKINS		7.12.44	
DD.878	VESOLE		29.12.44	
DD.879	LEARY		20. 1.45	
DD.880	DYESS		26. 1.45	
DD.881	BORDELON	Consoli-	3. 3.45	
DD.882	FURSE	dated	9. 3.45	
DD.883	NEWMAN K. PERRY	(Orange, Tex.):	17. 3.45	
DD.884	FLOYD B. PARKS	G.E.*	31. 3.45	
DD.885	JOHN R. CRAIG		14. 4.45	
DD.886	ORLECK		12. 5.45	
DD.887	BRINKLEY BASS		26. 5.45	
DD.888	STICKELL		16. 6.45	
DD.889	O'HARE		22. 6.45	
DD.890	MEREDITH		28. 6.45	

*DD.713, 716, 719-721 engined G.E.; 764-5, 789 Allis-Chalmers; 822-23, 859, 868-69, 879-80, 886 Westinghouse.

Notes:—Modified Sumner class with 14 ft. extra section amidships. The following unnamed vessels were also cancelled in 1945: DD.809-816, 854-856, 891-926. As completed many of these ships differed from armament details as given, some were not commissioned until long after the war. DD.742-743, 805-808, 829-835, 873-883 had a light tripod mast between funnels (radar picket ships).

DESTROYER ESCORTS

The first destroyer escorts built in the United States were ordered under lend-lease for the United Kingdom early in 1941. The original 50 was expanded to 250 early in 1942, but ironically only 55 of this group were actually transferred, the remainder being retained by the U.S. Navy which had not planned to build any.

Of the 1,005 destroyer escorts finally ordered by 1943, only 563 were completed, including 56 completed as high speed transports (APD), and 84 transferred under lend-lease. Except for the original " short-hull " design, all were to be of the same design. However, priority in construction was given to landing ships resulting in a shortage of machinery. In order to get them to sea, 254 were completed with only half the designed horsepower (**Edsall, Cannon** and **Evarts classes**), resulting in a speed of only 21 knots instead of the designed 24. In these ships, turbines were replaced by diesel engines. The early types mounted three 3-inch guns; later units were armed with two 5-inch guns. All except the short hull type (and units transferred to the United Kingdom and France) also had three 21-inch T.T. in a new triple mounting.

In the North Atlantic, the DE's served admirably as convoy escorts and with the escort carrier hunter-killer groups. They replaced the old World War I flush-deckers which had done good service, but which after 1943 were steadily retired to training duties.

In the Pacific, DE's were used in similar fashion as escorts and in anti-submarine work. A notable although unintended exception to this unheralded duty was the action of DENNIS, JOHN C. BUTLER, RAYMOND and SAMUEL B. ROBERTS in attacking the main Japanese fleet off Samar during the Battle of Leyte Gulf.

Destroyer escorts are denoted by the symbol DE, and named in similar fashion to destroyers.

(GMT) Evarts (Short Hull) class

Displacement: 1,140 tons.
Dimensions: $289\frac{1}{2}$ (wl) $283\frac{1}{2}$ (oa) $\times$ 35 $\times$ $8\frac{1}{4}$ ft.
Machinery: 2-shaft diesel-electric motors, S.H.P. 6,000 = 21 knots.
Armament: 3—3 in., 4—40 mm., 5—20 mm. guns.
Complement: 170.

DE.5	EVARTS			7.12.42	Scrapped 7/46.
DE.6	WYFFELS			7.12.42	Chinese TAI KANG (8/45).
			Boston N.Yd.		
DE.7	GRISWOLD			9. 1.43	Scrapped 1/47.
DE.8	STEELE			9. 1.43	Scrapped 1/47.
DE.9	CARLSON			9. 1.43	Scrapped 12/46.

Destroyer escort dropping depth charges at Pacific Fleet base at Ulithi, 20th November 1944.

DE.10	BEBAS	} Boston N.Yd.	9. 1.43	Scrapped 2/47.
DE.11	CROUTER		26. 1.43	Scrapped 12/46.
DE.13	BRENNAN		22. 8.42	Scrapped 8/46.
DE.14	DOHERTY		29. 8.42	Scrapped 12/46.
DE.15	AUSTIN		25. 9.42	Scrapped 2/47.
DE.16	EDGAR G. CHASE		26. 9.42	Scrapped 4/47.
DE.17	EDWARD C. DALY		21.10.42	Scrapped 2/47.
DE.18	GILMORE		22.10.42	Scrapped 3/47.
DE.19	BURDEN R. HASTINGS		20.11.42	Scrapped 3/47.
DE.20	LE HARDY		21.11.42	Scrapped 1/47.
DE.21	HAROLD C. THOMAS	} Mare Island N.Yd.	18.12.42	Scrapped 2/47.
DE.22	WILEMAN		19.12.42	Scrapped 2/47.
DE.23	CHARLES R. GREER		18. 1.43	Scrapped 3/47.
DE.24	WHITMAN		19. 1.43	Scrapped 2/47.
DE.25	WINTLE		18. 2.43	Scrapped 8/47.
DE.26	DEMPSEY		19. 2.43	Scrapped 5/47.
DE.27	DUFFY		16. 4.43	Scrapped 8/47.
DE.28	EMERY (ex-Eisner)		17. 4.43	Scrapped 8/47.
DE.29	STADTFELD		17. 5.43	Scrapped 8/47.
DE.30	MARTIN		18. 5.43	Scrapped 7/47.
DE.31	SEDERSTROM (ex-Gillette)		15. 6.43	Scrapped 2/48.
DE.32	FLEMING		16. 6.43	Scrapped 2/48.
DE.33	TISDALE		28. 6.43	Scrapped 3/48.
DE.34	EISELE		29. 6.43	Scrapped 2/48.
DE.35	FAIR		27. 7.43	Sold 6/47.
DE.36	MANLOVE		28. 7.43	Scrapped 3/48.
DE.37	GREINER		20. 5.43	Scrapped 3/47.
DE.38	WYMAN		3. 6.43	Scrapped 6/47.
DE.39	LOVERING	} Puget Sound N.Yd.	18. 6.43	Scrapped 1/47.
DE.40	SANDERS		18. 6.43	Scrapped 6/47.
DE.41	BRACKETT		1. 8.43	Scrapped 6/57.
DE.42	REYNOLDS		1. 8.43	Scrapped 5/47.
DE.43	MITCHELL		1. 8.43	Scrapped 1/47.
DE.44	DONALDSON		1. 8.43	Scrapped 8/46.
DE.45	ANDRES		24. 7.42	Scrapped 2/46.
DE.47	DECKER	} Philadelphia N.Yd.	24. 7.42	Chinese TAI PING (8/45) lost 14/11/54.
DE.48	DOBLER		24. 7.42	Scrapped 7/46.
DE.49	DONEFF		24. 7.42	Scrapped 1/47.
DE.50	ENGSTROM		24. 7.42	Scrapped 1/47.
DE.256	SEID		22. 2.43	Scrapped 2/47.
DE.257	SMARTT		22. 2.43	Scrapped 8/46.
DE.258	WALTER S. BROWN	} Boston N.Yd.	22. 2.43	Scrapped 8/46.
DE.259	WILLIAM C. MILLER		22. 2.43	Scrapped 5/47.
DE.260	CABANA		10. 3.43	Scrapped 6/47.
DE.261	DIONNE		10. 3.43	Scrapped 7/47.

U.S.S. Sederstrom (DE31: Evarts Class) December 1943.

U.S.S. Mason (DE529: Evarts Class). Short-hull type in dazzle camouflage, August 1944.

DE.262	CANFIELD		6. 4 43	Scrapped 7/47.
DE.263	DEEDE	Boston	6. 4 43	Scrapped 7/47.
DE.264	ELDEN	N.Yd.	6. 4 43	Scrapped 7/47.
DE.265	CLOUES		6. 4 43	Scrapped 6/47.
DE.301	LAKE		18. 8.43	Scrapped 1/47.
DE.302	LYMAN		19. 8.43	Scrapped 1/47.
DE.303	CROWLEY		22. 9.43	Scrapped 1/47.
DE.304	RALL		23. 9.43	Scrapped 4/47.
DE.305	HALLORAN		14. 1.44	Scrapped 4/47.
DE.306	CONNOLLY		15. 1.44	Scrapped 6/46.
DE.307	FINNEGAN		22. 2.44	Scrapped 6/46.
DE.308	CREAMER	Mare	23. 2.44	Cancelled 9/44.
DE.309	ELY	Island	10. 4.44	Cancelled 9/44.
DE.310	DELBERT W. HALSEY	N.Yd.	11. 4.44	Cancelled 9/44.
DE.311	KEPPLER			Cancelled 3/44.
DE.312	LLOYD THOMAS			Cancelled 3/44.
DE.313	WILLIAM C. LAWE			Cancelled 3/44.
DE.314	WILLARD KEITH			Cancelled 3/44.
DE.315	(Unnamed)			Cancelled 3/44.
DE.527	O'TOOLE		2.11.43	Scrapped 3/46.
DE.528	JOHN J. POWERS	Boston	2.11.43	Scrapped 2/46.
DE.529	MASON	N.Yd.	17.11.43	Scrapped 4/47.
DE.530	JOHN M. BER-MINGHAM		17.11.43	Scrapped 3/46.

All engined General Motors.

Notes:—DE.1-50 were originally ordered for the Royal Navy under lend-lease as BDE.1-50, but only DE.1-4, 12 and 46 were transferred. 26 later ships of this class (DE.266-280 and 516-526) were also transferred. Originally designed with 12,000 shaft horsepower and speed of 24 knots.

(TE) Buckley class

Displacement: 1,400 tons.
Dimensions: 300 (wl) 306 (oa) × 37 × 9½ ft.
Machinery: 2-shaft turbo-electric drive, S.H.P. 12,000 = 23.5 knots.
Armament: 3—3 in., 6—40 mm. A.A. guns; 3—21 in. T.T.
Complement: 220.

DE.51	BUCKLEY		9. 1.43	
DE.53	CHARLES LAWRENCE		16. 2.43	APD 37 (10/44). Discarded 9/64
DE.54	DANIEL T. GRIFFIN	Bethlehem (Hing-	23. 2.43	APD 38 (10/44).
DE.56	DONNELL	ham)	13. 3.43	IX 182 (7/44); sold 4/46.
DE.57	FOGG		20. 3.43	
DE.59	FOSS		10. 4.43	

DE.60	GANTNER	⎫	17. 4.43	APD 42 (2/45).
DE.62	GEORGE W. INGRAM		8. 5.43	APD 43 (2/45).
DE.63	IRA JEFFERY		15. 5.43	APD 44 (2/45). Discarded 1960.
DE.65	LEE FOX	Bethlehem (Hing- ham)	29. 5.43	APD 45 (2/45). Discarded 9/64.
DE.66	AMESBURY		5. 6.43	APD 46 (2/45). Discarded 1960.
DE.68	BATES		6. 6.43	APD 47 (7/44); lost 25/5.45.
DE.69	BLESSMAN		19. 6.43	APD 48 (7/44).
DE.70	JOSEPH E. CAMPBELL		26. 6.43	APD 49 (7/44).
DE.153	REUBEN JAMES	⎱	6. 2.43	
DE.154	SIMS		6. 2.43	APD 50 (9/44). Discarded 1960.
DE.155	HOPPING		10. 3.43	APD 51 (9/44). Discarded 9/64.
DE.156	REEVES	Norfolk N.Yd.	22. 4.43	APD 52 (9/44). Discarded 1960.
DE.157	FECHTELER		22. 4.43	Lost 4/5.44.
DE.158	CHASE		24. 4.43	APD 54 (11/44); sold 11/46.
DE.159	LANING		4. 7.43	APD 55 (11/44).
DE.160	LOY		4. 7.43	APD 56 (10/44). Discarded 9/64.
DE.161	BARBER		20. 5.43	APD 57 (10/44).
DE.198	LOVELACE		4. 7.43	
DE.199	MANNING	⎱	1. 6.43	
DE.200	NEUENDORF		1. 6.43	
DE.201	JAMES E. CRAIG		22. 7.43	
DE.202	EICHEN- BERGER		22. 7.43	
DE.203	THOMASON		23. 8.43	
DE.204	JORDAN		23. 8.43	Scrapped 7/47.
DE.205	NEWMAN		9. 8.43	APD 59 (7/44). Discarded 9/64.
DE.206	LIDDLE	Charleston N.Yd.	9. 8.43	APD 60 (7/44).
DE.207	KEPHART		6. 9.43	APD 61 (7/44).
DE.208	COFER		6. 9.43	APD 62 (7/44).
DE.209	LLOYD		23.10.43	APD 63 (7/44).
DE.210	OTTER		23.10.43	
DE.211	JOSEPH C. HUBBARD		11.11.43	APD 53 (6/45).
DE.212	HAYTER		11.11.43	APD 80 (6/45).
DE.213	WILLIAM T. POWELL		27.11.43	
DE.214	SCOTT	⎱	3. 4.43	
DE.215	BURKE	Philadel- phia N.Yd.	3. 4.43	APD 65 (1/45).
DE.216	ENRIGHT		29. 5.43	APD 66 (1/45).
DE.217	COOLBAUGH		29. 5.43	
DE.218	DARBY	⎭	29. 5.43	

U.S.S. Robert I. Paine (DE578: Buckley Class) 1945. Notice cluster of A.A. guns abaft funnel.

159

U.S.S. Gillette (DE681: Buckley Class). Turbo-electric type with 3in. guns, June 1944.

U.S.S. Weber (DE675: Buckley Class) September 1943.

DE.219	J. DOUGLAS BLACKWOOD	⎫	29. 5.43	
DE.220	FRANCIS M. ROBINSON	Philadel-phia	29. 5.43	
DE.221	SOLAR	N.Yd.	29. 5.43	Lost 30/4/46.
DE.222	FOWLER		3. 7.43	
DE.223	SPANGEN-BERG	⎭	3. 7.43	
DE.575	AHRENS	⎫	21.12.43	
DE.576	BARR		28.12.43	APD 39 (7/44). Discarded 1960.
DE.577	ALEXANDER J. LUKE	Bethlehem (Hing-ham)	28.12.43	
DE.578	ROBERT I. PAINE	⎭	30.12.43	
DE.633	FOREMAN	⎫	1. 8.43	
DE.634	WHITEHURST		5. 9.43	
DE.635	ENGLAND		26. 9.43	Scrapped 11/46.
DE.636	WITTER		17.10.43	Scrapped 11/46.
DE.637	BOWERS		31.10.43	APD 40 (6/45); Philippine RAJAH SOLIMAN (4/61).
DE.638	WILLMARTH	Bethlehem (San Francisco)	21.11.43	
DE.639	GENDREAU		12.12.43	
DE.640	FIEBERLING		2. 4.44	
DE.641	WILLIAM C. COLE		29.12.43	
DE.642	PAUL G. BAKER		12. 3.44	
DE.643	DAMON M. CUMMINGS		18. 4.44	
DE.644	VAMMEN	⎭	21. 5.44	
DE.665	JENKS	⎫	11. 9.43	
DE.666	DURIK	Dravo (Pitts-burgh)	9.10.43	
DE.667	WISEMAN	⎭	6.11.43	
DE.675	WEBER	⎫	1. 5.43	APD 75 (12/44). Discarded 1960.
DE.676	SCHMITT		29. 5.43	APD 76 (1/45).
DE.677	FRAMENT		28. 6.43	APD 77 (12/44). Discarded 1960.
DE.678	HARMON	Bethlehem (Quincy)	25. 7.43	
DE.679	GREENWOOD		21. 8.43	
DE.680	LOESER		11. 9.43	
DE.681	GILLETTE		25. 9.43	
DE.682	UNDERHILL		15.10.43	Lost 24/7/45.
DE.683	HENRY R. KENYON	⎭	30.10.43	
DE.693	BULL	⎫	25. 3.43	APD 78 (7/44).
DE.694	BUNCH		29. 5.43	APD 79 (7/44). Scrapped 1965.
DE.695	RICH	Defoe (Bay City Mich.)	22. 6.43	Lost 8/6/44.
DE.696	SPANGLER		15. 7.43	
DE.697	GEORGE		14. 8.43	
DE.698	RABY		4. 9.43	
DE.699	MARSH	⎭	25. 9.43	

U.S.S. George A. Johnson (DE583: Rudderow Class). Turbo-electric type with 5in. guns. August 1944.

U.S.S. McNulty (DE581: Rudderow Class) August 1944.

162

DE.700	CURRIER	⎫	14.10.43	
DE.701	OSMUS	⎪	4.11.43	
DE.702	EARL V. JOHNSON	Defoe (Bay City Mich.)	24.11.43	
DE.703	HOLTON		15.12.43	
DE.704	CRONIN		5. 1.44	
DE.705	FRYBARGER	⎭	25. 1.44	
DE.789	TATUM		7. 8.43	APD 81 (12/44).
DE.790	BORUM		14. 8.43	
DE.791	MALOY		18. 8.43	
DE.792	HAINES		26. 8.43	APD 84 (12/44). Discarded 1960.
DE.793	RUNELS	Consolidated (Orange, Tex.)	4. 9.43	APD 85 (1/45). Discarded 1960.
DE.794	HOLLIS		11. 9.43	APD 86 (1/45).
DE.795	GUNASON		16.10.43	
DE.796	MAJOR		23.10.43	
DE.797	WEEDEN		27.10.43	
DE.798	VARIAN		6.11.43	
DE.799	SCROGGINS		6.11.43	
DE.800	JACK W. WILKE		18.12.43	

All engined G.E.

Notes:—46 of this class (DE.52, 55, 58, 61, 64, 67, 71-94, 563-574) were transferred to the Royal Navy. 37 were converted to High Speed Transports (APD) following completion. Conversion of 7 others (DE.214, 635-636, 665-666, 790-791) did not proceed. During 1945, DE.217-219, 678-680, 696-698, 700-701 were rearmed with 2—5 in., 10—40 mm. guns, no T.T. ENGLAND sank six Japanese submarines within twelve days in the Central Pacific, 18-30/5/44. DONNEL torpedoed 3/5/44, was used as a floating power station at Cherbourg during 1944.

(TEV) Rudderow class

Displacement: 1,450 tons.
Dimensions: 300 (wl) 306 (oa) × 37 × $9\frac{3}{4}$ ft.
Machinery: 2-shaft turbo-electric drive, S.H.P. 12,000 = 24 knots.
Armament: 2—5 in., 10—40 mm. A.A. guns; 3—21 in. T.T.
Complement: 200.

DE.224	RUDDEROW	⎫ Philadelphia N.Yd.	14.10.43	
DE.225	DAY		14.10.43	
DE.230	CHAFFEE	Charleston N.Yd.	27.11.43	Scrapped 6/48.
DE.231	HODGES		9 .12.43	
DE.579	RILEY		29.12.43	
DE.580	LESLIE L. B. KNOX		8. 1.44	
DE.581	McNULTY		8. 1.44	
DE.582	METIVIER		12. 1.44	
DE.583	GEORGE A. JOHNSON	Bethlehem (Hingham)	12. 1.44	
DE.584	CHARLES J. KIMMEL		15. 1.44	
DE.585	DANIEL A. JOY		15. 1.44	
DE.586	LOUGH		22. 1.44	

DE.587	THOMAS F. NICKEL	⎫	Bethlehem (Hingham)	22. 1.44	
DE.588	PEIFFER	⎬		26. 1.44	
DE.589	TINSMAN			29. 1.44	
DE.684	DE LONG			23.11.43	
DE.685	COATES		Bethlehem (Quincy)	9.12.43	
DE.686	EUGENE E. ELMORE	⎬		23.12.43	
DE.706	HOLT			15. 2.44	Korean CHUNG NAM (6/63).
DE.707	JOBB		Defoe (Bay City, Mich.)	4. 3.44	
DE.708	PARLE	⎬		25. 3.44	
DE.709	BRAY			15. 4.44	APD 139 (7/45); sunk as target 26/3/63.

All engined G.E.

Notes:—Basically similar to **Buckley** class but with 5 in. guns. A further 50 ships of this class completed as High Speed Transports (DE.226-229, 232-237, 281-283, 590-606, 674, 687-692, 710-722). Conversion of DE.684-685 cancelled. The following unnamed vessels were cancelled during 1943-44: DE.284-300, 607-632, 645-664, 723-738, 905-1005.

(DET) Cannon class

Displacement: 1,240 tons.
Dimensions: 300 (wl) 306 (oa) × 36½ × 8¾ ft.
Machinery: 2-shaft diesel-electric drive, S.H.P. 6,000 = 21 knots.
Armament: 3—3 in., 6—40 mm. A.A. guns; 3—21 in. T.T.
Complement: 200.

DE.99	CANNON	⎫		25. 5.43	Brazilian BAEPENDI (12/44).
DE.100	CHRISTOPHER			19. 6.43	Brazilian BENAVENTE (12/44).
DE.101	ALGER			8. 7.43	Brazilian BABITONGA (3/45).
DE.102	THOMAS	⎬	Dravo; Wilmington (Del.)	31. 7.43	Chinese TAI HO (10/48).
DE.103	BOSTWICK			30. 8.43	Chinese TAI TSANG (12/48).
DE.104	BREEMAN			4. 9.43	Chinese TAI HU (10/48).
DE.105	BURROWS			2.10.43	Dutch VAN AMSTEL (6/50).
DE.112	CARTER			29. 2.44	Chinese TAI CHAO (12/48).
DE.113	CLARENCE L. EVANS			22. 3.44	French BERBERE (3/52).
DE.162	LEVY	⎫		28. 3.43	
DE.163	McCONNELL			28. 3.43	
DE.164	OSTERHAUS			18. 4.43	
DE.165	PARKS			18. 4.43	
DE.166	BARON	⎬	Federal (Newark, N.J.)	9. 5.43	Uruguayan URUGUAY (5/52).
DE.167	ACREE			9. 5.43	
DE.168	AMICK			27. 5.43	Japanese ASAHI (6/55).
DE.169	ATHERTON			27. 5.43	Japanese HATSUHI (6/55).

U.S.S. Pennewill (DE175: Cannon Class). A.A. guns not fitted abaft torpedo tubes, October 1943.

U.S.S. Cates (DE763: Cannon Class) June 1945.

DE.170	BOOTH		21. 6.43	
DE.171	CARROLL		21. 6.43	
DE.172	COONER		25. 7.43	
DE.173	ELDRIDGE		25. 7.43	Greek LEON (1/51).
DE.714	MARTS		8. 8.43	Brazilian BOCAINA (3/45).
DE.175	PENNEWILL		8. 8.43	Brazilian BERTIOGA (8/44).
DE.176	MICKA		22. 8.43	
DE.177	REYBOLD		22. 8.43	Brazilian BRACUI (8/44).
DE.178	HERZOG		5. 9.43	Brazilian BEBERIBE (8/44).
DE.179	McANN		5. 9.43	Brazilian BAURU (8/44).
DE.180	TRUMPETER		19. 9.43	
DE.181	STRAUB		19. 9.43	
DE.182	GUSTAFSON		3.10.43	Dutch VAN EWIJCK (10/50).
DE.183	SAMUEL S. MILES		3.10.43	French ARABE (8/50).
DE.184	WESSON	Federal (Newark, N.J.)	17.10.43	Italian ANDROMEDA (1/51).
DE.185	RIDDLE		17.10.43	French KABYLE (8/50).
DE.186	SWEARER		31.10.43	French BAMBARA (9/50).
DE.187	STERN		31.10.43	Dutch VAN ZIJLL (5/51).
DE.188	O'NEILL		14.11.43	Dutch DUBOIS (10/50).
DE.189	BRONSTEIN		14.11.43	Uruguayan ARTIGAS (5/52).
DE.190	BAKER (ex-Raby)		28.11.43	French MALGACHE (3/52).
DE.191	COFFMAN		28.11.43	
DE.192	EISNER		12.12.43	Dutch DE ZEEUW (5/51).
DE.193	GARFIELD THOMAS (ex-William G. Thomas)		12.12.43	Greek PANTHIR (1/51).
DE.194	WINGFIELD		30.12.43	French SAKALAVE (9/50).
DE.195	THORNHILL		30.12.43	Italian ALDEBARAN (1/51).
DE.196	RINEHART		9. 1.44	Dutch DE BITTER (6/50).
DE.197	ROCHE		9. 1.44	Sunk as target 11/3/46.
DE.739	BANGUST		6. 6.43	Peruvian CASTILLA (2/52).
DE.740	WATERMAN	Western Pipe & Steel (San Pedro)	20. 6.43	Peruvian AGUIRRE (10/51).
DE.741	WEAVER		4. 7.43	Peruvian RODRIGUEZ (10/51).
DE.742	HILBERT		18. 7.43	
DE.743	LAMONS		1. 8.43	

DE.744	KYNE		15. 8.43	
DE.745	SNYDER		29. 8.43	
DE.746	HEMMINGER		12. 9.43	Thai PIN KLAO (7/59).
DE.747	BRIGHT		26. 9.43	French TOUAREG
		Western		(11/50).
DE.748	TILLS	Pipe &	3.10.43	
DE.749	ROBERTS	Steel	14.11.43	
DE.750	McCLELLAND	(San	28.11.43	
DE.751	GAYNIER	Pedro)	1943	Cancelled 9/44.
DE.752	CURTIS W. HOWARD		1943	Cancelled 9/44.
DE.753	JOHN J. VAN BUREN		1943	Cancelled 9/44.
DE.763	CATES		10.10.43	French SOUDANAIS (11/50).
DE.764	GANDY		12.12.43	Italian ALTAIR (1/51).
DE.765	EARL K. OLSEN		13. 2.44	
DE.766	SLATER		13. 2.44	Greek AETOS (3/51).
DE.767	OSWALD	Tampa	25. 4.44	
DE.768	EBERT	Sbdg.	11. 5.44	Greek IERAX (3/51).
DE.769	NEAL A. SCOTT		4. 6.44	
DE.770	MUIR		4. 6.44	S. Korean KYONG KI (/56).
DE.771	SUTTON		6. 8.44	S. Korean KANK WON (/56).
DE.772	MILTON LEWIS		1944	Cancelled 9/44.
DE.773	GEORGE M. CAMPBELL		1944	Cancelled 9/44.
DE.774	RUSSELL M. COX		1944	Cancelled 9/44.

All engined General Motors.

Notes:—Originally designed with 12,000 shaft horsepower and speed of 24 knots. The following unnamed vessels were also cancelled during 1943: DE.114-128, 754-762, 775-788, 801-904. DE.106-111 were built for France under lend-lease. Very similar to **Edsall** class but less successful.

(FMR) Edsall class

Displacement: 1,200 tons.
Dimensions: 300 (wl) 306 (oa) $\times$ $36\frac{3}{4}$ $\times$ $8\frac{3}{4}$ ft.
Machinery: 2-shaft geared diesels, S.H.P. 6,000 = 21 knots.
Armament: 3—3 in., 8—40 mm. A.A. guns; 3—21 in. T.T.
Complement: 200.

DE.129	EDSALL		1.11.42
DE.130	JACOB JONES		29.11.42
DE.131	HAMMANN (ex-Langley)	Consolidated	13.12.42
DE.132	ROBERT E. PEARY	Orange, Tex.)	3. 1.43
DE.133	PILLSBURY		10. 1.43
DE.134	POPE		12. 1.43

DE.135	FLAHERTY		17. 1.43	
DE.136	FREDERICK C. DAVIS		24. 1.43	Lost 24/4/45.
DE.137	HERBERT C. JONES		19. 1.43	
DE.138	DOUGLAS L. HOWARD		24. 1.43	
DE.139	FARQUHAR		13. 2.43	
DE.140	J. R. Y. BLAKELY	Consolidated	7. 3.43	
DE.141	HILL	(Orange,	28. 2.43	
DE.142	FESSENDEN	Tex.)	9. 3.43	
DE.143	FISKE		14. 3.43	Lost 2/8/44.
DE.144	FROST		21. 3.43	
DE.145	HUSE		23. 3.43	
DE.146	INCH		4. 4.43	
DE.147	BLAIR		6. 4.43	
DE.148	BROUGH		10. 4.43	
DE.149	CHATELAIN		21. 4.43	
DE.150	NEUNZER		27. 4.43	
DE.151	POOLE		8. 5.43	
DE.152	PETERSON		15. 5.43	
DE.238	STEWART		22.11.42	
DE.239	STURTEVANT		3.12.42	
DE.240	MOORE		21.12.42	
DE.241	KEITH (ex-Scott)		21.12.42	
DE.242	TOMICH		28.12.42	
DE.243	J. RICHARD WARD (ex-James R. Ward)	Brown	6. 1.43	
DE.244	OTTERSTETTER	Sbdg.	19. 1.43	
DE.245	SLOAT	(Houston)	21. 1.43	
DE.246	SNOWDEN		19. 2.43	
DE.247	STANTON		21. 2.43	
DE.248	SWASEY		18. 3.43	
DE.249	MARCHAND		20. 3.43	
DE.250	HURST		14. 4.43	
DE.251	CAMP		16. 4.43	
DE.252	HOWARD D. CROW		26. 4.43	
DE.253	PETTIT		28. 4.43	
DE.254	RICKETTS		10. 5.43	
DE.255	SELLSTROM		12. 5.43	
DE.316	HARVESON		22. 5.43	
DE.317	JOYCE		26. 5.43	
DE.318	KIRKPATRICK		5. 6.43	
DE.319	LEOPOLD		12. 6.43	Lost 10/3/44.
DE.320	MENGES	Consolidated	15. 6.43	
DE.321	MOSLEY	(Orange	26. 6.43	
DE.322	NEWELL	Tex.)	29. 6.43	
DE.323	PRIDE		3. 7.43	
DE.324	FALGOUT		24. 7.43	
DE.325	LOWE		28. 7.43	
DE.326	THOMAS J. GARY (ex-Gary)		21. 8.43	

U.S.S. Brister
(DE327: Edsall Class)
June 1945.

U.S.S. Kretchmer
(DE329: Edsall Class).
Diesel type with re-
duced horsepower.
1944.

DE.327	BRISTER		24. 8.43	
DE.328	FINCH		28. 8.43	
DE.329	KRETCHMER		31. 8.43	
DE.330	O'REILLY		2.10.43	
DE.331	KOINER		5.10.43	
DE.332	PRICE		30.10.43	
DE.333	STRICKLAND		2.11.43	
DE.334	FORSTER		13.11.43	
DE.335	DANIEL		16.11.43	
DE.336	ROY O. HALE		20.11.43	
DE.337	DALE W. PETERSON		22.12.43	
DE.338	MARTIN H. RAY		29.12.43	
DE.382	RAMSDEN	Consoli-	24. 5.43	
DE.383	MILLS	dated	26. 5.43	
DE.384	RHODES	(Orange,	29. 6.43	
DE.385	RICHEY	Tex.)	30. 6.43	
DE.386	SAVAGE		15. 7.43	
DE.387	VANCE		16. 7.43	
DE.388	LANSING		2. 8.43	
DE.389	DURANT		3. 8.43	
DE.390	CALCATERRA		16. 8.43	
DE.391	CHAMBERS		17. 8.43	
DE.392	MERRILL		29. 8.43	
DE.393	HAVERFIELD		30. 8.43	
DE.394	SWENNING		13. 9.43	
DE.395	WILLIS		14. 9.43	
DE.396	JANSSEN		4.10.43	
DE.397	WILHOITE		5.10.43	
DE.398	COCKRILL		29.10.43	
DE.399	STOCKDALE		30.10.43	
DE.400	HISSEM		26.12.43	
DE.401	HOLDER		27.11.43	Lost 11/4/44.

All engined Fairbanks-Morse.

Notes:—Originally designed with 12,000 shaft horsepower, speed of 24 knots and turbines. CAMP rearmed in 4/45: 2-5 in., 10-40 mm. AA guns, no T.T. MENGES, torpedoed 3/5/44, was repaired with the stern of HOLDER. A boarding party from PILLSBURY captured U-505, 4/6/44.

(WGT) John C. Butler class

Displacement: 1,350 tons.
Dimensions: 300 (wl) 306 (oa) $\times$ 36$\frac{3}{4}$ $\times$ 9$\frac{1}{2}$ ft.
Machinery: 2-shaft geared turbines, S.H.P. 12,000 = 24 knots.
Armament: 2—5 in., 10—40 mm. guns; 3—21 in. T.T. (371-2, 448-50, 510 537-540, no T.T.).
Complement: 200.

DE.339	JOHN C. BUTLER	Consoli- dated	11.12.43
DE.340	O'FLAHERTY	(Orange,	14.12.43
DE.341	RAYMOND	Tex.)	8. 1.44

170

U.S.S. Doyle C.
Barnes (DE353:
John C. Butler Class)
September 1944.

U.S.S. Decatur
(DD341) 1944, still
retaining four fun-
nels.

DE.342	RICHARD W. SUESENS	11. 1.44	
DE.343	ABERCROMBIE	14. 1.44	
DE.344	OBERRENDER	18. 1.44	Lost 9/5/45.
DE.345	ROBERT BRAZIER	22. 1.44	
DE.346	EDWIN A. HOWARD	25. 1.44	
DE.347	JESSE RUTHERFORD	29. 1.44	
DE.348	KEY	12. 2.44	
DE.349	GENTRY	15. 2.44	
DE.350	TRAW	12. 2.44	
DE.351	MAURICE J. MANUEL	19. 2.44	
DE.352	NAIFEH	29. 2.44	
DE.353	DOYLE C. BARNES	4. 3.44	
DE.354	KENNETH M. WILLETT	7. 3.44	
DE.355	JACCARD	18. 3.44	
DE.356	LLOYD E. ACREE	21. 3.44	
DE.357	GEORGE E. DAVIS	8. 4.44	
DE.358	MACK	11. 4.44	Consolidated (Orange, Tex.)
DE.359	WOODSON	29. 4.44	
DE.360	JOHNNIE HUTCHINS	2. 5.44	
DE.361	WALTON	20. 5.44	
DE.362	ROLF	23. 5.44	
DE.363	PRATT	1. 6.44	
DE.364	ROMBACH	6. 6.44	
DE.365	McGINTY	5. 8.44	
DE.366	ALVIN C. COCKRELL	8. 8.44	
DE.367	FRENCH	17. 6.44	
DE.368	CECIL J. DOYLE	1. 7.44	
DE.369	THADDEUS PARKER	26. 8.44	
DE.370	JOHN L. WILLIAMSON	29. 8.44	
DE.371	PRESLEY	19. 8.44	
DE.372	WILLIAMS	22. 8.44	
DE.373	WILLIAM C. LAWE		Cancelled 6/44.
DE.374	LLOYD THOMAS		Cancelled 6/44.
DE.375	KEPPLER		Cancelled 6/44.
DE.376	KLEINSMITH		Cancelled 6/44.
DE.377	HENRY W. TUCKER		Cancelled 6/44.
DE.378	WEISS		Cancelled 6/44.
DE.379	FRANCOVICH		Cancelled 6/44.

U.S.S. Howard F. Clark (DE533: John C. Butler Class) 1944.

U.S.S. Haas (DE424: John C. Butler Class) 5th October 1944.

DE.402	RICHARD S. BULL		16.11.43	
DE.403	RICHARD M. ROWELL		17.11.43	
DE.404	EVERSOLE		3.12.43	Lost 28/10/44.
DE.405	DENNIS		4.12.43	
DE.406	EDMONDS		17.12.43	
DE.407	SHELTON		18.12.43	Lost 3/10/44.
DE.408	STRAUS		30.12.43	
DE.409	LA PRADE		31.12.43	
DE.410	JACK MILLER		10. 1.44	
DE.411	STAFFORD		11. 1.44	
DE.412	WALTER C. WANN		19. 1.44	
DE.413	SAMUEL B. ROBERTS		20. 1.44	Lost 25/10/44.
DE.414	LE RAY WILSON	Brown Sbdg. (Houston)	28. 1.44	
DE.415	LAWRENCE C. TAYLOR		29. 1.44	
DE.416	MELVIN R. NAWMAN		7. 2.44	
DE.417	OLIVER MITCHELL		8. 2.44	
DE.418	TABBERER		18. 2.44	
DE.419	ROBERT F. KELLER		19. 2.44	
DE.420	LELAND E. THOMAS		28. 2.44	
DE.421	CHESTER T. O'BRIEN		29. 2.44	
DE.422	DOUGLAS A. MUNRO		8. 3.44	
DE.423	DUFILHO		9. 3.44	
DE.424	HAAS		20. 3.44	
DE.438	CORBESIER		13. 2.44	
DE.439	CONKLIN		13. 2.44	
DE.440	McCOY REYNOLDS		22. 2.44	Portuguese CORTE REAL (2/57).
DE.441	WILLIAM SEIVERLING		7. 3.44	
DE.442	ULVERT M. MOORE		7. 3.44	
DE.443	KENDALL C. CAMPBELL	Federal	19. 3.44	
DE.444	GOSS		19. 3.44	
DE.445	GRADY		2. 4.44	
DE.446	CHARLES E. BRANNON		23. 4.44	
DE.447	ALBERT T. HARRIS		16. 4.44	
DE.448	CROSS		4. 7.44	
DE.449	HANNA		4. 7.44	
DE.450	JOSEPH E. CONNOLLY		6. 8.44	

DE.451	WOODROW R. THOMPSON			Cancelled 6/44.
DE.452	STEINAKER			Cancelled 6/44.
DE.508	GILLIGAN (ex-Donaldson)	Federal	22. 2.44	
DE.509	FORMOE		2. 4.44	Portuguese DIEGO CAO (2/57).
DE.510	HEYLIGER		6. 8.44	
DE.531	EDWARD H. ALLEN		7.10.43	
DE.532	TWEEDY		7.10.43	
DE.533	HOWARD F. CLARK		8.11.43	
DE.534	SILVERSTEIN		8.11.43	
DE.535	LEWIS		7.12.43	
DE.536	BIVIN		7.12.43	
DE.537	RIZZI		7.12.43	
DE.538	OSBERG		7.12.43	
DE.539	WAGNER		27.12.43	
DE.540	VANDIVIER		27.12.43	
DE.541	SHEEHAN		27.12.43	
DE.542	OSWALD A. POWERS		27.12.43	Cancelled 1/46.
DE.543	GROVES		1944	Cancelled 9/44.
DE.544	ALFRED WOLF	Boston N.Yd.	1944	Cancelled 9/44.
DE.545	HAROLD J. ELLISON			Cancelled 6/44.
DE.546	MYLES C. FOX			Cancelled 6/44.
DE.547	CHARLES R. WARE			Cancelled 6/44.
DE.548	CARPELLOTTI			Cancelled 6/44.
DE.549	EUGENE A. GREENE			Cancelled 6/44.
DE.550	GYATT			Cancelled 6/44.
DE.551	BENNER			Cancelled 6/44.
DE.552	KENNETH D. BAILEY			Cancelled 6/44.
DE.553	DENNIS J. BUCKLEY			Cancelled 6/44.
DE.554	EVERETT F. LARSEN			Cancelled 6/44.

All engined Westinghouse or G.E.

Notes:—The following unnamed vessels were also cancelled during 1943-44: DE.380-381, 425-437 453-507, 511-515, 555-562. WAGNER and VANDIVIER were not completed until 1955, as radar pickets.

SUBMARINES

112 submarines were in commission at the outbreak of the Pacific war in December 1941, and an additional 65 were on order.

Over half were of the small, old " O," " R " and " S " classes of World War I. Many of these had been in reserve during the twenties and thirties, but were recommissioned in 1941 for training duties. Nine of these were transferred to the Royal Navy in 1941-42. The old " S " class had been designed primarily as a defensive weapon and was not properly equipped for the long-range operations required by Pacific distances. Nevertheless, six of the twenty-eight Asiatic Fleet submarines in late 1941 were of this class.

During the 1920's a succession of various types of submarines were built known collectively as the " V " class. Originally given numbers only, they were named in 1931. It was believed that size and heavy guns were advantageous following the experience of World War I. The **Barracuda** class represented a considerable advance in size over the S-48 type, and the earlier unsuccessful " T " class of fleet submarines. These were followed by the ARGONAUT and NARWHAL. The former was the largest submarine built by the U.S.N. until the nuclear TRITON of 1958, and was unique in being a minelayer. She and the slightly smaller NARWHAL class carried 6 in. guns. The DOLPHIN and CACHALOT types represented later experiments in a smaller size.

The " P," new " S " and " T " classes stabilized the standard fleet submarine at about 300 feet in length. They and all later submarines had all-electric drive with the diesels connected to the generators rather than directly to the propellors. Experience with these classes led to the GATO class which remained the standard design for all wartime construction, 195 boats being completed. They were among the finest submarines of their time, of all-welded construction, with excellent sea-keeping qualities, oceanic cruising range and a designed diving depth of 400 feet (300 in earlier units).

After a rather lack-luster beginning caused in part by poor torpedoes which failed to explode upon contact, as well as by lack of submarines, the contribution of the submarine force grew to become the principal cause of enemy ship sinkings. Submarines are credited with sinking 1,152 Japanese merchant ships (of over 500 tons) totalling 4,861,317 gross tons*. An impressive number of warships of all sizes were also sunk by submarines. As the war progressed the Japanese suffered an almost total lack of proper escort vessels, their destroyer forces having been whittled away in fruitless surface and air actions and by submarine attacks. Towards the end of the war, major units were unable to put to sea partly because of the lack of adequate anti-submarine protection.

American submarines were very active in other types of service, minelaying, rescuing carrier pilots downed at sea, reconnaissance, and landing and supplying guerillas in the Philippines.

Submarines are designated by the symbol SS and are named after fish. It is reported that during the war the Navy ran out of fish names and suitable names were given submarines which could be given to newly discovered types of fish.

---

* About 2% of these figures were credited to British and Dutch submarines.

176

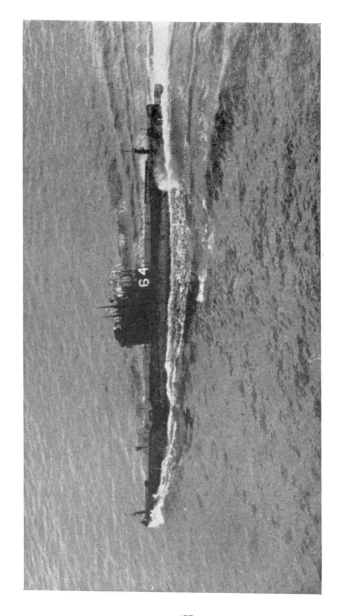

U.S.S. O-3 (SS64) "O" Class, 17th July 1944.

177

U.S.S. R-12 (SS89) "R" Class, April 1942.

U.S.S. S-20 (SS125) Old "S" Class—1st group, 26th March 1945.

178

SUBMARINES

" O " class

Displacement: 500/650 tons.
Dimensions: 164 (wl) 172½ (oa) × 18 × 13¼ ft.
Machinery: 2-shaft Diesels, S.H.P. 880/740 = 14/10.5 knots.
Armament: 4—18 in. T.T. (bow); 1—50 cal. M.G.
Complement: 32.

SS.63	O-2	Puget Sound N.Yd.	24. 5.18	Scrapped 1945.
SS.64	O-3		29. 9.17	Scrapped 1946.
SS.65	O-4		20.10.17	Scrapped 1/46.
SS.67	O-6		25.11.17	Scrapped 1946.
SS.68	O-7	Fore River	16.12.17	Scrapped 1946.
SS.69	O-8		31.12.17	Scrapped 1946.
SS.70	O-9		27. 1.18	Lost 20/6/41.
SS.71	O-10		21. 2.18	Scrapped 1946.

Notes:—Originally a class of 16 boats. 0-5 lost in 1923; others discarded prior to the war.

" R " class

Displacement: 540/695 tons.
Dimensions: 179 (wl) 186¼ (oa) × 17½ × 13¾ ft.
Machinery: 2-shaft Diesels, S.H.P. 1200/934 = 14.7/10.5 knots.
Armament: 4—18 in. T.T. (bow); 1—3 in. gun.
Complement: 33.

SS.78	R-1		24. 8.18	Scrapped 1946.
SS.79	R-2		23. 9.18	Scrapped 1946.
SS.80	R-3		18. 1.19	H.M.S. P-511 (11/41). Scrapped 2/48.
SS.81	R-4		26.10.18	Scrapped 1946.
SS.82	R-5		24.11.18	Scrapped 1946.
SS.83	R-6		1. 3.19	Scrapped 1946.
SS.84	R-7	Fore River	5. 4.19	Scrapped 1946.
SS.86	R-9		24. 5.19	Scrapped 1946.
SS.87	R-10		28. 6.19	Scrapped 1946.
SS.88	R-11		21. 7.19	Scrapped 1946.
SS.89	R-12		15. 8.19	Lost 12/6/43.
SS.90	R-13		27. 8.19	Scrapped 1946.
SS.91	R-14		10.10.19	Scrapped 1945.
SS.92	R-15		10.12.17	Scrapped 1946.
SS.93	R-16	Union Iron Works	15.12.17	Scrapped 1946.
SS.94	R-17		24.12.17	H.M.S. P-512 (3/42). Scrapped 12/45.
SS.95	R-18		8. 1.18	Scrapped 1946.

179

SS.96	R-19		Union	28. 1.18	H.M.S. P-514 (3/42). Lost 21/6/42.
		}	Iron		
SS.97	R-20		Works	21. 1.18	Scrapped 1946.

Notes:—Refitted 1940-41

Old " S " class (1st Group)

Displacement: 850/1,090 tons.
Dimensions: 211 (wl) 219¼ (oa) × 20½ × 15¼ ft.
Machinery: 2-shaft Diesels, S.H.P. 1200/1500 = 14.5/11 knots.
Armament: 4—21 in. T.T. (bow); 1—4 in. gun, except S.23, 30-34, 40, 1—3in. gun.
Complement: 42.

SS.105	S-1		26.10.18	H.M.S. P-552 (4/42). Scrapped 6/46.
SS.123	S-18		29. 4.20	Scrapped 1946.
SS.125	S-20		9. 6.20	Scrapped 1946.
SS.126	S-21		18. 8.20	H.M.S. P-553 (9/42). Scuttled 20/3/45.
SS.127	S-22		15. 7.20	H.M.S. P-554 (6/42). Scrapped 1945.
SS.128	S-23		27.10.20	Scrapped 1946.
SS.129	S-24		27. 6.22	H.M.S. P-555 (8/42). Sunk as target 25/8/47.
SS.130	S-25	Bethlehem (Quincy)	29. 5.22	Polish JASTRZAB (P-551, 11/41); lost 2/5/42.
SS.131	S-26		22. 8.22	Lost 24/1/42.
SS.132	S-27		18.10.22	Lost 19/6/42.
SS.133	S-28		20. 9.22	Lost 4/7/44.
SS.134	S-29		9.11.22	H.M.S. P-556 (6/42). Sold 1/49.
SS.135	S-30		21.11.18	Scrapped 1947.
SS.136	S-31		28.12.18	Scrapped 1947.
SS.137	S-32		11. 1.19	Scrapped 1946.
SS.138	S-33		5.12.18	Scrapped 1947.
SS.139	S-34		13. 2.19	Scrapped 1946.
SS.140	S-35	Bethlehem (San Francisco)	27. 2.19	Sunk as target 4/4/46.
SS.141	S-36		3. 6.19	Lost 20/1/42.
SS.142	S-37		20. 6.19	Scuttled 20/2/45.
SS.143	S-38		17. 6.19	Scuttled 20/2/45.
SS.144	S-39		2. 7.19	Lost 14/8/42.
SS.145	S-40		5. 1.21	Scrapped 1946.
SS.146	S-41		21. 2.21	Scrapped 1946.

Notes:—S-1 carried an experimental seaplane in 1923; S-19 discarded 1936. Refitted 1940-41.

U.S.S. S-17 (SS122) Old "S" Class—2nd group, July 1944.

U.S.S. S-11 (SS116) Old "S" Class—2nd group, September 1935.

181

U.S.S. S-47 (SS158) Old "S" Class—3rd group, 25th January 1944, entering dry dock at an Alaskan port.

" S " class (2nd Group)

Displacement: 840/1,150 tons.
Dimensions: 231 (wl and oa) × 21½ × 12¼ ft.
Machinery: 2-shaft Diesels, S.H.P. 2,000/1,200 = 15/11 knots.
Armament: 4—21 in. T.T. (bow); 1—4 in. gun.
Complement: 42.

SS.116	S-11	⎫ Ports-mouth N.Yd. Lake Torpedo Boat Co. ⎬ ⎭	7. 2.21	Scrapped 1945.
SS.117	S-12		4. 8.21	Scrapped 1945.
SS.118	S-13		20.10.21	Scrapped 1945.
SS.119	S-14		22.10.19	Scrapped 1945.
SS.120	S-15		8. 3.20	Scrapped 1946.
SS.121	S-16		23.12.19	Scuttled 3/4/45.
SS.122	S-17		22. 5.20	Scuttled 5/4/45.

Notes:—S-4 and S-5 lost in accidents in the 1920's; S-3 and 6-10 discarded before the war.

" S " class (3rd Group)

Displacement: 870/1,135 tons.
Dimensions: 216 (wl) 225¼ (oa) × 20½ × 15¼ ft.
Machinery: 2-shaft Diesels, S.H.P. 2,000/1,500 = 15/11 knots.
Armament: 4—21 in. T.T. (bow); 1—3 in. gun (S-47, 1—4 in.).
Complement: 42.

SS.153	S-42	⎫ Bethlehem (Quincy) ⎬ ⎭	30. 4.23	Scrapped 1947.
SS.154	S-43		31. 3.23	Scrapped 1947.
SS.155	S-44		27.10.23	Lost 7/10/43.
SS.156	S-45		26. 6.23	Scrapped 1947.
SS.157	S-46		11. 9.23	Scrapped 1947.
SS.158	S-47		5. 1.24	Scrapped 1947.

" S " class (4th Group)

Displacement: 1,010/1,460 tons.
Dimensions: 267 (oa) × 21½ × 11 ft.
Machinery: 2-shaft Diesels, S.H.P. 2,000/1,500 = 14.5/11 knots.
Armament: 5—21 in. T.T. (4 bow, 1 stern); 1—4 in. gun.
Complement: 45.

SS.159	S-48	⎫ Lake Torpedo Boat Co. ⎬ ⎭	26. 2.21	Scrapped 1947.

Notes:—S-51 lost in 1925; S-49 and S-50 discarded 1931.

183

U.S.S. S-48 (SS159) Old "S" Class—4th group, 14th April 1942.

U.S.S. Nautilus (SS168) Narwhal Class, 3rd August 1943, with deck tubes and 6in. guns.

U.S.S. Barracuda (SS163). Barracuda Class, 29th October 1943, with deck gun removed.

U.S.S. Argonaut (SS166). Minelayer. Shown shortly after completion when still known as V-4, July 1929.

185

Barracuda class

Displacement: 2,000/2,620 tons.
Dimensions: 326 (wl) 341½ (oa) × 27¼ × 14¾ ft.
Machinery: 2-shaft Diesels, S.H.P. 6,700/2,400 = 18/11 knots.
Armament: 6—21 in. T.T. (4 bow, 2 stern); 1—5 in. gun, except BASS 1—3 in.
Complement: 80.

SS.163	BARRACUDA (ex-V-1)	⎫ Ports-mouth N.Yd. ⎬	17. 7.24	Scrapped 1945.
SS.164	BASS (ex-V-2)		27.12.24	Scuttled 14/7/45.
SS.165	BONITA (ex-V-3)	⎭	9. 6.25	Scrapped 1945.

Notes:—BASS lost half her crew in engine room fire while at sea, 17/8/42. Scheduled conversion of these ships to transport submarines (APS.2-4) cancelled. Pre-war pendant No.: B-1 to 3.

Argonaut (Minelayer)

Displacement: 2,710/4,080 tons.
Dimensions: 358 (wl) × 381 (oa) × 34 × 15½ ft.
Machinery: 2-shaft Diesels, S.H.P. 3,175/2,400 = 15/8 knots.
Armament: 4—21 in. T.T. (bow); 2—6 in. guns; 80 mines.
Complement: 89.

SS.166	ARGONAUT (ex-V-4)	Portsmouth N.Yd.	10.11.27	APS 1 (9/42); Lost 10/1/43.

Notes:—The U.S. Navy's only minelaying-submarine (SM.1), ARGONAUT was converted to a transport submarine immediately after Pearl Harbor. Pre-war pendant No.: A-1.

Narwhal class

Displacement 2,730/4,050 tons.
Dimensions: 349 (wl) 371 (oa) × 33¼ × 15¾ ft.
Machinery: 2-shaft Diesels, H.P. 5,450/2,540 = 17/8 knots.
Armament: 6—21 in. T.T. (4 bow, 2 stern); 2—6 in. guns.
Complement: 90.

SS.167	NARWHAL (ex-V-5)	Portsmouth N.Yd.	17.12.29	Scrapped 1945.
SS.168	NAUTILUS (ex-V-6)	Mare Island N.Yd.	15. 3.30	Scrapped 1945.

Notes:—4—21 in. external T.T. added during the war. Re-engined 1941. NAUTILUS and ARGONAUT took part in the raid on Makin 16/8/42. Pre-war pendant No.: N-1 and 2.

U.S.S. Cachalot (SS170) Cachalot Class, May 1944.

U.S.S. Dolphin (SS169). Showing its pre-war pendant number of D.I.

U.S.S. Skipjack (SS184) New "S" Class — 1st group, April 1944.

U.S.S. Pike (SS173) "P" Class, February 1944.

Dolphin

Displacement: 1,540/2,240 tons.
Dimensions: 307 (wl) 319¼ (oa) × 27¾ × 13½ ft.
Machinery: 2-shaft Diesels, H.P. 4,250/1,750 = 17/8 knots.
Armament: 6—21 in. T.T. (4 bow, 2 stern); 1—3 in. gun.
Complement: 60.

SS.169	DOLPHIN	Portsmouth N.Yd.	8. 3.32	Scrapped 1946.

Notes:—Not very successful; used for training. Pre-war pendant No.. D-1.

Cachalot class

Displacement: 1,120/1,680 tons.
Dimensions: 260 (wl) 272 (oa) × 24¾ × 12¾ ft.
Machinery: 2-shaft Diesels, H.P. 3,100/1,600 = 17/8 knots.
Armament: 6—21 in. T.T. (4 bow, 2 stern); 1—3 in. gun.
Complement: 50.

SS.170	CACHALOT	Portsmouth N.Yd.	19.10.33	Scrapped 1947.
SS.171	CUTTLEFISH	Electric Boat	21.11.33	Scrapped 1947.

Notes:—Of all-welded construction. Re-engined in 1936. Pre-war pendant No.: C-1 and 2.

" P " class (1st Group)

Displacement: 1,310/1,960 tons.
Dimensions: 283 (wl) 301 (oa) × 25 × 13 ft.
Machinery: 2-shaft Diesels, H.P. 4,300/2,085 = 19/8 knots.
Armament: 6—21 in. T.T. (4 bow, 2 stern); 1—3 in. gun.
Complement: 55.

SS.172	PORPOISE	} Ports- mouth N.Yd.	20. 6.35	Scrapped 1957.
SS.173	PIKE		12. 9.35	Scrapped 1957.

" P " class (2nd Group)

Displacement: 1,315/1,968 tons.
Dimensions: 287 (wl) 298 (oa) × 25¼ × 14 ft.
Machinery: 2-shaft Diesels, H.P. 4,300/2,085 = 19/8 knots.
Armament: 6—21 in. T.T. (4 bow, 2 stern); 1—4 in. gun.
Complement: 55.

SS.174	SHARK	} Electric Boat	21. 5.35	Lost 11/2/42.
SS.175	TARPON		4. 9.35	Lost en route to ship-breakers 26/8/57.

" P " class (3rd Group)

Displacement: 1,330/2,005 tons (SS.179-180: 1,335/2,020 tons).
Dimensions: 298 (wl) 300½ (oa) × 25¼ × 14 ft.
Machinery: 2-shaft Diesels, H.P. 4,300/2,085 = 19/8 knots.
Armament: 6—21 in. T.T. (4 bow, 2 stern); 1—4 in. gun.
Complement: 55.

SS.176	PERCH	} Electric Boat	9. 5.36	Lost 3/3/42.
SS.177	PICKEREL		7. 7.36	Lost 4/43.
SS.178	PERMIT (ex-Pinna)		5.10.36	Scrapped 1957.
SS.179	PLUNGER	} Ports- mouth N.Yd.	8. 7.36	Scrapped 1957.
SS.180	POLLACK		15. 9.36	Scrapped 1947.
SS.181	POMPANO	Mare Island N.Yd.	11. 3.37	Lost 8/43.

Notes:—2—21 in. external T.T. added in PORPOISE, PIKE, TARPON, PICKEREL and PERMIT Pre-war pendant No. P-1 to 10.

New " S " class (1st Group)

Displacement: 1,435/2,210 tons.
Dimensions: 308 × 26¼ × 14¼ ft.
Machinery: 2-shaft Diesels, S.H.P. 5,500/3,300 = 21/9 knots.
Armament: 8—21 in. T.T. (4 bow, 4 stern); 1—4 in. gun, except STURGEON 1—3 in.
Complement: 70.

SS.180	SALMON	} Electric Boat	12. 6.37	Scrapped 1946.
SS.183	SEAL		25. 8.37	Scrapped 1957.
SS.184	SKIPJACK		23.10.37	Bikini target ship (7/46). Sunk 16/10/48.
SS.185	SNAPPER	} Ports- mouth N.Yd.	24. 8.37	Scrapped 1948.
SS.186	STINGRAY		6.10.37	Scrapped 1947.
SS.187	STURGEON	Mare Island N.Yd.	15. 3.38	Scrapped 1948.

Notes:—As " P " class with 8 T.T. Pre-war pendant No.: S-1 to 6.

U.S.S. Tuna (SS203)
"T" Class.

U.S.S. Sargo (SS188)
New "S" Class—2nd
group, August 1944.

191

U.S.S. Marlin (SS205) "M" Class, June 1943.

U.S.S. Thresher (SS200) "T" Class, 6th October 1943.

New " S " class (2nd Group)

Displacement: 1,460/2,350 tons except SS.193-194 1,450/2,340 tons, SS.192 1,475/2,340 tons.
Dimensions: 310½ × 27¼ × 13¾ ft.
Machinery: 2-shaft Diesels, S.H.P. 5,500/3,300 = 21/9 knots.
Armament: 8—21 in. T.T. (4 bow, 4 stern); 1—4 in. gun.
Complement: 70.

SS.188	SARGO		6. 6.38	Scrapped 1947.
SS.189	SAURY	Electric	20. 8.38	Scrapped 1947.
SS.190	SPEARFISH	Boat	29.10.38	Scrapped 1947.
SS.191	SCULPIN	Ports-	27. 7.38	Lost 19/11/43.
SS.192	SQUALUS	mouth N.Yd.	14. 9.38	Renamed SAILFISH (1940). Scrapped 1948.
SS.193	SWORDFISH	Mare Island N.Yd.	1. 4.39	Lost 1/45.
SS.194	SEADRAGON	Electric	21. 4.39	Scrapped 1948.
SS.195	SEALION	Boat	25. 5.39	Lost 25/12/41.
SS.196	SEARAVEN	Ports-	21. 6.39	Sunk as target 11/9/48.
SS.197	SEAWOLF	mouth N.Yd.	15. 8.39	Lost 3/10/44.

Notes:—SQUALUS sank while on trials off Portsmouth, N.H., 23/5/39, recommissioned as SAILFISH 5/40. Pre-war pendant No.: S-7 to 16.

" T " class

Displacement: 1,475/2,370 tons.
Dimensions: 307¼ × 27¼ × 13¾ ft.
Machinery: 2-shaft Diesels, S.H.P. 5,400/2,740 = 20/8.7 knots.
Armament: 10—21 in. T.T. (6 bow, 4 stern); 1—5 in., 1—40 mm. guns.
Complement: 85.

SS.198	TAMBOR		20.12.39	Scrapped 3/60.
SS.199	TAUTOG	Electric	27. 1.40	Scrapped 1960.
SS.200	THRESHER	Boat	27. 3.40	Scrapped 1948.
SS.201	TRITON	Ports-	25. 3.40	Lost 15/3/43.
SS.202	TROUT	mouth N.Yd.	21. 5.40	Lost 29/2/44.
SS.203	TUNA	Mare Island N.Yd.	2.10.40	Sunk as target 25/9/48.
SS.206	GAR		7.11.40	Scrapped 1959.
SS.207	GRAMPUS	Electric	23.12.40	Lost 5/3/43.
SS.208	GRAYBACK	Boat	31. 1.40	Lost 27/2/44.
SS.209	GRAYLING	Ports-	4. 9.40	Lost 9/9/43.
SS.210	GRENADIER	mouth N.Yd.	29.11.40	Lost 22/4/43.
SS.211	GUDGEON	Mare Island N.Yd.	25. 1.41	Lost 4/44.

Notes:—TAUTOG sank 26 ships during the war, the largest toll exacted by an American submarine.

U.S.S. Flying Fish (SS229) returning to Pearl Harbor, 1945, with other units of wolf-pack.

" M " class

Displacement: 835/1,190 and 800/1,165 tons respectively.
Dimensions: 243¼ × 22¼ × 11¾ and 239 × 21¾ × 11¾ ft. respectively.
Machinery: 2-shaft Diesels, H.P. 3,360/1,500 = 16/11 knots.
Armament: 6—21 in. T.T. (4 bow, 2 stern); 1—3 in. or 5 in., 1—40 mm. guns.
Complement: 42.

| SS.204 | MACKEREL | Electric Boat | 28. 9.40 | Scrapped 1947. |
| SS.205 | MARLIN | Portsmouth N.Yd. | 29. 1.41 | Scrapped 1946. |

Notes:—An experimental coastal type. MARLIN was modernized during the war.

Gato class

Displacement: 1,525/2,415 tons.
Dimensions: 307 (wl) 311¾ (oa) × 27¼ × 15¼ ft.
Machinery: 2-shaft Diesels, H.P. 5,400/2,740 = 20¼/10 knots.
Armament: 10—21 in. T.T. (6 bow, 4 stern); 1—5 in., 1—40 mm. guns.
Complement: 80.

SS.212	GATO		21. 8.41	Discarded 1960.
SS.213	GEENLING		20. 9.41	Discarded 1960.
SS.214	GROUPER		27.10.41	SSK (1/51), AGSS (6/58).
SS.215	GROWLER		22.11.41	Lost 8/11/44.
SS.216	GRUNION		22.12.41	Lost 30/7/42.
SS.217	GUARDFISH		20. 1.42	Sunk as target 1961.
SS.218	ALBACORE		17. 2.42	Lost 7/11/44.
SS.219	AMBERJACK		6. 3.42	Lost 16/2/43.
SS.220	BARB	Electric Boat	2. 4.42	Italian ENRICO TAZZOLI (1/55).
SS.221	BLACKFISH		18. 4.42	Discarded 1959.
SS.222	BLUEFISH		21. 2.43	Discarded 1959.
SS.223	BONEFISH		7. 3.43	Lost 18/6/45.
SS.224	COD		21. 3.43	AGSS (12/62).
SS.225	CERO		4. 4.43	AGSS (12/62).
SS.226	CORVINA		9. 5.43	Lost 16/11/43.
SS.227	DARTER		6. 6.43	Lost 24/10/44.
SS.228	DRUM		12. 5.41	AGSS (12/62).
SS.229	FLYING FISH		9. 7.41	AGSS (1/51), scrapped 1960.
SS.230	FINBACK	Ports-mouth N.Yd.	25. 8.41	Scrapped 1959.
SS.231	HADDOCK		20.10.41	Discarded 1959.
SS.232	HALIBUT		3.12.41	Scrapped 1947.
SS.233	HERRING		15. 1.42	Lost 1/6/44.
SS.234	KINGFISH		2. 3.42	Discarded 1960.
SS.235	SHAD	Mare Island N.Yd.	15. 4.42	Discarded 1960.
SS.236	SILVERSIDES		26. 8.41	AGSS (12/62).
SS.237	TRIGGER		22.10.41	Lost 28/3/45.

U.S.S. Bream (SS243) Gato Class, June 1945, returning to base with periscopes raised and war flags flying.

U.S.S. Growler (SS215) Gato Class, May 1943, with 3in. gun forward.

196

SS.238	WAHOO	Mare	14. 2.42	Lost 12/10/43.
SS.239	WHALE	Island	14. 3.42	Discarded 1960.
SS.240	ANGLER	N.Yd.	4. 7.43	SSK (8/51), AGSS (6/63).
SS.241	BASHAW		25. 7.43	SSK (8/51), AGSS (9/62).
SS.242	BLUEGILL		8. 8.43	SSK (8/51).
SS.243	BREAM	Electric	17.10.43	SSK (8/51), AGSS (4/65).
SS.244	CAVALLA	Boat	14.11.43	SSK (8/51), AGSS (7/63).
SS.245	COBIA		28.11.43	AGSS (12/62).
SS.246	CROAKER		19.12.43	SSK (8/51), AGSS (6/63).
SS.247	DACE		25. 4.43	Italian LEONARDO DA VINCI (12/54).
SS.248	DORADO		23. 5.43	Lost 12/10/43.
SS.249	FLASHER		20. 6.43	Scrapped 1963.
SS.250	FLIER		11. 7.43	Lost 13/8/44.
SS.251	FLOUNDER		22. 8.43	Discarded 1960.
SS.252	GABILAN		19. 9.43	Discarded 1960.
SS.253	GUNNEL		17. 5.42	Discarded 1959.
SS.254	GURNARD		1. 6.42	Discarded 1960.
SS.255	HADDO		21. 6.42	Scrapped 1959.
SS.256	HAKE	Electric	17. 7.42	AGSS (12/62).
SS.257	HARDER	Boat	19. 8.42	Lost 24/8/44.
SS.258	HOE		17. 9.42	Discarded 1960.
SS.259	JACK		16.10.42	Greek AMFITRITI (4/58).
SS.260	LAPON		27.10.42	Greek POSEIDON (8/57).
SS.261	MINGO		30.11.42	Japanese KUROSHIO (8/55).
SS.262	MUSKALLUNGE		13.12.42	Brazilian HUMAITA (1/57).
SS.263	PADDLE		30.12.42	Brazilian RIACHUELO (1/57).
SS.264	PARGO		24. 1.43	Scrapped 1961.
SS.265	PETO		30. 4.42	Scrapped 1961.
SS.266	POGY		23. 6.42	Discarded 1959.
SS.267	POMPON		15. 8.42	SSR (3/51), discarded 1960.
SS.268	PUFFER		22.11.42	Scrapped 1961.
SS.269	RASHER	Manitowoc	20.12.42	SSR (3/51), AGSS (7/60).
SS.270	RATON		24. 1.43	SSR (3/51), AGSS (7/60).
SS.271	RAY		28. 2.43	SSR (3/51), discarded 1960.
SS.272	REDFIN		4. 4.43	SSR (3/51), AGSS (6/63).
SS.273	ROBALO		9. 5.43	Lost 26/7/44.
SS.274	ROCK		20. 6.43	SSR (3/51), AGSS (7/60).
SS.275	RUNNER		30. 5.42	Lost 6/63.
SS.276	SAWFISH		23. 6.42	Discarded 1960.
SS.277	SCAMP	Ports-	20. 7.42	Lost 16/11/44.
SS.278	SCORPION	mouth	20. 7.42	Lost 2/44.
SS.279	SNOOK	N.Yd.	15. 8.42	Lost 4/45.
SS.280	STEELHEAD		11. 9.42	Discarded 1960.
SS.281	SUNFISH		2. 5.42	Discarded 1960.
SS.282	TUNNY	Mare	30. 6.62	SSG (1/51).
SS.283	TINOSA	Island	7.10.42	Training hulk; lost 1961.
SS.284	TULLIBEE		11.11.42	Lost 26/3/44.

U.S.S. Flasher (SS249) Gato Class, 4th November 1943.

U.S.S. Hoe (SS258) Gato Class, 16th February 1943.

		Builder	Date	Notes
SS.285	BALAO		27.10.42	AGSS (1960), discarded 1963.
SS.286	BILLFISH		12.11.42	AGSS (12/62).
SS.287	BOWFIN	Ports-	7.12.42	AGSS (12/62).
SS.288	CABRILLA	mouth	24.12.42	AGSS (12/62).
SS.289	CAPELIN	N.Yd.	20. 1.43	Lost 12/43.
SS.290	CISCO		24.12.42	Lost 28/9/43.
SS.291	CREVALLE		22. 2.43	AGSS (1961).
SS.292	DEVILFISH		30. 5.43	AGSS (12/62).
SS.293	DRAGONET		18. 4.43	Sunk as target 1961.
SS.294	ESCOLAR		18. 4.43	Lost 10/44.
SS.295	HACKLEBACK		30. 5.43	AGSS (12/62).
SS.296	LANCETFISH		15. 8.43	Sank before completion 20/2/45; not repaired; scrapped 1958.
SS.297	LING	Cramp	15. 8.43	AGSS (12/62).
SS.298	LIONFISH		7.11.43	AGSS (12/62).
SS.299	MANTA		7.11.43	AGSS (8/49).
SS.300	MORAY		14. 5.44	AGSS (12/62).
SS.301	RONCADOR		14. 5.44	AGSS (12/62).
SS.302	SABALO		4. 6.44	
SS.303	SABLEFISH		4. 6.44	
SS.304	SEAHORSE		9. 1.43	AGSS (12/62).
SS.305	SKATE	Mare Island	4. 3.43	Bikini target ship (7/46); sunk 16/10/48.
SS.306	TANG	N.Yd.	17. 8.43	Lost 24/10/44.
SS.307	TILEFISH		25.10.43	Venezuelan CARITE (5/60).
SS.308	APOGON (ex-Abadejo)		10. 3.43	Bikini target ship; sunk 26/7/46.
SS.309	ASPRO (ex-Acedia)		7. 4.43	AGSS (7/60), discarded 1962.
SS.310	BATFISH (ex-Acoupa)		5. 5.43	AGSS (12/62).
SS.311	ARCHERFISH		28. 5.43	AGSS (1960).
SS.312	BURRFISH (ex-Arnillo)		18. 6.43	SSR (1/48); HMCS GRILSE (5/61).
SS.313	PERCH		12. 9.43	Transport (1/48).
SS.314	SHARK		17.10.43	Lost 24/10/44.
SS.315	SEALION		31.10.43	Transport (3/48).
SS.316	BARBEL		14.11.43	Lost 4/2/45.
SS.317	BARBERO	Electric Boat	12.12.43	Cargo submarine (3/48); SSG (10/55), discarded 1964.
SS.318	BAYA		2. 1.44	AGSS (8/49).
SS.319	BECUNA		30. 1.44	
SS.320	BERGALL		16. 2.44	Turkish TURGUT REIS (10/58).
SS.321	BESUGO		27. 2.44	AGSS (12/62).
SS.322	BLACKFIN		12. 3.44	
SS.323	CAIMAN (ex-Blanquillo)		30. 3.44	
SS.324	BLENNY		9. 4.44	
SS.325	BLOWER		23. 4.44	Turkish DUMLUPINAR (2/50), lost 3/4/53.

U.S.S. Runner
(SS476) Tench Class,
March 1945.

U.S.S. Blackfin
(SS332) Gato Class,
4th August 1944.

200

Hull No.	Name	Builder	Date	Notes
SS.326	BLUEBACK		7. 5.44	Turkish IKINCI INONU (5/48).
SS.327	BOARFISH		21. 5.44	Turkish SAKARYA (5/48).
SS.328	CHARR (ex-Boccaccio)	Electric Boat	28. 5.44	
SS.329	CHUB (ex-Bonaci)		18. 6.44	Turkish GUR (5/48).
SS.330	BRILL		25. 6.44	Turkish BIRINCI INONU (5/48).
SS.331	BUGARA		2. 7.44	
SS.332	BULLHEAD		16. 7.44	Lost 6/8/45.
SS.333	BUMPER		6. 8.44	Turkish CANAKKALE (2/50).
SS.334	CABEZON		27. 8.44	AGSS (12/62).
SS.335	DENTUDA (ex-Capidoli)		10. 9.44	AGSS (12/62).
SS.336	CAPITAINE		1.10.44	AGSS (7/60).
SS.337	CARBONERO		15.10.44	
SS.338	CARP		12.11.44	
SS.339	CATFISH		19.11.44	
SS.340	ENTEMEDOR (ex-Chickwick)		17.12.44	
SS.341	CHIVO		14. 1.45	
SS.342	CHOPPER		4. 2.45	
SS.343	CLAMAGORE		25. 2.45	
SS.344	COBBLER		1. 4.45	
SS.345	COCHINO		20. 4.45	Lost 26/8/49.
SS.346	CORPORAL		10. 6.45	
SS.347	CUBERA	Electric Boat	17. 6.45	
SS.348	CUSK		28. 7.45	SSG (1/48).
SS.349	DIODON		10. 9.45	
SS.350	DOGFISH		27.10.45	
SS.351	GREENFISH (ex-Doncella)		21.12.45	
SS.352	HALFBEAK (ex-Dory)		19. 2.46	
SS.353	DUGONG			Cancelled 23/10/44.
SS.354	EEL			Cancelled 23/10/44.
SS.355	ESPADA			Cancelled 23/10/44.
SS.356	JAWFISH (ex-Fanegal)			Cancelled 29/7/44.
SS.357	ONO (ex-Friar)			Cancelled 29/7/44.
SS.358	GARLOPA			Cancelled 29/7/44.
SS.359	GARRUPA			Cancelled 29/7/44.
SS.360	GOLDRING			Cancelled 29/7/44.
SS.361	GOLET		1. 8.43	Lost 14/6/44.
SS.362	GUAVINA		29. 8.43	Oiler Submarine (8/48).
SS.363	GUITARRO		26. 9.43	Turkish PREVEZE (8/54).
SS.364	HAMMERHEAD	Manitowoc	24.10.43	Turkish CERBE (8/54).
SS.365	HARDHEAD		12.12.43	
SS.366	HAWKBILL		9. 1.44	Dutch ZEELEEUW (4/53).
SS.367	ICEFISH		20. 2.44	Dutch WALRUS (2/53).
SS.368	JALLAO		12. 3.44	

SS.369	KETE		9. 4.44	Lost 3/45.
SS.370	KRAKEN		30. 4.44	Spanish ALMIRANTE GARCIA DE LOS REYES (10/59).
SS.371	LAGARTO		28. 5.44	Lost 3/5/45.
SS.372	LAMPREY		18. 6.44	Argentine SANTA FE (7/60).
SS.373	LIZARDFISH		16. 7.44	Italian EVANGELISTA TORRICELLI (1/60).
SS.374	LOGGERHEAD	Manitowoc	13. 8.44	AGSS (12/62).
SS.375	MACABI		19. 9.44	Argentine SANTIAGO DEL ESTERO (9/60).
SS.376	MAPIRO		9.11.44	Turkish PIRI REIS (3/60).
SS.377	MENHADEN		20.12.44	
SS.378	MERO		17. 1.45	Turkish HIZIR REIS (4/60).
SS.379	NEEDLEFISH			Cancelled 29/7/44.
SS.380	NERKA			Cancelled 29/7/44.
SS.381	SAND LANCE (ex-Ojanco, ex-Orca)		25. 6.43	Brazilian RIO GRANDE DO SUL (1963).
SS.382	PICUDA (ex-Obispo)		12. 7.43	
SS.383	PAMPANITO		12. 7.43	AGSS (12/62).
SS.384	PARCHE		24. 7.43	AGSS (12/62).
SS.385	BANG		30. 8.43	
SS.386	PILOTFISH		30. 8.43	Bikini target ship (7/46). Sunk 16/10/48.
SS.387	PINTADO		15. 9.43	
SS.388	PIPEFISH		12.10.43	AGSS (12/62).
SS.389	PIRANHA		27.10.43	AGSS (12/62).
SS.390	PLAICE		15.11.43	Brazilian BAHIA (1963).
SS.391	POMFRET		27.10.43	
SS.392	STERLET (ex-Pudiano)	Portsmouth N.Yd.	27.10.43	
SS.393	QUEENFISH		30.11.43	AGSS (7/60), sunk as target 1963
SS.394	RAZORBACK		27. 1.44	
SS.395	REDFISH		27. 1.44	AGSS (7/60).
SS.396	RONQUIL		27. 1.44	
SS.397	SCABBARDFISH		27. 1.44	Greek TRIANA (2/65).
SS.398	SEGUNDO		5. 2.44	
SS.399	SEA CAT		21. 2.44	AGSS (8/49).
SS.400	SEA DEVIL		28. 2.44	AGSS (7/60), disc. 1964.
SS.401	SEA DOG		28. 3.44	AGSS (12/62).
SS.402	SEA FOX		28. 3.44	
SS.403	ATULE		6. 3.44	
SS.404	SPIKEFISH (ex-Shiner)		26. 4.44	AGSS (7/62), discarded 1963.
SS.405	SEA OWL		7. 5.44	SSK (1963).
SS.406	SEA POACHER		20. 5.44	
SS.407	SEA ROBIN		25. 5.44	
SS.408	SENNET		6. 6.44	
SS.409	PIPER (ex-Awa)		26. 6.44	

SS.410	THREADFIN (ex-Sole)	⎫ Ports- ⎬ mouth	26. 6.44	
SS.411	SPADEFISH	⎱ N.Yd.	8. 1.44	AGSS (12/62).
SS.412	TREPANG (ex-Senorita)	Mare	23. 3.44	AGSS (12/62).
SS.413	SPOT	⎬ Island	19. 5.44	Chilean SIMPSON (1/62
SS.414	SPRINGER	N.Yd.	3. 8.44	Chilean THOMSON (1/61).
S.S415	STICKLEBACK	⎭	1. 1.45	Lost 29/5/58.
SS.416	TIRU	⎭	16. 9.47	

Notes:—The standard U.S. submarine of **W.W.II,** carried 24 torpedoes. Some were completed in as little as 9 months. FLASHER sank 100,231 tons of shipping (21 ships) and RASHER, BARB, TANG and SILVERSIDES all sank over 90,000 tons.

Tench class

Displacement: 1,570/2,415 tons.
Dimensions: 307 (wl) 311¾ (oa) × 27¼ × 15¼ ft.
Machinery: 2-shaft Diesels, S.H.P. 5,400/2,740 = 20¼/10 knots.
Armament: 10—21 in. T.T. (6 bow, 4 stern); 1—5 in., 1—40 mm. guns.
Complement: 85.

SS.417	TENCH	⎫	7. 7.44	
SS.418	THORNBACK		7. 7.44	
SS.419	TIGRONE		20. 7.44	SSR (3/48), AGSS (12/63).
SS.420	TIRANTE		9. 8.44	
SS.421	TRUTTA (ex-Tomatate)	⎬ Ports- mouth	18. 8.44	
SS.422	TORO	N.Yd.	23. 8.44	AGSS (7/62); scrapped 1965.
SS.423	TORSK		6. 9.44	
SS.424	QUILLBACK (ex-Trembler)	⎭	1.10.44	
SS.425	TRUMPETFISH	⎱	13. 5.45	
SS.426	TUSK		8. 7.45	
SS.427	TURBOT			Cancelled 12/8/45; test hull.
SS.428	ULUA			Cancelled 12/8/45; test hull; scrapped 1958.
SS.429	UNICORN	⎬ Cramp		Cancelled 29/7/44.
SS.430	VANDACE			Cancelled 29/7/44.
SS.431	WALRUS			Cancelled 29/7/44.
SS.432	WHITEFISH			Cancelled 29/7/44.
SS.433	WHITING			Cancelled 29/7/44.
SS.434	WOLFFISH	⎭		Cancelled 29/7/44.
SS.435	CORSAIR	⎱	3. 5.46	AGSS (4/60); scrapped 1964.
SS.436	UNICORN	⎬ Electric Boat	1. 8.46	Scrapped incomplete 1958.
SS.437	WALRUS	⎭	20. 9.46	Scrapped incomplete 1958.

SS.475	ARGONAUT		1.10.44	
SS.476	RUNNER		17.10.44	AGSS (1962); discarded
SS.477	CONGER		17.10.44	1963.
SS.478	CUTLASS		5.11.44	AGSS (7/62); Pakistani
SS.479	DIABLO	Ports-	1.12.44	GHAZI (6/64).
		mouth		
SS.480	MEDREGAL	N.Yd.	15.12.44	SSR (1/48).
SS.481	REQUIN		1. 1.45	
SS.482	IREX		26. 1.45	
SS.483	SEA LEOPARD		2. 3.45	
SS.484	ODAX		10. 4.45	
SS.485	SIRAGO		11. 5.45	
SS.486	POMODON		12. 6.45	
SS.487	REMORA		12. 7.45	
SS.488	SARDA		24. 8.45	AGSS (7/62); scrapped
				1965.
SS.489	SPINAX		20.11.45	SSR (1/48).
SS.490	VOLADOR	Ports-	17. 1.46	
SS.491	POMPANO	mouth		Cancelled 12/8/45.
SS.492	GRAYLING	N.Yd.		Cancelled 12/8/45.
SS.493	NEEDLEFISH			Cancelled 12/8/45.
SS.494	SCULPIN			Cancelled 12/8/45.
SS.516	WAHOO	Mare Island		Cancelled 7/1/46.
		N.Yd.		
SS.522	AMBERJACK		15.12.44	
SS.523	GRAMPUS		15.12.44	
SS.524	PICKEREL		15.12.44	
SS.525	GRENADIER	Boston	15.12.44	
SS.526	DORADO	N.Yd.		Cancelled 29/7/44.
SS.527	COMBER			Cancelled 29/7/44.
SS.528	SEA PANTHER			Cancelled 29/7/44.
SS.529	TIBURON			Cancelled 29/7/44.

Notes:—Improved **Gato** class. SS.438-474, 495-515, 517-521, 530-562, all unnamed, were cancelled in 1944-45.

MINE CRAFT

This category comprises the ships equipped primarily for the laying and removal of mines, either in defensive minefields or in enemy-controlled water.

In 1941 the only minelayers on the list were two old coastal passenger ships converted during World War I, which were joined by four similar vessels converted in that year. There were also eight flush-deck destroyers fitted as minelayers for offensive minelaying. Of the three large minelayers under construction, only one was finally completed as such. In 1944, eight small Army minelayers were acquired by the Navy; they had formerly been operated for defensive minelaying by the Coast Artillery Corps. Twelve **Sumner** class destroyers were completed as light minelayers in 1944. Minelayers were named after Civil War monitors.

The largest minesweepers on the list were the eighteen flush-deck destroyers converted in 1940-42 by a reduction in armament including removal of torpedo tubes and the addition of sweeping gear. Twenty-four **Livermore** class destroyers were similarly converted in 1944-45; these proved most useful during operations on Okinawa.

Pre-war minesweepers included the twenty-two remaining vessels of the **Bird** class, forty-nine of which had been completed. Most of these saw service in the removal of the North Sea Mine Barrage in 1919. Their numbers had been augmented by fifteen large trawlers acquired and converted in 1940.

In the same year the prototypes of a new class, **Raven** and **Osprey**, were launched. These were sturdy steel-hulled minesweepers of which ninety-five were completed, twenty-two being transferred to the Royal Navy. Larger and faster than the British corvette, these ships proved most useful as escorts for coastal convoys and other patrol duties, as well as for minesweeping in amphibious operations. The smaller, slower **Admirable** class, of which 123 units were completed, was of the same design as the PCE submarine chasers. Ten were transferred to the Soviet Union on completion in 1943, and 24 others followed in 1945. Eighteen other vessels of the **Adroit** class (AM.82-99) built in 1942, minesweeper variations of the steel-hulled submarine chaser, were reclassified as PC.1586-1603 in 1944.

Coastal minesweepers (AMc) included a number of converted fishing boats and seventy wooden-hulled boats built in 1941-42. Motor minesweepers (YMS) were most valuable boats and were used in the forefront of amphibious operations for inshore sweeping.

Minesweepers were originally named after birds but when the number of ships outran this category, 'action' nouns and adjectives were used.

MINELAYERS

Displacement: 5,875 tons.
Dimensions: 440 (wl) 454¾ (oa) × 60¼ × 19½ ft.
Machinery: 2-shaft geared turbines, S.H.P. 11,000 = 21 knots.
Armament: 4—5 in., 16—40 mm. A.A. guns; 800 mines.
Complement: 400.

CM.5	TERROR	Philadelphia N.Yd.	6. 6.41	
CM.6	CATSKILL	Willaimette	19. 5.42	Completed as LSV 1 (6/44).
CM.7	OZARK	Willaimette	15. 6.42	Completed as LSV 2 (9/44).

Notes:—TERROR was at North Africa, then Pacific 1944-45 (*Kamikaze* 30/4/45).

U.S.S. Miantonomah (CM10). Converted coastal steamer, 29th April 1944.

U.S.S. Terror (CM5).

U.S.S. Salem (CM11). Former Florida East Coast train ferry, 29th April 1944.

U.S.S. Keokuk (AKN4). Net Cargo Ship, formerly minelayer, 27th November 1944.

207

U.S.S. Wassuc (CMc3). Coastal minelayer, July 1944.

U.S.S. Trapper (ACM9). Auxiliary minelayer after transfer from the Army.

Converted types:

CM.8	KEOKUK (ex-CMc 6, ex-Columbia Heights)	2699/14	7.41	AN 5 (5/42); AKN 4 (11/43); merc. HENRY M. FLAGLER (1947), FLAGLER ODICA (1961).
CM.9	MONADNOCK (ex-CMc 4, ex-Cavalier)	3056/38	6.41	ACM 10 (7/45); merc. KARUKARA (1949); MONTE DE LA ESPERANZA (1952).
CM.10	MIANTONOMAH (ex-CMc 5, ex-Quaker)	3056/38	5.41	Lost 25/9/44.
CM.11	SALEM (ex-Joseph R. Parrott)	2406/16	6.42	SHAWMUT (8/45); returned 6/46.
CM.12	WEEHAWKEN (ex-Estrada Palma)	2639/20	6.42	Lost 8/10/45.
CMc.3	WASSUC (ex-Yale)	1670/24	12.40	Sold 7/46.

Notes:—AROOSTOOK (CM.3) became AK.44 but did not serve in the war. OGLALA (CM.4) sunk at Pearl Harbor 7/12/41, was recommissioned as ARG.1. CMc.1 and 2 were yachts.

AUXILIARY MINELAYERS

Displacement: 880 tons.
Dimensions: 189 (oa) × 37 × 12 ft.
Machinery: 2-shaft Diesel, S.H.P. 1,200 = 10 knots.
Armament: 1—40 mm. gun.
Complement: 70.

ACM.1	CHIMO (ex-Bundy)	⎫	1942	Merc. DAY ISLAND (1963).
ACM.2	PLANTER (ex-Ricker)		1942	Merc. SAN JUAN (1963)
ACM.3	BARRICADE (ex-Story)		1942	MAGNOLIA (WAGL 328) (6/46).
ACM.5	BARBICAN (ex-Armistead)	⎬ Marietta	1942	IVY (WAGL 329) (6/46).
ACM.6	BASTION (ex-Hunt)		1942	JONQUIL (WAGL 330) (6/46).
ACM.7	OBSTRUCTOR (ex-Sylvester)		1942	HEATHER (WAGL 331) (6/46).
ACM.8	PICKET (ex-Knox)		1942	WILLOW (WAGL 332) (6/46).
ACM.9	TRAPPER (ex-Murray)	⎭	1942	YAMACRAW (WARC 333) (6/46).

Notes:—Former Army mine-planters transferred in 1944-45. ACM.4 was named BUTTRESS (ex-PCE.878).

U.S.S. Montgomery (DM17). Flush-deck destroyer converted to light minelayer prior to the war at Dutch Harbor, Alaska, March 1943.

U.S.S. Shannon (DM25). Sumner class destroyer completed as light minelayer, September 1944.

U.S.S. Tolman (DM28). Light minelayer, 1945.

LIGHT MINELAYERS

Displacement:	1,160 tons.			
Dimensions:	310 (wl) 314¼ (oa) × 31¾ × 15¼ ft.			
Machinery:	2-shaft geared turbines, S.H.P. 25,000 = 30 knots.			
Armament:	3—3 in., 2—40 mm. A.A. guns; 80 mines.			
Complement:	122.			

DM.15	GAMBLE (ex-DD 123)	⎫	11. 5.18	Lost 17/2/45.
DM.16	RAMSAY (ex-DD 124)	⎬ Newport News	8. 6.18	AG 98 (6/45); scrapped 1947.
DM.17	MONT-GOMERY (ex-DD 121)		23. 3.18	Lost 17/10/44.
DM.18	BREESE (ex-DD 122)	⎭	11. 5.18	Scrapped 1946.
DM.19	TRACY (ex-DD 214)	Cramp	12. 8.19	Scrapped 1946.
DM.20	PREBLE (ex-DD 345)	⎫	8. 3.20	AG 99 (6/45); scrapped 1947.
DM.21	SICARD (ex-DD 346)	⎬ Bath Iron Works	20. 4.20	AG 100 (6/45); scrapped 1946.
DM.22	PRUITT (ex-DD 347)	⎭	2. 8.20	AG 101 (6/45); scrapped 1946.

Notes:—Flush-deck destroyers converted to minelayers in 1930-37.

Displacement:	2,200 tons.			
Dimensions:	369 (wl) 376½ (oa) × 40¾ × 18¾ ft.			
Machinery:	2-shaft geared turbines, S.H.P. 60,000 = 34 knots.			
Armament:	6—5 in. (3 × 2), 12—40 mm. A.A. guns; 100 mines.			
Complement:	350.			

DM.23	ROBERT H. SMITH	⎫	25. 5.44	
DM.24	THOMAS E. FRASER		10. 6.44	
DM.25	SHANNON	⎬ Bath Iron Works	24. 6.44	
DM.26	HARRY F. BAUER		9. 7.44	
DM.27	ADAMS		23. 7.44	
DM.28	TOLMAN		13. 8.44	
DM.29	HENRY A. WILEY	⎫	21. 4.44	
DM.30	SHEA	⎬ Bethlehem (Staten I.)	20. 5.44	
DM.31	J. WILLIAM DITTER	⎭	4. 7.44	Scrapped 1946.
DM.32	LINDSEY	⎫ Bethlehem (San Pedro, Cal.)	5. 3.44	
DM.33	GWIN	⎬	9. 4.44	
DM.34	AARON WARD	⎭	5. 5.44	Scrapped 1946.

Notes:—**Sumner** class destroyers converted during construction. Ex-DD.735-40, 749-51, 771-73 respectively. Served as picket destroyers at Okinawa, where AARON WARD, LINDSEY and J. WILLIAM DITTER were severely damaged by *Kamikaze* and SHEA by *Baka* bomb.

U.S.S. Hogan (DMS6). Flush-deck destroyer as high speed mine-sweeper, 29th July 1943.

U.S.S. Shea (DM30). Former Sumner class destroyer as light minelayer, 18th October 1944. Note absence of T.T.

U.S.S. Chandler (DMS9). High speed minesweeper, 23rd May 1945. Note squared-off stern, sweeping gear.

U.S.S. Endicott (DMS35). Livermore class destroyer converted to high speed minesweeper, 1945. Note sweeping gear at stern in place of "Y" turret. T.T. have also been removed.

HIGH SPEED MINESWEEPERS

Displacement: 1,060 to 1,190 tons.
Dimensions: 310 (wl) 314½ (oa) × 31½ × 11½ ft.
Machinery: 2-shaft geared turbines, S.H.P. 26,000 = 32.5 knots.
Armament: 3—3 in., 2—40 mm. A.A. guns.
Complement: 140.

DMS.1	DORSEY (ex-DD 117)	Cramp	9. 4.18	Lost 9/10/45.
DMS.2	LAMBERTON (ex-AG 21, ex-DD 119)	Newport News	30. 3.18	AG 21 (6/45); scrapped 1947.
DMS.3	BOGGS (ex-AG 19, ex-DD 136)	Mare Island N.Yd.	25. 4.18	AG 19 (6/45); scrapped 1947.
DMS.4	ELLIOT (ex-DD 146)	Cramp	4. 7.18	AG 104 (6/45); scrapped 1946.
DMS.5	PALMER (ex-DD 161)	Bethlehem; Fore R.	18. 8.18	Lost 7/1/45.
DMS.6	HOGAN (ex-DD 178)	⎫	12. 4.19	AG 105 (6/45); sunk as target 8/11/45.
DMS.7	HOWARD (ex-DD 179)	Union Iron Works	26. 4.19	AG 106 (6/45); scrapped 1946.
DMS.8	STANSBURY (ex-DD 180)		16. 5.19	AG 107 (6/45); scrapped 1946.
DMS.9	CHANDLER (ex-DD 206)	⎫	19. 3.19	AG 108 (6/45); scrapped 1947.
DMS.10	SOUTHARD (ex-DD 207)	Cramp	31. 3.19	Lost 9/10/45.
DMS.11	HOVEY (ex-DD 208)		26. 4.19	Lost 6/1/45.
DMS.12	LONG (ex-DD 209)		26. 4.19	Lost 6/1/45.
DMS.13	HOPKINS (ex-DD 249)	New York Sbdg. Co.	26. 6.20	Scrapped 1947.
DMS.14	ZANE (ex-DD 337)	⎫	12. 8.19	AG 109 (6/45); scrapped 1946.
DMS.15	WASMUTH (ex-DD 338)		15. 9.20	Lost 29/12/42.
DMS.16	TREVER (ex-DD 339)	Mare Island N.Yd.	15. 9.20	AG 110 (6/45); scrapped 1947.
DMS.17	PERRY (ex-DD 340)		29.10.21	Lost 13/9/44.
DMS.18	HAMILTON (ex-DD 141)		15. 1.19	AG 111 (6/45); scrapped 1947.

Notes:—Flush-deck destroyers converted in 1940-42. 24 **Livermore** class destroyers were converted to minesweepers in 1944-45 (DMS.19-42). For names and details see pp. 132 and 135. Armament was 3—5 in., 4—40 mm. A.A. guns, no T.T.

U.S.S. Harding (DMS28). High speed minesweeper, 17th December 1944.

U.S.S. Cormorant (AM40). Bird class minesweeper, 12th February 1942, later converted to fleet tug.

U.S.S. Owl (AM2). Bird class minesweeper, 1940.

U.S.S. Bluebird (AM72). Trawler converted to minesweeper, January 1942.

MINESWEEPERS
Bird class

Displacement: 840 tons.
Dimensions: 174 (wl) 188 (oa) × 35½ × 9 ft.
Machinery: 1-shaft reciprocating (VTE), S.H.P. 1,400 = 14 knots.
Armament: 2—3 in. A.A. guns.
Complement: 72.

AM.2	OWL	Todd (Brooklyn)	4. 3.18	ATO 137 (6/42); sold 7/47.
AM.3	ROBIN		17. 6.18	ATO 140 (6/42); sold 2/48.
AM.5	TANAGER	Staten Island	2. 3.18	Lost 4/5/42.
AM.7	ORIOLE		3. 7.18	ATO 136 (6/42); merc. (1947).
AM.9	FINCH	Standard Sbdg.	30. 3.18	Lost 10/4/42. Salved by Japan, lost 12/1/45.
AM.13	TURKEY		30. 4.18	ATO 143 (6/42); sold 12/46.
AM.14	WOODCOCK		12. 5.18	ATO 145 (6/42); sold 1/48.
AM.15	QUAIL	Chester Sbdg.	6.10.18	Lost 5/5/42.
AM.16	PARTRIDGE		15.10.18	ATO 138 (6/42); lost 11/6/44.
AM.20	BOBOLINK	Baltimore D.D.	15. 6.18	ATO 131 (6/42); sold 10/46.
AM.21	LARK		6. 8.18	ATO 168 (3/44); sold 1/47.
AM.24	BRANT	Sun	30. 5.18	AT 132 (6/42); ARS 32 (9/42).
AM.25	KINGFISHER	Puget Sound N.Yd. Gas Engine & Power Co.	30. 3.18	ATO 135 (6/42); sold 6/47.
AM.26	RAIL		25. 4.18	ATO 139 (6/42); sold 1/47.
AM.30	SEAGULL		24.12.18	ATO 141 (6/42); sold 4/47.
AM.31	TERN		22. 3.19	ATO 142 (6/42); sold 7/47.
AM.33	PENGUIN	New Jersey Sbdg.	12. 6.18	Lost 8/12/41.
AM.35	WHIPPOOR-WILL	Alabama Sbdg.	28. 1.19	ATO 169 (3/44); sold 11/46.
AM.36	BITTERN		15. 2.19	Lost 10/12/41.
AM.40	CORMORANT	Todd (Brooklyn)	5. 2.19	ATO 133 (6/42); sold 3/47.
AM.43	GREBE	Staten Island	17.12.18	ATO 134 (6/42); lost 5/12/42.
AM.52	VIREO	Philadelphia N.Yd.	26. 5.19	ATO 144 (6/42); sold 2/47.

Notes:—Survivors of a class of 54 vessels. CONDOR, PLOVER, GOSHAWK, RAVEN and SHRIKE cancelled 1919. SWALLOW, CARDINAL, CURLEW, SANDERLING and PEACOCK lost before the war. Six transferred to other government agencies were re-acquired in 1941 as salvage vessels. Others were converted to submarine rescue vessels and seaplane tenders. EIDER converted to gate vessel. Remaining vessels converted to fleet tugs in 1942.

Converted types:

AM.66	BULLFINCH (ex-Villanova)	262/37	7.40	Returned 7/45.
AM.67	CARDINAL (ex-Jeanne d'Arc)	262/37	8.40	Returned 8/45.
AM.68	CATBIRD (ex-Bittern)	355/38	8.40	IX 183 (8/44); merc. SALHUS (1947).
AM.69	CURLEW (ex-Kittiwake)	355/37	8.40	IX 170 (6/44); merc. RAGAN (1946).
AM.70	FLICKER (ex-Delaware)	303/37	8.40	IX 165 (4/44); Dept. of Interior DELAWARE (1945).
AM.71	ALBATROSS (ex-Illinois)	256/31	8.40	IX 171 (6/44); returned 11/45.
AM.72	BLUEBIRD (ex-Maine)	256/31	8.40	IX 172 (6/44); merc. RYTTER (1946).
AM.73	GRACKLE (ex-Notre Dame)	255/29	9.40	Returned 1/46.
AM.74	GULL (ex-Boston College)	241/28	8.40	Merc. GUDRUN (5/46); lost 14/1/51.
AM.75	KITE (ex-Holy Cross)	299/28	9.40	Sold 3/45.
AM.76	LINNET (ex-Georgetown)	229/28	9.40	Merc. CAMBRIDGE IX 166 (4/44); (1945).
AM.77	GOLDFINCH (ex-Fordham)	255/29	9.40	Returned 1/46.
AM.79	GOSHAWK (ex-Penobscot)	522/19	9.40	IX 195 (10/44); merc. BERING SEA (1946).
AM.80	GOLDCREST (ex-Shawmut)	235/28	11.40	Merc. BATAVIA (1946).
AM.81	CHAFFINCH (ex-Trimount)	235/28	12.40	Merc. MEDAN (1946).
AM.132	EAGLE (ex-Wave)	320/27	1.42	CAPTOR (PYC 40, 4/42); sold 2/45.
AM.133	HAWK (ex-Gale)	320/37	1.42	Returned 9/44.
AM.134	IBIS (ex-Tide)	320/37	1.42	Returned 9/44.
AM.135	MERGANSER (ex-Ocean)	320/37	1.42	Returned 9/44.

Notes:—AM.78 was a converted yacht (PYc.4);

Raven-Auk class

Displacement: 890 tons (except AM.55-56, 810 tons).
Dimensions: 215 (wl) 221¼ (oa) × 32 × 10¾ ft.
Machinery: 2-shaft diesel-electric drive, S.H.P. 2,900 to 3,500 = 18.1 knots.
Armament: 1—3 in., 2—40 mm. guns (except AM.314-341, 4—40 mm. guns).
Complement: 100.

AM.55	RAVEN	⎫ Norfolk	24. 8.40	
AM.56	OSPREY	⎬ N.Yd.	24. 8.40	Lost 5/6/44.
AM.57	AUK	⎭	26. 8.41	Discarded 1959.

U.S.S. Osprey (AM56). Raven class, 1943.

U.S.S. Speed (AM116). Raven class, February 1943.

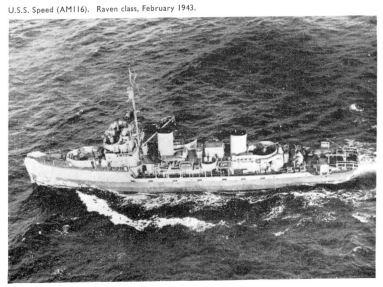

AM.58	BROADBILL	⎫	21. 5.42	
AM.59	CHICKADEE	⎬ Defoe	20. 7.42	
AM.60	NUTHATCH	(Bay City)	16. 9.42	
AM.61	PHEASANT	⎭	24.10.42	
AM.62	SHELDRAKE	⎫	12. 2.42	AGS 19 (1952).
AM.63	SKYLARK		12. 3.42	Lost 28/3/45.
AM.64	STARLING		11. 4.42	
AM.65	SWALLOW	⎬ General	6. 5.42	Lost 22/4/45.
AM.100	HEED	Engin-	19. 6.42	
AM.101	HERALD	eering	4. 7.42	
AM.102	MOTIVE		17. 8.42	
AM.103	ORACLE	⎭	30. 9.42	
AM.104	PILOT	⎫	5. 7.42	
AM.105	PIONEER	Pennsyl-	26. 7.42	
AM.106	PORTENT	⎬ vania	16. 8.42	Lost 23/1/44.
AM.107	PREVAIL	Shipyard	13. 9.42	AGS 20 (1952);
				scrapped 1965.
AM.108	PURSUIT	⎭	12. 6.42	AGS 17 (1952);
				discarded 1960.
AM.109	REQUISITE	Winslow	25. 7.42	AGS 18 (1952).
		Marine		scrapped 1965.
AM.110	REVENGE		7.11.42	
	(ex-Right)			
AM.111	SAGE	⎭	21.11.42	
AM.112	SEER		23. 5.42	Norwegian ULLER
		American		(1962).
AM.113	SENTINEL	⎬ Sbdg.	4. 6.42	Lost 10/7/43.
AM.114	STAFF	(Lorain)	17. 6.42	
AM.115	SKILL	⎭	22. 6.42	Lost 25/9/43.
AM.116	SPEED		18. 4.42	
AM.117	STRIVE	American	16. 5.42	Norwegian GOR (1959)
AM.118	STEADY	⎬ Sbdg.	6. 6.42	
AM.119	SUSTAIN	(Cleve-	23. 6.42	Norwegian TYR
		land)		(1959).
AM.120	SWAY	John	29. 9.42	
AM.121	SWERVE	⎬ H.	25. 2.43	Lost 9/7/44.
AM.122	SWIFT	⎭ Mathis	5.12.42	
AM.123	SYMBOL	Savannah	2. 7.42	
		Machine		
AM.124	THREAT	& Fdry.	15. 8.42	
AM.125	TIDE	Co.	7. 9.42	Lost 7/6/44.
AM.126	TOKEN	⎫	28. 3.42	
AM.127	TUMULT		19. 4.42	
AM.128	VELOCITY	⎬ Gulf	19. 4.42	
AM.129	VITAL	Sbdg.	7. 9.42	H.M.S. STRENUOUS
		(Madison-		(1943).
AM.130	USAGE	ville)	4.10.42	H.M.S. TOURMALINE
AM.131	ZEAL	⎭	15. 9.42	(1943).
AM.314	CHAMPION	⎫	12.12.42	
	(ex-Akbar)			
AM.315	CHIEF	⎬ General	5. 1.43	
	(ex-Alice)	Engin-		
AM.316	COMPETENT	⎭ eering	9. 1.43	
	(ex-Amelie)			

U.S.S. Toucan (AM387). Raven class, February 1945.

U.S.S. Firm (AM98). Adroit class mine-sweeper, February 1944, later reclassi-fied to submarine chaser.

222

AM.317	DEFENSE (ex-Amity)	General Engineering	18. 2.43	
AM.318	DEVASTATOR (ex-Augusta)		19. 4.43	
AM.319	GLADIATOR (ex-Blaze)		7. 5.43	
AM.320	IMPECCABLE (ex-Brutus)		21. 5.43	
AM.321	OVERSEER		25. 1.43	H.M.S. ELFREDA (1943).
AM.322	SPEAR (ex-Errant)		25. 2.43	
AM.323	TRIUMPH (ex-Éspoir)	Associated	25. 2.43	Norwegian BRAGE (1/61).
AM.324	VIGILANCE (ex-Exploit)		5. 4.43	
AM.340	ARDENT (ex-Buffalo)	General Engineering	22. 6.43	
AM.341	DEXTROUS (ex-Sepoy)	Gulf Sbdg. (Madisonville)	17. 1.43	
AM.371	MINIVET		8.11.44	Lost 29/12/45.
AM.372	MURRELET		29.12.44	Philippine (1965).
AM.373	PEREGRINE	Savannah Machine & Fdry Co.	17. 2.45	AG 176 (4/64).
AM.374	PIGEON		28. 3.45	
AM.375	POCHARD		11. 6.44	
AM.376	PTARMIGAN		15. 7.44	Korean SHIN SONG (7/63).
AM.377	QUAIL		20. 8.44	
AM.378	REDSTART		18.10.44	Chinese (1965).
AM.379	ROSELLE		29. 8.44	
AM.380	RUDDY	Gulf Sbdg. (Madisonville)	29.10.44	Peruvian GALVEZ (11/60).
AM.381	SCOTER		26. 9.44	
AM.382	SHOVELLER		10.12.44	Peruvian DIEZ CANSECO (11/60).
AM.383	SURFBIRD	American Sbdg. (Lorain)	31. 8.44	ADG 383 (5/57).
AM.384	SPRIG		15. 9.44	
AM.385	TANAGER		9.12.44	C.G.WTR 385 (11/63).
AM.386	TERCEL		16.12.44	
AM.387	TOUCAN	American Sbdg. (Cleveland)	15. 9.44	Chinese (1965).
AM.388	TOWHEE		6. 1.45	AGS 28 (4/64).
AM.389	WAXWING		10. 3.45	Chinese (1965).
AM.390	WHEATEAR		21. 4.45	

Notes:—Of 32 additional ships built for R.N. under lend-lease (BAM.1-32), BAM.1-8, 22-24 and 30 were retained by U.S.N. as AM.314-320, 340, 322-324 and 341 respectively.

U.S.S. Buoyant (AM153). Admirable class, 11th June 1944, in dazzle camouflage, with smoke pipe instead of funnel.

U.S.S. Dour (AM223). Admirable class, 18th December 1944, with small funnel.

Admirable class

Displacement: 650 tons.
Dimensions: 180 (wl) 184½ (oa) × 33 × 9¾ ft.
Machinery: 2-shaft Diesel, S.H.P. 1,710 = 14.8 knots.
Armament: 1—3 in., 4—40 mm. A.A. guns.
Complement: 100.

AM.136	ADMIRABLE		18.10.42	U.S.S.R. (7/45).
AM.137	ADOPT		18.10.42	U.S.S.R. (7/45).
AM.138	ADVOCATE		1.11.42	U.S.S.R. (6/43).
AM.139	AGENT		1.11.42	U.S.S.R. (7/43).
AM.140	ALARM		7.12.42	U.S.S.R. (8/43).
AM.141	ALCHEMY		7.12.42	U.S.S.R. (8/43), lost.
AM.142	APEX		7.12.42	U.S.S.R. (8/43).
AM.143	ARCADE	Tampa	7.12.42	U.S.S.R. (8/43).
AM.144	ARCH	Sbdg.	7.12.42	U.S.S.R. (9/43).
AM.145	ARMADA		7.12.42	U.S.S.R. (9/43), lost.
AM.146	ASPIRE		27.12.42	U.S.S.R. (9/43).
AM.147	ASSAIL		27.12.42	U.S.S.R. (10/43).
AM.148	ASTUTE		23. 2.43	U.S.S.R. (7/45).
AM.149	AUGURY		23. 2.43	U.S.S.R. (7/45).
AM.150	BARRIER		23. 2.43	U.S.S.R. (7/45).
AM.151	BOMBARD		23. 2.43	U.S.S.R. (7/45).
AM.152	BOND		21.10.42	U.S.S.R. (8/45).
AM.153	BUOYANT		24.11.42	Sold 5/46.
AM.154	CANDID		14.10.42	U.S.S.R. (8/45).
AM.155	CAPABLE		16.11.42	U.S.S.R. (8/45).
AM.156	CAPTIVATE		1.12.42	U.S.S.R. (8/45).
AM.157	CARAVAN	Willa-	27.10.42	U.S.S.R. (8/45).
AM.158	CAUTION	mette	7.12.42	U.S.S.R. (8/45).
AM.159	CHANGE	Iron &	15.12.42	Discarded 1960.
AM.160	CLAMOUR	Steel	24.12.42	Discarded 1959.
AM.161	CLIMAX		9. 1.43	Discarded 1959.
AM.162	COMPEL		16. 1.43	Discarded 1959.
AM.163	CONCISE		6. 2.43	Discarded 1959.
AM.164	CONTROL		28. 1.43	Discarded 1958.
AM.165	COUNSEL		17. 2.43	
AM.214	CRAG		21. 3.43	Mexican DM-15 (1962).
	(ex-Craig)			
AM.215	CRUISE		21. 3.43	
AM.216	DEFT		28. 3.43	Chinese (8/48), scrapped (1/59).
AM.217	DELEGATE	Tampa	28. 3.43	Chinese YUNG HO (5/46).
		Sbdg.		
AM.218	DENSITY		6. 2.44	Discarded 1960.
AM.219	DESIGN		6. 2.44	Discarded 1960.
AM.220	DEVICE		21. 5.44	Mexican DM-11 (1962).
AM.221	DIPLOMA		21. 5.44	Mexican DM-17 (1962).
AM.222	DISDAIN		25. 3.44	U.S.S.R. (5/45).
AM.223	DOUR		25. 3.44	Mexican DM-16 (1962).
AM.224	EAGER	American	10. 6.44	Mexican DM-06 (1962).
AM.225	ELUSIVE	Sbdg.	10. 6.44	Chinese YUNG KANG (5/46).
		(Lorain)		
AM.226	EMBATTLE		17. 9.44	Chinese YUNG HSING (5/46).

225

U.S S. Improve (AM247). Admirable class, June 1945. Note 3in. gun forward, twin 40mm. mounts aft of funnel.

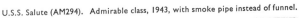

U.S.S. Salute (AM294). Admirable class, 1943, with smoke pipe instead of funnel.

AM.227	EMBROIL			Cancelled 6/44.
AM.228	ENHANCE	American		Cancelled 6/44.
AM.229	EQUITY	Sbdg.		Cancelled 6/44.
AM.230	ESTEEM	(Lorain)		Cancelled 6/44.
AM.231	EVENT			Cancelled 6/44.
AM.232	EXECUTE		22. 6.44	Mexican DM-03 (1962).
AM.233	FACILITY		22. 6.44	Mexican DM-04 (1962).
AM.234	FANCY	Puget	4. 9.44	U.S.S.R. (5/45).
AM.235	FIXITY	Sound	4. 9.44	Mercantile COMMER-
		Bridge		CIAL DIXIE (1949).
AM.236	FLAME			Cancelled 6/44.
AM.237	FORTIFY			Cancelled 6/44.
AM.238	GARLAND		20. 2.44	Discarded 1960.
AM.239	GAYETY		19. 3.44	Vietnamese CHI LANG
				II (6/62).
AM.240	HAZARD	Commer-	21. 5.44	
AM.241	HILARITY	cial Ship	30. 7.44	Mexican DM-02 (1962).
AM.242	INAUGURAL	Repair	1.10.44	Discarded 1961.
AM.243	ILLUSIVE			Cancelled 6/44.
AM.244	IMBUE			Cancelled 6/44.
AM.245	IMPERVIOUS			Cancelled 6/44.
AM.246	IMPLICIT		6. 9.43	Chinese YUNG CHIA
				(6/48).
AM.247	IMPROVE		26. 9.43	Merc. ECUADOR(1948),
				lost 16/3/53.
AM.248	INCESSANT		22.10.43	Merc. COMMERCIAL
				OHIOAN (1949).
AM.249	INCREDIBLE	Savannah	21.11.43	Discarded 1959.
AM.250	INDICATIVE	Machine	12.12.43	U.S.S.R. (5/45).
AM.251	INFLICT	& Fdry	16. 1.44	Merc. MANABI (1948),
		Co.		lost 24/4/53.
AM.252	INSTILL		5. 3.44	Mexican DM-10 (1962).
AM.253	INTRIGUE		8. 4.44	Mexican DM-19 (1962).
AM.254	INVADE		2. 6.44	Mexican DM-18 (1962).
AM.255	JUBILANT		20. 2.43	Mexican DM-01 (1962).
AM.256	KNAVE		13. 3.43	Mexican DM-13 (1962).
AM.257	LANCE		10. 4.43	Chinese YUNG SHENG
				(8/45).
AM.258	LOGIC		10. 4.43	Chinese YUNG SHUN
				(8/45).
AM.259	LUCID	American	5. 6.43	Chinese YUNG TING
		Sbdg.		(8/45); YANG MING
		(Lorain)		(1964).
AM.260	MAGNET		5. 6.43	Chinese YUNG NING
				(8/45).
AM.261	MAINSTAY		31. 7.43	Discarded 1959.
AM.262	MARVEL		31. 7.43	U.S.S.R. (5/45).
AM.263	MEASURE		23.10.43	U.S.S.R. (5/45).
AM.264	METHOD		23.10.43	U.S.S.R. (5/45).
AM.265	MIRTH		24.12.43	U.S.S.R. (5/45).
AM.266	NIMBLE		24.12.43	Chinese (6/48).
AM.267	NOTABLE	Gulf	12. 6.43	Discarded 1946.
AM.268	NUCLEUS	Sbdg.	26. 6.43	U.S.S.R. (5/45).
AM.269	OPPONENT	(Madison-	12. 6.43	Discarded 1960.
AM.270	PALISADE	ville)	26. 6.43	U.S.S.R. (5/45).

AM.271	PENETRATE	⎫ Gulf	11. 9.43	U.S.S.R. (5/45).
AM.272	PERIL	Sbdg.	25. 7.43	U.S.S.R. (5/45).
AM.273	PHANTOM	⎬ (Madison-	25. 7.43	Chinese (6/48).
AM.274	PINNACLE	ville)	11. 9.43	Chinese YUNG HSIU (6/48).
AM.275	PIRATE	⎫	16.12.43	Lost 12/10/50.
AM.276	PIVOT		11.11.43	Chinese YUNG SHOU (8/48).
AM.277	PLEDGE		23.12.43	Lost 12/10/50.
AM.278	PROJECT		20.11.43	Philippine SAMAR (5/48).
AM.279	PRIME	Gulf ⎬ Sbdg. (Madison-	22. 1.44	Chinese YUNG FENG (5/46).
AM.280	PROWESS	ville)	17. 2.44	
AM.281	QUEST		16. 3.44	Philippine PAGASA (6/48); SANTA MARIA (1955).
AM.282	RAMPART	⎱	30. 3.44	U.S.S.R. (5/45).
AM.283	RANSOM	⎰	18. 9.43	Mexican DM-12 (1963).
AM.284	REBEL		28.10.43	Mexican DM-14 (1963).
AM.285	RECRUIT		11.12.43	Mexican DM-07 (1963).
AM.286	REFORM		29. 1.44	Chinese (6/48).
AM.287	REFRESH		12. 4.44	Chinese YUNG CHANG (6/48).
AM 288	REIGN		29. 5.44	Discarded 1959.
AM.289	REPORT		8. 7.44	Discarded 1963.
AM.290	REPROOF	General ⎬ Engineer- ing	8. 8.44	Completed as merc. HARCOURT MAT-COLM (1947), COL-TON BAY (1953), STRATFORD (1960).
AM.291	RISK		7.11.44	Completed as GEORGE GAMBLIN (1947), WINDING BAY (1953), PINGUINO (1962).
AM.292	RIVAL			Cancelled 6/44.
AM.293	SAGACITY			Cancelled 6/44.
AM.294	SALUTE	⎱	6. 2.43	Lost 8/6/45.
AM.295	SAUNTER		20. 2.43	Sold (4/47).
AM.296	SCOUT		2. 5.43	Mexican DM-09 (1963).
AM.297	SCRIMMAGE	Commer-	16. 5.43	Merc. GIANT II (1962).
AM.298	SCUFFLE	⎬ cial Ship	8. 8.43	Mexican DM-05 (1963).
AM.299	SENTRY	Repair	15. 8.43	Vietnamese KY HOA (7/62).
AM.300	SERENE		31.10.43	Vietnamese NHUT TAO (8/63).
AM.301	SHELTER		14.11.43	Vietnamese CHI LINH (8/63).
AM.302	SIGNET	⎱	16. 8.43	
AM.303	SKIRMISH		16. 8.43	
AM.304	SCURRY (ex-Skurry)	⎬ Associated	1.10.43	
AM.305	SPECTACLE		1.10.43	Sold 5/47.
AM.306	SPECTER	⎰	15. 2.44	

U.S.S. Waxbill (AMc15). Converted fishing boat as coastal minesweeper, 14th July 1941.

U.S.S. Combat (AMc69). Navy-built coastal minesweeper, January 1942.

U.S.S. YMS-86. Motor minesweeper, 12th May 1942. Original type with two funnels, broken hull line.

U.S.S. YMS-260. Modified type of motor minesweeper, 12th April 1943, with single squat funnel, unbroken hull line.

U.S.S. YMS-449. Third type of motor minesweeper, 15th July 1944, with no funnel.

AM.307	STAUNCH			15. 2.44	
AM.308	STRATEGY			28. 3.44	
AM.309	STRENGTH	Associated		28. 3.44	
AM.310	SUCCESS			11. 5.44	Mexican DM-08 (1963).
AM.311	SUPERIOR			11. 5.44	
AM.351	ADJUTANT			17. 6.44	Cancelled 11/45.
AM.352	BITTERN			21. 6.44	Cancelled 11/45.
AM.353	BREAKHORN			4. 7.44	Cancelled 11/45.
AM.354	CARIAMA			1. 7.44	Cancelled 11/45.
AM.355	CHUKOR	Willa-		15. 7.44	Cancelled 11/45.
AM.356	CREDDOCK	mette		22. 7.44	
AM.357	DIPPER	Iron &		26. 7.44	Sold 1/61.
AM.358	DOTTEREL	Steel		5. 8.44	Cancelled 11/45.
AM.359	DRAKE			12. 8.44	Completed as Degaussing Vessel (YDG 11).
AM.360	DRIVER			19. 8.44	Cancelled 11/45.
AM.361	DUNLIN			26. 8.43	Discarded 1946.
AM.362	GADWALL			15. 7.43	
AM.363	GAVIA			18. 9.43	Chinese YUNG CHUN (5/46).
AM.364	GRAYLAG			4.12.43	
AM.365	HARLEQUIN	Puget		3. 6.44	Mexican DM-20 (1962).
AM.366	HARRIER	Sound		7. 6.44	Discarded 1959.
AM.367	HUMMER	Bridge			Cancelled 6/44.
AM.368	JACKDAW				Cancelled 6/44.
AM.369	MEDRICK				Cancelled 6/44.
AM.370	MINAH				Cancelled 6/44.

Notes:- In addition, AM.391-420 of this class were cancelled in 1945.

Motor Minesweepers: YMS.1-481.

Displacement: 215 tons.
Dimensions: 130 (wl) 136 (oa) × 24½ × 6 ft.
Machinery: 2-shaft Diesel motors; S.H.P. 1,000 = 12 knots.
Armament: 1—3 in., 2—20 mm. guns.
Complement: 50.
War losses: YMS 14, 19, 21, 24, 30, 39, 48, 50, 70, 71, 84, 103, 133, 304, 350, 365, 378, 385, 409, 481.

Notes:—Built 1942-45. YMS.450-452, 474 and 476 completed as submarine chasers (PCS). YMS.195, 242, 262 and 263 were converted to surveying vessels and renamed CHAUVENET, HARKNESS, JAMES M. GILLIS and SIMON NEWCOMB (AGS.11-14) respectively. YMS.344 and 480 became degaussing vessels (YDG.6-7). Of the same design as sweeper-type submarine chasers. YMS.137, 141-142, 148-150, 152-157, 161-162, 167-168, 171-175, 181-182, 185-191 194, 202-206, 209-214, 217, 221, 223, 225, 229-230, 232-234, 236, 240, 244, 252-258, 261, 264, 277-280, 282 and 284 transferred to R.N. together with an additional eighty (BYMS.1-80) of a separate series. YMS.33, 38, 42, 59, 75, 85, 88, 100, 135, 139, 143-145, 178, 180, 184, 216, 237, 241, 260, 266, 272-273, 285, 287-288, 295, 301, 332, 428, 435, 447-448, 453, 455-457, 460, 462, 464-466 and 469 transferred to U.S.S.R.; YMS.3, 13, 15-16, 18, 20, 23, 26-29, 31, 34, 36-37, 43, 55, 58, 62-64, 69, 77-78, 82-83, 169, 207-208, 226-227 to France; and YMS.247, 305, 377 and 379-382 to Norway.

BUILDERS

Associated (Seattle): YMS 287-296.
Astoria Marine: YMS 100-103, 135-142, 422-425.
Ballard (Seattle): YMS 326-333.
Bellingham Iron Works: YMS 269-276, 342-345, 410-413, 480-481.
Burger (Manitowoc): YMS 107-112, 155-162.
Campbell (San Diego): YMS 151-154.
Colberg (Stockton, Cal.): YMS 94-99, 383-388.
Dachel-Carter (Benton Hbr., Mich.): YMS 163-170.
Gibbs Gas Engine (Jacksonville): YMS 54-65, 346-357, 464-472.
Henry C. Grebe (Chicago): YMS 84-85, 171-182, 279-280, 405-409, 418-421.
Greenport Basin: YMS 20-31, 183-194, 375-382, 453-459.
Harbor Boat (Terminal I., Cal.): YMS 117-120, 313-316, 393-396, 473-474.
Herreshoff (Bristol, R.I.): YMS 18-19.
Hiltebrant (Kingston, N.Y.): YMS 32-38, 195-206, 442-445, 462-463.
Robert Jacob (N.Y.): YMS 39-41, 207-215, 358-362, 438-441, 446-448.
Kruse & Banks (North Bend, Ore.): YMS 121-124, 265-268.
Al Larson (Terminal I., Cal.): YMS 86-87, 320-325.
J. M. Martinac (Tacoma): YMS 125-128, 216-221, 277-278.
Mojean & Ericson (Tacoma): YMS 222-225, 426-429, 479.
Henry B. Nevins (N.Y.): YMS 1-11, 308-312, 397-404.
Northwestern (Bellingham): YMS 285-286.
Rice Bros. (E. Boothbay, Me.): YMS 12-17, 303-307.
Frank L. Sample (Boothbay Hbr., Me.): YMS 104-106, 226-234.
San Diego Marine: YMS 113-116, 143-146, 475-476.
Seattle Sbdg.: YMS 334-341.
South Coast (Newport Bch., Cal.): YMS 88-93, 259-264, 317-319, 449-452.
Stadium (Cleveland): YMS 76-83, 235-240, 389-392, 414-417, 460-461.
Wm. F. Stone (Oakland): YMS 299-302.
Tacoma Boat: YMS 129-132, 241-246, 297-298, 430-433, 477-478.
Weaver (Orange, Tex.): YMS 66-75, 247-258, 371-374.
Western (Tacoma): YMS 133-134, 147-150.
Wheeler (Brooklyn): YMS 42-53.

PATROL CRAFT

A very diverse category, patrol craft ranged in size from the large **Erie** class gunboats to motor torpedo boats. During the war many types fitted for diverse duties joined the comparatively few pre-war vessels. In addition, Coast Guard cutters served in similar roles under Navy Control (see p. 363).

In 1941, the list included seven large gunboats, five of which were of World War I vintage or older, five Yangtze River gunboats, and a number of converted yachts. There were also eight old Eagle Boats, slow, weak and of little value, and eight submarine chasers left over from World War I.

Because of the shortage of anti-submarine craft in the early days of 1942, the U.S. Navy commissioned ten corvettes reverse lend-leased from the Royal Navy. Twenty-two A/S trawlers were also loaned with British crews. Eight additional corvettes were built in Canada. The next development of this type was the frigate, of which ten were ordered in Canada (PG 101-110). Only two were retained by the U.S. Navy, but one hundred were ordered from U.S. yards. They were built by the Maritime Commission for the Navy having been originally designed as small freighters. Twenty-one were built for Great Britain, and twenty-eight were later loaned to the Soviet Union. They were unbearably hot below decks in the tropics and were quickly disposed of after the war.

A number of yachts were taken over for patrol and escort duties classified as PG, PY or PYc according to size. Although the type had proved not very successful during World War I, six ships were fitted out as Q-ships, heavily armed vessels disguised as innocent merchantmen. These were the trawler EAGLE (PYc 40), tanker BIG HORN (AO 45), small freighters ASTERION (AK 63), ANACAPA (AG 49) and ATIK (unnumbered) and schooner IRENE FORSYTE (IX 93). Only ATIK ever saw a U-boat (which sank her) and the others were later returned to more routine duties. ANACAPA served off the Pacific coast.

A program of steel and wooden hulled submarine chasers was put in hand and this group spawned a number of distinctive types. The steel-hulled class (PC) were useful as patrol vessels but of little value as convoy escorts, being too slow and weakly armed. The bigger PCE escorts for coastal convoys came out too late and many were converted to small gunboats for amphibious operations and as rescue vessels. The wooden-hulled SC's were similar to the British motor launches and were useless for fighting submarines, but proved most valuable for lesser duties. A patrol version of the YMS motor minesweeper was classified as a submarine chaser (PCS).

The motor torpedo boats received much public notice, such as the famous PT-109 commanded by the late President Kennedy, but space does not permit much elaboration on the various types. There were two major American-built types, designed by Elco and Higgins. A substantial number of the British-designed Vosper type were also built.

Gunboats and frigates were named after small cities and the yachts after precious stones.

GUNBOATS

Displacement: 990 tons.
Dimensions: 173 (wl) 200½ (oa) × 35 × 12¼ ft.
Machinery: 2-shaft reciprocating (VTE), I.H.P. 1,000 = 10 knots.
Armament: 1—5 in., 2—4 in., 1—3 in. guns.
Complement: 170.

PG.17	DUBUQUE	⎫ Gas	15. 8.04	Sold 1/47.
PG.18	PADUCAH	⎬ Engine &	11.10.04	Merc. (12/46); scrapped
		⎭ Power Co.		1950.

Notes:—Used for training after 1921.

Displacement: 1,025 tons.
Dimensions: 210 (wl) 226¼ (oa) × 40¾ × 9½ ft.
Machinery: 1-shaft reciprocating (VTE), I.H.P. 950 = 12.5 knots.
Armament: 2—4 in., 1—3 in. guns.
Complement: 153.

PG. 19 SACRAMENTO	Cramp	21. 2.14	Merc. FERMINA (8/47).

U.S.S. Dubuque (PG17). Gunboat, 15th June 1943, as rearmed with 3—5in. guns. Sister Paducah retained twin funnels.

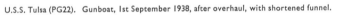

U.S.S. Tulsa (PG22). Gunboat, 1st September 1938, after overhaul, with shortened funnel.

U.S.S. Erie (PG50). Gunboat, May 1940, in pre-war paint with "E" (for Engineering) on funnel.

U.S.S. Charleston (PG51). Gunboat, March 1944, with 6in. guns in shields and depth charge racks on stern.

Wreck of gunboat Erie at Willemstad, Curacao, 2nd December 1942.

U.S.S. Plymouth (PG57). Large yacht classed as a gunboat, 17th February 1943, later converted to m.t.b. tender.

U.S.S. St. Augustine (PG54). Large yacht classed as a gunboat, 22nd May 1943, and used as escort for coastal convoys.

237

Displacement:	1,200 tons.			
Dimensions:	225 (wl) 241¼ (oa) × 41¼ × 10 ft.			
Machinery:	1-shaft geared turbines, S.H.P. 1,200 = 12 knots.			
Armament:	3—4 in., 4—3 in. guns.			
Complement:	175.			

PG.21	ASHEVILLE	Charleston	4. 7.18	Lost 3/3/42.
PG.22	TULSA	N.Yd.	25. 8.22	TACLOBAN (11/44); sold 10/46.

Notes:—Both Asiatic Fleet, 1941.

Displacement:	1,900 tons.			
Dimensions:	308 (wl) 328½ (oa) × 41¼ × 11½ ft.			
Machinery:	2-shaft geared turbines, S.H.P. 6,200 = 20 knots.			
Armament:	4—6 in. (4 × 1), 16—40 mm. A.A. guns, 1 seaplane.			
Complement:	236.			

PG.50	ERIE	New York N.Yd.	29. 1.36	Lost 12/11/42.
PG.51	CHARLESTON	Charleston	25. 2.36	Massachusetts State Trng. Ship (3/48).

Notes:—CHARLESTON served in the Aleutian and Alaska area.

Converted types:

		Gross ton'age /Year Built	Acquired	Fate
PG.52	NIAGARA (ex-Hi-Esmaro)	1333/29	10.40	AGP 1 (1/43).
PG.53	VIXEN (ex-Orion)	3060/29	11.40	Returned 1/47.
PG.54	ST. AUGUSTINE (ex-Noparo)	1300/28	12.40	Lost 6/1/44.
PG.55	JAMESTOWN (ex-Alder)	2076/27	12.40	AGP 3 (1/43).
PG.56	WILLIAMSBURG (ex-Aras)	1332/30	4.41	Presidential Yacht (11/45), Merc. ANTON BRUUN (1963).
PG.57	PLYMOUTH (ex-Alva)	2265/31	11.41	Lost 5/8/43.
PG.58	HILO (ex-Moana)	1839/31	11.41	AGP 2 (1/43).
PG.59	SAN BERNADINO (ex-Vanda)	1250/28	1.42	Merc. VANDA (1946).
PG.60	BEAUMONT (ex-Carola)	1108/30	1.42	Merc. ELPETAL (1947).

238

U.S.S. Nourmahal (PG72). Large yacht, July 1942, later transferred to the Coast Guard.

U.S.S. Siren (PY13). Yacht armed as coastal convoy escort, July 1943.

PG.61	DAUNTLESS (ex-Delphine)	1363/21	1.42	Returned 6/46.
PG.72	NOURMAHAL	1969/28	3.42	U.S.C.G. WPG 122 (1/44); sold 5/46.
PY.10	ISABEL	710/17	19.17	Scrapped 3/46.
PY.12	SYLPH (ex-Intrepid)	596/30	7.40	Merc. SYLPH (1947); scrapped 1960.
PY.13	SIREN (ex-Lotosland)	662/30	10.40	Merc. (1946).
PY.14	ARGUS (ex-Haida)	704/29	10.40	Sold 10/46.
PY.15	CORAL (ex-Yankee Clipper)	726/13	11.40	Expended as target 1944.
PY.16	ZIRCON (ex-Nakhoda)	958/30	12.40	Merc. NEW YORK (1951).
PY.17	JADE (ex-Doctor Brinkley)	582/26	12.40	Merc. SANTA MARIA (1946).
PY.18	TURQUOISE (ex-Entropy)	513/22	8.40	Ecuadorian 9 DE OCTUBRE (1/44); lost 7/9/53.
PY.19	CARNELIAN (ex-Seventeen)	502/30	5.41	Merc. WILLIAM JOHNSON (19).
PY.20	TOURMALINE (ex-Sylvia)	502/30	5.41	Merc. SYLVIA (1946), ADELPHIC (1946), KYKNOS (1948).
PY.21	RUBY (ex-Placida)	502/30	6.41	Merc. PLACIDA (1947); lost 2/12/56.
PY.22	AZURLITE (ex-Vagabondia)	854/28	12.41	Merc. (1947).
PY.23	BERYL (ex-Rene)	945/30	12.41	Merc. BALTIMORE (1947).
PY.24	ALMANDITE (ex-Happy Days)	545/27	1.42	Sold 12/46.
PY.25	CRYSTAL (ex-Vida)	1030/29	1.42	Merc. (1947).
PY.26	CYTHERA (i)	602/07	12.41	Lost 2/5/42.
PY.27	GIRASOL (ex-Firenze)	535/26	3.42	Merc. SOUTH SEAS (1947).
PY.28	MARCASITE (ex-Ramfis)	968/28	2.42	Merc. COMANDO (1946), WESTMIN-STER (1947), STAR OF MALTA (1952).
PY.29	MIZPAH (ex-Allegro)	559/26	3.42	Merc. (1945).
PY.31	CYTHERA (ii) (ex-Abril)	800/31	7.42	Merc. ABRIL (1945), Israel : BEN HECHT SANTA MARIA DEL MARE (1950).
PY.32	SOUTHERN SEAS (ex-Lyndonia)	954/20	11.42	Lost 9/10/45.

U.S.S. Captor (PYc40). Trawler classed as coastal yacht, August 1944, having served in 1942 as Q-ship.

U.S.S. Mindanao (PR8). River gunboat, on trials, June 1928.

U.S.S. Temptress (PG62). Corvette, 9th October 1944.

U.S.S. Fury (PG69). Corvette, 1942, immediately following transfer to U.S.N. Note camouflage, uncharacteristic number. [I.W.M.

U.S.S. Surprise (PG63). Corvette, May 1944.

RIVER GUNBOATS

Details for all: 2—3 in. guns; complement 70; all built by Kiangnan, Shanghai.
Displacement: 370 tons.
Dimensions: 150 (wl) 159¾ (oa) × 27¼ × 5¼ ft.
Machinery: 2-shaft reciprocating (VTE), S.H.P. 1,950 = 14.5 knots.

PR.3	WAKE (ex-Guam)		28. 5.27	Captured 7/12/41; Japanese TATARA; Chinese TAI YUAN (1946).
PR.4	TUTUILA		14. 6.27	Chinese MEI YUAN (3/42).

Displacement: 450 tons.
Dimensions: 180 (wl) 191¼ (oa) × 28¼ × 5¼ ft.
Machinery: 2-shaft reciprocating (VTE), S.H.P. 2,250 = 15 knots.

PR.5	PANAY		11.11.27	Lost 12/12/37.
PR.6	OAHU		26.11.27	Lost 6/5/42.

Displacement: 560 tons.
Dimensions: 198 (wl) 210¾ (oa) × 31¼ × 5¾ ft.
Machinery: 2-shaft reciprocating (VTE), S.H.P. 3,150 = 16 knots.

PR.7	LUZON		12. 9.27	Lost 6/5/42; Japanese KARATSU (salved); lost 3/2/45.
PR.8	MINDANAO		28. 9.27	Lost 5/5/42.

Notes:—PANAY was sunk in the Yangtze by Japanese aircraft. OAHU, LUZON and MINDANAO arrived in Manila 5/12/41. TUTUILA remained at Chungking throughout the war.

CORVETTES

Displacement: 925 tons.
Dimensions: 190 (wl) 205 (oa) × 33 × 14½ (PG.86-100, 208¼ (oa)) ft.
Machinery: 1-shaft reciprocating (VTE), S.H.P. 2,750 = 16 knots.
Armament: 1—4 in., 1—3 in. guns (PG.86-100, 2—3 in.).
Complement: 87.

PG.62	TEMPTRESS (ex-H.M.S. Veronica)	Smiths Dock	17.10.40	Mercantile VEROLOCK (1947); lost 1/47.
PG.63	SURPRISE (ex-H.M.S. Heliotrope)	Crown	5. 6.40	Merca. HELIOLOCK (1946), ZIANG TEH (1947), Comm. Chinese LIN I.
PG.64	SPRY (ex-H.M.S. Hibiscus)	Harland & Wolff	6. 4.40	Merc. MADONNA (1947).
PG.65	SAUCY (ex-H.M.S. Arabis)	Harland & Wolff	14. 2.40	H.M.S. SNAPDRAGON merc. KATINA (1947), TEWFIK (1950).

PG.66	RESTLESS (ex-H.M.S. Periwinkle)	Harland & Wolff	24. 2.40	Merc. PERILOCK (1947).
PG.67	READY (ex-H.M.S. Calendula)	Harland & Wolff	21. 3.40	Merc. VILLA CISNER-OS (1948), VILLA BENS (1949).
PG.68	IMPULSE (ex-H.M.S. Begonia)	Cook Welton	18. 9.40	Merc. BEGONLOCK (1946), FUNDICION, ES MOLINAO (1949), ASTILUZU (1951), RIO MERO (1956).
PG.69	FURY (ex-H.M.S. Larkspur)	Fleming & Ferguson	5. 9.40	Merc. LARKSLOCK (1946).
PG.70	COURAGE (ex-H.M.S. Heartsease, ex-Pansy)	Harland & Wolff	20. 4.40	Merc. ROSKVA (1951), DOUGLAS (1956), SEABIRD (1958), lost 12/58.
PG.71	TENACITY (ex-H.M.S. Candytuft)	Grange-mouth	8. 7.40	Merc. MAW HWA (1947).
PG.86	ACTION (ex-H.M.S. Comfrey)	Colling-wood	28. 7.42	Merc. ARNE PRESTHUS (1952).
PG.87	ALACRITY (ex-H.M.S. Cornel)	Colling-wood	4. 9.42	Merc. RIO MARINA (1948), PORTO FERRAIO (1951).
PG.88	BEACON (ex-H.M.S. Dittany)	Colling-wood	31.10.42	H.M.S. DITTANY (3/43); merc. OLYM-PIC CRUISER (1950), OTORI MARU No. 2 (1956).
PG.89	BRISK (ex-H.M.S. Flax)	Kingston	15. 6.42	Merc. BRISK (1947), ARIANA (1951), ARVIDA BAY (1955).
PG.90	CAPRICE (ex-H.M.S. Honesty)	Kingston	28. 9.42	H.M.S. HONESTY (5/43); sold 12/46.
PG.91	CLASH (ex-H.M.S. Linaria)	Midland	18.11.42	H.M.S. LINARIA (6/43); merc. PORTO OFFU-RO (1948)?
PG.92	HASTE (ex-H.M.S. Mandrake)	Morton	22. 8.42	Merc. PORTO AZZURO (1949).
PG.93	INTENSITY (ex-H.M.S. Milfoil)	Morton	5. 8.42	Merc. OLYMPIC PROMOTER (1950), OTORI MARU No. 5 (1956).
PG.94	MIGHT (ex-H.M.S. Musk)	Morton	15. 7.42	Merc. OLYMPIC EXPLORER (1950), OTORI MARU No. 3 (1956), KYO MARU No. 12 (1957).

U.S.S. Intensity (PG93). Canadian-built corvette, 7th September 1943.

U.S.S. Asheville (PF1). Canadian-built frigate, 3rd November 1943.

PG.95	PERT (ex-H.M.S. Nepeta)	Morton	27.11.42	Merc. OLYMPIC LEADER (1950), OTORI MARU No. 1 (1956), KYO MARU No. 15 (1957).
PG.96	PRUDENT (ex-H.M.S. Privet)	Morton	4.12.42	Italian ELBANO (1949), STAFFETTA (1951).
PG.97	SPLENDOR (ex-H.M.S. Rosebay)	Collingwood	11. 2.43	H.M.S. ROSEBAY (7/43), merc. BENMARK (1947), FRIDAY (1950).
PG.98	TACT (ex-H.M.S. Smilax)	Collingwood	24.12.42	H.M.S. SMILAX (6/43), Argentine REPUBLICA (1946).
PG.99	VIM (ex-H.M.S. Statice)	Collingwood	10. 4.43	H.M.S. STATICE (9/43). sold 5/47.
PG.100	VITALITY (ex-H.M.S. Willowherb)	Midland	24. 3.43	H.M.S. WILLOWHERB (8/43); sold 5/47.

Notes:—PG.62-71 transferred from R.N. under reverse lend-lease, Spring 1942. PG.86-100 built in Canada for U.S.N. but seven of these as noted above were turned over to R.N. PG.62-71 were returned to R.N. 8/45 and unless otherwise noted resumed their original names.

FRIGATES

Displacement: 1,000 tons.
Dimensions: 283 (wl) $301\frac{1}{2}$ (oa) $\times$ $36\frac{1}{2}$ $\times$ $11\frac{1}{2}$ ft. max.
Machinery: 2-shaft reciprocating (VTE), S.H.P. 5,500 = 20 knots.
Armament: 3—3 in., 4—40 mm. guns.
Complement: 180.

| PF.1 | ASHEVILLE (ex-H.M.S. Adur) | Canadian Vickers | 22. 8.42 | Argentine HERCULES (6/46). |
| PF.2 | NATCHEZ (ex-H.M.S. Annan) | | 12. 9.42 | Dominican JUAN PABLO DUARTE (7/47). |

Notes:—Ex-PG.101-102. PG.103-110 of this class transferred to R.N. on completion. Canadian *River* class.

Displacement: 1,430 tons.
Dimensions: $285\frac{1}{2}$ (wl) 304 (oa) $\times$ $37\frac{1}{2}$ $\times$ 12 ft.
Machinery: 2-shaft reciprocating (VTE), S.H.P. 5,500 = 20 knots.
Armament: 2 or 3—3 in., 10—20 mm. A.A. or 3—3 in., 4—40 mm., 9—20 mm. guns.
Complement: 180.

| PF.3 | *TACOMA | Kaiser (Richmond. Cal.) | 7. 7.43 | S. Korean TAEDONG (10/51). |
| PF.4 | *SAUSALITO | | 20. 7.43 | S. Korean IMCHIN (/53). |

U.S.S. Pasco (PF6)
9th January 1945

U.S.S. Rockford (PF48). In dazzle camouflage, with funnel cap. [Ted Stone

PF.5	*HOQUIAM		31. 7.43	S. Korean NAKTONG (10/51).
PF.6	*PASCO		17. 8.43	Japanese KASHI (/53).
PF.7	*ALBU-QUERQUE	Kaiser (Rich-mond, Cal.)	14. 9.43	Japanese TOCHI (/53).
PF.8	*EVERETT		29. 9.43	Japanese KIRI (3/53).
PF.9	POCATELLO		17.10.43	Sold 9/47.
PF.10	BROWNSVILLE		14.11.43	Sold 9/47.
PF.11	GRAND FORKS		27.11.43	Sold 5/47.
PF.12	CASPER		27.12.43	Sold 5/47.
PF.13	PUEBLO		20. 1.44	Dominican PRESI-DENTE PEYNADO (9/47).
PF.14	GRAND ISLAND		19. 2.44	Cuban MAXIMO GOMEZ (6/47).
PF.15	ANNAPOLIS	American Sbdg. (Lorain)	16.10.43	Mexican USUMACIN-TA (11/47).
PF.16	BANGOR		6.11.43	Mexican TEHUANTE-PEC (11/47).
PF.17	KEY WEST		29.12.43	Sold 5/47.
PF.18	ALEXANDRIA		15. 1.44	Scrapped 1947.
PF.19	HURON	American Sbdg. (Cleve-land)	3. 7.43	Merc. JOSE MARCE-LINO (1948).
PF.20	GULFPORT		21. 8.43	Scrapped 1947.
PF.21	*BAYONNE		11. 9.43	Japanese BUNA (/53).
PF.22	*GLOUCESTER		12. 7.43	Japanese TSUGE (/53)
PF.23	SHREVEPORT		15. 7.43	Scrapped 1947.
PF.24	MUSKEGON		25. 7.43	French MERMOZ (3/47).
PF.25	*CHARLOTTES-VILLE	Walter Butler (Superior, Wis.)	30. 7.43	Japanese MAKI (1/53).
PF.26	*POUGHKEEP-SIE		12. 8.43	Japanese MOMI (/53).
PF.27	*NEWPORT		15. 8.43	Japanese KAEDE (/53).
PF.28	EMPORIA		30. 8.43	French LE VERRIER (3/47).
PF.29	GROTON		14. 9.43	Colombian ALMIRAN-TE PADILLA (3/47).
PF.30	HINGHAM		27. 8.43	Scrapped 1947.
PF.31	GRAND RAPIDS		10. 9.43	Scrapped 1947.
PF.32	WOONSOCKET		27. 9.43	Peruvian GALVEZ (9/48).
PF.33	DEARBORN (ex-Toledo)		27. 9.43	Sold 7/47.
PF.34	*LONG BEACH	Consoli-dated Steel (San Pedro, Cal.)	5. 5.43	Japanese SHII (/53).
PF.35	*BELFAST		20. 5.43	Lost 17/11/48 under Soviet control.
PF.36	*GLENDALE		28. 5.43	Thai TACHIN (/51).
PF.37	*SAN PEDRO		11. 6.43	Japanese KAYA (/53).
PF.38	*CORONADO		17. 6.43	Japanese SUGI (1/53).
PF.39	*OGDEN		23. 6.43	Japanese KUSU (/53).
PF.40	EUGENE		6. 7.43	Cuban JOSE MARTI (6/47).

U.S.S. Eagle 57 (PE57). World War I patrol boat still in service, August 1944.

U.S.S. PC-588. Steel-hull submarine chaser, February 1943.

U.S.S. PC-797. Steel-hull submarine chaser, April 1945, with 40mm. A.A. gun aft.

PF.41	EL PASO		16. 7.43	Sold 10/47.
PF.42	VAN BUREN		27. 7.43	Scrapped 1947.
PF.43	ORANGE		6. 8.43	Sold 9/47.
PF.44	CORPUS CHRISTIE		17. 8.43	Sold 10/47.
PF.45	HUTCHINSON	Consoli-dated Steel (San Pedro, Cal.)	27. 8.43	Mexican CALIFORNIA (11/47).
PF.46	*BISBEE		7. 9.43	Colombian CAPITAN TONO (2/52).
PF.47	*GALLUP		17. 9.43	Thai PRASAE (10/51)
PF.48	*ROCKFORD		27. 9.43	S. Korean APNOK (11/50), const. total loss 21/5/52.
PF.49	*MUSKOGEE		18.10.43	S. Korean DUMAN (11/50).
PF.50	*CARSON CITY		13.11.43	Japanese SAKURA (4/53).
PF.51	*BURLINGTON		7.12.43	Colombian ALMIRAN-TE BRION (/53).
PF.52	*ALLENTOWN	Froem-ming (Milwau-kee)	3. 7.43	Japanese UME (4/53).
PF.53	*MACHIAS		22. 8.43	Japanese NARA (/53).
PF.54	*SANDUSKY		5.10.43	Japanese NIRE (/53).
PF.55	*BATH		14.11.43	Japanese MATSU (12/53).
PF.56	COVINGTON	Globe (Superior, Wis.)	15. 7.43	Ecuadorian GUAYAS (8/47).
PF.57	SHEBOYGAN		31. 7.43	Belgian VICTOR BILLET (3/47).
PF.58	ABILENE (ex-Bridgeport)		21. 8.43	Dutch CIRRUS (5/47).
PF.59	BEAUFORT		9.10.43	Scrapped 1947.
PF.60	CHARLOTTE		30.10.43	Merc. BAHIA (1948).
PF.61	MANITOWOC	Globe (Duluth)	30.11.43	French LE BRIX (3/47).
PF.62	GLADWYNE (ex-Worcester)		7. 1.44	Mexican PAPALOA-PAN (11/47).
PF.63	MOBERLY (ex-Scranton)		26. 1.44	Sold 12/47.
PF.64	KNOXVILLE	Leatham D. Smith Sbdg. (Superior Wis.)	10. 7.43	Dominican PRESI-DENTE TRONCOSO (9/47).
PF.65	UNIONTOWN (ex-Chattanooga)		7. 8.43	Argentine SARANDI (6/46).
PF.66	READING		28. 8.43	Argentine HEROINA (6/46).
PF.67	PEORIA		2.10.43	Cuban ANTONIO MACEO (6/47).
PF.68	BRUNSWICK		6.11.43	Scrapped 1947.
PF.69	DAVENPORT		8.12.43	Sold 6/46.
PF.70	*EVANSVILLE		27.11.43	Japanese KEYAKI (10/53).
PF.71	NEW BEDFORD		29.12.43	Sold 11/47.
PF.93	LORAIN (ex-Roanoke)	American Sbdg. (Lorain)	18. 3.44	French LAPLACE (3/47); lost 16/9/50.

U.S.S. PGM-12. 173ft. submarine chaser converted to motor gunboat, 28th April 1945, with funnel and depth charge racks removed.

U.S.S. PCE-898. Steel-hull escort, January 1945.

U.S.S. PCE(R)-854. Steel-hull escort adapted as rescue vessel, 1945, with hull line extended aft providing increased accommodation.

				5. 4.44	Sold 4/47.
PF.94	MILLEDGE-VILLE (ex-Sitka)		American Sbdg. (Lorain)		
PF.95	STAMFORD				Cancelled 12/43.
PF.96	MACON				Cancelled 12/43.
PF.97	LORAIN (ex-Sitka)				Cancelled 12/43.
PF.98	VALLEJO				Cancelled 12/43.
PF.99	ORLANDO		American Sbdg. (Cleveland)	1.12.43	Sold 11/47.
PF.100	RACINE			15. 3.44	Sold 12/47.
PF.101	GREENSBORO			9. 3.44	Sold 2/48.
PF.102	FORSYTH			20. 5.44	Dutch CUMULUS (7/47)

Notes:—Units marked (*) were loaned to the Soviet Union, Summer 1945, the survivors being returned during 1949. PF.72-92 were transferred to R.N. (" **Colony** " class). 75 frigates were Coast Guard manned.

EAGLE BOATS

PE.19, 27, 32, 38, 48, 55–57.

Displacement: 430 tons.
Dimensions: 194 (wl) 200$\frac{3}{4}$ (oa) $\times$ 25$\frac{3}{4}$ $\times$ 6$\frac{1}{2}$ ft.
Machinery: 1-shaft geared turbine, S.H.P. 2,500 = 18 knots.
Armament: 1—4 in. gun (PE.27; 48: 1—3 in.).
Complement: 68
War loss: PE.56.

Notes:—Built in 1919 by Ford Motor Co. Survivors of a class of 60.

SUBMARINE CHASERS

Steel hull type: PC.461–496, 542–627, 776–825, 1077–1265, 1546–1603.

Displacement: 280 tons.
Dimensions: 170 (wl) 174$\frac{3}{4}$ (oa) $\times$ 23 $\times$ 7$\frac{1}{2}$ ft.
Machinery: 2-shaft Diesel motors, S.H.P. 2,880 = 20 knots.
Armament: 1—3 in., 1—40 mm. A.A. guns.
Complement: 80.
War losses: PC.496, 558, 1129, 1261, 1603.

Notes:—PC.1092-1118 and 1570-1585 cancelled. 317 were completed. PC.1586-1603 were originally built as minesweepers (AM.82-99) but sweeping gear was removed and they were fitted as the others in 6/44. PC.1124 renamed CHOCURA (IX.206) and PC.488, EUREKA (IX.221). Thirty-five were adapted as amphibious control vessels (PCC); displacement was increased to 315 tons. Twenty-four completed as motor gunboats (PGM.9-32, see p. 255). PC.471-475, 480-482, 542-543, 545-546, 550-551, 556-557, 559, 562, 591, 621, 625-627, 1226-1227, 1235, 1248-1250 were transferred to France in 1944; PC.544, 547, 554, 561, 604-605, 607 and 1236 to Brazil in 1942-43; and PC.467 to Norway, PC.468 to Netherlands, PC.622 to Greece and PC.1234 to Uruguay.

U.S.S. SC-1009. Wood-hull submarine chaser, 1st June 1943, at full speed on trials.

U.S.S. SC-1497. Wood-hull submarine chaser.

U.S.S. SC-1472. Fairmile type submarine chaser, 24th October 1943, transferred from R.C.N. as reverse lend-lease.

Escort type: PCE.827–960.

Displacement: 795 tons.
Dimensions: 180 (wl) 184½ (oa) × 33 × 9½ ft.
Machinery: 2-shaft Diesel motors, S.H.P. 1,800 = 16 knots.
Armament: 2—3 in., 2—40 mm. A.A. guns.
Complement: 110.
War losses: Nil.

Notes:—PCE.861-866, 887-890, 905-960 cancelled. Forty-nine were completed (as U.S.N. ships). 848-866 were rescue vessels (PCE(R)). Six were adapted as amphibious control vessels (PCE(C)). PCE.878 was converted to a minelayer in 1944 and re-named BUTTRESS (ACM.4). PCE.901 became an auxiliary and was re-named PARRIS ISLAND (AG.72). PCE.876, 879 and 883 became degaussing vessels as YDG.8-10. PCE.827-841 were built for R.N. ('' Kil '' class). PCE(R).858 and 860 became C. G. JACKSON and BEDLOE (WPG.120-121). Same hull design as **Admirable** class minesweepers.

Wooden hull type: SC.497–508, 511–522, 524–541, 628– 775, 977–1076, 1266–1375, 1474–1545.

Displacement: 95 tons.
Dimensions: 107½ (wl) 110¾ (oa) × 17 × 6 ft.
Machinery: 2-shaft diesel motors, B.H.P. 2,400 = 20 knots.
Armament: 1—3 in. gun.
Complement: 28
War losses: SC.521, 694, 696, 700, 709, 740, 744, 751, 984, 1019, 1024, 1059, 1067.

Notes:—SC.1494-1495, 1500-1501, 1509, 1513-1516 and 1518-1545 cancelled. 435 were completed. Thirty-four were adapted as amphibious control vessels (SCC), and seventy-two were transferred in 1945 to the Coast Guard as aircraft rescue vessels (AVR). SC.501 re-named RACER (IX.100). Eight became motor gunboats (PGM.1-8, see p. 255). SC.497-498, 503 506-508, 515-517, 519, 522, 524-526, 529-530, 532-535, 638-639, 649, 651, 655, 666, 676, 690-693, 695, 697, 770-771, 977-979, 1029-1030, 1043-1044, 1331, 1335-1337, 1344-1346, 1359 transferred to France in 1943-44; SC.500, 537-538, 634, 643, 646-647, 657, 660-661, 663, 673-675, 685, 687, 713, 719-721, 752, 754, 756, 774, 986, 997, 1007, 1011, 1021, 1060, 1073-1076, 1283-1287, 1295, 1324, 1364-1365, 1475-1493, 1496-1499, 1502-1508, 1510-1512 and 1517 to U.S.S.R. in 1943-45; SC.762-767 and 1288-1289 to Brazil.

Fairmile type: SC.1466–1473.

Displacement: 73 tons.
Dimensions: 111½ (oa) × 17¾ × 5¼ ft.
Machinery: 2-shaft gasoline motors, B.H.P. 1,200 = 16 knots.
Armament: 1—40 mm. A.A. gun.
Complement: 28.

Notes:—Built by Le Blanc Sbdg. in 1942 as R.C.N. ML.392-399 and transferred upon completion. SC.1470 re-named PANTHER (IX.105). SC.1466, 1469 and 1471 transferred to Mexico.

Sweeper type: PCS.1376–1465.

Displacement: 267 tons.
Dimensions: 130 (wl) 136 (oa) × 24½ × 8½ ft.
Machinery: 2-shaft Diesel motors, S.H.P. 800 = 14.5 knots.
Armament: 1—3 in., 1—40 mm. A.A. guns.
Complement: 57.
War losses: Nil.

Notes:—PCS.1393-1395, 1398, 1406-1412, 1415-1416, 1427-1428, 1432-1440, 1443, 1447, 1453-1454, 1456 and 1462-1463 cancelled, and 1464-1465 completed as coastal minesweepers (AMc.203-204). Fifty-seven were completed. PCS.1458, 1388, 1396, 1404 and 1457 were converted to surveying vessels and re-named DERICKSON, LITTLEHALES, DUTTON, ARMISTEAD RUST and JOHN BLISH (AGS.6-10) respectively. Thirteen were adapted as amphibious control vessels (PCS(C)). Same hull design as YMS-type motor minesweepers.

Miscellaneous types:

Notes:—SC.64, 102, 185, 330, 412, 428, 432 and 440 remained from 448 wooden-hulled chasers ordered during World War I. They were of 75 tons, 110 ft. in length and made 15 knots. PC.451 and 452 were experimental steel-hulled vessels built in 1940, the first having diesel-power, a broken hull line and was 165 ft. in length. PC.452 had geared turbines, and was re-named CASTINE (IX.211) 3/45. SC.449-450 and 453 were experimental wooden-hulled vessels. Eleven yachts taken over were numbered PC.454-460, 509-510, 523 and 826, but were later given other numbers, except PC.457, lost.

MOTOR GUNBOATS

Wooden hull type: PGM.1–8 (ex-SC.644, 757, 1035, 1053, 1056, 1071-1072, 1366).

Armament modified to include 1—3 in. gun and 1—60 mm. mortar. War loss: PGM 7. Converted in 1944.

Steel hull type: PGM.9–32 (ex-PC.1548, 805–806, 1088–1091, 1148, 1189, 1255, 1550–1559, 1565–1568).

Armament modified to include 1—3 in. gun, 1—60 mm. mortar and rocket launchers. War losses: PGM 17, 18. Converted in 1944-45.

BUILDERS OF SUBMARINE CHASERS

American Car & Foundry: SC.449.
Walter E. Abrams (Halesite, N. Y.): SC.672-673, 678-681, 1333-1340.
Albina (Portland, Ore.): PC.569-572, 578-582, 815-820, 1077-1082; PCE.867-890.
American Cruiser (Detroit): SC.511-512, 658-659, 682-687.
Annapolis Yacht: SC.521-522, 688-691, 1309-1314.
Astoria Marine: PCS.1464-1465.
Ballard (Seattle): PCS.1457-1458.
Bellingham Iron Works: PCS.1461-1463.
Brown (Houston): PC.565-568, 608-611, 1251-1254.
Burger (Manitowoc): SC.660-661, 1059-1060; PCS.1423-1424, 1449-1450.
Calderwood (Manchester, Mass.): SC.692-693, 1358-1361, 1502-1503.
Colberg (Stockton, Cal.): PCS.1402-1404.
Commercial Iron Works (Portland, Ore.): PC.596-599, 776-814, 1586-1592.
Consolidated Sbdg. (New York): PC.483-487, 563-564, 600-603, 1191-1210, 1237-1240, 1264-1265, 1546-1559.
Dachel-Carter (Benton Hbr., Mich.): SC.664-665,; PCS.1417-1420.
Daytona Beach: SC.668-669, 694-697, 1302-1308, 1484-1487.
Defoe (Bay City): PC.451-452, 471-482, 542-549, 583-587, 1119-1166.
Delaware Bay (Leesburg, N.J.): SC.648-649, 698-703, 1325-1328.
Dingle Boat (St. Paul, Minn.): SC.1000-1002.
Donovan (Burlington, Vt.): SC.1029-1030, 1504-1506.
Dooleys Basin (Ft. Lauderdale): SC.710-711.
Dravo (Pittsburgh): PC.490-494, 573, 592-595, 1593-1597.
Dravo (Wilmington, Del.): PC.495, 574-577.
Elizabeth City: SC.515-518, 638-641, 704-709, 1276-1287, 1488-1491.
Fellows & Stewart (Wilmington, Cal.): SC.1003-1012, 1370-1375.

Fisher (Detroit): SC.499-500, 662-663, 712-721, 1347-1350.
Gibbs Gas Engine (Jacksonville): PC.612-615, 1181-1190; PCS.1429-1440.
Greenport Basin: PCS.1405-1412.
Gulf Marine Ways (Galveston): SC.1057-1058.
Harbor Boat (Terminal I., Cal.): SC.722-729; PCS.1441-1444.
Harris & Parsons (Greenwich, R.I.): SC.1061-1062, 1321-1324, 1507-1509.
Hiltebrant (Kingston, N.Y.): SC.674-675, 730-733; PCS.1425-1428.
Inland Waterways (Duluth): SC.670-671, 1059-1060.
Island Docks (Kingston, N.Y.): SC.996-999.
Robert Jacob (New York): PCS.1388-1395.
Jakobson (Oyster Bay): PC.1598-1599.
Jeffersonville: PC.559-562, 624-627
Geo. W. Kneass (San Francisco): SC.990-995.
Thomas Knutson (Halesite, N.Y.): SC.1498-1501.
Al Larson (Terminal I., Cal.): SC.734-735.
Geo. Lawley (Neponset, Mass.): PC.461-470, 616-619, 1083-1118.
Liberty (Brooklyn): SC.736-737.
Luders Marine (Stamford): PC.556-558, 604-607, 1211-1220, 1255-1259; SC.449,
   505-506, 532-535, 1013-1022, 1355-1357.
Mathis Yacht (Camden): SC.507-508, 524-529, 630-635, 1023-1028, 1067-1072.
John E. Matton (Waterford, N.Y.): SC.985-989.
Mojean & Ericson (Tacoma): PCS.1455-1456.
Nashville Bridge: PC.620-623, 1241-1250, 1600-1601.
Penn-Jersey (Camden): PC.1221-1224, 1602-1603.
Peterson Boat (Sturgeon Bay): SC.536-539, 642-645, 1031-1038, 1517-1520.
Julius Peterson (Nyack): SC.652-653, 738-743, 1315-1320.
Perkins & Vaughan (Wickford, R.I.): SC.1065-1066, 1298-1301, 1510-1516.
Peyton (Newport Bch., Cal.): SC.772-775, 1362-1365.
Pullman Standard Car (Chicago): PCE.827-866.
Quincy Adams (Quincy): SC.513-514, 628-629, 744-751, 1266-1275, 1474-1479.
Rice Bros. (E. Boothbay, Me.): SC.503-504, 1039-1046, 1314-1346, 1480-1483.
Robinson Marine (Benton Hbr., Mich.): SC.540-541, 646-647, 752-759.
W. A. Robinson (Ipswich, Mass.): SC.676-677, 760-767, 1288-1297.
San Diego Marine: PCS.1445-1448.
Seabrook Yacht: SC.501-502, 768-771.
Simms Bros. (Dorchester, Mass.): SC.977-980, 1329-1332, 1492-1495.
Leathem D. Smith (Sturgeon Bay): PC.496, 550-551, 588-591, 821-825, 1171-1180,
   1225-1230, 1260-1263, 1560-1585.
Snow (Rockland, Me.): SC.656-657.
South Coast (Newport Bch., Cal.): PCS.1396-1401.
Stadium (Cleveland): PCS.1413-1416.
Wm. F. Stone (Oakland): PCS.1421-1422.
Sullivan (Brooklyn): PC.488-489, 552-555, 1167-1170, 1231-1236.
Tacoma Boat: PCS.1451-1454.
John Trumpy (Gloucester, N.J.): SC.1073-1076.
Ventnor: SC.1047-1052.
Victory (Holland, Mich.): SC.1063-1064.
Vineyard (Milford, Del.): SC.519-520, 636-637, 981-984, 1351-1354, 1496-1497.
Weaver (Orange, Tex.): SC.666-667.
Westergard (Rockport, Tex.): SC.497-498, 530-531, 650-651, 654-655.
Western (Tacoma): PCS.1459-1460.
Wheeler (Brooklyn): PCS.1376-1387.
Willamette (Portland, Ore.): PCE.891-934.
Wilmington Boat (Cal.): SC.1053-1056, 1366-1369.

U.S.S. PCS-1397. Wood-hull 136ft. submarine chaser, 4th May 1944, of same characteristics as YMS-type motor minesweepers.

U.S.S. PT-105. Elco type 80ft. m.t.b., 12th July 1942.

U.S.S. PT-139. Elco type 80ft. m.t.b., 1942, in zebra camouflage.

MOTOR TORPEDO BOATS

PT.20–68.

Displacement:	35 tons.
Dimensions:	77 × 20 × 5½ ft.
Machinery:	3-shaft gasoline engines, H.P. 4,050 = 40 knots.
Armament:	4—18 in. T.T., 4 M.G.
Complement:	12.
War losses:	PT.22, 28, 31-35, 37, 41, 43-44, 63, 67-68.

Notes:—Built 1941-42 by Elco. PT.33-44, 57-68 were originally designated PTC.13-36. PT.49-58 transferred to R.N. on completion as MTB.307-316. PT.59-68, scheduled for transfer, were retained by U.S.N.

Higgins type: PT.71–94, 197–254, 265–313, 450–485, 625–660, 791–808.

Displacement:	35 tons.
Dimensions:	78 × 20¾ × 5¼ ft.
Machinery:	3-shaft gasoline engines, H.P. 4,500 = 41 knots.
Armament:	4—21 in. T.T., 1—40 mm. & 2—20 mm. guns.
Complement:	17.
War losses:	PT.73, 77, 79, 200, 202, 218-219, 239, 247, 251, 279, 283, 300-301, 311.

Notes:—Built 1942-45. PT.797-808 cancelled. Earlier boats carried 4—21 in. tubes. PT.88, 90-94, 198, 201, 203-217 were transferred to R.N. in 1943-44 becoming MTB.419-423 and MGB.177-192 (not respectively). Of these, PT.201, 204. 207-209, 211, 213 and 217 were transferred to Yugoslavia. PT.85-87, 89, 197, 265-276, 289-294, 625-656 transferred to U.S.S.R. in 1943-45.

Huckins type: PT.95–102, 255–264.

Displacement:	34 tons.
Dimensions:	78 × 19½ × 5 ft.
Machinery:	3-shaft gasoline engines, H.P. 4,050 = 40 knots.
Armament:	4—21 in. T.T., 2—20 mm. guns.
Complement:	12.
War losses:	Nil.

Notes:—Built 1942-43.

Elco type: PT.103–196, 314–367, 372–383, 486–563, 565–624, 731–790.

Displacement:	38 tons.
Dimensions:	80 × 20¾ × 5 ft.
Machinery:	3-shaft gasoline engines, S.H.P. 4,050 = 40 knots.
Armament:	4—21 in. T.T., 2—20 mm. A.A. guns.
Complement:	14.
War losses:	PT.107, 109-113, 117-119, 121, 123, 133, 135-136, 145, 147, 153, 158, 164-166, 172-173 193, 320-323, 337-339, 346-347, 353, 363, 493, 509, 555.

U.S.S. PT-533. Elco type 80ft. m.t.b.

[*Robert S. Weinberg*

U.S.S. PT-78. Higgins type 78ft. m.t.b., 26th January 1943.

U.S.S. PT-337. Elco type 80ft. m.t.b., 7th July 1943.

Vosper type: PT.368–371, 384–449, 661–730.

Displacement:	33 tons.
Dimensions:	70 × 19 × 4¾ ft.
Machinery:	3-shaft gasoline engines, H.P. 4,050 = 40 knots.
Armament:	2—21 in. T.T.
Complement:	12.
War losses:	PT.368, 371.

Notes:—Built 1943-45 by Fyff's Shipyard (368-371), Robert Jacob (384-399), Annapolis Yacht (400-429, 661-730) and Herreshoff (430-449). PT.368-371 were formerly Dutch TM.32 and 35-37, transferred before completion. PT.384-399 transferred to R.N. in 1944 as MTB 396-411, together with BPT.21-68, sisters built under *Lend/Lease*. PT.400-449 and 661-687 transferred to U.S.S.R. in 1944-45.

Experimental types:

	Builder	Displ.	Dimens.	H.P.	
PT.1-2	Miami	25	59 × 18		
PT.3-4	Fisher	25	59 × 18		
PT.5-6	Higgins	34	81 × 26	3750	
PT.6(i)	Higgins	34	81 × 20	4050	
PT.7-8	Phila. N.Yd.		81 × 18		
PT.9	Br. Power		70 × 20	3300	
PT.69	Huckins		72 × 18	4050	
PT.70	Higgins	35	78 × 21	4050	
PT.564	Higgins	35	70 × 15	4050	

Notes:—Other boats included the 70 ft. PT.10-19 and PTC.1-12 built by Elco and transferred to R.N. upon completion. There were also RPC.1-80 of 63 ft. built for and transferred to U.S.S.R. under Lend-Lease.

AMPHIBIOUS CRAFT

Of all the new types of ships developed during the war, perhaps the most striking innovations were the landing vessels. In both the European and Pacific Theatres of Operations, amphibious operations were undertaken on a scale never before envisaged. The huge fleets that carried out the landings in North Africa, Normandy, the Solomons, Leyte, Okinawa and all the other major and minor operations, would have been irrelevant but for the specialized ships and craft which had been conceived to put the troops and equipment on the beaches.

In 1938, the old destroyer MANLEY had been converted to a high speed transport (APD 1), two smokestacks and two boilers being removed to make way for troop space and small landing craft. She was the prototype of thirty-two flush deck destroyers which were actually converted. The success of this type resulted in ninety-four destroyer escorts being similarly converted or completed as transports.

Larger transports and cargo ships were also equipped for amphibious operations with davits for landing craft and greater anti-aircraft protection. In 1943, these were given separate classifications as attack transports (APA) and attack cargo ships (AKA).

Designed to carry flag and general officers and their staffs were the Amphibious Force Flagships (AGC). They were originally called Combined Operations Communications Headquarters Ships but with their great capability for communications were also used as fleet headquarters ships.

One of the most radical innovations was the Dock Landing Ship (LSD), which combined a ship and a floating drydock. Of the original fifteen, which were first designated Mechanized Artillery Transports (APM), seven were ordered for the Royal Navy. Only four were actually transferred.

The well-known Tank Landing Ship (LST), which was the largest vessel designed to beach herself and discharge tanks and troops, was the mainstay of the amphibious forces. The first LST's set sail in early 1943 and they were soon to be seen in every theatre of war, landing troops and vehicles directly on the beach in the initial assault and continually bringing in supplies and reinforcements. They proved most useful as supply ships for bases where there was no port or harbor.

The Medium Landing Ship (LSM), a development of the smaller Tank Landing Craft, proved to be a most versatile type. Smaller and more manoeuverable than the LST, it carried tanks and had bow doors. Twelve were converted to rocket launching ships (LSMR) and forty-eight later vessels were redesigned and lengthened during construction, being completed powerfully armed with guns, mortars and rockets for amphibious support.

The Infantry Landing Craft (LCI) was the next smaller size. It carried 200 troops who debarked by means of catwalks and ramps. Later versions eliminated the ramps and had bow doors. There were several conversions of the LCI, with varying armaments, including gunboat (LCIG), mortar ship (LCIM), rocket ship (LCIR) and force flagship (LCFF). The Support Landing Craft (LCS) was a similar type but started a new series of numbers. The LCI's should not be confused with the British Infantry Landing Ships (LSI) which were converted liners similar to the American APA's.

In this section it has been necessary to limit discussion to vessels with sea-going capability. Therefore no reference is made to the numerous types of smaller landing craft, each of which was as important in its own function as the larger vessels.

VEHICLE LANDING SHIPS

Displacement: 5,625 tons except LSV.1-2, 5,875 tons.
Dimensions: 440 (wl) 451¼ (oa) × 60¼ × 20 ft, except LSV.1-2, 455½ ft. (oa).
Machinery: 2-shaft geared turbines, S.H.P. 11,000 = 20.3 knots.
Armament: 2—5 in., 8—40 mm. A.A. guns.
Complement: 564.

LSV.1	CATSKILL (ex-CM 6)	⎫	19. 5.42	
LSV.2	OZARK (ex-CM 7)	⎬ Willamette	15. 6.42	
LSV.3	OSAGE (ex-AN 3)	⎭	30. 6.43	Discarded 1961.
LSV.4	SAUGUS (ex-AN 4)	⎫ Ingalls	4. 9.43	Discarded 1961.
LSV.5	MONITOR (ex-AN 1)	⎬	29. 1.43	Discarded 1961.

U.S.S. Montauk (LSV6). Vehicle landing ship.

U.S.S. Gunston Hall (LSD5). Dock landing ship, March 1944.

LSV.6	MONTAUK (ex-AN 2)	}Ingalls	14. 4.43	GALILEA (AKN 6) (10/46), discarded 1961

Notes:—Laid down as minelayers or netlayers and converted while building. Redesignated Mine Warfare Command and Support Vessels in 1955. Designed to carry vehicles which can be unloaded over the side or aft by the stern ramp.

DOCK LANDING SHIPS

Displacement: 4,500 tons.
Dimensions: 454 (wl) 457¾ (oa) × 72¼ × 18 ft.
Machinery: 2-shaft geared turbines, S.H.P. 7,400 = 15.4 knots (except LSD.1-8, steam reciprocating, 17 knots).
Armament: 1—5 in., 12—40 mm. A.A. guns.
Complement: 240.

LSD.1	ASHLAND		21.12.42	
LSD.2	BELLE GROVE		17. 2.43	
LSD.3	CARTER HALL		4. 3.43	
LSD.4	EPPING FOREST		2. 4.43	MCS 7 (11/62).
LSD.5	GUNSTON HALL	}Moore (Oakland)	1. 5.43	
LSD.6	LINDENWALD		11. 6.43	
LSD.7	OAK HILL		25. 6.43	
LSD.8	WHITE MARSH		19. 7.43	Chinese TUNG HAI (11/60).
LSD.13	CASA GRANDE (ex-H.M.S. Portway, ex-Spear)		11. 4.44	
LSD.14	RUSHMORE (ex-H.M.S. Swashway, ex-Sword)		10. 5.44	
LSD.15	SHADWELL (ex-H.M.S. Waterway, ex-Tomahawk)	}Newport News	24. 5.44	
LSD.16	CABILDO		22.12.44	
LSD.17	CATAMOUNT		27. 1.45	
LSD.18	COLONIAL		28. 2.45	
LSD.19	COMSTOCK		28. 4.45	
LSD.20	DONNER	}Boston N.Yd.	6. 4.45	
LSD.21	FORT MANDAN		2. 6.45	
LSD.22	FORT MARION		22. 5.45	
LSD.23	FORT SNELLING	}Gulf Sbdg.	8.46	Completed as merc. CARIB QUEEN; U.S.N. TAURUS (AK 273, 1959).

U.S.S. Oak Hill (LSD7). Dock landing ship, 21st March 1944.

U.S.S. LST-477. 30th March 1943.

U.S.S. LST-909. 12th May 1944. Note bizarre camouflage, bow gun.

U.S.S. LST-493. April 1945, low in the water with a full load.

LSD.24	POINT DEFIANCE (ex-Hilton Head)	} Gulf Sdbg.		Cancelled 8/45.
LSD.25	SAN MARCOS	Philadelphia N.Yd.	10. 1.45	
LSD.26	TORTUGA	} Boston N.Yd.	21. 1.45	
LSD.27	WHETSTONE		18. 7.45	

Notes:—LSD.9-12 built for R.N. LSD.1-15 were originally designated APM.1-8 and BAPM.1-7 respectively. A remarkable innovation, these ships were half floating drydock with gates in the stern. They served as landing craft tenders and serviced and repaired other small craft such as PT-boats. One funnel is placed on each side of the dock with machinery and boilers in the side walls.

TANK LANDING SHIPS

LST.1–1152.

Displacement:	1,625 tons.
Dimensions:	316 (wl) 328 (oa) $\times$ 50 $\times$ 11$\frac{1}{4}$ ft.
Machinery:	2-shaft Diesel motors, S.H.P. 1,700 = 11.6 knots
Armament:	8—40 mm. A.A. (some had 1—5 in.).
Complement:	110.
War losses:	LST.6, 43, 69, 158, 167, 179, 203, 228, 282, 313-314, 318, 333, 342, 348-349, 353, 359, 376, 396, 447-448, 460, 472, 480, 493, 496, 499, 507, 523, 531, 563, 577, 738, 749-750, 906.

Notes:—Built 1942-45. LST.85-116, 142-156, 232-236, 248-260, 296-300 and 431-445 were cancelled. 982 were completed. Designated ATL until late 1942. Thirty-nine were converted for the evacuation of casualties (LST(H)) in 1945. Eighty-three others were converted to or completed as repair ships, M.T.B. tenders, and service craft (see respective pages). LST.129, 278 and 340 were re-named COHASSET (IX.198), SEAWARD (IX.209) and SPARK (IX.196) following damage and were used as storage hulks. LST.2-5, 8-9, 11-13, 62-65, 76-77, 79-80, 159-165, 173, 178, 180, 198-200, 214-217, 237-239, 280, 289, 301-305, 311, 315, 319-324, 326, 331, 336-337, 346-347, 351-352, 358, 360-369, 371, 373, 380-383, 385-386, 394, 401-430, 538 and 1021 transferred to R.N. 1942-44, and LST.33 and 35-37 to Greece.

BUILDERS

American Bridge: LST.137-156, 261-300, 653-681, 754-771, 829-849, 1081-1095.
Bethlehem (Fairfield): LST.401-445.
Bethlehem (Hingham): LST.906-979, 1060-1080.
Bethlehem (Quincy): LST.361-382, 1004-1027.
Charleston N.Yd.: LST.353-360.
Chicago Bridge: LST.132-136, 197-236, 511-522, 600-652, 772-774, 850-860, 1115-1152.
Dravo (Pittsburgh): LST.1-60, 730-753, 775-796, 884-905, 1038-1059.
Jeffersonville: LST.61-121, 181-196, 501-510, 523-530 682-729, 797-805, 861-873, 1096-1100.
Kaiser (Richmond, Cal.): LST.476-490.
Kaiser (Vancouver, Wash.): LST.446-475.
Missouri Valley: LST.122-131, 157-180, 237-260, 491-500, 531-599, 806-828, 874-883, 1101-1114.
New York N.Yd.: LST.311-318.
Newport News: LST.383-400.
Norfolk N.Yd.: LST.333-352.
Philadelphia N.Yd.: LST.319-332.

U.S.S. LSM-233. 27th July 1944, with bow doors open but ramp not lowered.

U.S.S. LSM(R)-194. Rocket ship conversion with 5in. gun aft.

LSM(R) firing rockets.

U.S.S. LSM(R)-401. Rocket ship built from the keel up, 1945. Note newer type rocket launchers, 5in. gun and superstructure aft.

MEDIUM LANDING SHIPS

LSM 1-187, 200-400, 413-500, 537-558.

Displacement:	520 tons.
Dimensions:	196½ (wl) 203½ (oa) × 34½ × 7¼ ft.
Machinery:	2-shaft Diesel motors, S.H.P. 2,800 = 12.5 knots.
Armament:	2—40 mm. A.A. guns.
Complement:	50.
War losses:	LSM.12, 20, 59, 135, 149, 318.

Notes:—Built 1944-45. Originally designated LCT(7).1466-2023.

MEDIUM LANDING SHIPS (ROCKET)
(EARLY TYPE)

LSM(R).188–199.

As above, except 1—5 in., 2—40 mm. A.A. guns, 4—4.2 in. mortars, 85 to 105 rockets.

War losses:	LSM(R).190, 194, 195.

Notes:—Converted during construction.

(LATER TYPE)

LSM(R).401–412, 501–536.

Displacement:	790 tons.
Dimensions:	204½ (wl) 206¼ (oa) × 34½ × 7¼ ft.
Machinery:	2-shaft Diesel motors, S.H.P. 2,800 = 13 knots.
Armament:	1—5 in., 4—40 mm. A.A. guns, 4—4.2 in. mortars, 10 automatic rocket launchers.
Complement:	75.

Notes:—Converted and lengthened during construction. The automatic rocket launchers fired thirty 5 in. rockets per minute.

BUILDERS

Brown Sbdg. (Houston): LSM.1-125, 354-388, 459-552.
Charleston N.Yd.: LSM.126-200, 295-309, 389-410, 413, 553-558.
Dravo (Wilmington, Del.): LSM.201-232, 414-446.
Federal (Newark): LSM.253-294.
Mare Island N.Yd.: LSM.411-412.
Pullman (Chicago): LSM.310-353.
Western Pipe: LSM.233-252, 447-458.

U.S.S. LCI(L)-87. Original type with squared superstructure debarking troops during manoeuvers.

U.S.S. LCI(L)-463. Revised version with larger superstructure amidships, rounded conning tower 19th October 1943.

U.S.S. LCI(L)-402. Third version with bow doors replacing ramps.

U.S.S. LCI.(L)-328 and 336 during landing operations on Rondova, 30th June 1943.

INFANTRY LANDING CRAFT (LARGE)

LCI(L).1–1139, LCS(L).1–130.

Displacement: 246 tons.
Dimensions: 153 (wl) 159 (oa) × 23¾ × 5¾ ft.
Machinery: 2-shaft Diesel motors, B.H.P. 2,320 = 14.4 knots.
War losses: LCI(L).1, 20, 32, 85, 91, 92, 93, 219, 232, 339, 416, 553, 684, 974, 1065. LCI(G).82, 459, 468, 474. LCS(L).7, 15, 26, 33, 49, 127.
Cancelled: LCI(L).49-60, 717-724, 781, 822-865, 885-942, 1034-1051, 1099-1139.

Type	Number converted	Armament	Comple-ment
LCI(L)	—	5—20 mm. A.A. guns.	25
LCI(G)	212	3—40 mm. A.A. guns, 10 rocket launchers.	65
LCI(M)	60*	1—40 mm. A.A. gun, 3—4.2 in. chemical mortars.	50
LCI(R)	52	1—40 mm. A.A. gun, 6—5 in. rocket launchers.	30
LC(FF)	49	5—20 mm. A.A. guns.	60
LCS(L)	—	6—40 mm. A.A. guns, 10 rocket launchers.	73

*Some LCI(G) were later converted to LCI(M).

Notes:—210 were transferred to R.N., 30 to the Soviet Union and 8 to France. LCI's were originally designed APY.

AMPHIBIOUS FORCE FLAGSHIPS

Displacement: 7,430 tons.
Dimensions: 435 (wl) 459¼ (oa) × 63 × 24 ft.
Machinery: 1-shaft geared turbines, S.H.P. 6,000 = 16.4 knots.
Armament: 2—5 in., 8—40 mm. A.A. guns.
Type: C2-S-AJ1 (AGC.1-3, 5: C2-S-B1).
Complement: 633

AGC.1	APPALACHIAN	Federal (Kearny)	29. 1.43	Scrapped 1960.
AGC.2	BLUE RIDGE		7. 3.43	Scrapped 1961.
AGC.3	ROCKY MOUNT		7. 3.43	Discarded 1960.
AGC.5	CATOCTIN (ex-Mary Whitridge)	Moore	23. 1.43	Scrapped 1960.
AGC.7	MOUNT KcKINLEY (ex-Cyclone)	North Carolina Sbdg.	27. 9.43	
AGC.8	MOUNT OLYMPUS (ex-Eclipse)		3.10.43	Discarded 1961.
AGC.9	WASATCH (ex-Fleetwing)		8.10.43	Scrapped 1961.
AGC.10	AUBURN (ex-Kathay)		19.10.43	Scrapped 1961.
AGC.11	ELDORADO (ex-Monsoon)		26.10.43	

U.S.S. LCS(L)-121, followed by a sister, 1945.

Tank landing craft, LCT(5) during manoeuvers in Chesapeake Bay, 1943.

U.S.S. Ancon (AGC4). Amphibious force flagship at Salerno with Italian submarine alongside, 11th September 1943.

AGC.12	ESTES (ex-Morning Star)		1.11.43	
AGC.13	PANAMINT (ex-Northern Light)	North Carolina Sbdg.	9.11.43	Scrapped 1961.
AGC.14	TETON (ex-Witch of the Wave)		5. 2.44	Discarded 1961.
AGC.15	ADIRONDACK		13. 1.45	Discarded 1961.
AGC.16	POCONO		25. 1.45	
AGC.17	TACONIC		10. 2.45	

Displacement: 6,812 tons.
Dimensions: 471½ (wl) 493 (oa) × 64 × 26¼ ft.
Machinery: 2-shaft geared turbines, S.H.P. 9,000 = 18 knots.
Armament: 2—5 in., 8—40 mm. A.A. guns.
Complement: 700.

AGC.4	ANCON (ex-AP 66)	Bethlehem (Quincy)	10.12.38	Returned 2/46.

Notes:—Panama R.R. liner taken over in 1942 as a transport and used as headquarters ship a Sicily, Salerno, Normandy and Okinawa. BISCAYNE (AGC.18, ex-AVP.11) was converted in 1943 and had 2—5 in., 6—20 mm. A.A. guns (see p. 305). Coast Guard cutters CAMPBELL, INGHAM DUANE, TANEY, SPENCER and BIBB were also converted to amphibious force flagships in 1944 retaining their C.G. numbers. Superstructure was extended aft and armament changed to 2—5 in. 6—40 mm. A.A. guns (see p. 373).

HIGH SPEED TRANSPORTS

Displacement: 1,020 to 1,190 tons.
Dimensions: 310 (wl) 314½ (oa) × 31¾ × 8¾ ft.
Machinery: 2-shaft geared turbines, S.H.P. 13,000 = 25 knots.
Armament: 3—3 in., 2—40 mm. A.A. guns.
Complement: 200.

APD.1	MANLEY (ex-DD.74)	Bath Iron Works	23. 8.17	Sold 11/46.
APD.2	COLHOUN (ex-DD.85)	Bethlehem (Quincy)	21. 2.18	Lost 30/8/42.
APD.3	GREGORY (ex-DD.82)		27. 1.18	Lost 5/9/42.
APD.4	LITTLE (ex-DD.79)		11.11.17	Lost 5/9/42.
APD.5	McKEAN (ex-DD.90)	Union Iron Works	4. 7.18	Lost 17/11/43.
APD.6	STRINGHAM (ex-DD.83)	Bethlehem (Quincy)	30. 3.18	Scrapped 3/46.

Notes:—Twenty-six additional ships of this class were converted during 1942-43 (APD.7-36). Of these, WARD, DICKERSON, NOA and BARRY were lost. For full details and names see pp. 103, 106, 109 and 112.

Displacement: 1,400 tons.
Dimensions: 300 (wl) 306 (oa) × 37 × 12¾ ft.
Machinery: 2-shaft turbo-electric, S.H.P. 12,000 = 23.6 knots.
Armament: 1—5 in., 6—40 mm. guns.
Complement: 204.

U.S.S. Blue Ridge (AGC2). Amphibious force flagship, October 1943.

U.S.S. Barr (APD39). High speed transport, 31st October 1944, converted from destroyer escort.

U.S.S. Roper (APD20). High speed transport, 4th February 1944

U.S.S. Colhoun (APD2). High speed transport, 1942, converted from flush-deck destroyer prior to the war.

278

APD.69	YOKES (ex-DE.668)	Dravo (Pitts-burgh)	27.11.43	
APD.70	PAVLIC (ex-DE.669)		18.12.43	
APD.71	ODUM (ex-DE.670)		19. 1.44	
APD.72	JACK C. ROBINSON (ex-DE.671)		8. 1.44	
APD.73	BASSETT (ex-DE.672)		15. 1.44	
APD.74	JOHN P. GRAY (ex-DE.673)		18. 3.44	
APD.87	CROSLEY (ex-DE.226)	Philadel. N.Yd.	12. 2.44	
APD.88	CREAD (ex-DE.227)		12. 2.44	Discarded 1960.
APD.89	RUCHAMKIN (ex-DE.228)		14. 6.44	Discarded 1960.
APD.90	KIRWIN (ex-DE.229)		15. 6.44	
APD.91	KINZER (ex-DE.232)	Charleston N.Yd.	9.12.43	
APD.92	REGISTER (ex-DE.233)		20. 1.44	
APD.93	BROCK (ex-DE.234)		20. 1.44	
APD.94	JOHN Q. ROBERTS (ex-DE.235)		11. 2.44	Discarded 1960.
APD.95	WILLIAM M. HOBBY (ex-DE.236)		11. 2.44	Discarded 1960.
APD.96	RAY K. EDWARDS (ex-DE.237)		19. 2.44	Discarded 1960.
APD.97	ARTHUR L. BRISTOL (ex-DE.281)		19. 2.44	Scrapped 1965.
APD.98	TRUXTUN (ex-DE.282)		9. 3.44	
APD.99	UPHAM (ex-DE.283)		9. 3.44	Discarded 1961.
APD.100	RINGNESS (ex-DE.590)	Bethlehem (Hing-ham)	5. 2.44	
APD.101	KNUDSON (ex-DE.591)		5. 2.44	
APD.102	REDNOUR (ex-DE.592)		12. 2.44	
APD.103	TOLLBERG (ex-DE.593)		12. 2.44	
APD.104	WILLIAM J. PATTI-SON (ex-DE.594)		15. 2.44	Discarded 1960.
APD.105	MYERS (ex-DE.595)		15. 2.44	Discarded 1960.
APD.106	WALTER B. COBB (ex-DE.596)		23. 2.44	
APD.107	EARLE B. HALL (ex-DE.597)		1. 3.44	
APD.108	HARRY L. CORL (ex-DE.598)		1. 3.44	
APD.109	BELET (ex-DE.599)		3. 3.44	Mexican H-3 (12/63).
APD.110	JULIUS A. RAVEN (ex-DE.600)		3. 3.44	
APD.111	WALSH (ex-DE.601)		28. 4.45	
APD.112	HUNTER MARSH-ALL (ex-DE.602)		5. 5.45	Discarded 1960.
APD.113	EARHART (ex-DE.603)		12. 5.45	Mexican H-4 (12/63).
APD.114	WALTER S. GORKA (ex-DE.604)		26. 5.54	Discarded 1960.

APD.115	ROGERS BLOOD (ex-DE.605)	Bethlehem (Hing-	2. 6.45	Discarded 1960.
APD.116	FRANCOVICH (ex-DE.606)	ham)	5. 6.45	Scrapped 1965.
APD.117	JOSEPH M. AUMAN (ex-DE.674)	Dravo	2. 5.44	Mexican H-5 (12/63).
APD.118	DON O. WOODS (ex-DE.721)	(Pitts- burgh)	19. 2.44	Mexican H-6 (12/63).
APD.119	BEVERLY W. REID (ex-DE.722)		4. 3.44	
APD.120	KLINE (ex-DE.687)		27. 6.44	
APD.121	RAYMON W. HERN- DON (ex-DE.688)		15. 7.44	
APD.122	SCRIBNER (ex-DE.689)	Bethlehem	1. 8.44	
APD.123	DIACHENKO (ex-Alex Diachenko, ex-DE.690)	(Quincy)	15. 8.44	
APD.124	HORACE A. BASS (ex-DE.691)		12. 9.44	
APD.125	WANTUCK (ex-DE.692)		25. 9.44	Discarded 3/58.
APD.126	GOSSELIN (ex-DE.710)		4. 5.44	
APD.127	BEGOR (ex-DE.711)		25. 5.44	
APD.128	CAVALLARO (ex-DE.712)		15. 6.44	Korean KYUNG NAM (10/59).
APD.129	DONALD W. WOLF (ex-DE.713)		22. 7.44	
APD.130	COOK (ex-DE.714)		26. 8.44	
APD.131	WALTER X. YOUNG (ex-DE.715)	Defoe	30. 9.44	Discarded 1962.
APD.132	BALDUCK (ex-DE.716)		27.10.44	
APD.133	BURDO (ex-DE.717)		25.11.44	
APD.134	KLEINSMITH (ex-DE.718)		27. 1.45	Chinese TIEN SHAN (5/60).
APD.135	WEISS (ex-DE.719)		17. 2.45	
APD.136	CARPELLOTTI (ex-DE.720)		10. 3.45	Scrapped 12/60.

Notes:—**Buckley** and **Rudderow** class destroyer escorts converted to high speed transports during construction. Built up amidships and fitted to carry four LCVP. Thirty-eight additional ships of this class were converted after completion during 1944-45 (APD.37-68, 75-86, 139). Of these, BATES (APD.47) was lost. For full details and names, see p. 157-164.

AUXILIARIES

As a result of the Spanish-American War of 1898, the United States acquired possessions and bases thousands of miles from North America. The responsibility of protecting these interests lay with the Navy, and important questions of servicing the fleet abroad arose. In 1898 at the outset of the war a number of merchant ships were purchased for use as colliers to supply the fleets in the Philippines and the West Indies. Many of these were retained after the war and some specialized types were developed for other uses. The new colliers ONTARIO and ERIE were completed as repair ships, and a number of auxiliary cruisers were used as destroyer tenders.

At the declaration of war by the United States, the small fleet of auxiliaries consisted only of the destroyer tenders DIXIE, PRAIRIE, BUFFALO, PANTHER (all former auxiliary cruisers), MELVILLE and LEONIDAS, submarine tenders FULTON, BUSHNELL and ALERT, repair ships PROMETHEUS and VESTAL, hospital ships RELIEF and SOLACE, transports HENDERSON and HANCOCK, and an assortment of colliers, oilers, and tugs.

Of the vast number of merchant vessels taken over in 1917-18, only a very few were retained for the postwar fleet. However a modest ship-building program had been undertaken resulting in the destroyer tenders DOBBIN and WHITNEY, submarine tender HOLLAND, repair ship MEDUSA, ammunition ships NITRO and PYRO, and hospital ship RELIEF, all near sisters, completed in the early 1920's. A number of war-built ships were also acquired in 1921 although some were not first commissioned until 1940.

New types developed between the wars pointed up the increasing importance given to aerial and undersea warfare. The seaplane tender WRIGHT was followed by the oiler PATOKA being fitted with a mooring mast for dirigibles. A number of minesweepers also were converted to seaplane tenders, and others to submarine rescue vessels, fitted with pumps and rescue chambers.

Coincident with the new fleet programs of the late 1930's, orders were placed for new service craft such as the large and similar DIXIE, FULTON and VULCAN class tenders, CURTISS and BARNEGAT class seaplane tenders, NAVAJO class fleet tugs and TREE class net tenders. Starting in 1940 many of the fine new ships being built by the Maritime Commission were acquired by the Navy for use as fleet tenders, cargo and storeships, fleet oilers and a proliferation of types which soon covered almost every need of a huge fleet serving of necessity far from its home bases for months on end.

The development of the service and supply forces enabled the fleet to remain at sea for long periods. Advance bases set up and built around service craft could be moved forward as the battle zone progressed across the Pacific. As new beachheads and islands were secured, the repair and service units moved in behind the assault forces to take care of damaged and tired ships.

Completely equipped ports were set up, lonely and unknown Pacific atolls, such as Manus and Ulithi, becoming major fleet bases. Everything needed was carried along, shells and fuel oil, floating drydocks, hospitals and spare parts, and so forth.

Despite limitations of space, it has been attempted to provide the reader with as complete as possible a description and listing of the large and small ships of this unheralded armada which supported the fighting fleets and made possible their wide range over the Pacific.

Oilers are named after rivers, cargo ships and attack transports after counties, repair ships have mythological names and tugs those of Indian tribes. Many cargo ships were named after stars and transports after signers of the Declaration of Independence and generals.

U.S.S. Melville (AD2). Destroyer tender, 3rd June 1944.

U.S.S. Altair (AD1). Destroyer tender, 25th July 1945.

282

DESTROYER TENDERS

Displacement:	5,250 tons.
Dimensions:	400 (wl) 417¼ (oa) × 54½ × 20 ft.
Machinery:	1-shaft geared turbines, S.H.P. 4,000 = 15 knots.
Armament:	2—5 in., 4—3 in., 4—40 mm. A.A. guns.
Complement:	600.

AD.2	MELVILLE	New York Sbdg.	2. 3.15	Scrapped 1949.

Notes:—Served in the Atlantic

Displacement:	8,325 tons.
Dimensions:	460 (wl) 483¾ (oa) × 61 × 24¼ ft.
Machinery:	1-shaft geared turbines, S.H.P. 7,000 = 16 knots.
Armament:	4—5 in., 8—40 mm. A.A. guns.
Complement:	600.

AD.3	DOBBIN	Philadelphia N.Yd.	5. 5.21	Scrapped 1951.
AD.4	WHITNEY	Boston N.Yd.	12.10.23	Scrapped 1947.

Notes:—Both served in Pacific.

Displacement:	5,600 tons.
Dimensions:	404½ (wl) 420¼ (oa) × 53¾ × 19¾ ft.
Machinery:	1-shaft reciprocating (VQE), S.H.P. 3,285 = 12.5 knots.
Armament:	4—3 in., 4—40 mm. A.A. guns.
Complement:	685.

AD.9	BLACK HAWK (ex-Santa Catalina)	Cramp	1913	Scrapped 1947.

Notes:—Acquired in 1917. Asiatic Fleet 1941-42; Aleutians 1942-45.

Displacement:	6,250 tons.
Dimensions:	410½ (wl) 423¾ (oa) × 54 × 21¼ ft.
Machinery:	1-shaft geared turbines, S.H.P. 2,500 = 10.5 knots.
Armament:	4—3 in., 6—40 mm. A.A. guns (ALTAIR also 1—5 in.).
Complement:	590.

AD.11	ALTAIR (ex-Edisto)	Skinner & Eddy	10. 5.19	Scrapped 1947.
AD.12	DENEBOLA (ex-Edgewood)		12. 4.19	Scrapped 1950.

Notes:—Acquired in 1921. RIGEL (AD.13) of this class converted to a repair ship (AR.11) 4/41. Both served in Atlantic.

Displacement:	9,450 tons.
Dimensions:	520 (wl) 530½ (oa) × 73¼ × 25½ ft.
Machinery:	2-shaft geared turbines, S.H.P. 12,000 = 19.6 knots.
Armament:	4—5 in., 8—40 mm. A.A. guns.
Complement:	1,262.

U.S.S. Cascade (AD16). Destroyer tender.

U.S.S. Yosemite (AD19). Destroyer tender, 23rd July 1944.

AD.14	DIXIE	} New York	27.-5.39	
AD.15	PRAIRIE	} Sbdg.	9.12.39	
AD.17	PIEDMONT		7.12.42	
AD.18	SIERRA	}Tampa	23. 2.43	
AD.19	YOSEMITE		16. 5.43	

Notes:—PRAIRIE damaged by fire 27/5/42. Later she and the others served in Pacific.

Displacement: 8,165 tons (AD.16: 9,800 tons; AD.20: 8,560 tons; AD.21: 7,919 tons; AD.26-29: 7,664 tons).
Dimensions: 465 (wl) 492 (oa) × $69\frac{1}{2}$ × $27\frac{1}{4}$ ft.
Machinery: 1-shaft geared turbines, S.H.P. 8,500 = 18.4 knots.
Armament: 1—5 in., 4—3 in., 4—4; mm. A.A. guns (AD.16: 2—5 in., 6—40 mm. A.A. guns).
Complement: 860.

AD.16	CASCADE	Western Pipe	7. 6.42	
AD.20	HAMUL (ex-AK.30, ex-Doctor Lykes)	Federal	6. 4.40	Discarded 1963.
AD.21	MARKAB (ex-AK.31, ex-Mormacpenn)	Ingalls	21.12.40	AR 23 (4/60).
AD.22	KLONDIKE	}	12. 8.44	AR 22 (2/60).
AD.23	ARCADIA	} Todd	19.11.44	
AD.24	EVERGLADES	} (San Pedro)	28. 1.45	
AD.25	FRONTIER		25. 3.45	
AD.26	SHENANDOAH	Todd (Tacoma)	29. 3.45	
AD.27	YELLOWSTONE	Todd (Seattle)	12. 4.45	
AD.28	GRAND CANYON	Todd (Tacoma)	27. 4.45	
AD.29	ISLE ROYALE	} Todd	19. 9.45	
AD.30	GREAT LAKES	} (Seattle)		Cancelled 1/46.
AD.31	TIDEWATER	Charleston N.Yd.	30. 6.45	
AD.32	NEW ENGLAND	Tampa Sbdg.		Cancelled 8/45.
AD.33	CANOPUS	Mare I. N.Yd.		Cancelled 8/45.
AD.35	ARROWHEAD	Puget Sd. N.Yd.		Cancelled 8/45.
AD.36	BRYCE CANYON	Charleston N.Yd.	7. 3.46	

Notes:—AD.20 and 21 acquired in 6/41 and converted in 1942. All were of a modified C3 type except AD.16, C3-S1-N2 and AD.20-21, C3-Cargo.

Displacement: 6,075 tons.
Dimensions: 426 (wl) 445 (oa) × 60 × $23\frac{1}{2}$ ft.
Machinery: 1-shaft geared turbines, S.H.P. 7,100 = 16.5 knots.
Armament: 4—3 in., 2—40 mm. A.A. guns.
Complement: 734.

AD.34	ALCOR (ex-AR.10, ex-AG.34, ex-Dixie)	Federal	29. 7.27	Scrapped 1949.

Notes:—Acquired 3/41 and served as flagship of the Service Force until 1942 when she was converted to a repair ship. Became a destroyer tender in 11/44. Served in Atlantic 1942-44, then to Pacific.

U.S.S. Fulton (AS11).   Submarine tender, January 1942.

U.S.S. Langley (AV3).   Seaplane tender, February 1937, following conversion from aircraft carrier.

SUBMARINE TENDERS

Displacement: 8,100 tons.
Dimensions: 460 (wl) 513 (oa) × 61 × 22¾ ft.
Machinery: 1-shaft geared turbines, S.H.P. 7,000 = 15.6 knots.
Armament: 8—5 in., 4—3 in. guns.
Complement: 400.

AS.3	HOLLAND	Puget Sd. N.Yd.	12. 4.26	ARG.18 (9/45); scrapped 1953.

Notes:—Armament changed during war to 4—5 in., 8—40 m m. A.A. guns. Asiatic Fleet 1941-42 Pacific 1944-45.

Displacement: 4,670 tons.
Dimensions: 357½ (wl) 380 (oa) × 47 × 20¼ ft.
Machinery: 1-shaft reciprocating (VTE), S.H.P. 4,500 = 16.5 knots.
Armament: 2—5 in., 4—3 in. guns.
Complement: 350.

AS.5	BEAVER	Newport News	27.11.09	ARG 19 (6/45); scrapped 1951.

Notes:—Acquired 1918. Atlantic 1942; Alaska 1943-44.

Displacement: 7,750 tons.
Dimensions: 360 (wl) 373¾ (oa) × 51½ × 21½ ft.
Machinery: 1-shaft reciprocating (VQE), S.H.P. 3,850 = 13 knots.
Armament: 2—5 in., 4—3 in. guns.
Complement: 317.

AS.9	CANOPUS (ex-Santa Leonora)	New York Sbdg.	1919	Lost 10/4/42.

Notes:—Acquired 1921. Asiatic Fleet 1941-42.

Displacement: 9,734 tons.
Dimensions: 520 (wl) 529¼ (oa) × 73½ × 23½ ft.
Machinery: 2-shaft Diesel-electric, S.H.P. 11,800 = 18 knots.
Armament: 4—5 in., 8—40 mm. A.A. guns.
Complement: 1300.

AS.11	FULTON		27.12.40	
AS.12	SPERRY		17.12.41	
AS.15	BUSHNELL	Mare I. N.Yd.	14. 9.42	
AS.16	HOWARD W. GILMORE (ex-Neptune)		16. 9.43	
AS.17	NEREUS		12. 2.45	
AS.18	ORION	Moore	14.10.42	
AS.19	PROTEUS		12.11.42	

Notes:—PROTEUS lengthened to 574½ ft. in 1960. All served in Pacific.

Displacement:	6,400 and 7,725 tons respectively.		
Dimensions:	465 (wl) 492 (oa) × 69½ × 24¼ ft.		
Machinery:	1-shaft Diesel, S.H.P. 8,900 = 16.5 knots.		
Armament:	1—5 in., 4—3 in. guns.		
Complement:	1513.		

AS.13	GRIFFIN (ex-Mormacpenn)	Sun	10.11.39	
AS.14	PELIAS (ex-Mormacyork)		14.11.39	

Notes:—Type C3-Cargo (D) acquired in late 1940. 5 in. gun removed.

Displacement:	3,600 tons.
Dimensions:	395 (wl) 417¾ (oa) × 60 × 18 ft.
Machinery:	1-shaft geared turbines, S.H.P. 4,000 — 14 knots.
Armament:	1—5 in., 4—3 in. guns.
Complement:	610.

AS.20	OTUS (ex-Fred Morris)	Federal	2.11.40	ARG 20 (6/45); sold 8/46.

Notes:—Type C1-B, acquired 3/41. Under conversion at Manila 7/12/41.

Displacement:	5,975 tons.
Dimensions:	387 (wl) 403 (oa) × 61 × 20 ft.
Machinery:	2-shaft geared turbines, S.H.P. 11,400 — 20 knots.
Armament:	1—4 in., 2—3 in. guns.
Complement:	440.

AS.21	ANTAEUS (ex-St. John)	Newport News	9. 1.32	AG 67 (9/43); RESCUE (AH 18, 1/45).

Notes:—Acquired 4/41; converted to transport in 1943.

Displacement:	7,728 tons (AS.22: 8,282 tons).
Dimensions:	465 (wl) 492 (oa) × 69½ × 23 ft.
Machinery:	1-shaft geared turbines, S.H.P. 8,500 — 18.5 knots. (AS 22: 16.5 knots).
Armament:	1—5 in., 4—3 in., 4—40 mm. A.A. guns.
Complement:	1460.

AS.22	EURYALE (ex-Hawaiian Merchant)	Federal	12. 4.41	
AS.23	AEGIR	Ingalls	15. 9.43	
AS.24	ANTHEDON		15.10.43	Discarded 1961.
AS.25	APOLLO		6.11.43	Discarded 1963.
AS.26	CLYTIE		26.11.43	Discarded 1961.

Notes:—Type C3-S-A2. EURYALE was a modified C3 acquired in 4/43. All served in Pacific.

SUBMARINE RESCUE VESSELS

Displacement: 1,060 tons.
Dimensions: 174 (wl) 188½ (oa) × 36¾ × 13¼ ft.
Machinery: 1-shaft reciprocating (VTE), S.H.P. 1,400 = 14 knots.
Armament: 1—3 in., gun (FALCON, 2—3 in. guns).
Complement: 75.

ASR.1	WIDGEON (ex-AM.22)	Sun	5. 5.18	Sold 3/48.
ASR.2	FALCON (ex-AM.28)	Gas Engine & Power Co.	7. 9.18	Sold 3/47.
ASR.3	CHEWINK (ex-AM.39)	Todd (Brooklyn)	21.12.18	Sunk as target 31/7/47.
ASR.4	MALLARD (ex-AM.44)	Staten Island	17.12.18	Scuttled 22/5/47.
ASR.5	ORTOLAN (ex-AM.45)	Staten Island	30. 1.19	Sold 9/47.
ASR.6	PIGEON (ex-AM.47)	Baltimore D.D.	29. 1.19	Lost 5/5/42.

Notes:—Former minesweepers of the " **Bird** " class converted in 1929.

Displacement: 1,653 tons.
Dimensions: 240 (wl) 251¼ (oa) × 42 × 14¾ ft.
Machinery: 1-shaft diesel-electric, S.H.P. 3,000 = 14.9 knots.
Armament: 2—3 in., 2—40 mm. guns.
Complement: 102.

ASR.7	CHANTICLEER		29. 5.42	
ASR.8	COUCAL		29. 5.42	
ASR.9	FLORIKAN	Moore	14. 6.42	
ASR.10	GREENLET		12. 7.42	
ASR.11	MACAW		12. 7.42	Lost 12/2/44.
ASR.13	KITTIWAKE		10. 7.45	
ASR.14	PETREL		26. 9.45	
ASR.15	SUNBIRD	Savannah	3. 4.46	
ASR.16	TRINGA	Machine &	25. 6.46	
ASR.17	VERDIN	Fdry. Co.		Cancelled 12/8/45.
ASR.18	WINDOVER			Cancelled 12/8/45.

Converted fleet tug:

ASR.12	PENGUIN (ex-AT.99, Chetco)	Charleston Sbdg.	20. 7.43	

MOTOR TORPEDO BOAT TENDERS

Displacement: 1,830 tons.
Dimensions: 300 (wl) 310¾ (oa) × 41 × 13½ ft.
Machinery: 2-shaft Diesel motors, S.H.P. 6,080 = 18.2 knots.
Armament: 2—5 in., 8—40 mm. A.A. guns.

AGP.6	OYSTER BAY (ex-AVP.28)	Lake Washing-ton	7. 9.42	Italian PIETRO CAVEZZALE (10/57).
AGP.7	MOBJACK (ex-AVP.27)		2. 8.42	C. & G.S. PIONEER (8/46).
AGP.8	WACHA-PREAGUE (ex-AVP.56)		10. 7.43	C.G. McCULLOCH (WAVP 386, 5/46).
AGP.9	WILLOUGHBY (ex-AVP.57)		21. 8.43	C.G. GRESHAM (WAVP 387, 6/46).

Notes:—Converted during construction from small seaplane tenders.

Displacement: 5,236 tons.
Dimensions: 412¼ (oa) × 60 × 23½ ft.
Machinery: 1-shaft geared turbines, S.H.P. 4,000 = 14.5 knots.
Armament: 1—5 in., 8—40 mm. A.A. guns.
Complement: 289.
Type: C1-A.

AGP.12	ACONTIUS (ex-Cape Carthage)	Pusey & Jones	12.10.43	Returned 3/46.
AGP.13	CYRENE (ex-Cape Farewell)		8. 2.44	Returned 7/46.

Converted yachts:

AGP.1	NIAGARA (ex-PG.52, ex-Hi-Esmaro)	1333/29	1.43*	Lost 23/5/43.
AGP.2	HILO (ex-PG.58, ex-Moana)	1534/31	1.43*	Merc. (1947).
AGP.3	JAMESTOWN (ex-PG.55, ex-Alder)	1730/27	1.43*	Merc. (1947), MAROSANNA (1953), lost 2/8/61.

* Date of conversion

Converted LST's:

AGP.4	PORTUNUS (ex-LST.330)	Sold 2/48.
AGP.5	VARUNA (ex-LST.14)	Merc. GUARAUNA (1947).
AGP.10	ORESTES (ex-LST.135)	Sold 3/48.
AGP.11	SILENUS (ex-LST.604)	Merc. ARZELL III (1948).
AGP.14	ALECTO (ex-LST.977)	Turkish ONARAN (5/48).
AGP.15	CALLISTO (ex-LST.966)	Merc. ELENA (1949), DAYTONA (1951), lost 20/11/55.
AGP.16	ANTIGONE (ex-LST.773)	Sold 2/48.
AGP.17	BRONTES (ex-LST.1125)	Merc. BARBARA (1947), DIANE (1948), XALAPA (1956), lost 27/10/59.

U.S.S. Vulcan (AR5). Repair ship, 10th January 1945.

U.S.S. Briareus (AR12). Repair ship, 17th February 1944, was a former American-Hawaiian Line cargo ship.

| AGP.18 | CHIRON (ex-LST.1133) | Merc. ALTAMAR (1948), lost 27/3/60. |
| AGP.20 | PONTUS (ex-LST.201) | Sold 11/47. |

Notes:—Armed with 8—40 mm. A.A. guns. ORESTES severely damaged by *Kamikaze* 30/12/44.

REPAIR SHIPS

Displacement:	8,125 tons.
Dimensions:	460 (wl) 483¾ (oa) × 70 × 20 ft.
Machinery:	1-shaft geared turbines, S.H.P. 7,000 = 14 knots.
Armament:	4—5 in., 2—3 in. guns.
Complement:	466.

| AR.1 | MEDUSA | Puget Sd. N.Yd. | 16. 4.23 | Scrapped 1951. |

Notes:—Rearmed during **W.W.II** with 6-3 in., 4-40 mm. AA guns. Served in Pacific.

Displacement:	6,625 tons.
Dimensions:	450 (wl) × 465¾ (oa) × 60 × 18 ft.
Machinery:	2-shaft reciprocating (VTE), S.H.P. 7,500 = 14 knots.
Armament:	4—5 in., 1—3 in. guns.
Complement:	450.

| AR.3 | PROMETHEUS (ex-Ontario) | Mare I. N.Yd. | 5.12.08 | Scrapped 1951. |
| AR.4 | VESTAL (ex-Erie) | New York N.Yd. | 19. 5.08 | Scrapped 1951. |

Notes:—Rearmed during **W.W.II** with 2—5 in., 4—3 in., 4—40 mm. A.A. guns. VESTAL damaged at Pearl Harbor 7/12/41; both served in Pacific.

Displacement:	9,140 tons.
Dimensions:	520 (wl) 529¼ (oa) × 73¼ × 23¼ ft.
Machinery:	2-shaft geared turbines, S.H.P. 11,000 = 19.2 knots.
Armament:	4—5 in., 8—40 mm. A.A. guns.
Complement:	1297.

AR.5	VULCAN	New York Sbdg.	14.12.40	
AR.6	AJAX	⎫ Todd	22. 8.42	
AR.7	HECTOR	⎬ (San	11.11.42	
ARH.1	JASON (ex-AR.8)	⎭ Pedro)	3. 4.43	AR.8 (9/57).

Notes:—All served in Pacific and VULCAN in Mediterranean 1943.

Displacement:	8,975 tons.
Dimensions:	465 (wl) 490½ (oa) × 69½ × 24¼ ft.
Machinery:	1-shaft geared turbines, S.H.P. 8,500 = 17 knots.
Armament:	1—5 in., 4—3 in., 4—40 mm. A.A. guns.
Complement:	903.

AR.9	DELTA (ex-AK.29, ex-Hawaiian Packer)	Newport News	2. 4.41	
AR.12	BRIAREUS (ex-Hawaiian Planter)		14. 2.41	

Notes:—Modified C3 type. DELTA acquired 6/41 as cargo ship and converted 7/42, served in Mediterranean. BRIAREUS acquired 2/43, served in Pacific.

Details same as destroyer tender ALTAIR (p. 283) except 1—5 in., 4—3 in., 4—40 mm. A.A. guns.

AR.11	RIGEL (ex-AD.13, ex-Edgecombe)	Skinner & Eddy	23.11.18	Scrapped 1950.

Notes:—Acquired 1921. Served in Pacific. ALCOR (AR.10) became AD.34, 11/44.

Displacement: 7,826 tons.
Dimensions: 465 (wl) 492 (oa) × 69½ × 27½ ft.
Machinery: 1-shaft geared turbines, S.H.P. 8,500 = 17 knots.
Armament: 2—5 in., 8—40 mm. A.A. guns.
Complement: 921.

AR.13	AMPHION		15. 5.45	
AR.14	CADMUS	Tampa Sbdg.	5. 8.45	
AR.15	DEUCALION			Cancelled 12/8/45.
AR.16	MARS			Cancelled 12/8/45.

Notes:—Modified C3 type.

Displacement: 3,476 tons.
Dimensions: 375 (wl) 395 (oa) × 52¼ × 15½ ft.
Machinery: 2-shaft reciprocating (VTE), S.H.P. 7,000 = 17 knots.
Armament: 1—5 in., 4—3 in., 4—40 mm. A.A. guns.
Complement: 350.

ARG.1	OGLALA (ex-CM.4, ex-Shawmut, ex-Massachusetts)	Cramp	29. 1.07	Sold 3/47.

Notes:—Acquired in 1917 as minelayer. Sunk 7/12/41 at Pearl Harbor and converted following salvage to repair ship for internal combustion engines.

Displacement: 5,801 tons (AR, 4,621 tons (ARG.2-9), 5,159 tons (ARG.10-11, 16-17), 6,225 tons (ARV), 5,371 tons (AG.68-71), 5,766 tons (AG.73-78).
Dimensions: 416 (wl) 441½ (oa) × 57 × 23 ft.
Machinery: 1-shaft reciprocating (VTE), S.H.P. 2,500 = 12.5 knots.
Armament: 1—5 in., 4—40 mm.A.A. guns (AR & ARG also 3—3 in.).
Complement: 524-583 (AG73-78: 891).

U.S.S. Mindanao (ARG3). Repair ship for internal combustion engines, November 1943. Was a Liberty Ship conversion.

U.S.S. Achelous (ARLI). LST converted to repair ship for landing craft, April 1943.

U.S.S. Zaniah (AG70). Repair and supply ship, 9th September 1944, another variant of the Liberty ship.

U.S.S. Swivel (ARS36). Steel-hulled salvage vessel, 28th September 1943.

AR.19	XANTHUS (ex-R.N. Hecla)		31. 7.44	Discarded 1962.
AR.20	LAERTES (ex-R.N. Dutiful)		13. 9.44	Discarded 1962.
AR.21	DIONYSUS (ex-R.N. Faithful)		10.10.44	Discarded 1961.
ARG.2	LUZON (ex-Samuel Bowles)		14. 5.43	Discarded 1961.
ARG.3	MINDANAO (ex-Elbert Hubbard)		13. 5.43	Discarded 1962.
ARG.4	TUTUILA (ex-Arthur P. Gorman)		12. 9.43	
ARG.5	OAHU (ex-Caleb C. Wheeler)		9. 9.43	Discarded 1963.
ARG.6	CEBU (ex-Francis P. Duffy)		18.10.43	Discarded 1962.
ARG.7	CULEBRA ISLAND (ex-John F. Goucher)	Bethlehem (Fairfield)	23.11.43	Discarded 1962.
ARG.8	LEYTE		18. 2.44	MAUI (5/45); discarded 1962.
ARG.9	MONA ISLAND		11. 5.44	Discarded 1962.
ARG.10	PALAWAN		12. 8.44	Discarded 1963.
ARG.11	SAMAR		19.10.44	Discarded 1962.
ARG.16	KERMIT ROOSEVELT (ex-Deal Island)		5.10.44	Scrapped 1960.
ARG.17	HOOPER ISLAND (ex-Bert McDowell)		18.10.44	Discarded 1960.
ARV.1	CHOURRE (ex-ARG.14, Dumaran)		22. 5.44	Discarded 1962.
ARV.2	WEBSTER (ex-ARG.15, Masbate)		5. 8.44	Discarded 1962.
AG.68	BASILAN (ex-ARG.12, ex-Jacques Philippe Villere)	Delta Sbdg.	21. 3.44	Discarded 1947.
AG.69	BURIAS (ex-ARG.13, ex-Mollie Moore Davis)		27. 3.44	Discarded 1947.
AG.70	ZANIAH (ex-AK.120, ex-Anthony F. Lucas)	Todd (Houston) St. Johns River	12.12.43	Discarded 1947.
AG.71	BAHAM (ex-AK.122, ex-Elizabeth C. Bellamy)		21.12.43	Discarded 1947.
AG.73	BELLE ISLE		3.11.44	Discarded 1960.
AG.74	COASTER'S HARBOR		17.11.44	Scrapped 3/61.
AG.75	CUTTYHUNK ISLAND	New England Sbdg.	26.11.44	Scrapped 1960.
AG.76	AVERY ISLAND		13.12.44	Scrapped 3/61.
AG.77	INDIAN ISLAND		19.12.44	Scrapped 1961.
AG.78	KENT ISLAND		9. 1.45	Scrapped 1961.

Notes:—Type EC2-S-C1 (Liberty Ships), completed as repair ships for internal combustion engines (ARG), aviation repair ships (ARV), repair and supply ships (AG.68-71) or electronics repair ships (AG.73-78). AR.17-18 of this class transferred to R.N. ARG.18-20 were the former submarine tenders HOLLAND, BEAVER and OTUS converted in 1945 (see pp. 287-8).

Converted LST's:

ARB.1	ARISTAEUS (ex-LST.329)	Sold 1962.
ARB.2	OCEANUS (ex-LST.328)	Sold 1962.
ARB.3	PHAON (ex-LST.15)	Sold 1962.
ARB.4	ZEUS (ex-LST.132)	
ARB.5	MIDAS (ex-LST.514)	
ARB.6	NESTOR (ex-LST.518)	Wrecked 8/10/45; scrapped 1947.
ARB.7	SARPEDON (ex-LST.956)	
ARB.8	TELAMON (ex-LST.976)	
ARB.9	ULYSSES (ex-LST.967)	W. German (6/61).
ARB.10	DEMETER (ex-LST.1121)	Merc. MOTONAVE (1961), DEMETER (1963), lost 12/1/64.
ARB.11	DIOMEDES (ex-LST.1119)	W. German (6/61).
ARB.12	HELIOS (ex-LST.1127)	Brazilian BELMONTE (1/62).
ARL.1	ACHELOUS (ex-LST.10)	
ARL.2	AMYCUS (ex-LST.489)	
ARL.3	AGENOR (ex-LST.490)	French VULCAIN (3/51); Chinese (9/57).
ARL.4	ADONIS (ex-LST.83)	Sold 1962.
ARL.5	(Unnamed) (ex-LST.81)	H.M.S. LSE-1 (7/43); Argentine INGENIERO IRIBAS (8/47).
ARL.6	(Unnamed) (ex-LST.82)	H.M.S. LSE-2 (8/43); Argentine INGENIERO GADDA (8/47).
ARL.7	ATLAS (ex-LST.231)	
ARL.8	EGERIA (ex-LST.136)	
ARL.9	ENDYMION (ex-LST.513)	
ARL.10	CORONIS (ex-LST.1003)	Sold 1961.
ARL.11	CREON (ex-LST.1036)	Sold 1961.
ARL.12	POSEIDON (ex-LST.1037)	Sold 1962.
ARL.13	MENELAUS (ex-LST.971)	Merc. MARYLAND CLIPPER (1961).
ARL.14	MINOS (ex-LST.644)	Sold 1961.
ARL.15	MINOTAUR (ex-LST 645)	Korean DUKSOO (10/55).
ARL.16	MYRMIDON (ex-LST.948)	Sold 1961.
ARL.17	NUMITOR (ex-LST.954)	Sold 1961.
ARL.18	PANDEMUS (ex-LST.650)	
ARL.19	PATROCLUS (ex-LST.955)	Turkish BASARAN (1952).
ARL.20	PENTHEUS (ex-LST.1115)	Merc. TMT SAN JUAN (1961).
ARL.21	PROSERPINE (ex-LST.116)	Sold 1962.
ARL.22	ROMULUS (ex-LST.962)	Philippine AKLAN (10/61).
ARL.23	SATYR (ex-LST.852)	
ARL.24	SPHINX (ex-LST.963)	
ARL.26	STENTOR (ex-LST.858)	Sold 1961.
ARL.27	TANTALUS (ex-LST.1117)	Sold 1/47.
ARL.28	TYPHON (ex-LST.1118)	Sold 1961.
ARL.29	AMPHITRITE (ex-LST.1124)	Merc. TMT BISCAYNE (1963).
ARL.30	ASKARI (ex-LST.1131)	
ARL.31	BELLEROPHON (ex-LST.1132)	
ARL.32	BELLONA (ex-LST.1136)	Lost 1/12/45.
ARL.33	CHIMAERA (ex-LST.1137)	Sold 1962.
ARL.35	DAEDALUS (ex-LST.1143)	Merc. VIRGINIA CLIPPER (1961).
ARL.36	GORDIUS (ex-LST.1145)	Iranian SOHRAB (2/61).

ARL.37	INDRA (ex-LST.1147)		
ARL.38	KRISHNA (ex-LST.1149)		
ARL.39	QUIRINUS (ex-LST.1151)	Venezuelan (6/62).	
ARL.40	REMUS (ex-LST.453)	Sold 12/47.	
ARL.41	ACHILLES (ex-LST.455)	Chinese HSING AN (9/47); Chinese (Comm.) (1950).	
ARST.1	LAYSAN ISLAND (ex-LST.1098)		
ARST.2	OKALA (ex-LST.1099)	Merc. SAIPAN (1947).	
ARST.3	PALMYRA (ex-LST.1100)		
ARVE.3	AVENTINUS (ex-LST.1092)	Chilean (1963)	
ARVA.4	CHLORIS (ex-LST.1094)		
ARVE.5	FABIUS (ex-LST.1093)		
ARVA.6	MEGARA (ex-LST.1095)		

Notes:—Converted from tank landing ships 1943-45. Conversion of AEOLUS (ex-LST.310), CERBERUS (316), CONSUS (317), FERONIA (332), CHANDRA (350) and MINERVA (374) to ARL.42-47 cancelled in 8/45.

SEAPLANE TENDERS

Displacement:	8,400 tons.
Dimensions:	448 (oa) $\times$ 58 $\times$ 19¼ ft.
Machinery:	1-shaft geared turbines, S.H.P. 6,000 = 15 knots.
Armament:	2—5 in., 2—3 in. guns.
Complement:	311

AV.1	WRIGHT	Hog Island	28. 4.20	SAN CLEMENTE (AG 79, 10/44); scrapped 1948.

Notes:—Served in Pacific.

Displacement:	11,050 tons.
Dimensions:	519 (wl) 542 (oa) $\times$ 65½ $\times$ 16½ ft.
Machinery:	2-shaft turbo-electric drive, S.H.P. 7,000 = 15 knots.
Armament:	4—5 in. guns.
Complement:	350.

AV.3	LANGLEY (ex-CV.1, ex-AC.3, Jupiter)	Mare Is. N.Yd.	24. 8.12	Lost 27/2/42.

Notes:—The first U.S.N. aircraft carrier converted in 1922 from collier JUPITER. Flight deck was cut down upon conversion to tender in 1937.

Displacement:	9,090 tons.
Dimensions:	508 (wl) 527¼ (oa) $\times$ 69¼ $\times$ 21 ft.
Machinery:	2-shaft geared turbines, S.H.P. 12,000 = 19.7 knots.
Armament:	4—5 in., 16—40 mm. A.A. guns.
Complement:	1,195.

U.S.S. Curtiss (AV4). Seaplane tender, 1945.

U.S.S. Albemarle (AV5). Seaplane tender, 5th May 1942.

U.S.S. Kenneth Whiting (AV14). Seaplane tender, 1945. Note seaplane on deck aft.

U.S.S. Barnegat (AVP10). Small seaplane tender, October 1941, as completed, with 2-5in. guns in single turrets.

AV.4	CURTISS	⎱ New York	20. 4.40	Discarded 1963.
AV.5	ALBEMARLE	⎰ Sbdg.	13. 7.40	

Notes:—CURTISS damaged at Pearl Harbor 7/12/41 and by *Kamikaze* 21/6/45. ALBEMARLE served in Atlantic.

Displacement: 9,106 tons.
Dimensions: 520 (wl) 540½ (oa) × 69¼ × 26 ft.
Machinery: 2-shaft geared turbines, S.H.P. 12,000 = 19.2 knots.
Armament: 4—5 in., 12—40 mm. A.A. guns.
Complement: 1,247.

AV.7	CURRITUCK	Philadel-phia N.Yd.	11. 9.43	
AV.11	NORTON· SOUND	⎫	28.11.43	AVM 1 (1952).
AV.11	PINE ISLAND	⎬ Todd (San Pedro)	26. 2.44	
AV.13	SALISBURY SOUND (ex-Puget Sound)	⎭	18. 6.44	

Notes:—CURRITUCK served in Pacific.

Displacement: 8,560 tons (AV.10: 9,031 tons).
Dimensions: 465 (wl) 492 (oa) × 69½ × 24½ ft.
Machinery: 1-shaft geared turbines, S.H.P. 8,500 = 16.5 knots.
Armament: 1—5 in., 4—3 in., 8—40 mm. A.A. guns.
Complement: 857.

AV.8	TANGIER (ex-Sea Arrow)	Moore	15. 9.39	Merc. DETROIT (1963).
AV.9	POCOMOKE (ex-Exchequer)	Ingalls	8. 6.40	Discarded 1961.
AV.10	CHANDELEUR	Western Pipe	29.11.41	

Notes:—TANGIER and POCOMOKE acquired in 1940, originally carried 4—5 in. guns. All served in Pacific. Type C3-Cargo (AV 10: C3-S1.B1)

Displacement: 8,510 tons.
Dimensions: 465 (wl) 492 (oa) × 69½ × 26 ft.
Machinery: 1-shaft geared turbines, S.H.P. 8,500 = 18.7 knots.
Armament: 2—5 in., 12—40 mm. A.A. guns.
Complement: 662.

AV.14	KENNETH WHITING	⎫	15.12.43	Discarded 1961.
AV.15	HAMLIN	⎪	11. 1.44	Discarded 1963.
AV.16	ST. GEORGE	⎬ Todd	14. 2.44	Discarded 1963.
AV.17	CUMBERLAND SOUND	⎪ (Tacoma)	23. 2.44	Scrapped 1964.
AV.18	TOWNSEND	⎭		Cancelled 8/45.

U.S.S. Ballard (AVD10). Flush-deck destroyer as converted to seaplane tender, 21st March 1941, in pre-war paint.

| AV.19 | CALIBOGUE | Puget Sd. N.Yd. | | Cancelled 10/44. |
| AV.20 | HOBE SOUND | Charleston N.Yd. | | Cancelled 10/44. |

Notes:—Modified C3 type.

EX-DESTROYERS

Displacement: 1,190 tons.
Dimensions: 310 (wl) 314½ (oa) × 30¾ × 9¼ ft.
Machinery: 2-shaft geared turbines, S.H.P. 13,500 = 25 knots.
Armament: 2—3 in. guns.

AVD.1	CHILDS (ex-DD.241)	New York Sbdg.	15. 9.20	Sold 5/46.
AVD.7	WILLIAM B. PRESTON (ex-DD.344)	Norfolk N.Yd.	9. 8.19	Sold 11/46.
ADV.10	BALLARD (ex-DD.267)	Bethlehem (Squantum)	7.12.18	Sold 5/46.
AVD.11	THORNTON (ex-DD.270)	Bethlehem (Squantum)	22. 3.19	Lost 5/4/45.
AVD.12	GILLIS (ex-DD.260)	Bethlehem (Quincy)	29. 5.19	Scrapped 1946.

Notes:—Fourteen flush-deck destroyers were converted in 1938-40; two boilers and T.T. removed. WILLIAMSON, GEORGE E. BADGER, CLEMSON, GOLDSBOROUGH, HULBERT, BELKNAP, OSMOND INGRAM, GREENE and McFARLAND reverted to destroyers in 11/43 (see pp. 106, 109 and 112).

SMALL SEAPLANE TENDERS

Displacement: 840 tons.
Dimensions: 174 (wl) 187¾ (oa) × 35½ × 8¾ ft.
Machinery: 1-shaft reciprocating (VTE), S.H.P. 1,400 = 12 knots.
Armament: 2—3 in. guns.
Complement: 72.

AVP.1	LAPWING (ex-AM.1)	Todd (Brooklyn)	14. 3.18	Sold 8/46.
AVP.2	HERON (ex-AM.10)	Standard Sbdg.	18. 5.18	Sold 7/47.
AVP.3	THRUSH (ex-AM.18)	Pusey & Jones	15. 9.18	Merc. SEMPER PARATUS (1947), CYRENAICA I (1950), lost 10/3/51.
AVP.4	AVOCET (ex-AM.19)	Baltimore	9. 3.18	Sold 12/46.
AVP.5	TEAL (ex-AM.23)	Sun	25. 5.18	Sold 1/48.

U.S.S. Rockaway (AVP29). Small seaplane tender, 5th October 1944, with "B" turret replaced by smaller A.A. gun, and smaller crane aft.

U.S.S. Vestal (AR4). Repair ship, listing following torpedo damage at Pearl Harbor, 7th December 1941.

AVP.6	PELICAN (ex-AM.27)	Gas Engine & Power Co.	15. 6.18	Sold 11/46.
AVP.7	SWAN (ex-AM.34)	Alabama Sbdg.	4. 7.18	Sold 10/46.
AVP.8	GANNET (ex-AM.41)	Todd (Brooklyn)	19. 3.19	Lost 7/6/42.
AVP.9	SANDPIPER (ex-AM.51)	Philadelphia N.Yd.	28. 4.19	Sold 10/46.

Notes:—Minesweepers of the **Bird** class converted in 1936.

Displacement:	1,766 tons.
Dimensions:	300 (wl) $310\frac{3}{4}$ (oa) $\times$ 41 $\times$ $13\frac{1}{2}$ ft.
Machinery:	2-shaft Diesel-electric drive, S.H.P. 6,080 = 18.2 knots.
Armament:	1—5 in., 8—40 mm. A.A. guns.
Complement:	215.

AVP.10	BARNEGAT		23. 5.41	Merc. KENTAVROS (1962).
AVP.11	BISCAYNE	Puget Sd. N.Yd.	23. 5.41	AGC 18 (10/44); C. G. DEXTER (WAVP 385) 6/46.
AVP.12	CASCO		15.11.41	C.G. WAVP 370 (4/49).
AVP.13	MACKINAC		15.11.41	C.G. WAVP 371 (/48).
AVP.21	HUMBOLDT	Boston N.Yd.	17. 3.41	C.G. WAVP 372 (/48).
AVP.22	MATAGORDA		18. 3.41	C.G. WAVP 373 (/48).
AVP.23	ABSECON		8. 3.42	C.G. WAVP 374 (1/49).
AVP.24	CHINCOTEAGUE	Lake Washington	15. 4.42	C.G. WAVP 375 (3/49).
AVP.25	COOS BAY		15. 5.42	C.G. WAVP 376 (1/49).
AVP.26	HALF MOON		12. 7.42	C.G. WAVP 378 (9/48).
AVP.29	ROCKAWAY		14. 2.42	C.G. WAVP 377 (12/48).
AVP.30	SAN PABLO	Associated	31. 3.42	
AVP.31	UNIMAK		27. 5.42	C.G. WAVP 379 (9/48).
AVP.32	YAKUTAT		2. 7.42	C.G. WAVP 380 (8/48).
AVP.33	BARATARIA		2.10.42	C.G. WAVP 381 (9/48).
AVP.34	BERING STRAIT		15. 1.44	C.G. WAVP 382 (9/48).
AVP.35	CASTLE ROCK		11. 3.44	C.G. WAVP 383 (9/48).
AVP.36	COOK INLET		13. 5.44	C.G. WAVP 384 (9/48).
AVP.37	CORSON		15. 7.44	
AVP.38	DUXBURY BAY		2.10.44	
AVP.39	GARDINERS BAY	Lake Washington	2.12.44	Norwegian HAAKON VII (5/58).
AVP.40	FLOYDS BAY		28. 1.45	Discarded 1960.
AVP.41	GREENWICH BAY		18. 3.45	
AVP.42	HATTERAS			Cancelled 4/43.
AVP.43	HEMPSTEAD			Cancelled 4/43.
AVP.44	KAMISHAK			Cancelled 4/43.
AVP.45	MAGOTHY			Cancelled 4/43.
AVP.46	MATANZAS			Cancelled 4/43.
AVP.47	METOMKIN			Cancelled 4/43.

U.S.S. Arided (AK73). Cargo ship. Liberty Ship type.

U.S.S. Nitro (AE2). Ammunition ship, 17th November 1943.

U.S.S. Hammondsport (AP√2). Transport and aircraft ferry, May 1942. A former Seatrain Lines train ferry.

AVP.48	ONSLOW	⎤		20. 9.42	Discarded 1960.
AVP.49	ORCA	⎮		4.10.42	Ethiopian ETHIOPIA (1961).
AVP.50	REHOBOTH	⎮ Lake		8.11.42	
AVP.51	SAN CARLOS	⎬ Washing-		20.12.42	GIBBS (AGOR 1, 12/58).
AVP.52	SHELIKOF	⎮ ton		31. 1.43	Discarded 1960.
AVP.53	SUISUN	⎮		14. 3.43	
AVP.54	TIMBALIER	⎮		18. 4.43	Discarded 1960.
AVP.55	VALCOUR	⎦		5. 6.43	

Notes:—AVP.27-28 and 56-57 were completed as M.T.B. tenders (see p. 290). Some early units had 2 or 4—5 in. guns, later removed. TIMBALIER and VALCOUR completed at Puget Sd. N.Yd. in 1946. Conversion of HUMBOLDT, MATAGORDA and ROCKAWAY to communications ships (AG.121-123) cancelled 9/45. Fifteen loaned to Coast Guard in 1948-49 retained navy names. AVP 14-20 became AVD 1-7 in 1940.

AVIATION SUPPLY SHIPS

During 1944-45, eight ships (AVS 1-8) were adapted for the carrying of aviation supplies and spare parts. These were FORTUNE and SUPPLY (IX.146-147), GRUMIUM and ALLIOTH (AK.112, 109), GWINNETT, NICOLLET and PONTOTOC (AK.185, 199, 206) and JUPITER (AK.43) respectively. Details will be found under former designations.

AIRCRAFT FERRIES

APV.1	KITTY HAWK (ex-Seatrain New York)	8067/32	6.41	AKV 1 (9/43); returned 1/46.
APV.2	HAMMONDS-PORT (ex-Seatrain Havana)	8067/32	7.41	AKV 2 (9/43); returned 3/46.
APV.3	LAKEHURST (ex-Seatrain New Jersey)	8108/40	10.42	APM 9 (12/42); Army (8/43); returned 1946.

Notes:—Conversion of LAFAYETTE (APV.4, ex-AP.53) was never carried out see (p. 340).

SALVAGE VESSELS

Displacement: 1,180 tons.
Dimensions: 174 (wl) 187$\frac{3}{4}$ (oa) × 35$\frac{1}{2}$ × 8$\frac{3}{4}$ ft.
Machinery: 1-shaft reciprocating (VTE), S.H.P. 1,400 = 12 knots.
Complement: 80.

ARS.1	VIKING (ex-Guide, ex-AM.32, Flamingo)	New Jersey Sbdg.	24. 8.18	Sold 1953.

ARS.2	CRUSADER (ex-Pioneer, ex-AM.29, Osprey)	Gas Engine & Power Co.	19.11.18	Merc. VICTORIA (1947).
ARS.3	DISCOVERER (ex-AM.38, Auk)	Todd (Brooklyn)	28. 8.18	Venezuelan FELIPE LARRAZABAL (1947).
ARS.4	REDWING (ex-C.G., ex-AM.48)	Baltimore Dry Dock	7. 6.19	Lost 27/6/43.
ARS.11	WARBLER (ex-AM.53)	Philadel- phia N.Yd.	30. 7.19	Scrapped 12/48.
ARS.12	WILLET (ex-AM.54)	Philadel- phia N.Yd.	11. 9.19	Sold 11/48.
ARS.32	BRANT (ex-AT.132, ex-AM.24)	Sun	30. 5.18	Sold 8/46.

Notes:—Former minesweepers of the **Bird** class. ARS.1-3 reacquired in 1941 from the U.S. Coast and Geodetic Survey, ARS.4 from the Coast Guard. ARS.11 and 12 reacquired from the Maritime Commission.

Displacement:	1,530 tons.
Dimensions:	207 (wl) 213½ (oa) × 39 × 14 ft.
Machinery:	2-shaft Diesel-electric motors, S.H.P. 2,400 = 14.8 knots.
Armament:	4—40 mm. A.A. guns.
Complement:	120.

ARS.5	DIVER		19.12.42	Merc. RESCUE (1949).
ARS.6	ESCAPE		22.11.42	
ARS.7	GRAPPLE		31.12.42	
ARS.8	PRESERVER		1. 4.43	
ARS.9	SHACKLE		1. 4.43	C.G. ACUSHNET (WAT 167) (6/46).
ARS.19	CABLE		1. 4.43	Merc. (1947).
ARS.20	CHAIN		3. 6.43	
ARS.21	CURB		24. 4.43	Merc. (1947).
ARS.22	CURRENT		25. 9.43	
ARS.23	DELIVER		25. 9.43	
ARS.24	GRASP		31. 7.43	
ARS.25	SAFEGUARD	Basalt Rock	20.11.43	
ARS.26	SEIZE		8. 4.44	C.G. YOCONA (WAT 168) (6/46).
ARS.27	SNATCH		8. 4.44	Merc. ARGO (1960).
ARS.33	CLAMP (ex-BARS.3, Atlantic Salvor)		24.10.42	Discarded 1963.
ARS.34	GEAR (ex-BARS.4, Pacific Salvor)		24.10.42	
ARS.38	BOLSTER		23.12.44	
ARS.39	CONSERVER		27. 1.45	
ARS.40	HOIST		31. 3.45	
ARS.41	OPPORTUNE		31. 3.45	

U.S.S. Protector (ARS14). Wooden-hull salvage vessel.

U.S.S. Buckthorn (YN9, later AN14). Net laying ship, March 1943.

ARS.42	RECLAIMER		25. 6.45	
ARS.43	RECOVERY		4. 8.45	
ARS.44	RETRIEVER			Cancelled 8/45.
ARS.45	SKILLFUL	Basalt		Cancelled 8/45.
ARS.46	SUPPORT	Rock		Cancelled 8/45.
ARS.47	TOILER			Cancelled 8/45.
ARS.48	URGENT			Cancelled 8/45.
ARS.49	WILLING			Cancelled 8/45.

Notes:—Two additional ships of this class transferred to R.N. (BARS.1-2).

Displacement: 1,089 tons.
Dimensions: 174 (wl) $183\frac{1}{4}$ (oa) $\times$ 37 $\times$ $14\frac{3}{4}$ ft.
Machinery: 2-shaft Diesel-electric motors, S.H.P. 1,200 = 12 knots.
Armament: 1—3 in. gun.
Complement: 65.

ARS.13	ANCHOR		13. 3.43	Sold 5/47.
ARS.14	PROTECTOR	Colberg Boat Works	27. 4.43	Merc. (1947), PAKIS-TAN PROTECTOR (1952).
ARS.15	EXTRACTOR		15. 6.43	Lost 24/1/45.
ARS.16	EXTRICATE		12. 9.42	Lost 9/10/45.
ARS.17	RESTORER	Snow S.Y.	24.10.42	Danish VITUS BERING (1947).
ARS.28	VALVE	Belling-ham I.W.	20. 5.43	Sold 7/48.
ARS.29	VENT		30. 6.43	Merc. WESTERN PIONEER (1949).
ARS.35	WEIGHT (ex-BARS.7, Plymouth Salvor)	Amer. Car & Fdry.	21. 4.43	Sold 7/47.
ARS.36	SWIVEL (ex-BARS.8, York Salvor)		6. 5.43	Merc. (1947).

Notes:—Four additional ships of this class transferred to R.N. (BARS.5-6 and 9-10). Wood hulls.

Converted Types:

ARS.18	RESCUER (ex-Caspar)	739/04	2.42	Lost 1/1/43.
ARS.30	ACCELERATE (ex-Walling)	449/21	4.42	Merc. MARIGO (1947), SEMARA II (1950), GEORGE (1951).
ARS.31	HARJURAND	812/19	6.42	Merc. DODECANESE (1946).
ARS.37	TACKLE (ex-W. R. Chamberlin Jr.)	2264/12	6.43	ARST 4 (2/45); 1X 217 (3/45); scrapped 1949.

NET LAYING VESSELS

Displacement: 560 tons.
Dimensions: 146 (wl) 163¼ (oa) × 30½ × 11¾ ft.
Machinery: 1-shaft Diesel-electric, S.H.P. 800 = 13 knots.
Armament: 1—3 in. gun.
Complement: 48.

AN.6	ALOE		11. 1.41	Discarded 1962.
AN.7	ASH	Lake	15. 2.41	Discarded 1962.
AN.8	BOXWOOD	Washing-	8. 3.41	Discarded 1962.
	(ex-Birch)	ton		
AN.9	BUTTERNUT		10. 5.41	
AN.10	CATALPA		22. 2.41	Discarded 1962.
AN.11	CHESTNUT	Com-	15. 3.41	Discarded 1962.
AN.12	CINCHONA	mercial	12. 7.41	Discarded 1962.
AN.13	BUCKEYE	I.W.	26. 7.41	Discarded 1963.
	(ex-Cottonwood)			
AN.14	BUCKTHORN		27. 3.41	Discarded 1963.
	(ex-Dogwood)			
AN.15	EBONY	General	4. 6.41	Discarded 1962.
AN.16	EUCALYPTUS	Eng.	3. 7.41	Discarded 1962.
AN.17	CHINQUAPIN		14. 7.41	Sold 11/46.
	(ex-Fir)			
AN.18	GUM TREE		20. 3.41	Merc. FALCON (1948); ZAPARITA (1948).
AN.19	HOLLY	Marietta	17. 4.41	Discarded 1962.
AN.20	ELDER		19. 6.41	Discarded 1962.
	(ex-Juniper)			
AN.21	LARCH		2. 7.41	Turkish AG-4 (5/48).
AN.22	LOCUST		1. 2.41	Discarded 1962.
AN.23	MAHOGANY		13. 2.41	Scuttled 19/4/46.
AN.24	MANGO	American	22. 2.41	Discarded 1962.
AN.25	HACKBERRY	Sbdg.	6. 3.41	French ARAIGNEE
	(ex-Maple)	(Cleveland)		(11/44).
AN.26	MIMOSA		15. 3.41	Discarded 1962.
AN.27	MULBERRY		26. 3.41	Discarded 1963.
AN.28	PALM		8. 2.41	Discarded 1962.
AN.29	HAZEL		15. 2.41	Discarded 1962.
	(ex-Poplar)			
AN.30	REDWOOD	American	22. 2.41	Discarded 1962.
AN.31	ROSEWOOD	Sbdg.	1. 3.41	Discarded 1962.
AN.32	SANDALWOOD	(Lorain)	16. 3.41	Discarded 1962.
AN.33	NUTMEG		13. 3.41	Discarded 1962.
	(ex-Sycamore)			
AN.34	TEABERRY		24. 5.41	Merc. PACIFIC SALVOR (1962).
AN.35	TEAK	Mathis	26. 7.41	Discarded 1962.
AN.36	PEPPERWOOD	(Camden)	25. 8.41	French TARENTULE
	(ex-Walnut)			(12/44).
AN.37	YEW		4.10.41	French SCORPION (11/44).

Notes:—Numbered YN.1-32 until 1/44.

Displacement: 1,175 tons.
Dimensions: 169½ (wl) 194½ (oa) × 34½ × 11¾ ft.
Machinery: 1-shaft Diesel-electric, S.H.P. 1,200 = 14 knots.
Armament: 1—3 in., 4—20 mm. A.A. guns.
Complement: 56.

AN.38	AILANTHUS		20. 5.43	Lost 26/2/44.
AN.39	BITTERBUSH (ex-Almond)		30. 6.43	Merc. CIUDAD BOLIVAR (1947); lost 27/5/54.
AN.40	ANAQUA		16. 8.43	Merc. (1947).
AN.41	BARETTA		9.10.43	Merc. (1947).
AN.42	CLIFFROSE		27.11.43	Sold 1/47.
AN.43	SATINLEAF	Everett-Pacific	15. 2.44	Merc. ROCKY RIVER (1948), FOUNDATION JOSEPHINE II (1952), NORTH STAR IV (1960); lost 14/8/61.
AN.44	CORKWOOD		29. 3.44	Sold 6/47.
AN.45	CORNEL		21. 4.44	Sold 1/47.
AN.46	MASTIC (ex-Gingko)		19. 5.44	Merc. ARCTIC MAID (1948).
AN.47	CANOTIA		4. 7.44	Sold 4/47.
AN.48	LANCEWOOD (ex-Ironwood)		2. 5.43	French COMMANDANT CHARCOT (1947).
AN.49	PAPAYA		23. 5.43	Merc. PACIFIC REEFER (1950), IRMA CATALINA (1956), MAYON I (1959), MAIGUS LUCK (1959); lost 11/2/64.
AN.50	CINNAMON (ex-Royal Palm)		6. 6.43	Sold 3/47.
AN.51	SILVER BELL	Pollock-Stockton	19. 6.43	Sold 1/47.
AN.52	SNOWBELL		14. 9.43	Lost 9/10/45.
AN.53	SPICEWOOD		6.12.43	Merc. (1948), lost 29/6/61.
AN.54	MANCHINEEL (ex-Sumac)		1. 1.44	Sold 6/47.
AN.55	TORCHWOOD		19. 2.44	Sold 10/46.
AN.56	WINTERBERRY (ex-Tupelo)		22. 3.44	Merc. TROJAN (1948), ATLANTIC REEFER (1950); lost 12/4/63.
AN.57	VIBURNUM		26. 4.44	Sold 8/47.
AN.58	ABELE	Barbour	15. 7.43	Merc. (1948), SUPERIOR STRAITS (1954).
AN.59	TEREBINTH (ex-Balm)		19. 8.43	Merc. CARIBBEAN (1949).
AN.60	CATCLAW		22. 5.43	Sold 4/46.
AN.61	CHINABERRY		19. 7.43	Sold 2/50.
AN.62	HOP TREE	Snow	14.10.43	Merc. (1950).
AN.63	WHITEWOOD		21. 4.44	AG 129 (1/47); sold 1951.

U.S.S. Hop Tree (AN62). Net laying ship, 22nd December 1944. Wooden-hull type.

U.S.S. Cohoes (AN78). Steeled-hulled net laying ship on trials.

AN.64	PALO BLANCO		17. 6.44	ATA 214 (8/44); sold 4/47.
AN.65	PAL VERDE	} Snow	2. 9.44	ATA 215 (8/44); discarded 12/48.
AN.66	PINON	Am. Car & Foundry	10. 1.44	Merc. ALASKA REEF-ER (1948); lost 28/8/61.
AN.67	SHELLBARK		31.10.43	Sold 4/46.
AN.68	SILVERLEAF		11.12.43	Sold 3/47.
AN.69	STAGBUSH		29. 1.44	Merc. ANNA LUCIA (1948), OMAR BABUN (19), lost 16/10/54.
AN.70	ALLTHORN	} Canulette	27. 5.44	ATA 216 (8/44), merc. KARNA GAY (1948), EL SOL (19).
AN.71	TESOTA		29. 7.44	ATA 217 (8/44), merc. REINA DEL MAR (1947), lost 17/2/49.
AN.72	YAUPON		16. 9.44	ATA 218 (8/44); sold 1/47.

Notes:—Originally numbered YN.57-96 until 1/44. Wooden hulls. AN.58-77 originally ordered for R.N. under Lend-Lease but only AN.73-77 were transferred. AN.64-65 and 70-72 were completed as auxiliary ocean tugs without names; they were armed with 2—40 mm. A.A. guns.

Displacement: 680 tons.
Dimensions: 146 (wl) 168½ (oa) × 33¾ × 10¾ ft.
Machinery: 1-shaft Diesel-electric, S.H.P. 1,500 = 12 knots.
Armament: 1—3 in. gun.
Complement: 46.

AN.78	COHOES		29.11.44	Discarded 1963.
AN.79	ETLAH		16.12.44	Discarded 1963.
AN.80	SUNCOCK	Commer-cial	16. 2.45	Discarded 1962.
AN.81	MANAYUNK	I.W.	30. 3.45	Discarded 1962.
AN.82	MARIETTA		27. 4.45	Venezuelan PUERTO SANTO (2/62).
AN.83	NAHANT		30. 6.45	
AN.84	NAUBUC		15. 4.44	Discarded 1962.
AN.85	ONEOTA	Marine Iron & Sbdg.	27. 5.44	Discarded 1962.
AN.86	PASSACONA-WAY		30. 6.44	Discarded 1963.
AN.87	PASSAIC		29. 6.44	Discarded 1963.
AN.88	SHAKAMAXON	} L. D. Smith	9. 9.44	Discarded 1963.
AN.89	TONAWANDA		14.11.44	Haitian JACQUES DESSALINES (5/60).
AN.90	TUNXIS	Zenith Dredge	18. 8.44	Venezuelan PUERTO DE NUTRIAS (1963).
AN.91	WAXSAW		15. 9.44	Venezuelan PUERTO MIRANDA (1963).
AN.92	YAZOO		18.10.44	Discarded 1963.

Notes:—Steel hulls. Twenty-one additional ships cancelled.

U.S.S. ATR-76. Rescue tug, 18th October 1944.

U.S.S. Brazos (AO4). Oiler, March 1944.

U.S.S. Bowditch (AGS4). Surveying vessel.

U.S.S. APc-15. Coastal transport, 1944.

SURVEYING VESSELS

AG.1	HANNIBAL (ex-Joseph Holland)	1785/98	4.98	Sunk as target 3/3/45.
AGS.1	PATHFINDER	2175/42	2.42	Returned 8/46.
AGS.2	HYDRO-GRAPHER	987/31	4.42	Returned 7/46.
AGS.3	OCEANO-GRAPHER (ex-PG.85, Natchez) ex-Corsair	1136/98	4.42	Scrapped 1944.
AGS.4	BOWDITCH (ex-AG.30, ex-Santa Inez)	4576/28	3.40	Discarded 1948; scrapped 1959.
AGS.5	SUMNER (ex-AG.32, ex-AS.2, Bushnell)	3142/15	.15	Scrapped 1947.

Notes:—AGS.1-3 were acquired from the U.S. Coast and Geodetic Survey. AGS.5 was converted from a submarine tender in 1940. Nine small coastal surveying vessels (AGS.6-14) were converted from YMS and PCS types. For names, see pp. 231 and 254.

OILERS

Displacement: 5,950 tons (AO.4-6, 5,723 tons).
Dimensions: 455 (wl) 475 (oa) × 56 × 26¼ ft.
Machinery: 2-shaft reciprocating (VTE) (AO.2, Diesel); S.H.P. 5,200 = 14 knots.
Armament: 2—5 in., 8—40 mm. A.A. guns.
Complement: 144.

AO.1	KANAWHA	Mare Is. N.Yd.	11. 7.14	Lost 7/4/43.
AO.2	MAUMEE		17. 4.15	AG.124 (8/45); Chinese OMEI (11/46).
AO.3	CUYAMA		17. 6.16	Scrapped 1946.
AO.4	BRAZOS	Boston N.Yd.	1. 5.19	Scrapped 1947.
AO.5	NECHES		2. 6.20	Lost 23/1/42.
AO.6	PECOS		23. 4.21	Lost 1/3/42.

Notes:—MAUMEE and PATOKA (see below) converted to Mine Craft Tenders, 1945.

Displacement: 5,422 tons.
Dimensions: 463¼ (wl) 477¾ (oa) × 60 × 26¼ ft.
Machinery: 1-shaft reciprocating (VTE) (AO.13 & 21, geared turbines). S.H.P. 2,900 = 10.5 knots.
Armament: 2—5 in., 8—40 mm. A.A. guns.
Complement: 107.

AO.9	PATOKA (ex-AV.6)	Newport News	26. 7.19	AG 125 (8/45); scrapped 1949.

U.S.S. Chemung (AO30). Oiler, April 1946, refuelling destroyer Steinaker (DD863). Aircraft carrier Princeton (CV37) on horizon.

318

U.S.S. Cimarron (AO22). Oiler, May 1942, at Pearl Harbor. 4-5in. guns carried in turrets.

U.S.S. Laramie (AO16). Oiler, 1942.

U.S.S. Platte (AO24). Oiler, 31st October 1944, with two 5in. guns in turrets visible forward and aft of funnel.

U.S.S. Schuylkill (AO76). Oiler, 1944, with small tube in place of funnel. Funnel-like object on forward superstructure houses electronic gear.

AO.11	SAPELO		24.12.19	Scrapped 1946.
AO.12	RAMAPO		11. 9.19	Merc. (1946); scrapped 1953.
AO.13	TRINITY	Newport News	3. 7.20	Merc. (1946), SEA-BEAVER (1951), ASYNETI (1952), scrapped 1953.
AO.18	RAPIDAN		25.10.19	Scrapped 1946.
AO.19	SALINAS		5. 5.20	Merc. (1946), scrapped 1960.
AO.20	SEPULGA		21. 4.20	Scrapped 1947.
AO.21	TIPPECANOE		5. 6.20	Scrapped 1947.

Notes:—AO.18-21 acquired in 1922, but TIPPECANOE not commissioned until 1940. SALINAS torpedoed 30/10/41.

Displacement: 5,450 tons.
Dimensions: 430 (wl) 446 (oa) × 58 × 25½ ft.
Machinery: 1-shaft reciprocating (VTE), S.H.P. 2,800 = 11 knots.
Armament: 2—5 in., 8—40 mm. A.A. guns.
Complement: 107.

AO.15	KAWEAH		14. 8.19	Scrapped 1946.
AO.16	LARAMIE	Cramp	.19	Scrapped 1946.
AO.17	MATTOLE		.20	Scrapped 1946.

Notes:—A fourth ship, ALAMEDA (AO.10), sold in 1922, was re-acquired in 1943 as SILVER CLOUD (IX.143). LARAMIE torpedoed 27/8/42.

Displacement: 7,256 tons (AO.105-109, 7,423 tons).
Dimensions: 525 (wl) 553 (oa) × 75 × 32 ft.
Machinery: 2-shaft geared turbines, S.H.P. 13,500 = 18.3 knots.
Armament: 1—5 in., 4—3 in., 8—40 mm. A.A. guns (AO.22, 24, 26: 4—5 in., 8—40 mm. A.A. guns).
Complement: 304.
Type: T3-S2-A1 (AO.105-109, T3-S2-A3).

AO.22	CIMARRON	Sun	7. 1.39	
AO.23	NEOSHO	Federal	29. 4.39	Lost 11/4/42.
AO.24	PLATTE	Sparrows Pt.	8. 7.39	
AO.25	SABINE (ex-Esso Albany)		27. 4.40	
AO.26	SALAMONIE (ex-Esso Columbia)	Newport News	18. 9.40	
AO.27	KASKASKIA (ex-Esso Richmond)		29. 9.39	
AO.28	SANGAMON (ex-Esso Trenton)	Federal	4.11.39	CVE 26 (2/42).
AO.29	SANTEE (ex-Seakay)	Sun	4. 3.39	CVE 29 (2/42).
AO.30	CHEMUNG (ex-Esso Annapolis)	Sparrows Pt.	9. 9.39	

AO.31	CHENANGO (ex-Esso New Orleans)	Sun	1. 4.39	CVE 28 (2/42).
AO.32	GUADALUPE (ex-Esso Raleigh)	Newport News	26. 1.40	
AO.33	SUWANEE (ex-Markay)	Federal	4. 3.39	CVE 27 (2/42).
AO.51	ASHTABULA	⎫	22. 5.43	
AO.52	CACAPON		12. 6.43	
AO.53	CALIENTE		25. 8.43	
AO.54	CHIKASKIA		2.10.43	
AO.55	ELOKOMIN		19.10.43	
AO.56	AUCILLA (ex-Escanaba)		20.11.43	
AO.57	MARIAS	⎬Sparrows Pt.	21.12.43	
AO.58	MANATEE		18. 2.44	
AO.59	MISSISSINEWA		28. 3.44	Lost 20/11/44.
AO.60	NANTAHALA		29. 4.44	
AO.61	SEVERN		31. 5.44	
AO.62	TALUGA		10. 7.44	
AO.63	CHIPOLA		21.10.44	
AO.64	TOLOVANA	⎭	6. 1.45	
AO.97	ALLAGASH		14. 4.45	
AO.98	CALOOSAHAT-CHEE		2. 6.45	
AO.99	CANISTEO	⎫	6. 7.45	
AO.100	CHUKAWAN		28. 8.45	
AO.105	MISPILLION	⎬	10. 8.45	
AO.106	NAVASOTA		30. 8.45	
AO.107	PASSUMPSIC	⎬Sun	31.10.45	
AO.108	PAWCATUCK		19. 2.46	
AO.109	WACCAMAW	⎭	30. 3.46	

Notes:—AO.26-33 acquired in 1940-41. See p. 49 for CVE.26-29. ASHTABULA torpedoed 24/10/44. SEVERN converted to water tanker.

Displacement: 5,958 tons.
Dimensions: 488 (wl) 501¾ (oa) × 68 × 30¾ ft. (AO 41-44, 47: 500 (wl) 526 (oa)).
Machinery: 1-shaft geared turbines, S.H.P. 12,000 = 16.7 knots (AO.68-72: S.H.P. 7,000 = 15.3 knots).
Armament: 1—5 in., 4—3 in., 8—40 mm. A.A. guns.
Complement: 215.
Type: T2-A (AO.68—72: T3-S-A1).

AO.36	KENNEBEC (ex-Corsicana)	⎫	19. 4.41	
AO.37	MERRIMACK (ex-Caddo)		1. 7.41	
AO.38	WINOOSKI (ex-Calusa)	⎬Sparrows Pt.	12.11.41	Merc. SAMUEL L. FULLER (1947).
AO.39	KANKAKEE (ex-Colina)		24. 1.42	
AO.40	LACKAWANNA (ex-Conastoga)	⎭	16. 5.42	Merc. TATARRAX (1947).

AO.41	MATTAPONI (ex-Kalkay)		17. 1.42	
AO.42	MONONGA-HELA (ex-Ellkay)		30. 5.42	Discarded 1957.
AO.43	TAPPAHAN-NOCK (ex-Jorkay)	Sun	18. 4.42	
AO.44	PATUXENT (ex-Emmkay)		25. 7.42	Merc. DAVID D. IRWIN (1947).
AO.47	NECHES (ex-Aekay)		11.10.41	
AO.48	NEOSHO (ex-Catawba)		23.12.41	Merc. TASCALUSA (1947).
AO.68	CHIWAWA (ex-Samoset)		25. 6.42	Merc. (1946).
AO.69	ENOREE (ex-Sachem)	Sparrows Pt.	29. 8.42	Discarded 1959.
AO.70	ESCALANTE (ex-Shabonee)		29. 9.42	Merc. GEORGE Mac-DONALD (1947), lost 30/6/60.
AO.71	NESHANIC (ex-Marqiette)		31.10.42	Merc. GULFOIL (1947).
AO.72	NIOBRARA (ex-Citadel)		28.11.42	

Displacement: 5,730 tons.
Dimensions: 503 (wl) 523½ (oa) × 68 × 30¾ ft.
Machinery: 1-shaft turbo-electric, S.H.P. 6,000 = 15.1 knots (AO.80 up.: S.H.P. 10,000 = 16.2 knots).
Armament: 1—5 in., 4—3 in., 8—40 mm. A.A. guns.
Complement: 225.
Type: T2-SE-A1 (AO.80 up.: T2-SE-A2).

AO.49	SUAMICO (ex-Harlem Heights)		30. 5.42	
AO.50	TALLULAH (ex-Valley Forge)		25. 6.42	
AO.65	PECOS (ex-Corsicana)		17. 8.42	
AO.67	CACHE (ex-Stillwater)		7. 9.42	
AO.73	MILLICOMA (ex-Kings Mountain)	Sun	21. 1.43	
AO.74	SARANAC (ex-Cowpens)		21.12.42	YFP 9 (1954), sold 4/57.
AO.75	SAUGATUCK (ex-Newtown)		7.12.42	
AO.76	SCHUYLKILL (ex-Louisberg)		16. 2.43	
AO.77	COSSATOT (ex-Fort Necessity)		28. 2.43	

AO.78	CHEPACHET (ex-Eutaw Springs)	⎫	10. 3.43	
AO.79	COWANESQUE (ex-Fort Duquesne)	⎬ Sun	11. 3.43	
AO.80	ESCAMBIA	⎫	25. 4.43	Discarded 1957.
AO.81	KENNEBAGO		9. 5.43	Discarded 1959.
AO.82	CAHABA (ex-Lackawaxen)		19. 5.43	Discarded 1958.
AO.83	MASCOMA		31. 5.43	Discarded 1959.
AO.84	OCKLAWAHA		9. 6.43	Discarded 1959.
AO.85	PAMANSET		25. 6.43	Discarded 1957.
AO.86	PONAGANSET		10. 7.43	Lost 9/12/47; scrapped 1949.
AO.87	SEBEC		29. 7.43	Discarded 1957.
AO.88	TOMAHAWK	⎬ Marinship	10. 8.43	Discarded 1961.
AO.91	PASIG		15. 7.44	AW 3 (8/44).
AO.92	ABATAN		6. 8.44	AW.4 (8/44).
AO.93	SOUBARISSEN		12. 8.44	Discarded 1961.
AO.94	ANACOSTIA		24. 9.44	Discarded 1957.
AO.95	CANEY		8.10.44	Discarded 1957.
AO.96	TAMALPAIS		29.10.44	Discarded 1958.
AO.101	COHOCTON		28. 6.45	Discarded 1958.
AO.102	CONCHO		25. 7.45	Cancelled 8/45.
AO.103	CONECUH		10. 8.45	Cancelled 8/45.
AO.104	CONTOCOOK	⎭	18. 9.45	Cancelled 8/45.

Notes:—PASIG and ABATAN completed as Distilling Ships; OCKLAWAHA, SOUBARISSEN and PONAGANSET converted to water tankers. SARANAC damaged by aircraft 18/6/44.

		Gross tonnage built	Acquired	
AO.34	CHICOPEE (ex-Esso Trenton)	10097/41	1.42	Merc. ESSO CHATTA-NOOGA (1947).
AO.35	HOUSATONIC (ex-Esso Albany)	10097/41	1.42	Merc. ESSO BETHLE-HEM (1947).
AO.45	BIG HORN (ex-Gulfdawn)	7096/36	3.42	C. G. WAO 124 (12/43); U.S.N. IX 207 (2/45); merc. C. B. WATSON (1947).
AO.46	VICTORIA (ex-George G. Henry)	6265/17	4.42	Returned 12/45.
AO.66	ATASCOSA (ex-Esso Columbia)	11344/42	4.42	Merc. ESSO SYRACU-SE (1947).
AO.89	PASIG (ex-J. C. Donnell)	9783/17	1.43	Returned 9/43.

Notes:— 15 in., 4-3 in., 8-40 mm AA guns.

GASOLINE TANKERS

Displacement: 1,850 tons.
Dimensions: 292 (wl) 310¾ (oa) × 48½ × 15¾ ft.
Machinery: 2-shaft diesel-electric drive, B.H.P. 3,300 = 14 knots.
Armament: 4—3 in. guns.
Complement: 124.

PATAPSCO, KERN (ex-Rappahannock), RIO GRANDE, WABASH, SUSQUEHANNA, AGAWAM, ELKHORN, GENESEE, KISHWAUKEE, NEMASKET, TOMBIGBEE (AOG.1-11), CHEHALIS, CHESTATEE, CHEWAUCAN, MAQUOKETA, MATTABESSET, NAMAKAGON, NATCHAUG, NESPELEN, NOXUBEE, PECATONICA, PINNEBOG, WACISSA (AOG.48-59).

Notes:—Built 1942-45 by Todd-Seattle (AOG 1-5) and Cargill (others). CHEHALIS lost 8/10/49.

Displacement: 845 tons.
Dimensions: 221 (oa) × 37 × 12¾ ft.
Machinery: 1-shaft diesel motor, B.H.P. 800 = 10 knots.
Armament: 1—3 in. gun.
Complement: 62.
Type: T1-M-A2.
War Loss: SHEEPSCOT.

METTAWEE, PASQUOTANK, SAKATONCHEE, SEEKONK, SEQUATCHIE, WAUTAUGA, AMMONUSUC, SHEEPSCOT (es-Androscoggin), CALAMUS, CHIWAUKUM, ESCATAWPA, GUALALA, HIWASSEE, KALAMAZOO, KANAWHA, NARRAGUAGUS, OCHLOCKONEE, OCONEE, OGEECHEE, ONTONAGON, YAHARA, PONCHATOULA, QUASTINET, SACANDAGA, TETONKAHA, TOWALIGA, TULAROSA, WAKULLA, YACONA, WAUPACA (AOG.17-46), MANOKIN, SAKONNET, CONEMAUGH, KLASKANINE (AOG.60-63).

Notes:—Built 1942-45 by Todd-Galveston (AOG 21-22), Todd-Houston (AOG 60-61) and East Coast Sbdg. (others). SACANDAGA lost 8/10/45; others sold 1946-48.

Displacement: 1,840 tons.
Dimensions: 325¼ (oa) × 48¼ × 19 ft.
Machinery: 1-shaft Diesel, S.H.P. 1,700 = 11 knots.
Armament: 1—3 in., 2—40 mm. A.A. guns.
Type: T1-M-BT1.

KLICKITAT, MICHIGAMME, NANTICOKE, PECONIC (AOG.64-66, 68).

Notes:—Cancelled: NODAWAY, PETALUMA, PISCATAQUA, QUINNEBAUG, SEBASTICOOK, KIAMICHI, TELLICO, TRUCKEE (AOG 67, 69-75). Built 1945 by St. John's River Sbdg.

Miscellaneous types:

		Gross tonnage built	Acquired	
AOG.12	HALAWA (ex-Blue Sunoco)	1588/28	4.42	Returned 10/45.
AOG.13	KALOLI (ex-Flying A)	1729/41	4.42	Returned 12/45.
AOG.14	AROOSTOOK (ex-Esso Delivery No.11)	1707/37	4.43	French LAC PAVIN (1/45).

U.S.S. Pasig (AW3). Distilling ship, 7th January 1945.

U.S.S. Porcupine (IX126). Station tanker, September 1944. The tanker version of the Liberty Ship.

AOG.15	CONASAUGA (ex-New York Socony)	1539/31	4.43	French LAC BLANC (12/44). Sold 12/45.
AOG.16	GUYANDOT (ex-Veedol No. 2)	1818/29	4.43	French LAC NOIR (1945).
AOG.47	SHIKELLAMY (ex-AO.90, ex-Daniel Pierce)	4887/43	4.43	Returned 1/46.

STATION TANKERS

Old or slow tankers taken over for fuel storage at Pacific bases and other duties not requiring the speed and mobility of fleet oilers.

Displacement:	3,665 tons.
Dimensions:	416 (wl) 441½ (oa) × 57 × 27¾ ft.
Machinery:	1-shaft reciprocating (VTE), S.H.P. 2,500 = 11 knots.
Armament:	1-5 in., 1-3 in. guns.
Complement:	79.
Type:	Z-ET1-S-C3.
War loss:	PORCUPINE.

ARMADILLO, BEAGLE, CAMEL, CARIBOU, ELK, GAZELLE, GEMSBOK, GIRAFFE, IBEX, JAGUAR, KANGAROO, LEOPARD, MINK, MOOSE, PANDA, PORCUPINE, RACCOON, STAG, WHIPPET, WILDCAT (IX.111-130).

Note:—STAG and WILDCAT completed as Distilling Ships (AW 1-2). Built 1943 by Calship (IX 111-120) and Delta Sbdg. (IX 121-130)

Miscellaneous types:

IX.131	ABARENDA (ex-Acme)	6878/16	2.44	Returned 2/46.
IX.132	ANDREW DORIA (ex-Alcibiades)	5169/08	8.44	Returned 2/46.
IX.133	ANTONA (ex-Birkenhead)	6690/21	5.44	Returned 5/46.
IX.134	ARAYAT (ex-Faireno)	5837/18	4.44	Returned 2/46.
IX.135	ARETHUSA (ex-Gargoyle)	7002/21	3.44	Returned 5/46.
IX.136	CARONDELET (ex-Gold Heels, ex-Brennero)	4945/21	4.44	Returned 2/46.
IX.137	CELTIC (ex-Kerry Patch, ex-Java Arrow)	8327/21	1.44	Returned 2/46.
IX.138	MALVERN (ex-Orissa)	5837/01	5.44	Returned 2/46.
IX.139	OCTORARA (ex-La Purisima)	5091/21	9.44	Returned 4/46.
IX.140	QUIROS (ex-Osmond)	6820/03	3.44	Returned 12/45.
IX.141	MANILENO (ex-Polonaise)	5812/21	4.44	Returned 2/46.
IX.142	SIGNAL (ex-Standard Arrow)	7794/16	4.44	Returned 2/46.
IX.143	SILVER CLOUD (ex-Sweep, ex-Olean, ex.-U.S.N. Alameda)	7223/19	7.44	Returned 3/46.
XI.144	CLYDE (ex-U.S.N. St. Mary, ex-Swivel)	5556/18	3.44	Returned 11/45.
XI.145	VILLALOBOS (ex-Typhoon)	4938/11	2.44	Returned 2/46.
IX.178	BANSHEE (ex-W.C. Fairbanks)	6353/17	12.44	Sold 2/46.
IX.179	KENWOOD (ex-Texas)	6368/15	12.44	Sold 1/46.
IX.184	CLIFTON (ex-Dilworth)	7045/19	5.45	Returned 2/46.
IX.185	STONEWALL (ex-Frank G. Drum)	7156/20	9.44	Returned 1/46.

IX.186	DAWN (ex-Vacuum)	7020/20	12.44	Returned 4/46.
IX.187	BELUSAN (ex-Vistula)	8537/20	2.45	Sold 1/47.
IX.188	CHOTAUK (ex-American Arrow)	8327/20	11.44	Returned 2/46.
IX.189	MARMORA (ex-J. C. Fitzsimmons)	6715/18	12.44	Returned 2/46.
IX.190	NAUSETT (ex-W. M. Irish)	7123/17	1.45	Returned 10/45.
IX.191	VANDALIA (ex-Walter Jennings)	9563/21	12.44	Lost 9/10/45.
IX.192	FLAMBEAU (ex-S. B. Hunt)	6840/19	1.45	Returned 9/46.
IX.193	MEREDOSIA (ex-Liebre)	7057/21	2.45	Returned 2/46.
IX.197	MARIVELES (ex-Jamestown)	7050/20	4.45	Sold 6/46.
IX.210	SEA FOAM (ex-Pennsylvania)	6390/17	5.45	Returned 2/46.
IX.213	SERAPIS (ex-District of Columbia)	7162/20	.45	Returned 10/45.
IX.214	YUCCA (ex-Utacarbon)	6878/20	7.45	Returned 2/46.
IX.218	GUARDOQUI (ex-E. T. Bedford)	9563/21	6.45	Returned 2/46.

Notes:—The majority were scrapped after the war. IX.132, 134, 136, 138, 140, 141, 144, 145 were Italian tankers seized in the Western Hemisphere in 1941.

AMMUNITION SHIPS

Navy built:

		Displacement Completed	
AE.1	PYRO	7040/20	Scrapped 1950.
AE.2	NITRO	7040/21	Scrapped 1949.
AE.8	MAUNA LOA	5450/43	
AE.9	MAZAMA	5450/44	
AE.13	AKUTAN	5450/45	Discarded 1960.

Converted types:

		Gross t'ge Built	Acquired	
AE.3	LASSEN (ex-Shooting Star)	6021/40	11.40	Discarded 1961.
AE.4	KILAUEA (ex-Surprise)	6022/40	11.40	MOUNT BAKER (1942).
AE.5	RAINIER (ex-Rainbow)	8051/41	4.41	
AE.6	SHASTA (ex-Comet)	8051/41	4.41	
AE.10	SANGAY (ex-Cape Sable)	5105/42	11.42	Discarded 1960.
AE.11	MOUNT HOOD (ex-Marco Polo)	8258/43	7.44	Lost 10/11/44.
AE.12	WRANGELL (ex-Midnight)	8258/44	5.44	
AE.14	FIREDRAKE (ex-Winged Racer)	8258/44	6.44	
AE.15	VESUVIUS (ex-Game Cock)	8258/44	7.44	
AE.16	MOUNT KATMAI	8258/45	2.45	
AE.17	GREAT SITKIN	8258/45	2.45	
AE.18	PARICUTIN	8258/45	3.45	
AE.19	DIAMOND HEAD	8258/45	3.45	

Notes:—1—5 in., 4—3 in., 4—40 mm. A.A. guns, except AE.1-2: 2—5 in., etc., and AE.10: 1—5 in. 6—40 mm. A.A. guns. AE.3-6 were type C2-T, 11-12 and 14-19, C2-S-AJ1, and AE.10, C1-A.

STORE SHIPS

Navy built:

		Displacement Completed	
AF.1	BRIDGE	5207/16	Merc. DON JOSE (1948); scrapped 3/53.

Converted types:

		Gross t'age Launched	Acquired	
AF.7	ARCTIC (ex-Yamhill)	5976/18	11.21	Scrapped 1947.
AF.8	BOREAS (ex-Yaquina)	6100/18	12.21	Scrapped 1946.
AF.9	YUKON (ex-Mehanno)	5970/19	11.21	Scrapped 1946.
AF.10	ALDEBARAN (ex-Stag Hound)	7169/39	12.40	
AF.11	POLARIS (ex-Donald McKay)	8222/39	1.41	Discarded 1/57.
AF.12	MIZAR (ex-Quirigua)	6982/32	6.41	Returned 4/46.
AF.13	TARAZED (ex-Chiriqui)	6963/31	6.41	Returned 1/46.
AF.14	URANUS (ex-Maria)	1369/33	8.41	Returned 5/46.
AF.15	TALAMANCA	6963/31	1.42	Returned 11/45.
AF.16	PASTORES	7241/12	12.41	Scrapped 1947.
AF.18	CALAMARES	7782/13	12.41	Scrapped 1947.
AF.19	ROAMER (ex-African Reefer)	1770/35	7.42	Returned 6/46.
AF.20	PONTIAC (ex-Australian Reefer)	2321/37	5.42	Lost 30/1/45; hulk scrapped 1949.
AF.21	MERAK (ex-Veragua)	6982/32	3.42	Returned 6/46.
AF.22	ARIEL (ex-U.S.S. Dione, ex-Jamaica)	6968/31	3.42	Returned 6/46.
AF.23	CYGNUS (ex-La Perla)	3792/25	8.42	Returned 7/46.
AF.24	DELPHINUS (ex-San Mateo)	3289/15	8.42	Scrapped 1946.
AF.25	TAURUS (ex-San Benito)	3724/21	10.42	Returned 12/45.
AF.26	OCTANS (ex-Ulua)	6494/17	5.43	Scrapped 1947.
AF.28	HYADES (ex-Iberville)	6165/43	9.43	
AF.29	GRAFFIAS (ex-Topa Topa)	6165/43	2.44	
AF.30	ADRIA	3770/44	11.44	Discarded 1960.
AF.31	AREQUIPA	3803/44	12.44	Discarded 1961.
AF.32	CORDUBA	3803/44	12.44	Discarded 1960.
AF.33	KARIN	3803/44	1.45	Discarded 1961.
AF.34	KERSTIN	3804/44	1.45	Discarded 1949.
AF.35	LATONA	3804/44	1.45	Discarded 1949.
AF.36	LIOBA	3804/44	2.45	Discarded 1960.
AF.37	MALABAR	3804/44	2.45	Discarded 1960.
AF.38	MERAPI	3804/44	3.45	Discarded 1960.
AF.39	PALISANA	3809/44	3.45	Merc. (1946).
AF.41	ATHANASIA (ex-Stevedore Knot)	3803/44	3.45	Returned 1/46.
AF.42	BONDIA (ex-Flemish Bend)	3805/44	3.45	Returned 7/46.
AF.43	GORDONIA (ex-Whale Knot)	3770/44	4.45	Returned 7/46.

U.S.S. Regulus (AK14). Cargo ship, 1942.

U.S.S. Admiral Hugh Rodman (AP126). Transport, 1945.

330

AF.44	LAURENTIA (ex-Wall and Crown)	3805/44	5.45	Returned 6/46.
AF.45	LUCIDOR	3809/45	6.45	Returned 5/46.
AF.46	OCTAVIA	3777/45	5.45	Merc. YARD-ARM KNOT (1946).
AF.47	VALENTINE	3777/45	6.45	Merc. PIER BEND (1946).

Notes:—BOREAS first commissioned in 1940. Acquisition of AF.17 and 27 cancelled. AF.30-39, 41-47 were type R1-M-AV3, and 28-29, C2-S-E1.

CARGO SHIPS

AK.13	CAPELLA (ex-Comerant)	5078/20	11.21	Scrapped 1947.
AK.14	REGULUS (ex-Glenora)	4980/20	11.21	Scrapped 1947.
AK.15	SIRIUS (ex-Saluda)	5581/19	12.21	Scrapped 1947.
AK.16	SPICA (ex-Shannock)	5562/19	11.21	Merc. PLEAMAR (1947). Scrapped 1964.
AK.17	VEGA (ex-Lebanon)	5058/19	12 21	Scrapped 1946.
AK.18	ARCTURUS (ex-Mormachawk)	6200/39	9.40	AKA 1; merc. STAR ARCTURUS (1947).
AK.19	PROCYON (ex-Sweepstakes)	7940/40	11.40	AKA 2; sold 7/46.
AK.20	BELLATRIX (ex-Raven)	8113/41	4.41	AKA 3; returned 6/46.
AK.21	ELECTRA (ex-Meteor)	8113/41	4.41	AKA 4; returned 3/47.
AK.22	FOMALHAUT (ex-Cape Lookout)	6750/41	5.41	ex-AKA 5; AE 20 (12/48); discarded 1962.
AK.23	ALCHIBA (ex-Mormacdove)	6198/39	6.41	AKA 6; merc. TJIPANAS (1948).
AK.24	ALCYONE (ex-Mormacgull)	6198/39	5.41	AKA 7; merc. STAR ALCYONE (1946).
AK.25	ALGORAB (ex-Mormacwren)	6198/39	6.41	AKA 8; merc. MONGALA (1948).
AK.26	ALHENA (ex-Robin Kettering)	7101/41	5.41	AKA 9; returned 9/46.
AK.27	ALMAACK (ex-Executor)	6736/40	5.41	AKA 10; merc. BUNKER HILL (1946).
AK.28	BETELGEUSE (ex-Mormaclark)	6198/39	5.41	AKA 11; merc. STAR BETELGEUSE (1946).
AK.41	HERCULES (ex-Exporter)	6736/39	7.41	Returned 7/46.
AK.42	MERCURY (ex-Mormactern)	7194/39	6.41	AKS 20 (7/45); discarded 1960.
AK.43	JUPITER (ex-Santa Catalina)	6085/39	6.41	AVS 8 (7/45). Discarded 1964.
AK.44	AROOSTOOK (ex-CM.3, ex-Bunker Hill)	4029/07	*5.41	Army (1/43).
AK.46	PLEIADES (ex-Mangalia)	3600/39	8.41	Merc. SCEPTER (1945).

AK.47	AQUILA (ex-Tunis)	1559/36	8.41	Returned 10/45.
AK.48	PEGASUS (ex-Lawrin)	1889/36	9.41	IX 222 (5/45); merc. RITA MAERSK (1946).
AK.49	SATURN (ex-Sting, ex-Arauca)	4354/39	4.42	AF 40 (4/44); returned 7/46.
AK.51	ARIES (ex-AG.37, Manomet)	1998/18	*1.42	Merc. ADELANTO (1947).
AK.53	LIBRA (ex-Jean Lykes)	6155/41	12.41	AKA 12.
AK.55	TITANIA (ex-Harry Culbreath)	7296/42	3.42	AKA 13; discarded 1961.
AK.56	OBERON (ex-Delalba)	7371/42	6.42	AKA 14; discarded 1960.
AK.63	ASTERION (ex-Evelyn)	3140/12	9.42	C. G. WAK 123 (1/44).
AK.80	ENCELADUS	2323/42	8.43	Sold 6/46.
AK.98	AURIGA (ex-Alcoa Partner)	6749/42	9.42	Returned 1/46.
AKS.1	CASTOR (ex-Challenge)	8097/39	10.40	
AKS.2	POLLUX (ex-Comet)	8097/39	1.41	Lost 18/2/42.
AKS.3	ANTARES (ex-AG.10, ex-Nedmac)	5698/19	*11.40	Scrapped 1947.
AKS.4	POLLUX (ex-Nancy Lykes)	6155/42	3.42	

* Converted.

Notes:—1—5 in., 4—3 in. guns, except AK.46-48, 51: 2—3 in.; AK.80: 1—3 in. AK.98: 1—5 in., 1—3 in., 4—40 mm. A.A.; AKS.3: 2—5 in., 4—3 in. REGULUS and SPICA first commissioned in 1940. Assault cargo ships equipped to carry landing craft reclassified AKA, 2/43, as noted above. ALCHIBA severely damaged 28/11/42.

Displacement: 4,023 to 4,846 tons.
Dimensions: 416 (wl) 441½ (oa) × 57 × 27½ ft.
Machinery: 1-shaft reciprocating (VTE), S.H.P. 2,500 = 12.5 knots.
Armament: 1—5 in., 1—3 in., 2—40 mm. A.A. guns.
　　　　　　(AKN: 1—5 in., 4—40 mm. A.A. guns.)
Complement: 198.
Type: EC2-S-C1.
War losses: ALUDRA, DEIMOS, SERPENS.

CRATER, ADHARA, ALUDRA, ARIDED, CARINA, CASSIOPEIA, CELENO, CETUS, DEIMOS, DRACO (AK.70-79), ALBIREO, COR CAROLI, ERIDANUS, ETAMIN, MINTAKA, MURZIM, STEROPE, SERPENS (AK.90-97), BOOTES, LYNX, LYRA, TRIANGULUM, SCULPTOR, GANYMEDE, NAOS, CAELUM, HYPERION, ROTANIN, ALLIOTH, ALKES, GIANSAR, GRUMIUM, RUTILICUS, ALKAID, CRUX, ALDERAMIN, ZAURAK, SHAULA, MATAR, (AK.99-119), SABIK (AK.121), MENKAR, AZIMECH, LESUTH, MEGREZ, ALNITAH, LEONIS, PHOBOS, ARKAB, MELUCTA, PROPUS, SEGINUS, SYRMA, VENUS, ARA, ASCELLA, CHELEB, PAVO, SITULA (AK.123-140), KENMORE, LIVINGSTON, DE GRASSE, PRINCE GEORGES, ALLEGAN, APPANOOSE (AK.221-226). INDUS, SAGITTARIUS, TUSCANA, ZEBRA (AKN.1-3, 5). ACUBENS, KOCHAB, LUNA, TALITA, VOLANS, CYBELE, GRATIA, HECUBA, HESPERIA, IOLANDA, LIGURIA (AKS.5-15).

Note:—ETAMIN, torpedoed 27/4/44, became storage hulk as IX 173. ALLIOTH and GRUMIUM converted to aviation store ships (AVS 4 and 3), 1944.

U.S.S. Artemis (AKA2I). Attack cargo ship, 8th September 1944.

U.S.S. Theenim (AKA63). Attack cargo ship.

Displacement:	2,382 tons.
Dimensions:	320 (wl) 338¾ (oa) × 50 × 21 ft.
Machinery:	1-shaft Diesel motors, B.H.P. 1,700 = 11.5 knots.
Armament:	1—3 in. gun.
Complement:	85.
Type:	C1-M-AV1.

ALAMOSA, ALCONA, AMADOR, ANTRIM, AUTAUGA, BEAVERHEAD, BELTRAMI, BLOUNT, BREVARD, BULLOCK, CABELL, CALEDONIA, CHARLEVOIX, CHATHAM, CHICOT, CLAIBORNE, CLARION, CODINGTON, COLQUITT, CRAIGHEAD (AK.156-175), FAIRFIELD, FARIBAULT, FENTRESS, FLAGLER, GADSDEN, GLACIER, GRAINGER, GWINNETT, HABERSHAM, HENNEPIN, HERKIMER, HIDALGO, KENOSHA, LEBANON, LEHIGH, LANCASTER, MARENGO, MIDLAND (AK.178-195), MUSCATINE, MUSKINGUM, NICOLLET, PEMBINA, PEMISCOT (AK.197-201), POINSETT, PONTOTOC, RICHLAND, ROCKDALE, SCHUYLER, SCREVEN, SEBASTIAN, SOMERSET, SUSSEX, TARRANT, TIPTON (AK.205-215).

Notes:—GWINNETT, NICOLLET and PONTOTOC converted to aviation store ships (AVS.5-7) 1945. Eleven additional hulls incomplete at end of war were not acquired: DODDRIDGE, DUVAL (AK.176-177), MINIDOKA (AK.196), PINELLAS, PIPESTONE, PITKIN (AK.202-204), TRAVERSE, TULARE, WASHTENAW, WESTCHESTER, WEXFORD (AK.216-220).

Displacement:	4,420 tons.
Dimensions:	436 (wl) 455¼ (oa) × 62 × 28½ ft.
Machinery:	1-shaft geared turbines, S.H.P. 8,500 = 17 knots.
Armament:	1—5 in., 1—3 in., 4—40 mm. A.A. guns.
Complement:	100.
Type:	VC2-S-AP2.

BOULDER VICTORY, PROVO VICTORY, LAS VEGAS VICTORY, MANDERSON VICTORY, BEDFORD VICTORY, MAYFIELD VICTORY, NEWCASTLE VICTORY, BUCYRUS VICTORY, RED OAK VICTORY, LAKEWOOD VICTORY (AK.227-236).

Notes:—Used for carriage of ammunition.

ATTACK CARGO SHIPS

Displacement:	6,556 tons.
Dimensions:	435 (wl) 459¼ (oa) × 63 × 25¾ ft.
Machinery:	1-shaft geared turbines, S.H.P. 6,000 = 16.4 knots.
Armament:	1—5 in., 8—40 mm. A.A. guns.
Complement:	404.
Type:	C2-S-B1.

ANDROMEDA, AQUARIUS, CENTAURUS, CEPHEUS, THUBAN, VIRGO (AKA.15-20), ACHERNAR, ALGOL, ALSHAIN, ARNEB, CAPRICORNUS, CHARA, DIPHDA, LEO, MULIPHEN, SHELIAK, THEENIM (AKA.53-63), UVALDE, WARRICK, WHITESIDE, WHITLEY, WYANDOT, YANCEY, WINSTON, MARQUETTE, MATHEWS, MFRRICK, MONTAGUE, ROLETTE, OGLETHORPE (AKA.88-100).

Note:—Cancelled: SAN JOAQUIN, SEDGWICK, WHITFIELD (AKA 109-111). Carried 15 LCVP 8 LCM(3) and 1 LCP(L).

As above, but 6,318 tons, draft 26¼ ft.; type C2-S-AJ3.

TOLLAND, SHOSHONE, SOUTHAMPTON, STARR, STOKES, SUFFOLK, TATE, TODD, CASWELL, NEW HANOVER, LENOIR, ALAMANCE, TORRANCE, TOWNER, TREGO, TROUSDALE, TYRRELL, VALENCIA, VENANGO, VINTON, WAUKESHA, WHEATLAND, WOODFORD, DUPLIN (AKA.64-87), OTTAWA, PRENTISS, RANKIN, SEMINOLE, SKAGIT, UNION, VERMILION, WASHBURN (AKA.101-108).

Displacement:	4,100 tons.
Dimensions:	400 (wl) 426 (oa) × 58 × 15½ ft.
Machinery:	2-shaft turbo-electric, S.H.P. 6,000 = 16.5 knots.
Armament:	1-5in., 8-40 mm. A.A. guns
Complement:	303.
Type:	S4-SE2-BE1.

ARTEMIS, ATHENE, AURELIA, BIRGIT, CIRCE, CORVUS, DEVOSA, HYDRUS, LACERTA, LUMEN, MEDEA, MELLENA, OSTARA, PAMINA, POLANA, RENATE, ROXANE, SAPPHO, SARITA, SCANIA, SELINUR, SIDONIA, SIRONA, SYLVANIA, TABORA, TROILUS, TURANDOT, VALERIA, VANADIS, VERITAS, XENIA, ZENOBIA (AKA.21-52).

Note:—Carried 12 LCVP, 2 LCM(3) and 1 LCP(L).

TRANSPORTS

AP.1	HENDERSON	7493/16	1916	BOUNTIFUL (AH.9, 3/44).
AP.2	DOYEN	6400/42	1942	APA 1; sold 6/46; BAY STATE (1963).
AP.5	CHAUMONT	7555/20	11.21	SAMARITAN (AH 10, 3/44).
AP.6	WILLIAM WARD BURROWS (ex-Santa Rita)	4576/29	2.40	Sold 6/46; scrapped 1957.
AP.7	WHARTON (ex-Southern Cross)	13788/19	11.39	Sold 3/47; scrapped 1951.
AP.8	HARRIS (ex-Pres. Grant)	14119/21	7.40	APA 2; scrapped 1947.
AP.9	ZEILIN (ex-Pres. Jackson)	14123/20	7.40	APA 3; scrapped 1947.
AP.10	McCAWLEY (ex-Santa Barbara)	7712/28	7.40	APA 4; lost 30/6/43.
AP.11	BARNETT (ex-Santa Maria)	7712/28	8.40	APA 5; merc. SURRIENTO (1947).
AP.12	HEYWOOD (ex-City of Baltimore)	8378/19	10.40	APA 6; sold 7/46, scrapped 1956.
AP.13	GEORGE F. ELLIOT (ex-City of Los Angeles)	7881/18	11.40	Lost 8/8/42.
AP.14	FULLER (ex-City of Newport News)	7610/19	11.40	APA 7; sold 6/46; scrapped 1957.
AP.15	WILLIAM P. BIDDLE (ex-City of San Francisco)	7884/18	11.40	APA 8; sold 7/46, scrapped 1957.
AP.16	NEVILLE (ex-City of Norfolk)	7894/18	12.40	APA 9; sold 7/46, scrapped 1957.

U.S.S. Sheepscot (AOG24). Gasoline tanker, August 1944.

U.S.S. Wakefield (AP21). The former United States Lines' *Manhattan*, 1945, shown after rebuilding following damage from fire at sea in 1942.　　　　　　　　　　　　　*[Official U.S. Coast Guard*

U.S.S. West Point (AP23). The former flagship of the U.S. merchant marine, as a transport, 7th June 1943.

U.S.S. General John Pope (AP110). Transport, 25th August 1943.

AP.17	HARRY LEE (ex-Exochorda)	9359/30	10.40	APA 10; merc. TARSUS (1948), lost 14/12/60.
AP.18	FELAND	6400/42	1942	APA 11; sold 6/46. scrapped 1964.
AP.19	CATLIN (ex-George Washington)	23788/07	1.41	Returned 9/41, lost 16/1/51.
AP.20	MUNARGO	6336/21	6.41	Army THISTLE (10/43).
AP.21	WAKEFIELD (ex-Manhattan)	24289/31	6.41	Discarded 1957, scrapped 1964.
AP.22	MOUNT VERNON (ex-Washington)	24289/32	6.41	Returned 1/46, scrapped 1964
AP.23	WEST POINT (ex-America)	23179/39	6.41	Merc. AMERICA (1946), AUSTRALIS (1965).
AP.24	ORIZABA	6937/17	6.41	Brazilian DUQUE DE CAXIAS (7/45).
AP.25	LEONARD WOOD (ex-Western World)	13712/21	6.41	APA 12; scrapped 1947.
AP.26	JOSEPH T. DICK-MAN (ex-Pres. Roosevelt)	13869/21	6.41	APA 13; scrapped 1948.
AP.27	HUNTER LIG-GETT (ex-Pan America)	13712/21	6.41	APA 14; scrapped 1948.
AP.28	KENT	4858/18	7.41	Army ERNEST HINDS (3/42).
AP.29	U.S. GRANT (ex-Army)	9410/07	6.41	Returned 11/45.
AP.30	HENRY T. ALLEN (ex-Pres. Jefferson)	14127/19	5.41	APA 15; AG 90 (2/45); scrapped 1948.
AP.31	CHATEAU THIERRY (ex-Army)	7556/20	7.41	Returned 9/43.
AP.32	ST. MIHIEL (ex-Army)	7556/20	7.41	Returned 11/43.
AP.33	REPUBLIC (ex-Army)	17886/06	7.41	Returned 2/45.
AP.34	J. FRANKLIN BELL (ex-Pres. McKinley)	14127/20	12.41	APA 16; scrapped 1949.
AP.35	AMERICAN LEGION	13736/19	8.41	APA 17; scrapped 1948.
AP.41	STRATFORD (ex-AK 45, ex-Catherine)	2286/18	7.41	Merc. GRANTON GLEN (1947).
AP.42	TASKER H. BLISS (ex-Pres. Cleveland)	12568/20	8.42	Lost 12/11/42.
AP.43	HUGH L. SCOTT (ex-Pres. Pierce)	12479/20	8.42	Lost 12/11/42.
AP.50	JOSEPH HEWES (ex-Excalibur)	9359/30	1.42	Lost 11/11/42.
AP.51	JOHN PENN (ex-Excambion)	9361/31	1.42	APA 23; lost 13/8/43.
AP.52	EDWARD RUT-LEDGE (ex-Exeter)	9360/31	1.42	Lost 12/11/42.

U.S.S. Joseph Hewes (AP50). Transport, 1942.

U.S.S. Hermitage (AP54). The former Italian liner Conte Biancamano as a naval transport, January 1943.

AP.53	LAFAYETTE (ex-Normandie)	83423/32	12.41	Burned 9/2/42; hulk scrapped 1947.
AP.54	HERMITAGE (ex-Conte Biancamano)	23254/25	4.42	Returned 8/46, scrapped 1960.
AP.61	MONTICELLO (ex-Conte Grande)	23861/27	4.42	Returned 5/46, scrapped 1961.
AP.62	KENMORE (ex-Pres. Madison)	10495/21	4.42	REFUGE (AH.11, 2/44).
AP.63	ROCHAMBEAU (ex-Marechal Joffre)	12063/30	12.41	Returned 3/45, scrapped 1960.
AP.67	DOROTHEA L. DIX (ex-Exemplar)	6736/40	9.42	Returned 4/46.
AP.69	ELIZABETH C. STANTON (ex-Mormacstar)	7864/39	9.42	Returned 4/46.
AP.70	FLORENCE NIGHTINGALE (ex-Mormacsun)	7864/40	9.42	Returned 5/46.
AP.71	LYON (ex-Mormactide)	7898/40	9.42	Returned 5/46.
AP.72	SUSAN B. AN-THONY (ex-Santa Clara)	8101/30	8.42	Lost 7/6/44.
AP.73	LEEDSTOWN (ex-Santa Lucia)	9135/33	8.42	Lost 9/11/42.
AP.74	LEJEUNE (ex-Windhuk)	16662/36	5.42	Discarded 1957.
AP.75	GEMINI (ex-AK 52, ex-AG 38, ex-Saginaw)	2153/19	9.41	Merc. RAMSDAL (1948).
AP.76	ANNE ARUNDEL (ex-Mormacyork)	7500/40	9.42	Returned 3/46.
AP.77	THURSTON (ex-Delsantos)	6131/42	8.42	Returned 8/46.
AP.102	LA SALLE (ex-Hotspur)	6221/42	3.43	Merc. STONEWALL JACKSON (1948).
AP.166	COMET	6221/42	2.44	Merc. PIONEER REEF (1948).
AP.167	JOHN LAND	6221/43	5.44	Merc. JEFF DAVIS (1949).
AP.168	WAR HAWK	6221/43	3.44	Merc. (1946).
AP.169	GOLDEN CITY	6214/43	5.44	Merc. (1946).
AP.170	WINGED ARROW	6125/43	4.44	Merc. FAIRHOPE (1948).
AP.171	STORM KING	8258/43	12.43	Merc. GULF FARMER (1947).
AP.172	CAPE JOHNSON	6711/43	6.44	Returned 7/46.
AP.173	HERALD OF THE MORNING	6214/43	4.44	Merc. CITRUS PACKER (1947).
AP.174	ARLINGTON (ex-Fred Morris)	6658/42	4.44	Returned 3/46.
AP.175	STARLIGHT	8166/43	2.44	Merc. FLORENCE LUCKENBACH (1947).
AP.177	EUROPA	49746/28	8.45	Merc. LIBERTE (1947).

| APA.89 | FREDERICK FUNSTON | 11971/41 | 4.43 | Army 4/46. |
| APA.90 | JAMES O'HARA | 11969/41 | 4.43 | Army 4/46. |

Notes:—AP.25-35 and 42-43 acquired from the Army. Assault transports equipped to carry landing craft were reclassified APA in 2/43 as noted above. AP.50 and 52 were lost before being reclassified APA.22 and 24. AP.2 and 18 carried 16 LCVP, 1,100 troops. Other APA's carried about 1,500 troops, 15-33 LCVP and 2-4 LCM(3). A number of famous large liners were commissioned as transports together with smaller coastal ships. Many other transports were operated by the Army and civilian agencies. WEST POINT carried 4—5 in., 4—3 in., 8—40 mm. A.A. guns; WAKEFIELD, 3—5 in., 12—40 mm.A.A.; HERMITAGE, MONTICELLO and LE JEUNE, 1—5 in., 4—3 in.; U.S.M.C. types, 1—5 in., 4—3 in., 4—40 mm. A.A. AP.67, 69-71, 76 were C3-Cargo; AP.77, C2-F; AP.102, 166-170 and 173, C2-S-B1; AP.171 and 175: C2-S-AJ1; AP.172 and 174: C1-B. WAKEFIELD, burned out at sea 3/9/42, was rebuilt and rejoined the fleet 10/2/44.

Displacement:	10,210 tons.		
Dimensions:	465 (wl) 491¾ (oa) × 69½ × 26½ ft.		
Machinery:	1-shaft geared turbines, S.H.P. 8,500 = 18.4 knots.		
Armament:	4—3 in., 4—40 mm. A.A. guns.		
	(AP.103-104 also 1—5 in. gun).		
Complement:	512.		
Type:	C3-A P. & C.		

AP.37	PRESIDENT JACKSON		7. 6.40	APA 18; discarded 1958.
AP.38	PRESIDENT ADAMS		31. 1.41	APA 19; discarded 1958.
AP.39	PRESIDENT HAYES		4.10.40	APA 20; discarded 1958.
AP.59	THOMAS STONE (ex-Pres. Van Buren)	Newport News	1. 5.41	Lost 25/11/42; hulk scrapped 1944.
AP.60	THOMAS JEFFERSON (ex-Pres. Garfield)		20.11.40	APA 30; discarded 1958.
AP.103	PRESIDENT POLK		28. 6.41	Returned 1/46.
AP.104	PRESIDENT MONROE		7. 8.40	Returned 2/46.

Type C3-P, as above, except 10,812 tons, 489 ft. (oa).

AP.55	ARTHUR MIDDLETON (ex-African Comet)		28. 6.41	APA 25; discarded 1958.
AP.56	SAMUEL CHASE (ex-African Meteor)	Ingalls	25. 8.41	APA 26; discarded 1958.
AP.57	GEORGE CLYMER (ex-African Planet)		27. 9.41	APA 27.

Type C3-Delta, as above, except, 8,429 tons, 65½ beam; S.H.P. 7,800 = 17ft. knots; 1—5 in., 4—3 in., 4—40 mm. A.A. guns (except AP.65, 3—3 in. guns).

AP.40	CRESCENT CITY (ex-Delorleans)		17. 2.40	APA 21; discarded 1958.
AP.58	CHARLES CARROLL (ex-Deluruguay)		24. 3.42	APA 28; discarded 1958.
AP.64	MONROVIA (ex-Deltargen-tino)	}Sparrows Pt.	19. 9.42	APA 31.
AP.65	CALVERT (ex-Delorleans)		22. 5.42	APA 32.
AP.105	GEORGE F. ELLIOT (ii) (ex-Delbrasil)		16.12.39	Merc. AFRICAN EN-DEAVOR (1949).

Notes:—Fast passenger-cargo liners of similar types which served continuously in every major landing from North Africa on. AP.37-40 acquired 6/41; 55-60 and 64-65 in 1942, and AP 103-105 in 1943. APA's carried 2 LCM(3) and 25 to 32 LCVP, 1400 troops.

Displacement:	11,450 tons.
Dimensions:	573 (wl) 622½ (oa) = 75½ × 25 ft.
Machinery:	2-shaft geared turbines, S.H.P. 17,000 = 20.6 knots.
Armament:	4—5 in., 8—40 mm. A.A. guns.
Type:	P2-S2-R2.

AP.110	GEN. JOHN POPE	21. 3.43	Army (1946-50).
AP.111	GEN. A. E. ANDERSON	2. 5.43	Sold 12/58.
AP.112	GEN. W. A. MANN	18. 7.43	
AP.113	GEN. H. W. BUTNER	19. 9.43	Sold 3/60.
AP.114	GEN. WILLIAM MITCHELL	31.10.43	
AP.115	GEN. G. M. RANDALL	30. 1.44	Sold 9/62.
AP.116	GEN. M. C. MEIGS	12. 3.44	Army (1946-50).
AP.117	GEN. W. H. GORDON	7. 5.44	Merc. (1946-51).
AP.118	GEN. W. P. RICHARDSON	6. 8.44	Merc. LA GUARDIA (1949), LEILANI (1956 PRES. ROOSEVELT (1961).
AP.119	GEN. WILLIAM WEIGEL (ex-Gen. C. H. Barth)	3. 9.44	Army (1946-50).
AP.176	GEN. J. C. BRECKINRIDGE	18. 3.45	

Notes:—All built by Federal (Kearny). Could carry 5,650 troops.

Displacement:	12,650 tons.
Dimensions:	573 (wl) 609 (oa) × 75½ × 29 ft.
Machinery:	2-shaft turbo-electric, S.H.P. 18,000 = 19 knots.
Armament:	4—5 in., 8—40 mm. A.A. guns.
Complement:	618.
Type:	P2-SE2-R1.

AP.120	ADM. W. S. BENSON	28.11.43	Army GEN. DANIEL I. SULTAN (6/46).
AP.121	ADM. W. L. CAPPS	20. 2.44	Army GEN. HUGH J. GAFFEY (5/46).
AP.122	ADM. R. E. COONTZ	22. 4.44	Army GEN. ALEXANDER M. PATCH (3/46)
AP.123	ADM. E. W. EBERLE	14. 6.44	Army GEN. SIMON B. BUCKNER (5/46).
AP.124	ADM. C. F. HUGHES	27. 8.44	Army GEN. EDWIN D. PATRICK (5/46).
AP.125	ADM. H. T. MAYO	26.11.44	Army GEN. NELSON M. WALKER (5/46); discarded 1959.
AP.126	ADM. HUGH RODMAN	25. 2.45	Army GEN. MAURICE ROSE (5/46).
AP.127	ADM. W. S. SIMS	4. 6.45	Army GEN. WILLIAM O. DARBY (6/46).
AP.128	ADM. D. W. TAYLOR		Completed as merc. PRES. CLEVELAND
AP.129	ADM. F. B. UPHAM		Completed as merc. PRES. WILSON.

Notes:—All built by Bethlehem (Alameda).

Displacement: 9,943 tons.
Dimensions: 496 (wl) 522¾ (oa) × 71½ × 26½ ft.
Machinery: 1-shaft geared turbines, S.H.P. 9,000 = 17 knots.
Armament: 4—5 in., 4—40 mm. A.A. guns.
Complement: 500.
Type: C4-S-A1.

AP.130	GEN. G. O. SQUIER	25.11.42	Merc. PENNMAR (1964).
AP.131	GEN. T. H. BLISS	19.12.42	Merc. SEAMAR (1964).
AP.132	GEN. J. R. BROOKE	21. 2.43	Merc. MARYMAR (1964).
AP.133	GEN. O. H. ERNST	23. 5.43	Merc. CALMAR (1964).
AP.134	GEN. R. L. HOWZE	23. 7.43	Army (1946-50).
AP.135	GEN. W. L. BLACK	23. 7.43	Army (1946-50).
AP.136	GEN. H. L. SCOTT	19. 9.43	Merc. YORKMAR (1964).
AP.137	GEN. S. D. STURGIS	12.12.43	Army (1946-50).
AP.138	GEN. C. G. MORTON	15. 3.44	Army (1946-50).
AP.139	GEN. R. E. CALLAN	23. 5.44	Army (1946-50); GEN. H. H. ARNOLD (AGM.9, 1964).
AP.140	GEN. M. B. STEWART	15.10.44	Army (1946-50).
AP.141	GEN. A. W. GREELY	5.11.44	Army (1946-50).
AP.142	GEN. C. H. MUIR	24.11.44	Army (1946-50).
AP.143	GEN. H. B. FREEMAN	11.12.44	Army (1946-50).
AP.144	GEN. H. F. HODGES	3. 1.45	Army (1946-50).
AP.145	GEN. HARRY TAYLOR	10.10.43	Army (1946-50); GEN. HOYT VANDENBERG (AGM 10, 1964).

U.S.S. Zeilin (APA3). The former American Mail liner President Jackson as an attack transport, 1944.

U.S.S. Aquarius (AKA16). Attack cargo ship.

U.S.S. Charles Carroll (APA28), Attack transport, 11th December 1944.

345

U.S.S. Kenton (APA122). Attack transport, 15th November 1944. Victory ship type

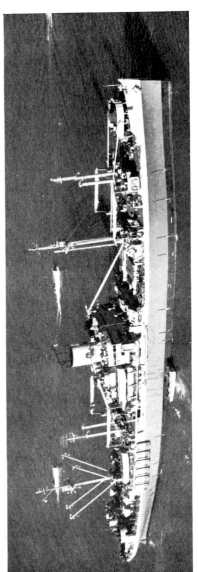

U.S.S. Leedstown (APA56). Attack transport, October 1943.

346

AP.146	GEN. W. F. HASE	15.12.43	Army (1946-50).
AP.147	GEN. E. T. COLLINS	22. 1.44	Army (1946-50).
AP.148	GEN. M. L. HERSEY	1. 4.44	Army (1946-50).
AP.149	GEN. J. H. McRAE	26. 4.44	Army (1946-50).
AP.150	GEN. M. M. PATRICK	21. 6.44	Army (1946-50).
AP.151	GEN. W. C. LANGFITT	17. 7.44	Army (1946-50).
AP.152	GEN. OMAR BUNDY	5. 8.44	Merc. PORTMAR (1964).
AP.153	GEN. R. M. BLATCHFORD	27. 8.44	Army (1946-50).
AP.154	GEN. LeROY ELTINGE	20. 9.44	Army (1946-50).
AP.155	GEN. A. W. BREWSTER	21. 1.45	Army (1946-50).
AP.156	GEN. D. E. AULTMAN	21. 2.45	Army (1946-50).
AP.157	GEN. C. C. BALLOU	7. 3.45	Army (1946-50).
AP.158	GEN. W. G. HAAN	20. 3.45	Army (1946-50).
AP.159	GEN. STUART HEINTZELMAN	21. 4.45	Army (1946-50).

Notes:—All built by Kaiser (Richmond, Cal.). Army ships were returned to Navy control in 1950.

ATTACK TRANSPORTS

Displacement: 7,845 tons.
Dimensions: 465 (wl) 492 (oa) × 69½ × 26½ ft.
Machinery: 1-shaft geared turbines, S.H.P. 8,500 = 18.4 knots.
Armament: 2—5 in., 8—40 mm. A.A. guns.
Complement: 575.
Type: C3-S-A2.

BAYFIELD, BOLIVAR, CALLAWAY, CAMBRIA, CAVALIER, CHILTON, CLAY, CUSTER, DU PAGE, ELMORE, FAYETTE, FREMONT, HENRICO, KNOX, LAMAR, LEON, ALPINE, BARNSTABLE, BURLEIGH, CECIL, DADE (ex-Lorain), MENDOCINO, MONTOUR, RIVERSIDE, WEST-MORELAND, HANSFORD (ex-Gladwin), GOODHUE, GOSHEN, GRAFTON, GRIGGS, GRUNDY, GUILFORD, SITKA, HAMBLEN, HAMPTON, HANOVER (APA.33-48, 92-93, 95-96, 99-102, 104, 106-116).

Notes:—HENRICO damaged by *Kamikaze* 2/4/45.

Displacement: 7,300 tons.
Dimensions: 445 (wl) 459¼ (oa) × 63 × 25¾ ft.
Machinery: 1-shaft geared turbines, S.H.P. 6,000 = 15.5 knots.
Armament: 2—5 in., 8—40 mm. A.A. guns.
Complement: 554.
Type: C2-S-B1.

ORMSBY, PIERCE, SHERIDAN (APA.49-51).

Displacement: 8,355 tons.
Dimensions: 000 (wl) 468¾ (oa) × 63 × 26 ft.
Machinery: 1-shaft geared turbines, S.H.P. 6,300 = 16 knots.
Armament: 2—5 in., 8—40 mm. A.A. guns.
Complement: 554.
Type: C2-S-E1.

SUMTER, WARREN, WAYNE, BAXTER (APA.52-54, 94).

Displacement: 7,970 tons.
Dimensions: 450 (wl) 473 (oa) × 66 × 20 ft.
Machinery: 1-shaft geared turbines, S.H.P. 8,000 = 16.5 knots.
Armament: 2—5 in., 8—40 mm. A.A. guns.
Complement: 554.
Type: C3-S-A3.

WINDSOR, LEEDSTOWN (ex-Wood), ADAIR, DAUPHIN, DUTCHESS,
QUEENS, SHELBY (APA.55-56, 91, 97-98, 103, 105).

Displacement: 4,247 tons.
Dimensions: 400 (wl) 426 (oa) × 58 × 15½ ft.
Machinery: 2-shaft turbo-electric drive, H.P. 6,600 = 16.5 knots.
Armament: 1—5 in., 8—40 mm. A.A. guns.
Complement: 320.
Type: S4-SE2-BD1.

GILLIAM, APPLING, AUDRAIN, BANNER, BARROW, BERRIEN,
BLADEN, BRACKEN, BRISCOE, BRULE, BRULESON, BUTTE,
CARLISLE, CARTERET, CATRON, CLARENDON, CLEBURNE,
COLUSA, CORTLAND, CRENSHAW, CRITTENDEN, CULLMAN,
DAWSON, ELKHART, FALLON, FERGUS, FILLMORE, GARRARD,
GASCONADE, GENEVA, NIAGARA, PRESIDIO (APA.57-88).

Displacement: 6,873 tons.
Dimensions: 436½ (wl) 455 (oa) × 62 × 24 ft.
Machinery: 1-shaft geared turbines, S.H.P. 8,500 = 17.7 knots.
Armament: 1—5 in., 12—40 mm. A.A. guns.
Complement: 536.
Type: VC2-S-AP5.

HASKELL, HENDRY, HIGHLANDS, HINSDALE, HOCKING, KENTON,
KITTSON, LA GRANGE, LANIER, ST. MARY'S, ALLENDALE, ARENAC,
MARVIN H. McINTYRE (ex-Arlington), ATTALA, BANDERA, BARN-
WELL, BECKHAM, BLAND, BOSQUE, BOTETOURT, BOWIE, BRAXTON,
BROADWATER, BROOKINGS, BUCKINGHAM, CLEARFIELD,
CLERMONT, CLINTON, COLBERT, COLLINGSWORTH, COTTLE,
CROCKETT, AUDUBON, BERGEN, LA PORTE, LATIMER, LAURENS,
LOWNDES, LYCOMING, MELLETTE, NAPA, NEWBERRY, DARKE,
DEUEL, DICKENS, DREW, EASTLAND, EDGECOMBE, EFFINGHAM,
FOND DU LAC, FREESTONE, GAGE, GALLATIN, GOSPER, GRAN-
VILLE, GRIMES, HYDE, JERAULD, KARNES, KERSHAW, KINGS-
BURY, LANDER, LAUDERDALE, LAVACA (APA.117-180). OCONTO,
OLMSTED, OXFORD, PICKENS, PONDERA, RUTLAND, SANBORN,
SANDOVAL, LENAWEE, LOGAN, LUBBOCK, McCRACKEN,
MAGOFFIN, MARATHON, MENARD, MENIFEE, MERIWETHER,
SARASOTA, SHERBURNE, SIBLEY, MIFFLIN, TALLADEGA, TAZE-
WELL, TELFAIR, MISSOULA, MONTROSE, MOUNTRAIL, NATRONA,
NAVARRO, NESHOBA, NEW KENT, NOBLE, OKALOOSA, OKANOGAN,
ONEIDA, PICKAWAY, PITT, RANDALL, BINGHAM, RAWLINS,
RENVILLE, ROCKBRIDGE, ROCKINGHAM, ROCKWALL, SAINT
CROIX, SAN SABA, SEVIER, BOLLINGER, BOTTINEAU, BRONX,
BEXAR, DANE, GLYNN (APA.187-239).

Notes:- Cancelled: HARNETT, HEMPSTEAD, IREDELL, LUZERNE, MADERA, MARICOPA,
McLENNAN, MECKLENBURG (APA.240-247).

U.S.S. Samaritan (AH10). Hospital ship, 13th March 1945.

U.S.S. Consolation (AH15). Hospital ship, 1945.

U.S.S. Rescue (AH18). Hospital ship, 1945, converted from submarine tender in 1944.

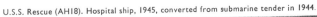

HOSPITAL SHIPS

AH.1	RELIEF	8288/19	1919	Scrapped 1947.
AH.5	SOLACE (ex-Iroquois)	6209/26	7.40	Merc. ANKARA (1947).
AH.6	COMFORT	6711/43	4.43	Army 4/46.
AH.7	HOPE	6711/43	9.43	Army 5/46.
AH.8	MERCY	6711/43	4.43	Army 5/46.
AH.9	BOUNTIFUL (ex-AP.1, Henderson)	7493/16	*3.44	Scrapped 1947.
AH.10	SAMARITAN (ex-AP.5, Chaumont)	7556/20	*3.44	Scrapped 1948.
AH.11	REFUGE (ex-AP.62, Kenmore, ex-Pres. Madison)	10501/21	*2.44	Scrapped 1947.
AH.12	HAVEN	13500/44	7.44	
AH.13	BENEVOLENCE	13500/44	8.44	Lost 25/8/50.
AH.14	TRANQUILLITY	13500/44	8.44	Discarded 1961.
AH.15	CONSOLATION	13500/44	9.44	Merc. HOPE (1960).
AH.16	REPOSE	13500/44	9.44	
AH.17	SANCTUARY	13500/44	9.44	Discarded 1961.
AH.18	RESCUE (ex-AG.67, ex-AS.21, Antaeus, ex-St. John)	6185/32	*1.45	Sold 6/46.

*Converted

Notes:—AH.12-17 type C4-S-B2; AH.6-8: C1-B. There were also twenty-four hospital ships operated by the U.S. Army and manned by civilian crews: ACADIA, ALEDA E. LUTZ (ex-Colombie), ALGONQUIN, BLANCHE F. SIGMAN, CHARLES A. STAFFORD (ex-Siboney), CHATEAU THIERRY, DOGWOOD, EMILY H. M. WEDER (ex-Pres. Buchanan), ERNEST HINDS, ERNESTINE KORANDA, FRANCES Y. SLANGER (ex-Saturnia), JARRETT M. HUDDLESTON, JOHN J. MEANY, JOHN L. CLEM, LARKSPUR (ex-U.S.S. Bridgeport), LOUIS A. MILNE, MARIGOLD (ex-Pres. Fillmore), REPUBLIC, St. MIHIEL, St. OLAF, SEMINOLE, SHAMROCK (ex-Agwileon), THISTLE (ex-Munargo), and WISTERIA.

EVACUATION TRANSPORTS

APH.1	TRYON (ex-Alcoa Courier)	7100/41	9.42	Army SGT. CHARLES E. MOWER (7/46).
APH.2	PINKNEY (ex-Alcoa Corsair)	7100/41	9.42	Army PVT. ELDEN H. JOHNSON (9/46).
APH.3	RIXEY (ex-Alcoa Cruiser)	7100/41	9.42	Army PVT. WILLIAM H. THOMAS (9/46).

Notes:—1—5 in., 8—40 mm. A.A. guns. Armed transports fitted for the evacuation of wounded from combat zones. A number of LST's were also so fitted. Type Z-C2-S1-A1.

FLEET TUGS

Displacement:	1,030 tons.
Dimensions:	149¼ (wl) 155¾ (oa) × 30 × 14½ ft.
Machinery:	1-shaft reciprocating (VTE), H.P. 1,800 — 13 knots.
Armament:	2—3 in. guns.
Complement:	60.

ATO.19	ALLEGHENY (ex-Huron)	American Sbdg. (Buffalo)	18.10.17	Sold 2/47.
ATO.10	SAGAMORE (ex-Comanche)		1917	Merc. JOHN E. McALLISTER (1948).
ATO.21	BAGADUCE (ex-Ammonoosuc)		5. 4.19	Sold 1/47.
ATO.23	KALMIA	Ferguson Steel	26. 8.19	Sold 1/47.
ATO.24	KEWAYDIN		25. 6.19	Sold 12/46.
ATO.25	UMPQUA		18. 9.19	Sold 12/46.
ATO.26	WANDANK		21.10.19	Merc. W. A. BISSO (1947).
ATO.27	TATNUCK (ex-Iosco)		21. 2.19	Sold 5/47.
ATO.28	SUNNADIN (ex-Katahdin)		28. 2.19	Sold 1/47.
ATO.29	MAHOPAC (ex-Kickapoo)	Puget Sound N.Yd.	27. 5.19	Sold 5/47.
ATO.30	SCIOTA (ex-Watauga)		11. 6.19	Sold 10/46.
AT.32	NAPA (ex-Yucca)		24. 7.19	Lost 8/4/42.
ATO.33	PINOLA (ex-Nipsic)		12. 8.19	Sold 11/47.
ATO.34	ALGORMA		12. 6.19	Sold 1/47.
ATO.37	IUKA		12. 1.20	Merc. (1948).
ATO.38	KEOSANQUA	Staten Island	26. 2.20	Merc. EDW. J. COYLE (1948), COMMODORE STRAITS (1960).
ATO.39	MONTCALM (ex-Kineo)		26. 2.20	Sold 2/47.

Notes:—Missing numbers were discarded prior to the war. AT.40-45 cancelled, 1919. Ex-AT.35 (CARRABASSETT) served in the Coast Guard having been transferred in 1924. Numerical series of tugs subdivided into ATA, ATF, and ATO, 5/44.

Displacement:	1,235 tons.	
Dimensions:	195 (wl) 205 (oa) $\times$ 38½ $\times$ 15¼ ft.	
Machinery:	1-shaft Diesel-electric motors, S.H.P. 3,000 = 16 knots.	
Armament:	1—3 in., 4—40 mm. A.A. guns.	
Complement:	85.	

AT.64	NAVAJO	Bethlehem (Staten Is.)	17. 8.39	Lost 11/9/43.
AT.65	SEMINOLE		15. 9.39	Lost 25/10/42.
ATF.66	CHEROKEE		10.11.39	C. G. WATF 165 (6/46).
ATF.67	APACHE		6. 5.42	
ATF.68	ARAPAHO (ex-Catawba)		22. 6.42	Argentine CDTE. GEN. ZAPIOLA (7/61).
ATF.69	CHIPPEWA	Charleston Sbdg.	25. 7.42	Discarded 1961.
ATF.70	CHOCTAW		18.10.42	Colombian PEDRO DE HEREDIA (12/60).
ATF.71	HOPI		7. 9.42	Discarded 1963.
ATF.72	KIOWA		5.11.42	

U.S.S. Bear (AG29). Arctic patrol and weather ship.

U.S.S. Bannock (ATF81). Fleet tug, 26th August 1944. Later units had no funnel.

ATF.73	MENOMINEE		14. 2.42	Indonesian RAKATA (1/61).
ATF.74	PAWNEE	United	31. 3.42	Discarded 1962.
ATF.75	SIOUX	(Alameda)	27. 5.42	
ATF.76	UTE		25. 6.42	
ATF.81	BANNOCK	Charleston	7. 1.43	Italian (10/62).
ATF.82	CARIB	Sbdg.	7. 2.43	Discarded 1963.
ATF.83	CHICKASAW		23. 7.42	
ATF.84	CREE		17. 8.42	
ATF.85	LIPAN	United	17. 9.42	
ATF.86	MATACO	(Alameda)	14.10.42	
ATF.87	MORENO		9. 7.42	Discarded 1961.
ATF.88	NARRAGAN-SETT		8. 8.42	Discarded 1961.
		Cramp		
AT.89	NAUSET	Sbdg.	7. 9.42	Lost 9/9/43.
ATF.90	PINTO		5. 1.43	Peruvian RIOS (12/60).
ATF.91	SENECA		2. 2.43	
ATF.92	TAWASA		22. 2.43	
ATF.93	TEKESTA	Com-	20. 3.43	Chilean YELCHO (5/60).
ATF.94	YUMA	mercial	17. 7.43	Pakistani MADADGAR (3/59).
		I.W.		
ATF.95	ZUNI		31. 7.43	C.G. TAMAROA (WATF 166) (6/46).
ATF.96	ABNAKI		22. 4.43	
ATF.97	ALSEA		22. 5.43	Discarded 1962.
ATF.98	ARIKARA		22. 6.43	
AT.99	CHETCO		20. 7.43	PENGUIN (ASR 12) (9/43).
ATF.100	CHOWONOC	Charleston	20. 8.43	
ATF.101	COCOPA	Sbdg.	5.10.43	
ATF.102	HIDATSA		29.12.43	Discarded 1963.
ATF.103	HITCHITI		29. 1.44	
ATF.104	JICARILLA		25. 2.44	Discarded 1963.
ATF.105	MOCTOBI		25. 3.44	
ATF.106	MOLALA		23.12.42	
ATF.107	MUNSEE		21. 1.43	
ATF.108	PAKANA		3. 3.43	Discarded 1963.
ATF.109	POTOWATOMI		3. 4.43	Chilean JANEQUEO (9/62).
ATF.110	QUAPAW		15. 5.43	
ATF.111	SARSI		12. 6.43	Lost 27/8/52.
ATF.112	SERRANO	United	24. 7.43	AGS 24 (6/60).
ATF.113	TAKELMA	(Alameda)	18. 9.43	
ATF.114	TAWAKONI		28.10.43	
ATF.115	TENINO		10. 1.44	Discarded 1962.
ATF.116	TOLOWA		17. 5.44	Venezuelan FELIPE LARRAZABAL (2/62).
ATF.117	WATEREE		14. 6.44	Lost 9/10/45.
ATF.118	WENATCHEE		7. 9.44	Discarded 1962.
ATF.148	ACHOMAWI		14. 6.44	Discarded 1962.
ATF.149	ATAKAPA		11. 7.44	
ATF.150	AVOYEL	Charleston	9. 8.44	C.G. WATF 150 (7/56).
ATF.151	CHAWASHA	Sbdg.	15. 9.44	Discarded 1963.
ATF.152	CAHUILLA		2.11.44	Argentine CDTE. GEN. IRIGOYEN (7/61).

ATF.153	CHILULA		1.12.44	C.G. WATF 153 (7/56).
ATF.154	CHIMARIKO		30.12.44	Discarded 1963.
ATF.155	CUSABO		26. 2.45	Ecuadorian LOS RIOS (11/60).
ATF.156	LUISENO		17. 3.45	
ATF.157	NIPMUC		12. 4.45	
ATF.158	MOSOPELEA		7. 5.45	
ATF.159	PAIUTE	Charleston	4. 6.45	
ATF.160	PAPAGO	Sbdg.	21. 6.45	
ATF.161	SALINAN		20. 7.45	
ATF.162	SHAKORI		9. 8.45	Discarded 1962.
ATF.163	UTINA		31. 8.45	
ATF.164	YUROK		15. 2.46	BLUEBIRD (ASR 19) (11/45); Turkish KURTARAN (8/50).
ATF.165	YUSTAGA		19. 3.46	SKYLARK (ASR 20) (11/45).

Miscellaneous types:

		Displac'nt Year built	Acquired	
ATO.12	SONOMA	1120/12	1912	Lost 24/10/44.
ATO.13	ONTARIO	1120/12	1912	Sold 4/47.
ATO.55	GENESEE (ex-Monocacy)	1000/05	11.17	Lost 5/5/42; Japanese PATROL BOAT No. 107, lost 5/11/44.
ATO.58	UNDAUNTED	450/17	2.18	Sold 3/47.
ATO.63	ACUSHNET (ex-C.G.)	604/08	5.36	Scrapped 1946.
ATO.147	ESSELEN (ex-New York)	800/93	6.43	Returned 11/44.
ATO.166	CHETCO (ex-Thomas E. Moran)	600/19	9.43	Merc. NEPTUNE (1947), lost 16/11/48.
ATA.167	CHATOT (ex-Buttercup)	554/19	10.43	Merc. ALBATROS (1945).

AUXILIARY TUGS

ATA.121–125, 146, 170–213 (ex-ATR.43–47, 90, 97–140), 219–238.

Displacement: 534 tons.
Dimensions: 134½ (wl) 143 (oa) × 33¾ × 13¼ ft.
Machinery: 1-shaft Diesel-electric drive, S.H.P. 1,500 = 13 knots.
Armament: 1—3 in. gun.
Complement: 49.
War loss: ATR.98 (was to become ATA.171).

Notes:—Built 1942-45. ATA.229-233 cancelled. ATA.219-238 originally ordered for transfer to U.S.S.R. but this never took place. ATA.191 lost 9/10/45, and 122, 124-125, 146, 170, 172-173, 180, 219-228 and 234-238 sold 1946-47. ATR.41-42 (ex-AT.119-120), 48-49 (ex-At.126-127), 91-96 and BAT.1, 3-14 of this class were transferred to R.N. under Lend/Lease. BAT.2 became ATA.146. ATA.194 and 202 became C. G. MODOC and COMANCHE in 1959.

BUILDERS:

Levingston: ATA.121-125, 174-198, 219-233, ATR.41-42, 43-49, 91-96, BAT.3-6, 11-12.
Gulfport: ATA.146, 170-173, 199-213, 234-238, BAT.1, 13-14.
Defoe: BAT.7-10.

RESCUE TUGS

ATR.1–40, 50–89.

Displacement:	852 tons.
Dimensions:	147 (wl) 165½ (oa) × 33¼ × 15½ ft.
Machinery:	1-shaft reciprocating (VTE), S.H.P. 1,500 = 12.5 knots.
Armament:	1—3 in. gun.
Complement:	52.
War loss:	ATR.15.

Notes:—Built 1943-45. All sold 1946-48. ATR.17-20 transferred to R.N. in 1944. Wooden hulls.

BUILDERS:

Bellingham: ATR.68-73.
Burger (Manitowoc): ATR.88-89.
Camden Sbdg. (Me.): ATR.17-22, 74-79.
Colberg (Stockton, Cal.): ATR.50-53.
Dachel-Carter (Benton Harbor, Mich.): ATR.54-57.
Delaware Bay Sbdg. (Leesburg, N.J.): ATR.13-14, 58-59.
Fulton (Antioch, Cal.): ATR.23-28.
Island Docks (Kingston, N.Y.): ATR.82-85.
Jakobson (Oyster Bay): ATR.15-16, 66-67.
Kruse & Banks (North Bend, Ore.): ATR.80-81, 86-87.
Lynch Sbdg. (San Diego): ATR.35-40.
Northwestern (Bellingham): ATR.31-34.
Frank L. Sample (Boothbay, Me.): ATR.7-12.
Wheeler (Brooklyn): ATR.1-6, 29-30, 60-65.

MISCELLANEOUS AUXILIARIES

Displacement:	19,700 tons.
Dimensions:	555½ (wl) 562 (oa) × 93 × 28¼ ft.
Machinery:	4-shaft geared turbines, S.H.P. 29,000 = 18 knots.
Armament:	6—12 in., 16—5 in., 8—3 in. guns.
Complement:	400.

AG.17	WYOMING (ex-BB.32)	Cramp	25.5.11	Scrapped Newark 1948.

Notes:—Gunnery training ship, converted in 1932. Sister to battleship ARKANSAS. Remaining turrets removed in 1944; re-armed with 10—5 in., 4—3 in., 11—40 mm. A.A. guns.

U.S.S. Wyoming (AG17). Gunnery training ship, 1945. Former battleship of Arkansas class. Note variety of types of guns.

Another view of the U.S.S. Wyoming (AG17). Note twin 5in. turrets on old barbettes.

U.S.S. Menemsha (AG39). Weather ship, 22nd January 1942, later transferred to Coast Guard.

Displacement:	19,800 tons.				
Dimensions:	512 (wl) 521½ (oa) × 106 × 29¼ ft.				
Machinery:	4-shaft geared turbines, S.H.P. 28,000 = 21 knots.				
Armament:	Unarmed.				

AG.16	UTAH (ex-BB.31)	New York Sbdg.	23.12.09	Lost 7/12/41.

Notes:—Mobile target ship converted in 1931.

		Tonnage Built	Acquired	
AG.12	GOLD STAR	5066/20	11.21	Scrapped 1946.
AG.23	SEQUOIA	100/25	3.33	
AG.24	SEMMES (ex-DD.189)	1190/18	*7.35	Sold 11/46.
AG.25	POTOMAC (ex-C.G.)	367/34	3.36	Merc. (1946).
AG.27	ROBERT L. BARNES (ex-AO.14)	1914/17	6.18	Captured 8/12/41.
AG.29	BEAR (ex-Bear of Oakland, ex-C.G. Bear)	648/74	12.41	Merc. ARCTIC BEAR (1948); lost 19/3/63.
AG.31	ARGONNE (ex-AS.10 ex-AP.4)	7556/20	11.21	Scrapped 1951.
AG.33	KAULA (ex-Cubahama)	932/38	1.41	Returned 7/46.
AG.35	CALYPSO (ex-C.G.)	367/33	5.41	Returned 1/42.
AG.36	MANASQUAN (ex-Aetna)	2016/18	10.41	C.G. WIX 273 (6/42).
AG.37	MANOMET (ex-John J. O'Hagan)	1998/18	9.41	ARIES (AK 51, 1/42).
AG.38	MATINICUS (ex-Saginaw)	2153/19	9.41	GEMINI (AK 52, 1/42).
AG.39	MENEMSHA (ex-John Gehm)	1991/18	9.41	C.G. WAG 274 (6/42).
AG.40	MONOMOY (ex-J. Floyd Massey)	2084/18	9.41	C.G. WAG 275 (6/42).
AG.41	MIDWAY (ex-Tyee)	1362/20	4.42	PANAY (5/43); merc. LLOYD QUINTO (1946)
AG.42	CAMANGA (ex-Oliver Olson)	2235/18)	4.42	Returned 12/45.
AG.43	MAJABA (ex-El Capitan)	2227/19	4.42	IX 102 (7/43); returned 3/46.
AG.44	MALANAO (ex-Florence Olson)	1437/12	5.42	Scrapped 1946.
AG.45	TAGANAK (ex-Olympic)	1876/18	5.42	Merc. GLENTO (1947).
AG.46	TULURAN (ex-Anna Schafer)	1985/17	10.42	Scrapped 1947.
AG.47	MANHASSET (ex-Wilton)	1827/23	1.42	C.G. WAG 276 (6/42).
AG.48	MUSKEGET (ex-Cornish)	1827/22	12.41	C.G. (6/42); lost 9/9/42.

AG.49	ANACAPA (ex-Coos Bay)	3321/19	6.42	Merc. GEORGE OLSON (1947).
AG.50	KOPARA (ex-AK.62)	679/38	8.42	Returned 1/45.
AG.66	BESBORO (ex-Lurline Burns)	2865/18	6.43	Merc. SHAPUR (1947).
AG.72	PARRIS ISLAND (ex-PCE.901)	795/43	*4.44	Merc. (1948).
	ATIK (ex-Carolyn)	3209/12	3.42	Lost 27/3/42.

* Converted

Notes:—ANACAPA and ATIK served as Q-ships. AG.36-40 and 47-48 were weather ships; AG.25, the presidential yacht; others were small cargo ships and transports used for coastal and inter-island service. ATIK never received a serial number. AG.61-65 were 176 ft. ice-breaking tugs built for U.S.S.R. AG.68-71 and 73-78 may be found under repair ships on p. 296. AG.1, 30 and 32 were surveying vessels (p. 317). Many old destroyers received AG numbers in 1944-45 upon being relegated to training duties.

UNCLASSIFIED VESSELS

Former combatant vessels retained on the navy list as relics, training ships or as adapted for other harbor duties.

IX.2	DESPATCH (ex-cruiser Boston)	3000/84	Scuttled 8/4/46.
IX.8	CUMBERLAND	1800/04	Sold 8/47.
IX.13	HARTFORD	2790/58	Scrapped 1958.
IX.15	PRAIRIE STATE (ex-BB.7, Illinois)	11500/98	Scrapped 1956.
IX.20	CONSTELLATION	1970/1797	Stricken 1956.
IX.21	CONSTITUTION	2200/1797	
IX.22	OREGON (ex-BB.3)	10300/93	Sold 12/42; hulk scrapped 1956.
IX.25	REINA MERCEDES (old Spanish cruiser)	2835/87	Scrapped 1958.
IX.28	WHEELING (ex-PG.14)	870/97	Sold 10/46.
IX.30	DOVER (ex-PG.8, Wilmington)	1280/95	Scuttled 1947.
IX.39	SEATTLE (ex-CA.11)	13700/05	Scrapped 1947.
IX.40	OLYMPIA (ex-cruiser 6)	5400/92	Discarded 1957.
IX.44	DCH-1 (ex-DD.163, Walker)	1190/18	Lost 28/12/41.
IX.46	TRANSFER	250/05	Merc. (1945).
IX.56	(unnamed) (ex-AT.52, Navajo)	800/07	Sold 2/46.
IX.98	MOOSEHEAD (ex-YW.56, ex-DD.259, Turner)	1190/19	Scrapped 1947.
AB.1	KEARSARGE (ex-BB.5)	11540/98	Scrapped 1955.

Former merchant vessels acquired for use as cargo ships, storage hulks, barracks ships, training ships and other harbor duties.

IX.29	WILMETTE (ex-Eastland)	1961/03	11.17	Scrapped 1947.

U.S.S. Ocelot (IX110). Barracks ship used as flagship of Service Squadron 10, 6th May 1944.

U.S.S. President Warfield (IX169). Barracks ship, July 1945. Formerly a Chesapeake Bay cruise ship, she ended her days as the Palestine blockade runner Exodus in 1947.

IX.33	NEWTON	5450/19	10.22	Scrapped 1946.
IX.42	CAMDEN (ex-AS.6, ex-Kiel)	4752/00	8.17	Sold 10/46.
IX.45	FAVORITE	1223/07	10.40	Sold 3/48.
IX.53	SEA OTTER II	1900/41	.41	Sold 6/42.
IX.55	BLACK DOUGLAS (ex-Fish & Wildlife Service)	371/30	.41	PYc 45 (4/43); returned 10/44.
IX.66	MIGRANT	661/29	5.42	Merc. FIMBER (1946); lost 13/7/53.
IX.67	GUINEVERE	508/21	6.43	Sold 4/46.
IX.71	KAILUA (ex-Dickinson)	831/23	5/43	Scuttled 7/2/46.
IX.72	LIBERTY BELLE (ex-City of Philadelphia)	622/09	4/42	Sold 4/47.
IX.80	CHRISTIANA (ex-Azalea)	393/91	8.42	YAG 32 (11/43); sold 2/46.
IX.96	RICHARD PECK	2906/92	1.41	Merc. ELISHA LEE (1947).
IX.99	SEA CLOUD (ex-C.G. WPG.284)	2323/31	4.43	Discarded 11/44.
IX.101	BIG CHIEF	382/97	5.43	Merc. B. O. COLONNA (1947).
IX.103	E. A. POE	7176/42	11.42	Scrapped 1949.
IX.104	P. H. BURNETT	7176/42	8.43	Returned 8/46.
IX.106	GREYHOUND (ex-Yale)	3818/06	4.43	Scrapped 1949.
IX.108	ATLANTIDA	4191/24	9.43	Returned 5/44.
IX.109	ANTELOPE (ex-M. H. de Young)	7176/43	10.43	Scrapped 1948.
IX.110	OCELOT (ex-Yomachichi)	5868/19	10.43	Lost 9/10/45; hulk scrapped 1949.
IX.146	FORTUNE (ex-City of Elwood)	6197/20	2.44	AVS 2 (5/45); scrapped 1946.
IX.147	SUPPLY (ex-Ward)	6167/21	2.44	AVS 1 (5/45); scrapped 1946.
IX.148	NORTH STAR (ex-C.G. WPG.59)	1435/32	1.44	Merc. (1946).
IX.155	MUSTANG (ex-William H. Smith)	566/99	1.44	Sold 11/46.
IX.156	CITY OF DALHART	5878/21	2.44	Scrapped 1947.
IX.157	ORVETTA (ex-Tampa)	5959/20	4.44	Scrapped 1949.
IX.167	LEYDEN (ex-Northland)	3336/10	5.44	Merc. HUNG CHONG (1946).
IX.168	SOUTHLAND	2081/08	5.44	Merc. HUNG YUNG (1946).
IX.169	PRESIDENT WARFIELD	1814/28	5.44	Merc. EXODUS (1947).
IX.205	CALLAO (ex-Externstiene)	1015/43	1.45	Scrapped 1951.
IX.208	DOMINO	3170/19	—	Cancelled 6/45.
IX.215	DON MARQUIS	7176/43	5.45	Returned 11/45.
IX.216	UNICOI	5875/20	4.45	Scrapped 1947

IX.223	TRIANA (ex-Elinor Wylie)	7176/44	5.45	Returned 2/46.
IX.225	HARCOURT (ex-John M. Clayton)	7176/42	6.45	Returned 5/46.
IX.226	ARANER (ex-Juan de Fuca)	7176/42	9.45	Returned 8/46.
IX.227	GAMAGE (ex-William B. Allison)	7176/43	7.45	Returned 4/46.
IX.228	JUSTIN (ex-Gus W. Darnell)	7247/44	9.45	Returned 1/46.

THE UNITED STATES COAST GUARD

The Coast Guard is a separate service, normally under the Treasury Department, which has customarily been transferred to the Navy Department in times of war. Between 1st November, 1941, and 31st December, 1945, the Coast Guard operated as part of the Navy.

The Revenue Cutter Service, established in 1790, was merged with the Lifesaving Service in 1915 and the new organization was titled the United States Coast Guard. On 1st July, 1939, the Lighthouse Service was merged with the Coast Guard. Its principal functions are enforcement of maritime and customs laws, ice patrol, navigational aids, lifesaving and similar services.

The large gunboat class cutters and patrol boats made excellent convoy escorts and were used in this service throughout the war. The smaller 83 ft. boats were used at Normandy as well as for coast patrols. A large number of trawlers were taken over early in the war to augment the strength of the Coast Guard.

Coast Guardsmen also manned 351 navy vessels, including 30 destroyer escorts, 75 frigates, 22 transports, 9 attack transports, 15 cargo ships, 5 attack cargo ships, 18 gasoline tankers, 76 LST's, 28 LCI's and 33 smaller craft; 288 army vessels were also C.G. manned.

Coast Guard cutters are rated by length, and those under 100 feet are known by numbers only, the first two digits of their number being the length. Early in the war the Coast Guard assigned a new series of numbers to its ships, using navy type symbols prefixed with the letter "G", later changed to "W".

GUNBOAT TYPE CUTTERS

Displacement: 1,090 tons.
Dimensions: 206 (oa) × 32 × 13½ ft.
Machinery: 1-shaft reciprocating (VTE), S.H.P. 2,400 = 16 knots.
Complement: 72.

| WPG.85 | GRESHAM | Globe I.W. | 1897 | Merc. T. V. McALLISTER (1945), TRADE WINDS (1947) |

Displacement: 1,181 tons.
Dimensions: 190 (oa) × 32 × 14¼ ft.
Machinery: 1-shaft reciprocating, S.H.P. 1,000 = 13 knots.
Armament: 2—3 in. guns.

U.S.C.G.C. Unalga (WPG53) 1945, with 2 single 3in. guns fore and aft.

U.S.C.G.C. Modoc (WPG46). Tampa class cutter.

WPG.53	UNALGA	Newport News	10. 2.12	Sold 7/46.

Displacement: 964 tons.
Dimensions: 165¾ (oa) × 32 × 11 ft.
Machinery: 1-shaft reciprocating, S.H.P. 1,000 = 12 knots.
Armament: 2—3 in. guns.
Complement: 74.

WPG.50	OSSIPEE	⎫ Newport	1. 5.15	Sold 9/46.
WPG.52	TALLAPOOSA	⎬ News	1. 5.15	Merc. SANTA MARIA (1947).

Displacement: 900 tons.
Dimensions: 158¼ (oa) × 30 × 13¾ ft.
Machinery: 1-shaft reciprocating, S.H.P. 1,800 = 13 knots.

WPG.54	SHAWNEE	General Engineering (Oakland)	15.11.21	Sold 11/47.

TAMPA CLASS

Displacement: 1,780 tons.
Dimensions: 240 (oa) × 39 × 16½ ft.
Machinery: 1-shaft turbo-electric drive, S.H.P. 2,600 = 16 knots.
Armament: 2—5 in., 2—3 in., 4—20 mm. guns.

WPG.45	HAIDA	⎫	19. 4.21	Sold 1/48.
WPG.46	MODOC	⎬ General Eng. (Oakland)	1.10.21	Merc. AMALIA V (1948), MACHALA (1950), scrapped 1964.
WPG.47	MOJAVE		7. 9.21	Sold 2/48.
WPG.48	TAMPA	⎭	19. 4.21	Merc. RIGEL KENT (1948), scrapped 1951.

NORTHLAND

Displacement: 2,065 tons.
Dimensions: 216 (oa) × 39 × 15 ft.
Machinery: 1-shaft Diesel-electric drive, B.H.P. 1,200 = 11 knots.
Armament: 2—3 in., 4—20 mm. guns; 1 seaplane.
Complement: 105.

U.S.C.G.C. Northland (WPG49). Specially designed for Arctic operations. Note seaplane aft.

U.S.C.G.C. Mojave (WPG47). Tampa class cutter, 1942, operating amid ice floes off Greenland.

U.S.C.G.C. Algonquin (WPG75). Algonquin class cutter. Masts and funnel of another ship appear behind forward gun.

U.S.C.G.C. Tahoma (WPG80).

U.S.C.G.C. Spencer (WPG36). Treasury class cutter, with flush-deck destroyer Bulmer (DD222) alongside, 14th April 1944. *[Official U.S. Navy*

U.S C.G.C. Ingham (WPG35), Treasury class cutter, in rough weather in the North Atlantic, 1943.

U.S.C.G.C. Bibb (WPG31), Treasury class cutter, 1942, with 2-5in. and 4-3in. guns.

U.S.C.G.C. Taney (WPG37). Treasury class cutter, 18th February 1944, with 4-5in. guns in single turrets, an arrangement which proved unsuccessful.

[*Official U.S. Navy*

U.S.C.G.C. Bibb (WPG31). Treasury class cutter, 1946, with reduced armament. (See page 369).

370

U.S.C.G.C. Duane (WAGC33). Treasury class cutter as amphibious force flagship.

U.S.C.G.C. Ingham (WAGC35). Treasury class cutter as amphibious force flagship, 1944.

U.S.C.G.C. Campbell (WAGC32). Treasury class cutter as amphibious force flagship, 1945. Mainmast has been added, forward 5in. gun moved to deck level, and amidships superstructure built up.

| WPG.49 | NORTHLAND Newport
News | 5. 2.27 | Merc. (1947), Israeli
MATZPEN (1948)
scrapped 1962. |

Notes:—Specially designed for operations in the Bering Sea.

The ten ships of the **Champlain** class, built in 1929-30, were transferred to R.N. in 1941.

Algonquin class

Displacement: 1,005 tons.
Dimensions: 165 (oa) × 36 × 13½ ft.
Machinery: 1-shaft geared turbines, S.H.P. 1,500 = 13 knots.
Armament: 2—3 in., 3—20 mm. guns.
Complement: 105.

WPG.75	ALGONQUIN	⎱ Pusey &	25. 7.34	Scrapped 1948.
WPG.75	COMANCHE	⎰ Jones	9.34	Merc. RELIEF (1949).
WPG.77	ESCANABA	Defoe	17. 9.32	Lost 13/6/43.
WPG.78	MOHAWK	Pusey & Jones	23.10.34	Sold 11/48.
WPG.79	ONONDAGA		2. 8.34	Sold 12/54.
WPG.80	TAHOMA	⎱ Defoe	5. 9.34	GUARD (1950); merc. STEERS M.K. (1955).

Treasury class

Displacement: 2,216 tons.
Dimensions: 308 (wl) 327 (oa) × 41 × 12½ ft.
Machinery: 2-shaft geared turbines, S.H.P. 6,200 = 20 knots.
Armament: 3—5 in., 3—3 in. guns.
Complement: 125.

WPG.31	BIBB	Charleston N.Yd.	14. 1.37	
WPG.32	CAMPBELL	⎱ Philadel-	3. 6.36	
WPG.33	DUANE	⎰ phia N.Yd.	3. 6.36	
WPG.34	ALEXANDER HAMILTON	New York N.Yd.	10.11.36	Lost 29/1/42.
WPG.35	INGHAM	Philadel- phia N.Yd.	3. 6.36	
WPG.36	SPENCER	New York N.Yd.	6. 1.37	
WPG.37	TANEY	Philadel- phia N.Yd.	3. 6.36	

Notes:—Named after Secretaries of the Treasury; names shortened to surnames only in 1942. Converted to amphibious force flagships in 1944-45, but retained C.G. numbers prefixed by WAGC; reverted to gunboat type in 1946. Construction of three additional projected vessels suspended in 1941.

U.S.C.G.C. Owasco (WPG39). Owasco class cutter, 18th July 1945, as completed.

U.S.C.G.C. Mendota (WPG69). Owasco class cutter, 1945.

U.S.C.G.C. Mayflower (WPG183). Former presidential yacht classed as a gunboat, 18th February 1944.
[*Official U.S. Navy*

U.S.C.G.C. Marita (WPY175). Patrol vessel, converted from small freighter, originally built in W.W.I as H.M.S. Kilmacrennan.

Owasco class

Displacement: 1,563 tons.
Dimensions: 255 (oa) × 43 × 15 ft.
Machinery: 1-shaft Diesel-electric drive, S.H.P. 1,400 = 18 knots.
Armament: 4—5 in. (2 × 2), 8—40 mm. guns.
Complement: 140.

WPG.39	OWASCO		18. 6.44	
WPG.40	WINNEBAGO		2. 7.44	
WPG.41	CHAUTAQUA		14. 5.44	
WPG.42	SEBAGO (ex-Wachusett)		28. 5.44	
WPG.43	IROQUOIS		22.10.44	Sold 1965.
WPG.44	WACHUSETT (ex-Huron)	Western Pipe (San Pedro)	5.11.44	
WPG.64	ESCANABA (ex-Otsego)		23. 3.45	
WPG.65	WINONA		22. 4.45	
WPG.66	KLAMATH		2. 9.45	
WPG.67	MINNETONKA (ex-Sunapee)		21.11.45	
WPG.68	ANDROS-COGGIN		16. 9.45	
WPG.69	MENDOTA	Coast Guard Yd. (Curtis Bay)	29. 2.44	
WPG.70	PONTCHAR-TRAIN (ex-Okeechobee)		29. 2.44	

Converted types:

		Gross t'age Built	Acquired	Fate
WPG.182	BODKIN (ex-Burke)	/34	—	Cancelled.
WPG.181	COBB (ex-Governor Cobb)	2522/06	7.43	Scrapped 1947.
WPG.183	MAYFLOWER (ex-PY.1)	/96	9.43	Sold 10/45.
WPG.59	NORTH STAR	1435/32	5.41	U.S.N. IX 148 (1/44).
WPG.122	NOURMAHAL (ex-PG.72)	1969/28	12.43	Sold 5/46.
WPG.284	SEA CLOUD	2323/31	4.42	U.S.N. IX 99 (4/43).

Notes:—COBB was fitted with an experimental helicopter landing deck, was armed with 2—5 in. guns. MAYFLOWER, the former presidential yacht, had 1—5 in., 2—3 in. and NOURMAHAL, 1—4 in. guns.

U.S.C.G.C. Southwind (WAG280). Wind class icebreaker. Note cranes and catapult abaft funnel.

U.S.C.G.C. Evergreen (WAGL295). One of 39 180ft. lighthouse tenders built during the war.

377

Wind class (Icebreakers)

Displacement: 3,500 tons.
Dimensions: 269 (oa) × 63½ × 25¾ ft.
Machinery: 3-shaft Diesel-electric drive (1 bow), S.H.P. 13,300 = 16 knots.
Armament: 4—5 in., 12—40 mm. guns; 1 aircraft.

WAG.278	NORTHWIND (i)		28.12.42	Russian SEVERNI VETER (1945); U.S.N. STATEN ISLAND (AGB 5) (1949).
WAG.279	EASTWIND		6. 2.43	
WAG.280	SOUTHWIND	Western Pipe (San Pedro)	8. 3.43	Russian KAPITAN BELUSOV (1945); U.S.N. ATKA (AGB 3) (1949).
WAG.281	WESTWIND		31. 3.43	Russian SEVERNI POLIUS (1945); returned 1949.
WAG.282	NORTHWIND (ii)		25. 2.45	

Note:- Two sisters, BURTON ISLAND and EDISTO (AG88-89), were completed after the war.

PATROL BOATS

Active class

Displacement: 220 tons.
Dimensions: 125 (oa) × 23½ × 9 ft.
Machinery: 2-shaft Diesel motors, S.H.P. 600 = 13 knots (except 125, 138, 141, 145, 150, 152, 155: 350 = 11 knots).
Armament: 1—3 in. gun.
Complement: 38.

WPC.125	ACTIVE		30.11.26	
WPC.126	AGASSIZ		30.11.26	
WPC.127	ALERT		30.11.26	
WPC.128	ANTIETAM		30.11.26	BEDLOE (1943); lost 14/9/44.
WPC.129	BONHAM		30.11.26	Merc. POLAR STAR (1959).
WPC.130	BOUTWELL	New York Sbdg.	27. 1.27	Merc. STATE BELL (1964).
WPC.131	CAHOONE		27. 1.27	
WPC.132	CARTIGAN		27. 1.27	
WPC.133	COLFAX (ex-Montgomery)		22. 3.27	Merc. (1956).
WPC.134	CRAWFORD		27. 1.27	Merc. (1947).
WPC.135	DILIGENCE		27. 1.27	Sold 1964.
WPC.136	DIX		27. 1.27	Merc. VALKYRIE (1948).

U.S.C.G.C. Active (WPC125). Active class cutter, 1945.

U.S.C.G.C. Harriet Lane (WPC141). Active class cutter, February 1944. [*Official U.S. Navy*

WPC.137	EWING	⎫	15. 3.27	
WPC.138	FAUNCE		15. 3.27	Merc. HUMBLE AC-2 (1948), MYRA WHITE (1961) VITOW II (1964).
WPC.139	FREDERICK LEE		15. 3.27	
WPC.140	GENERAL GREENE		14. 2.27	
WPC.141	HARRIET LANE		30.11.26	Merc. HUMBLE AC-4 (1949).
WPC.142	JACKSON		14. 2.27	Lost 14/9/44.
WPC.143	KIMBALL		25. 4.27	
WPC.144	LEGARE		14. 2.27	
WPC.145	MARION		15. 3.27	Merc. TOP CAT (1963).
WPC.146	McLANE		22. 3.27	
WPC.147	MORRIS		4. 4.27	
WPC.148	NEMAHA	New York Sbdg.	4. 4.27	Merc. (1948), SEA MONARCH II (1952), LE ROI (1958).
WPC.149	PULASKI		4. 4.27	Merc. (1948), CEMENTOS No. 1 (1957).
WPC.150	RELIANCE		18. 4.27	Sold 6/48.
WPC.151	RUSH		18. 4.27	Merc. HUMBLE AC-1 (1948), VITOW I (1964).
WPC.152	TIGER		18. 4.27	Merc. (1948).
WPC.153	TRAVIS		18. 4.27	Sold 1963.
WPC.154	VIGILANT		25. 4.27	Merc. (1956), BUNKER HILL (19).
WPC.155	WOODBURY		2. 5.27	Merc. HUMBLE AC-3 (1948), CHALLENGE (1963).
WPC.156	YEATON		2. 5.27	
WIX.157	CUYAHOGA (ex-WPC, ex-AG.26, ex-C.G.)	⎭	27. 1.27	Sold 1964.

Notes:—CUYAHOGA served in U.S.N. 1933-1941.

Argo class

Displacement:	337 tons.	
Dimensions:	165 (oa) × 25¼ × 9½ ft.	
Machinery:	2-shaft Diesel motors, B.H.P. 1,340 = 16 knots.	
Armament:	2—3 in., 2—20 mm. A.A. guns.	
Complement:	50.	

WPC.100	ARGO	Mathis	12.11.32	Merc. CIRCLE LINE XII (1955).
WPC.101	ARIADNE	⎱Lake	21. 7.34	
WPC.102	ATALANTA	⎰ Union	16. 6.34	Sold 12/54.
WPC.103	AURORA		28.11.31	
WPC.104	CALYPSO (ex-AG.35)	⎱Bath I.W.	6. 1.32	Merc. CIRCLE LINE XI (1955).
WPC.105	CYANE	Lake Union	30. 8.34	Sold 12/54.

U.S.C.G.C. Seabird (WYP330). Patrol vessel, May 1943.

U.S.C.G.C. Nike (WPC112). Argo class cutter, November 1943. [*Official U.S. Navy*

U.S.C.G.C. 83306. 83ft. patrol boat.

U.S.C.G.C. Eastwind (WAG279). Wind class icebreaker.

WPC.106	DAPHNE	Bath I.W.	27. 1.32	Merc. (1955).
WPC.107	DIONE	Manitowoc	30. 6.34	
WPC.108	GALATEA	Mathis	10.12.32	Dominican RESTAUR-ACION (1948).
WPC.109	HERMES	⎫	23. 2.32	Sold 5/58.
WPC.110	ICARUS	⎬ Bath I.W.	19. 3.32	Dominican INDEPEN-DENCIA (1948).
WPC.111	NEMESIS	⎰ Marietta	7. 7.34	
WPC.112	NIKE	⎱	.34	
WPC.113	PANDORA	Manitowoc	30. 6.34	Discarded 1959.
WPC.114	PERSEUS	⎫	11. 4.32	Merc. CIRCLE LINE XV (1962).
WPC.115	THETIS	⎬ Bath I.W.	9.11.31	Dominican LIBERTAD (1948).
WPC.116	TRITON	Marietta	.34	

Notes:—ELECTRA of this class was transferred to U.S.N. as presidential yacht POTOMAC (AG.25) in 1935.

83 ft. Type

Nos. 83300–83529.

Displacement: 50 tons.
Dimensions: 83 (oa) × 15¾ × 4½ ft.
Machinery: 2-shaft gasoline motors, H.P. 1,200 = 23.5 knots.
Armament: 1—20 mm. gun.
Complement: 10.
War losses: 83301, 83415, 83421, 83471.

Notes:— Built 1941-44. Eight were transferred to Cuba, two to Colombia, six to Peru, and three to Mexico. In this (and following) classes, the first two digits of the number refer to the length. Twelve additional boats of this type were built with U.S.N. numbers (C-56189 to 56200) and transferred to Cuba (4), Venezuela (4), Dominican Republic (3) and Haiti (1). 83300-83383 were originally numbered CG-450-489, 491-499, 600-634.

80 ft. Type

Nos. 80300–80308.

Displacement: 52 tons.
Dimensions: 80¾ (oa) × 15¾ × 4 ft.
Machinery: 2-shaft gasoline motors, H.P. 1,600 = 25 knots.
Armament: 1—1 pdr. gun.

Notes:—Built 1937. Originally numbered CG-406-414.

78 ft. Type

Nos. 78300–78305.

Displacement: 78¾ (oa) × 14½ × 4 ft.
Machinery: 2-shaft gasoline motors, H.P. 1,070 = 21.7 knots.
Armament: 1—1 pdr. gun.

Notes:—Built 1929-31. Originally numbered CG-400-405.

74 ft. Type

Nos. 74300–74351.

Displacement: 37 tons.
Dimensions: 74¾ (oa) × 13¼ × 4 ft.
Machinery: 2-shaft gasoline motors, H.P. 400 = 13.5 knots.
Armament: 1—1 pdr. gun.
War loss: 74327.

Notes:—Built 1924-25. Originally numbered between CG-100-302. Fifty-one of this class had been transferred to U.S.N. as patrol craft prior to the war.

Converted vessels:

		Gross t'age Built	Acquired	
WYP.164	AIVIK (ex-Arlington)	251/36	6.42	Returned 9/44.
WYP.168	AKLAK (ex-Weymouth)	170/41	7.42	Returned 4/44.
WYP.172	ALATOK (ex-Hekla)	386/22	6.42	Returned 3/44.
WYP.166	AMAROK (ex-Lark)	237/38	8.42	Returned 2/44.
WYP.167	ARLUK (ex-Atlantic)	163/34	7.42	Returned 7/44.
WYP.165	ARVEK (ex-Triton)	172/36	7.42	Returned 8/44.
WYP.163	ATAK (ex-Winchester)	243/37	6.42	Returned 7/44.
WPYc.346	BEDFORD (ex-Condor)	201/13	7.42	U.S.N. PER-SEVERANCE (PYc 44).
WYP.373	BELLEFONT (ex-F. & W.S. Albatross III)	341/26	4.44	Returned Fish & Wildlife Service 8/44.
WPC.372	BELLEVILLE (ex-Liberty II, ex-SC-258)	79/19	3.42	Returned 5/45.
WYP.341	BELMONT (ex-Thorarinn)	249/29	12.42	Returned.
WYP.367	BLACK ROCK (ex-The Boys)	78/24	9.42	Haitian AMIRAL KILLICK (11/55)
WPYc.369	BLANCHARD (ex-Nedra B.)	101/10	.42	Returned 5/45.
WPYc.343	BLANCO (ex-Atlantic)	198/23	8.42	Returned.
WPC.336	BLAZE (ex-SC-231)	/91	.42	Lost.
WYP.342	*BODEGA (ex-Thordr)	249/30	11.42	Lost 20/12/43.
WPC.335	BOONE (ex-SC-229)	/19	1.43	Returned.
WPYc.352	BOULDER (ex-Elkhorn)	/	6.42	Returned.
WPC.365	BOWSTRING (ex-SC-238)	/19		
WYP.340	BRONCO (ex-Star XVIII)	249/30	12.42	Returned.
WYP.312	*BRUSSTAR (ex-William S. Brusstar)	202/02	7.42	Returned.
WYP.174	CADDO (ex-Tanginak)	151/07	.42	Returned.
WYP.320	*CONANT (ex-Henry W. Conant)	260/19	7.42	Returned.
WYP.314	*COVINGTON (ex-William T. Covington, Jr.)	263/23	7.42	Returned.
WYP.353	*DOW (ex-Annie Dow)	241/24	10.42	Lost 15/10/43.

384

WPY.357	*EDWARDS (ex-Wilbert A. Edwards)	343/12	10.42 Returned.
WYP.360	*EUPHANE (ex-Helen Euphane)	168/02	10.42 Returned.
WPYc.386	GERTRUDE L. THEBAUD	137/30	11.42 Returned. Returned.
WYP.381	GLOBE (ex-Globe II)	/37	
WYP.380	GLOBE VIII	297/36	12.43 Returned.
WYP.325	*HUMPHREYS (ex-H. R. Humphreys)	211/19	.42 Discarded. Returned.
WYP.356	*JOE (ex-Little Joe)	250/22	10.42
WYP.173	KODIAK	148/12	.42 Returned.
WPYc.345	MADALAN	357/28	8.42 Returned.
WYP.323	*MARGARET	268/12	7.42 Returned.
WPY.175	MARITA (ex-Kaspar, ex-H.M.S. Kilmacrennan)	632/18	11.42 Returned 11/44.
WYP.358	*MESSICK (ex-W. L. Messick)	326/11	10.42 Returned.
WPYc.159	MICAWBER (ex-My Nevada)	153/26	7.42 Discarded.
WYP.169	NANOK (ex-North Star)	220/41	6.42 Returned.
WYP.170	NATSEK (ex-Belmont)	225/41	5.42 Lost 17/12/42.
WPYc.337	NELLWOOD (ex-Nellwood II)	244/29	8.42 Returned.
WYP.171	NOGAK (ex-St. George)	176/40	7.42 Returned.
WYP.361	*NORTHUMBERLAND	169/97	8.42 Returned.
WYP.379	OTTERN	361/37	Returned.
WYP.329	*PELICAN	384/19	5.42 Returned.
WYP.362	*POCAHONTAS	286/14	9.42 Returned.
WYP.382	POL (ex-Pol VII)	338/36	12.42 Returned.
WYP.322	*REED (ex-E. Warren Reed)	167/99	7.42 Returned.
WYP.328	*ROWE (ex-W. R. Rowe)	218/01	7.42 Returned.
WYP.330	*SEABIRD	386/19	8.42 Returned.
WYP.363	*STEPHEN McKEEVER	223/11	10.42 Returned.
WPYc.348	THALASSA	104/30	8.42 Returned; lost 31/12/48.
WYP.383	THORFINN	249/29	9.42
WYP.384	THORFJELL	313/34	12.42
WYP.377	THORGAUT	313/39	12.42
WYP.378	THORIS	305/36	1.43 Returned.
WYP.318	*VERNON McNEAL	265/04	7.42 Returned.
WYP.354	*WARREN EDWARDS	231/18	10.42 Returned.
WPYc.158	WICOMICO (ex-Dupont)	303/14	10.42 Returned.
WYP.333	*WILCOX (ex-Rowland H. Wilcox).	247/11	10.42 Lost 30/9/43.

* Name prefixed with EM (Emergency Manning).

LIGHTHOUSE TENDERS

WAGL.200	ACACIA (ex-Army Gen. John P. Story)	1130/19	Lost 15/3/42.
WAGL.216	ALDER	80/17	Merc. LUMMI (1948).

WAGL.177	ALMOND (ex-merc. La Salle)	677/22	Returned 8/46.
WAGL.223	ALTHEA	120/30	
WAGL.201	AMARANTH	975/92	Merc. SOUTH WING (1946).
WAGL.202	ANEMONE	1057/08	Philippine (7/47).
WAGL.203	ARBUTUS	960/33	
WAGL.176	ARROWWOOD (ex-merc. Cadillac)	1147/28	Merc. LADY HAMILTON (1946).
WAGL.204	ASPEN	415/06	Sold 1/48.
WAGL.269	ASTER	109/21	Sold 10/46.
WAGL.262	AZALEA	/15	Sold 1/46.
WAGL.294	BARBERRY	178/42	
WAGL.205	BEECH	255/28	
WAGL.256	BIRCH	76/39	
WAGL.313	BLUEBELL	178/44	
WAGL.257	BLUEBONNET	184/39	
WAGL.299	BRIER	178/43	
WAGL.206	CAMELLIA	377/11	Dominican CAPOTILLO (1948).
WAGL.207	CEDAR	1370/17	Sold 6/55.
WAGL.178	CHAPARRAL (ex-merc. Halcyon)	/25	Sold 12/46.
WAGL.258	CHERRY	202/32	
WAGL.286	CLEMATIS	93/44	
WAGL.208	COLUMBINE	323/31	
WAGL.293	COSMOS	178/42	
WAGL.209	COTTONWOOD (ex-Le Clair)	243/15	Sold 5/47.
WAGL.210	CROCUS	910/04	Sold 7/46.
WAGL.211	CYPRESS	1057/08	Merc. DRAFIN (1947).
WAGL.288	DAHLIA	175/33	
WAGL.259	DOGWOOD	230/41	
WAGL.260	ELM	69/37	
WAGL.304	FERN	350/42	
WAGL.212	FIR	885/39	
WAGL.63	FORSYTHIA	230/40	
WAGL.160	FORWARD	210/25	Sold 7/47.
WAGL.285	FOXGLOVE	350/44	
WAGL.213	GOLDENROD	193/38	
WAGL.214	GREENBRIER	440/24	Merc. MISSISSIPPI (1948).
WAGL.215	HAWTHORN	875/21	
WAGL.217	HEMLOCK	960/34	Sold 1958.
WAGL.218	HIBISCUS	1057/08	Sold 6/47.
WAGL.219	HICKORY	400/33	
WAGL.220	HOLLYHOCK	885/37	
WAGL.221	HYACINTH	950/03	Sold 10/46.
WAGL.236	HYDRANGEA (ex-Mayflower)	668/97	Sold 10/45.
WAGL.222	ILEX (ex-Army Gen. Edmund Kirby)	1130/19	Sold 10/47.
WAGL.261	JASMINE	184/35	
WAGL.179	JONQUIL (ex-merc. Lucinda Clark)	107/37	Returned 12/43.

WAGL.224	JUNIPER	790/40	
WAGL.56	KICKAPOO (ex-Baldridge)	840/19	Sold 7/47.
WAGL.225	KUKUI	1057/08	Sold 4/47.
WAGL.310	LANTANA	273/43	
WAGL.226	LARKSPUR	703/03	Sold 2/46.
WAGL.227	LILAC	770/33	
WAGL.228	LINDEN	323/31	
WAGL.229	LOTUS (ex-Army Col. Albert Todd)	1130/19	Sold 6/47.
WAGL.230	LUPINE (ex-Army Gen. W. P. Randolph)	1130/19	Sold 11/47.
WAGL.231	MAGNOLIA	916/04	Lost 24/8/45.
WAGL.232	MANGROVE	821/97	Sold 3/47.
WAGL.233	MANZANITA	1057/08	Sold 4/47.
WAGL.234	MAPLE	342/39	
WAGL.235	MARIGOLD	696/90	Sold 10/46.
WAGL.237	MISTLETOE	770/39	
WAGL.263	MYRTLE	186/32	Sold 1964.
WAGL.238	NARCISSUS	342/39	
WAGL.239	OAK	875/21	
WAGL.264	OLEANDER	80/41	
WAGL.240	ORCHID	1057/08	Philippine (12/45).
WAGL.265	PALMETTO	170/17	Sold 4/59.
WAGL.161	PHLOX (ex-Nansemond)	210/26	Merc. SALVOR (1949).
WAGL.162	PINE (ex-Petrel)	210/26	Merc. (1948).
WAGL.266	POINCIANA	120/30	
WAGL.241	POPLAR	193/39	
WAGL.316	PRIMROSE	178/44	
WAGL.298	RAMBLER	178/43	
WAGL.267	RHODODENDRON	114/35	Sold 1959.
WAGL.242	ROSE	567/16	Sold 6/48.
WAGL.243	SEQUOIA	1057/08	Philippine (7/47).
WAGL.287	SHADBUSH	93/44	
WAGL.244	SHRUB	356/12	Merc. (1948).
WAGL.315	SMILAX	178/44	
WAGL.245	SPEEDWELL (ex-Army Col. John V. White)	1130/20	Sold 12/47.
WAGL.246	SPRUCE (ex-Army Col. Garland N. Whistler)	1130/20	Sold 5/50.
WAGL.311	SUMAC	350/44	
WAGL.247	SUNFLOWER	1246/06	Sold 2/47.
WAGL.268	SYCAMORE	230/41	
WAGL.248	TAMARACK	400/34	
WAGL.249	TULIP	1057/08	Philippine (7/47).
WAGL.317	VERBENA	178/44	
WAGL.250	VIOLET	1012/30	Sold 1963.
WAGL.251	WAKEROBIN	575/27	Sold 4/55.
WAGL.252	WALNUT	885/39	
WAGL.253	WILLOW	1070/27	Sold 3/45.
WAGL.254	WISTARIA	323/33	
WAGL.255	ZINNIA	342/39	

Notes:—All the older vessels were acquired from the Lighthouse Service when that service became part of the Coast Guard in 1939. ARROWWOOD, ALMOND, CHAPARRAL and JONQUIL were temporary wartime acquisitions. COTTONWOOD, GREENBRIER and WAKEROBIN were stern-wheelers, and WILLOW, a side-wheeler.

Displacement: 935 tons.
Dimensions: 180 × 37 × 12 ft.
Machinery: 1-shaft Diesel-electric drive, B.H.P. 1,200 = 14 knots.
Armament: 1—3 in., 2 or 4—40 mm. A.A. guns.

BALSAM, CACTUS, COWSLIP, WOODBINE, GENTIAN, LAUREL, CLOVER, EVERGREEN, SORREL, IRONWOOD, CITRUS, CONIFER, MADRONA, TUPELO, MESQUITE, BUTTONWOOD, PLANE-TREE, PAPAW, SWEETGUM, BASSWOOD, BITTERSWEET, BLACKHAW, BLACKTHORN, BRAMBLE, FIREBUSH, HORNBEAM, IRIS, MALLOW, MARIPOSA, REDBUD, SAGEBRUSH, SALVIA, SASSAFRAS, SEDGE, SPAR, SUNDEW, SWEETBRIAR, ACACIA (ex-Thistle), WOODRUSH. (WAGL.62, 270, 277, 289-292, 295-297, 300-303, 305-309, 388-407).

Notes:—Built 1941-44 by Zenith Dredge (Duluth) and Marine Iron & Sbdg. (Duluth).

TUGS

Displacement: 290 tons.
Dimensions: 110½ (oa) × 24 × 10½ ft.
Machinery: 1-shaft Diesel S.H.P. 1,000 = 12 knots.

WYT.86	CALUMET	Charleston N.Yd.	.34
WYT.87	HUDSON	Portsmouth N.Yd.	.34
WYT.88	NAVESINK	Charleston N.Yd.	.34
WYT.89	TUCKAHOE	Charleston N.Yd.	.34

Displacement: 328 tons.
Dimensions: 110 (oa) × 26½ × 10½ ft.
Machinery: 1-shaft diesel-electric drive, S.H.P. 800 = 12 knots.

WYT.90	ARUNDEL	Gulfport	24. 6.39
WYT.91	MAHONING	Gulfport	22. 7.39
WYT.92	NAUGATUCK	Defoe	23. 3.39
WYT.93	RARITAN	Defoe	23. 3.39
WYT.60	MANITOU	⎰ Coast Guard Yd.	29. 9.42
WYT.61	KAW	⎱ (Curtis Bay)	6.10.42
WYT.71	APALACHEE	⎰	.43
WYT.72	YANKTON	⎱	.43
WYT.73	MOHICAN	⎱	7,43
WYT.96	CHINOOK	⎭ Bushey	7.43
WYT.97	OJIBWAY	⎱	10. 8.43
WYT.98	SNOHOMISH	⎱	10. 8.43
WYT.99	SAUK	⎱	10. 8.43⁻

Miscellaneous tugs:

WYT.55	CARRABASSETT (ex-U.S.N. AT.35)	1133/19	5.24	Sold 7/46.
WYT.74	TIOGA (ex-Calumet)	170/94	10.94	Merc. JOHN F. DREWS (1947).
WYT.81	DAVEY	182/08	0.08	Sold 7/45.
WYT.84	WINNISIMMET	182/02	7.03	Merc. SOPHIA (1946).

U.S.C.G.C. Cobb (WPG181) Coastal steamer, classed as a gunboat, converted for experimental use with the Coast Guard's first helicopter unit.

U.S.C.G.C. Big Horn (WAO124). Navy oiler serving with the Coast Guard as a weather ship, 1944.

MISCELLANEOUS VESSELS

WIX.184	ALEXANDER GRAHAM BELL	7176/42		Returned 1945.
WAK.123	ASTERION (ex-AK.63, ex-Evelyn)	3140/12	1/44	Scrapped 7/46.
WIX.271	ATLANTIC	303/03	3/41	Sold 6/48.
WIX.272	BETA (ex-Alexander Hamilton, ex-U.S.S. Vicksburg, PG 11)	1000/96	8/21	Sold 3/46.
WAO.124	BIG HORN (ex-AO 45, ex-Gulfdawn)	6395/36	12/43	U.S.N. IX 207 (2/45).
WIX.347	BISON (ex-President)	730/10		Discarded.
WIX.344	BYRON (ex-City of New York)			Cancelled.
WIX.375	BONNEVILLE (ex-Islander, ex-SC 438)	/18		Discarded.
WIX.283	DANMARK	777/33	/41	Returned 1945.
WIX.180	MacNICHOL (ex-David C. MacNichol)	/91		Discarded.
WAG.27	MANASQUAN (ex-AG 36, ex-Aetna)	2016/18	10/43	Scrapped 1946.
WAG.276	MANHASSET (ex-AG 47, ex-Wilton)	1827/23	10/43	Merc. MAN-HASSET (1946)
WAG.274	MENEMSHA (ex-AG 39, ex-John Gehm)	1991/18	10/43	Scrapped 1951.
WAG.275	MONOMOY (ex-AG 40, ex-J. Floyd Massey Jr)	2084/18	10/43	Scrapped 1951.
WIX.338	NAVIGATION (ex-U.S.S. Sard, PYc 23, ex-Navigation)	212/22	3/42	U.S.N. YP 271.
WAK.169	NETTLE (ex-Army FS-396)	550/45	2/45	
WARC.58	PEQUOT (ex-Army Gen. Samuel M. Mills)	950/19	4/22	Scrapped 1947.
WAK.170	TRILLIUM (ex-Army FS 397)	550/45	2/45	Korean MOCK-PO (7/55).
WIX.339	TYRER	149/28		Returned 1945.

Notes:—NAVIGATION and TYRER acquired from Bureau of Marine Inspection and Navigation. DANMARK was the Danish sail training ship.

Displacement: 1,715 tons.
Dimensions: 230 (oa) × 43 × 14 ft.
Machinery: 1-shaft Diesel-electric drive, S.H.P. 1,800 = 13.5 knots.
Armament: 2—3 in., 4—20 mm. A.A. guns.

WAG.38	STORIS (ex-Eskimo)	Toledo	.43	

Displacement: 5,252 tons.
Dimensions: 290 (oa) × 75 × 19 ft.
Machinery: 3-shaft Diesel-electric drive, S.H.P. 10,000 = 16 knots.
Armament: Nil.

WAG.83	MACKINAW (ex-Manitowoc)	Toledo	6. 3.44	

Note:—On Great Lakes.

U.S. NAVY STANDARD NOMENCLATURE

In 1921, the United States Navy adopted a method of classifying all ships which also provides an official identification number for each vessel. Each type of vessel is given a letter symbol and each ship a hull number. As no number is generally used more than once, ships are easily identified by simple reference to the symbol and number.

Below follow the various standard symbols in use during the period of World War II:

Major Combatant Vessels

BB	*Battleship*
BM	*Monitor*
CV	*Aircraft carrier*
CVB	*Aircraft carrier,* (*Large*)
CVL	*Aircraft carrier,* (*Small*)
CVE	*Aircraft carrier,* (*Escort*)
CVS	*Seaplane carrier*
CC	*Battle cruiser*
CB	*Large cruiser*
CA	*Heavy cruiser*
CL	*Light cruiser*
DD	*Destroyer*
DL	*Destroyer leader*
DE	*Destroyer escort*
SS	*Submarine*
SM	*Submarine minelayer*

Minecraft

CM	*Minelayer*
CMc	*Coastal minelayer*
ACM	*Auxiliary minelayer*
DM	*Light minelayer*
DMS	*High speed minesweeper*
AM	*Minesweeper*
AMc	*Coastal minesweeper*
AMc(U)	*Coastal minesweeper* (*underwater locator*)

Patrol Craft

PG	*Gunboat*
PR	*River gunboat*
PF	*Frigate*
PY	*Yacht*
PYc	*Coastal yacht*
PC	*Submarine chaser (173 ft.)*
PCC	*Submarine chaser (control)*
PCE	*Escort*
PCEC	*Escort, control*
PCE(R)	*Escort (rescue)*
PCS	*Submarine chaser (136 ft.)*
PCSC	*Submarine chaser (control)*
SC	*Submarine chaser (110 ft.)*
SCC	*Submarine chaser (control)*
PGM	*Motor gunboat*
PT	*Motor torpedo boat*
PTC	*Motor boat, submarine chaser*

Auxiliary Vessels

AB	*Crane ship*
AC	*Collier*
AD	*Destroyer tender*
AE	*Ammunition ship*
AF	*Store ship*
AG	*Auxiliary (miscellaneous)*
AGC	*Amphibious force flagship*
AGD	*Seagoing dredger*
AGL	*Lighthouse tender*
AGP	*Motor torpedo boat tender*
AGS	*Surveying ship*
AGSc	*Coastal surveying ship*
AH	*Hospital ship*
AK	*Cargo ship*
AKA	*Attack cargo ship*
AKL	*Light cargo ship*
AKN	*Net cargo ship*
AKS	*General stores-issue ship*
AKV	*Cargo ship & aircraft ferry*
AL	*Lightship*
AN	*Netlaying ship*
AO	*Oiler*
AOG	*Gasoline tanker*
AP	*Transport*
APA	*Attack transport*
APB	*Barracks ship*
APc	*Coastal transport*
APD	*High speed transport*
APH	*Transport fitted for evacuation of wounded*
APL	*Labor transport (non self-propelled)*
APS	*Transport submarine*
APV	*Transport & aircraft ferry*

AR	*Repair ship*
ARB	*Repair ship, battle damage*
ARC	*Cable ship*
ARG	*Repair ship, internal combustion engines*
ARH	*Heavy-hull repair ship*
ARL	*Repair ship, landing craft*
ARS	*Salvage vessel*
ARS(D)	*Salvage lifting vessel*
ARS(T)	*Salvage craft tender*
ARV	*Aircraft repair ship*
AS	*Submarine tender*
ASR	*Submarine rescue vessel*
ATA	*Ocean Tug, auxiliary*
ATF	*Ocean Tug, fleet*
ATO	*Ocean Tug, old*
ATR	*Ocean Tug, rescue*
AV	*Seaplane tender*
AVC	*Catapult lighter*
AVD	*Seaplane tender (destroyer)*
AVP	*Seaplane tender, small*
AVR	*Aircraft rescue vessel*
AVS	*Aviation supply ship*
AW	*Distilling ship*
AWK	*Water tanker*
IX	*Unclassified vessel*

Landing Ships & Craft

LSD	*Landing ship, dock*
LSM	*Landing ship, medium*
LSM(R)	*Landing ship, medium (rocket)*
LST	*Landing ship, tank*
LST(H)	*Landing ship, tank (evacuation)*
LSV	*Landing ship, vehicle*
LCI(L)*	*Landing craft, infantry (large)*
LCI(G)*	*Landing craft, infantry (gun)*
LCI(M)*	*Landing craft, infantry (mortar)*
LCI(R)*	*Landing craft, infantry (rocket)*
LC(FF)*	*Landing craft (flotilla flagship)*
LCS(L)*	*Landing craft, support (large)*
LCT*	*Landing craft, tank*
LCC	*Landing craft, control*
LCM	*Landing craft, mechanised*
LCP(L)	*Landing craft, personnel (large)*
LCP(N)	*Landing craft, personnel (nested)*
LCP(R)	*Landing craft, personnel (ramp)*
LCR	*Landing craft, rubber*
LCV	*Landing craft, vehicle*
LCVP	*Landing craft, vehicle-personnel*
LVT	*Landing vehicle, tracked*

* Later re-classed as landing ships.

WAR LOSSES

BATTLESHIPS

ARIZONA (BB 39)   Destroyed by aircraft bombs, Pearl Harbor, 7th December, 1941.

OKLAHOMA (BB 37)   Capsized and sank after being torpedoed by aircraft, Pearl Harbor, 7th December, 1941. Raised, March, 1943 but not repaired.

AIRCRAFT CARRIERS

HORNET (CV 8)   Sunk after being damaged by aircraft torpedoes, Battle of Santa Cruz, 26th October, 1942.

LEXINGTON (CV 2)   Sunk by aircraft torpedoes, Battle of Coral Sea, 8th May, 1942.

PRINCETON (CVL 23)   Sunk after being damaged by aircraft bombs east of Luzon, Battle of Leyte Gulf, 24th October, 1944.

WASP (CV 7)   Torpedoed and sunk by Japanese submarine *I—19* south of Guadalcanal, 15th September, 1942.

YORKTOWN (CV 5)   Damaged by aircraft, Battle of Midway, 4th June and sank after being torpedoed by Japanese submarine *I—168*, 7th June, 1942.

ESCORT CARRIERS

BLOCK ISLAND (CVE 21)   Torpedoed and sunk by German submarine *U—549* northwest of Canary Is., 29th May, 1944.

BISMARCK SEA (CVE 95)   Sunk by Kamikaze attack off Iwo Jima, 21st February, 1945.

GAMBIER BAY (CVE 73)   Sunk by gunfire of Japanese warships off Samar, Battle of Leyte Gulf, 25th October, 1944.

LISCOME BAY (CVE 56)   Torpedoed and sunk by Japanese submarine *I—175* off Guilbert Is., 24th November, 1943.

OMMANEY BAY (CVE 79)   Sunk by Kamikaze attack south of Mindoro, 4th January, 1945.

ST. LO (CVE 63)   Sunk by Japanese aircraft off Samar, Battle of Leyte Gulf, 25th October, 1944.

CRUISERS

ASTORIA (CA 34)
Sunk by gunfire of Japanese warships off Savo Island, 9th August, 1942.

ATLANTA (CL 51)
Torpedoed and sunk by Japanese warships during Battle of Guadalcanal, 13th November, 1942.

CHICAGO (CA 29)
Torpedoed by Japanese aircraft 29th January off Rennel Island, Solomon Is., and again 30th January, 1943, when she sank.

HELENA (CL 50)
Torpedoed and sunk by Japanese warships during Battle of Kula Gulf, 6th July, 1943.

HOUSTON (CA 30)
Sunk by gunfire and torpedoes of Japanese warships in Sunda Strait, N.E.I., 1st March, 1942.

INDIANAPOLIS (CA 35)
Torpedoed and sunk by Japanese submarine *I—58* in Philippine Sea, 29th July, 1945.

JUNEAU (CL 52)
Torpedoed and sunk by Japanese submarine *I—26* after being torpedoed during the Battle of Guadalcanal, 13th November, 1942.

NORTHAMPTON (CA 26)
Torpedoed by Japanese destroyer *Oyashio* during Battle of Tassafaronga, 30th November, and sank 1st December, 1942.

QUINCY (CA 39)
Sunk by torpedoes and gunfire of Japanese warships off Savo Island, 9th August, 1942.

VINCENNES (CA 44)
Torpedoed and sunk by Japanese warships off Savo Island, 9th August, 1942.

DESTROYERS

AARON WARD (DD 483)
Bombed and sunk in Lunga Roads, Guadalcanal, 7th April, 1943.

ABNER READ (DD 526)
Sunk by Kamikaze attack off Leyte, 1st November, 1944.

BARTON (DD 599)
Torpedoed and sunk by Japanese warships during Battle of Guadalcanal, 13th November, 1942.

BEATTY (DD 640)
Torpedoed and sunk by German aircraft off Philippeville, Algeria, 6th November, 1943.

BENHAM (DD 397)
Torpedoed and sunk by Japanese warships during Battle of Guadalcanal, 15th November, 1942.

BLUE (DD 387)
Torpedoed and sunk by Japanese destroyer *Kawakaze* off Guadalcanal, 22nd August, 1942.

BORIE (DD 215)
Sank as result of damage received (1st November) by ramming German submarine *U—405* north of Azores, 2nd November, 1943.

BRISTOL (DD 453)
Torpedoed and sunk by German submarine *U—371* off Algiers, 12th October, 1943.

BROWNSON (DD 518)	Sunk by Japanese aircraft off Cape Gloucester, New Britain, 26th December, 1943.
BUCK (DD 420)	Torpedoed and sunk by German submarine *U—616* off Salerno, 9th October, 1943.
BUSH (DD 529)	Hit by 3 Kamikaze planes off Okinawa and sunk, 6th April, 1945.
CALLAGHAN (DD 792)	Sunk by Kamikaze attack off Okinawa, 28th July, 1945.
CHEVALIER (DD 451)	Torpedoed and sunk by Japanese destroyer *Yugumo* in action off Vella Lavella, Solomon Is., 7th October, 1943.
COLHOUN (DD 801)	Hit by 4 Kamikaze planes off Okinawa and sunk, 6th April, 1945.
COOPER (DD 695)	Torpedoed and sunk in Ormoc Bay, Leyte, 3rd December, 1944.
CORRY (DD 463)	Sunk by mine off Utah Beach, Normandy, 6th June, 1944.
CUSHING (DD 376)	Sunk by gunfire during Battle of Guadalcanal, 13th November, 1942.
DE HAVEN (DD 469)	Bombed and sunk off Cape Esperance, Guadalcanal, 1st February, 1943.
DREXLER (DD 741)	Hit by 2 Kamikaze planes off Okinawa and sunk, 28th May, 1945.
DUNCAN (DD 485)	Sunk by gunfire during Battle of Cape Esperance, 12th October, 1942.
EDSALL (DD 219)	Sunk by Japanese warships south of Java, 1st March, 1942.
GLENNON (DD 620)	Sunk by mine and shore batteries off Normandy, 8th to 10th June, 1944.
GWIN (DD 433)	Torpedoed and sunk by Japanese destroyers during Battle of Kolombangara, 13th July, 1943.
HALLIGAN (DD 584)	Sunk by mine off Okinawa, 26th March, 1945.
HAMMANN (DD 412)	Torpedoed and sunk by Japanese submarine *I—168* following Battle of Midway, 6th June, 1942.
HENLEY (DD 391)	Torpedoed and sunk by Japanese submarine *RO—108* off Finschafen, New Guinea, 3rd October, 1943.
HOEL (DD 533)	Sunk by Japanese warships off Samar, Battle of Leyte Gulf, 25th October, 1944.
HULL (DD 350)	Foundered in typhoon off Luzon, 18th December, 1944.
INGRAHAM (DD 444)	Sunk in collision with oiler *Chemung* in fog off Nova Scotia, 22nd August, 1942.
JACOB JONES (DD 130)	Torpedoed and sunk by German submarine *U—578* off Cape May, N.J., 28th February, 1942.
JARVIS (DD 393)	Sunk by Japanese aircraft off Guadalcanal, 9th August, 1942.
JOHNSTON (DD 557)	Sunk by Japanese warships off Samar, Battle of Leyte Gulf, 25th October, 1944.
LAFFEY (DD 459)	Sunk by Japanese battleship *Hiyei* during Battle of Guadalcanal, 13th November, 1942.

LANSDALE (DD 426)	Torpedoed and sunk by German aircraft off Cap Bengut, Algeria, 20th April, 1944.
LEARY (DD 158)	Torpedoed and sunk by German submarine *U—275* in North Atlantic, 24th December, 1943.
LITTLE (DD 803)	Hit by 4 Kamikaze planes off Okinawa and sunk, 3rd May, 1945.
LONGSHAW (DD 559)	Ran aground off Naha, Okinawa, and destroyed by shore batteries, 18th May, 1945.
LUCE (DD 522)	Hit by 2 Kamikaze planes off Okinawa and sunk, 3rd May, 1945.
MADDOX (DD 622)	Bombed and sunk off Gela, Sicily, 10th July, 1943.
MAHAN (DD 364)	Hit by 3 Kamikaze planes off Ormoc, Leyte, and sunk, 7th December, 1944.
MANNERT L. ABELE (DD 733)	Sunk by Kamikaze and glider bomb attack off Okinawa, 12th April, 1945.
MEREDITH (DD 434)	Sunk by Japanese aircraft south of Guadalcanal, 15th October, 1942.
MEREDITH (DD 726)	Damaged by mine and later sunk by German aircraft off Normandy, 8th to 9th June, 1944.
MONAGHAN (DD 354)	Foundered in typhoon off Luzon, 18th December, 1944.
MONSSEN (DD 436)	Sunk by gunfire of Japanese warships during Battle of Guadalcanal, 13th November, 1942.
MORRISON (DD 560)	Hit by 4 Kamikaze planes off Okinawa and sunk, 4th May, 1945.
O'BRIEN (DD 415)	Torpedoed by Japanese submarine *I—15* north of Espiritu Santo, 15th September, and foundered off Samoa en route to base, 19th October, 1942.
PARROTT (DD 218)	Irreparably damaged in collision with s.s. *John Norton* at Norfolk, Va., 2nd May, 1944, and scrapped.
PEARY (DD 226)	Sunk by Japanese aircraft at Port Darwin, Australia, 19th February, 1942.
PERKINS (DD 377)	Sunk in collision with m.v. *Duntroon* off Buna, New Guinea, 29th November, 1943.
PILLSBURY (DD 227)	Sunk by Japanese warships south of Java, 1st March, 1942.
POPE (DD 225)	Sunk by Japanese aircraft in Java Sea, 1st March, 1942.
PORTER (DD 356)	Torpedoed and sunk by Japanese submarine *I—21* off Santa Cruz Is., 26th October, 1943.
PRESTON (DD 379)	Sunk by Japanese cruiser *Nagara* during Battle of Guadalcanal, 14th November, 1942.
PRINGLE (DD 477)	Sunk by Kamikaze attack off Okinawa, 16th April, 1945.
REID (DD 369)	Hit by 2 Kamikaze planes off Ormoc, Leyte, and sunk, 11th December, 1944.

REUBEN JAMES (DD 245)	Torpedoed and sunk by German submarine *U—562* 600 miles southwest of Iceland, 31st October, 1941.
ROWAN (DD 405)	Torpedoed and sunk by German m.t.b. off Salerno, 10th September, 1943.
SIMS (DD 409)	Sunk by Japanese aircraft during Battle of the Coral Sea, 7th May, 1942.
SPENCE (DD 512)	Capsized in typhoon off Luzon, 18th December, 1944.
STRONG (DD 467)	Torpedoed and sunk in destroyer action off Bairoko, Solomon Is., 5th July, 1943.
STURTEVANT (DD 240)	Sunk by mine off Marquesas Key, Fla., 26th April, 1942.
TRUXTUN (DD 229)	Wrecked in gale, Placentia Bay, Nfld., 18th February, 1942.
TUCKER (DD 374)	Sunk by mine off Espiritu Santo, New Hebrides, 4th August, 1942.
TURNER (DD 648)	Sunk by explosion off Ambrose Light, N.Y., 3rd January, 1944.
TWIGGS (DD 591)	Sunk by Kamikaze and aerial torpedo off Okinawa, 16th June, 1945.
WALKE (DD 416)	Sunk by torpedoes and gunfire during Battle of Guadalcanal, 14th November, 1942.
WARRINGTON (DD 383)	Foundered in hurricane off the Bahamas Islands, 13th September, 1944.
WILLIAM D. PORTER (DD 579)	Sunk by Kamikaze attack off Okinawa, 10th June, 1945.
WORDEN (DD 352)	Wrecked on Amchitka Island, Aleutians, 12th January, 1943.

In addition, CASSIN (DD 372), SHAW (DD 373) and DOWNES (DD 375) were sunk at Pearl Harbor, 7th December, 1942, but were salvaged and rebuilt. Also, STEWART (DD 224) was scuttled in drydock at Surabaya, 2nd March, 1942; she was recovered at the end of the war after serving in the Japanese Navy.

The following seriously damaged destroyers were not repaired following the end of the war:

EVANS (DD 552)	By Kamikaze, Okinawa, 11th May, 1945.
HAGGARD (DD 555)	By Kamikaze, Okinawa, 29th April, 1945.
HUGH W. HADLEY (DD 774)	By Kamikaze, Okinawa, 11th May, 1945.
HUTCHINS (DD 476)	By Kamikaze, Okinawa, 27th April, 1945.
LEUTZE (DD 481)	By Kamikaze, Okinawa, 6th April, 1945.
MORRIS (DD 417)	By Kamikaze, Okinawa, 6th April, 1945.
NEWCOMBE (DD 586)	By Kamikaze, Okinawa, 6th April, 1945.
SHAW (DD 373)	By grounding, Leyte, 2nd April, 1945.
SHUBRICK (DD 639)	By Kamikaze, Okinawa, 29th May, 1945.
THATCHER (DD 514)	By Kamikaze, Okinawa, 19th July, 1945.

DESTROYER ESCORTS

EVERSOLE (DE 404)	Torpedoed and sunk by Japanese submarine *I—45* east of Leyte, 28th October, 1944.
FECHTELER (DE 157)	Torpedoed and sunk by German submarine *U—967* northeast of Oran, 5th May, 1944.

FISKE (DE 143)	Torpedoed and sunk by German submarine *U—804* north of Azores, 2nd August, 1944.
FREDERICK C. DAVIS (DE 136)	Torpedoed and sunk by German submarine *U—546* in North Atlantic, 24th April, 1945.
HOLDER (DE 401)	Torpedoed by German aircraft off Algiers, 11th April, 1944, and scrapped.
LEOPOLD (DE 319)	Torpedoed and sunk by German submarine *U—255* south of Iceland, 10th March, 1944.
OBERRENDER (DE 344)	Irreparably damaged by Kamikaze attack off Okinawa, 9th May, 1945.
RICH (DE 695)	Sunk by mine off Normandy, 8th June, 1944.
SAMUEL B. ROBERTS (DE 413)	Sunk by Japanese warships off Samar, Battle of Leyte Gulf, 25th October, 1944.
SHELTON (DE 407)	Torpedoed and sunk by Japanese submarine *RO—41* off Morotai, 3rd October, 1944.
UNDERHILL (DE 682)	Sunk by Japanese human torpedo northeast of Luzon, 24th July, 1945.

In addition, ENGLAND (DE 635), seriously damaged by Kamikaze at Okinawa, 9th May, 1945, was not repaired following the end of the war, and DONNELL (DE 56), torpedoed 3rd May, 1944, became a floating power plant at Cherbourg.

SUBMARINES

ALBACORE (SS 218)	Probably sunk by mine north of Hokkaido, 7th November, 1944.
AMBERJACK (SS 219)	Probably sunk by Japanese torpedo boat *Hiyodori* and submarine chaser *No. 18* off Rabaul, 16th February, 1943.
ARGONAUT (APS 1)	Sunk by Japanese destroyers off Rabaul, 10th January, 1943.
BARBEL (SS 316)	Sunk by Japanese aircraft southwest of Palawan Island, Philippines, 4th February, 1945.
BONEFISH (SS 223)	Sunk by Japanese warships in Toyama Wan, Honshu, 18th June, 1945.
BULLHEAD (SS 332)	Probably sunk by Japanese aircraft off Bali, 6th August, 1945.
CAPELIN (SS 289)	Missing off Halmahera Island, December 1943.
CISCO (SS 290)	Sunk by Japanese warships and aircraft in Sulu Sea, 28th September, 1943.
CORVINA (SS 226)	Torpedoed and sunk by Japanese submarine *I-176* southwest of Truk, 16th November, 1943.
DARTER (SS 227)	Stranded off Palawan Island, 24th October, 1944, and destroyed to prevent capture.
DORADO (SS 248)	Probably sunk in error by U.S. aircraft in Caribbean Sea, 12th October, 1943.
ESCOLAR (SS 294)	Probably sunk by mine in Yellow Sea, October 1944.

FLIER (SS 250)	Sunk by mine while on surface in Balabac Strait, 13th August, 1944.
GOLET (SS 361)	Sunk by Japanese warships off north Honshu, 14th June, 1944.
GRAMPUS (SS 207)	Probably sunk by Japanese destroyers *Minegumo* and *Murasame* off New Georgia, 5th March, 1943.
GRAYBACK (SS 208)	Sunk by Japanese aircraft in East China Sea, 26th February, 1944.
GRAYLING (SS 209)	Probably sunk by Japanese freighter *Hokuan Maru* west of Luzon, 9th September, 1943.
GRENADIER (SS 210)	Sunk by Japanese aircraft off Penang, 22nd April, 1943.
GROWLER (SS 215)	Probably sunk by Japanese warships in South China Sea, 8th November, 1944.
GRUNION (SS 216)	Missing off Kiska, end July 1942. Probably sunk by Japanese submarine *I-25*, 30th July, 1942.
GUDGEON (SS 211)	Missing off Marianas Islands, April 1944.
HARDER (SS 257)	Sunk by Siamese destroyer *Pra Ruang* off Caiman Point, 24th August, 1944.
HERRING (SS 233)	Sunk by Japanese shore batteries off Matsuwa Island, Kuriles, 1st June, 1944.
KETE (SS 369)	Missing in Central Pacific, March 1945.
LAGARTO (SS 371)	Sunk by Japanese minelayer *Hatsutaka* in Gulf of Siam, 3rd May, 1954.
PERCH (SS 176)	Damaged by Japanese warships north of Java and scuttled at sea, 3rd March, 1942.
PICKEREL (SS 177)	Missing off northern Honshu, April 1943.
POMPANO (SS 181)	Missing east of Honshu, August 1943.
R-12 (SS 89)	Foundered during exercises off Key West, Fla., 12th June, 1943.
ROBALO (SS 273)	Sunk by internal explosion or mine off Palawan, 26th July, 1944.
RUNNER (SS 275)	Missing off Kurile Islands, June 1943.
S-26 (SS 131)	Sunk in collision with submarine chaser *PC-460* in Gulf of Panama, 24th January, 1942.
S-27 (SS 132)	Lost by grounding on reef at Amchitka Island, Aleutians, 19th June, 1942.
S-28 (SS 133)	Failed to surface during training exercises off Pearl Harbor, 4th July, 1944.
S-36 (SS 141)	Lost by grounding on Taka Bakang Reef, Makassar Strait, 20th January, 1942.
S-39 (SS 144)	Lost by grounding south of Rossel Island, Louisiade Archipelago, 14th August 1942.
S-44 (SS 155)	Sunk by Japanese destroyer off Paramushiru, 7th October, 1943.
SCAMP (SS 277)	Probably sunk by Japanese patrol vessel off Tokyo Bay, 6th November, 1944.
SCORPION (SS 278)	Missing in Western Pacific, February 1944.
SCULPIN (SS 191)	Sunk by Japanese destroyer *Yamagumo* off Truk, 19th November, 1943.

SEALION (SS 195)	Sunk by Japanese aircraft at Cavite, 10th December, and destroyed to prevent capture, 25th December, 1941.
SEAWOLF (SS 197)	Sunk in error by destroyer escort *Richard M. Rowell* off Morotai, 3rd October, 1944.
SHARK (SS 174)	Sunk by Japanese warships east of Menado, Celebes, 11th February, 1942.
SHARK (SS 314)	Sunk by Japanese warships in Luzon Strait, 24th October, 1944.
SNOOK (SS 279)	Missing in Okinawa area, April 1945 (possibly sunk by Japanese submarine).
SWORDFISH (SS 193)	Missing south of Kyushu, January 1945.
TANG (SS 306)	Sunk by own torpedo off Formosa, 24th October, 1944.
TRIGGER (SS 237)	Sunk by Japanese aircraft and warships in Nansei Shoto, 28th March, 1945.
TRITON (SS 201)	Sunk by Japanese destroyers north of Admiralty Islands, 15th March, 1943.
TROUT (SS 202)	Sunk by Japanese warships southeast of Okinawa, 29th February, 1944.
TULLIBEE (SS 284)	Sunk by own torpedo north of Palau, 26th March, 1944.
WAHOO (SS 238)	Sunk by Japanese aircraft in La Perouse Strait, 12th October, 1943.

MINELAYERS

GAMBLE (DM 15)	Damaged by aircraft bombs off Iwo Jima, 18th February, and scuttled off Saipan, 16th July, 1945.
MIANTONOMAH (CM 10)	Sunk by mine off Le Havre, 25th September, 1944.
MONTGOMERY (DM 17)	Damaged by mine off Palau, 17th October, 1944, and scrapped.

HIGH SPEED MINESWEEPERS

EMMONS (DMS 22)	Hit by 5 Kamikaze planes off Okinawa and sunk, 6th April, 1945.
HOVEY (DMS 11)	Torpedoed and sunk by Japanese aircraft in Lingayen Gulf, 6th January, 1945.
LONG (DMS 12)	Sunk by Kamikaze attack in Lingayen Gulf, 6th January, 1945.
PALMER (DMS 5)	Sunk by Japanese aircraft in Lingayen Gulf, 7th January, 1945.
PERRY (DMS 17)	Sunk by mine off Palau, 13th September, 1944.
WASMUTH (DMS 15)	Sunk by explosion of depth charges during gale off Aleutian Islands, 29th December, 1942.

The following seriously damaged minelayers and minesweepers were not repaired following the war:

AARON WARD (DM 34)	by Kamikaze, Okinawa, 3rd May, 1945.
BUTLER (DMS 29)	,,	,,	25th May, 1945.
FORREST (DMS 24)	,,	,,	27th May, 1945.
HARDING (DMS 28)	,,	,,	16th April, 1945.
J. WILLIAM DITTER (DM 31)	,,	,,	6th June, 1945.

MINESWEEPERS

BITTERN (AM 36) — Sunk by aircraft bombs at Cavite, 10th December, 1941.

FINCH (AM 9) — Sunk by Japanese aircraft off Corregidor, 11th April, 1942 (salvaged and sunk as Japanese *Patrol Boat No. 103* by U.S. aircraft, 12th January, 1945).

MINIVET (AM 371) — Sunk by mine in Tsushima Strait, 29th December, 1945.

OSPREY (AM 56) — Sunk by mine off Normandy, 5th June, 1944.

PENGUIN (AM 33) — Sunk by Japanese aircraft off Guam, 8th December 1941.

PORTENT (AM 106) — Sunk by mine off Anzio, 22nd January, 1944.

QUAIL (AM 15) — Scuttled off Corregidor, 6th May, 1942.

SALUTE (AM 294) — Sunk by mine off Brunei, Borneo, 8th June, 1945.

SENTINEL (AM 113) — Sunk by German aircraft off Licata, Sicily, 12th July, 1943.

SKILL (AM 115) — Torpedoed and sunk by German submarine *U-593* south of Capri, 25th September, 1943.

SKYLARK (AM 63) — Sunk by mine off Okinawa, 28th March, 1945.

SWALLOW (AM 65) — Sunk by Kamikaze attack off Okinawa, 22nd April, 1945.

SWERVE (AM 121) — Sunk by mine off Anzio, 9th July, 1944.

TANAGER (AM 5) — Sunk by shore batteries off Corregidor, 4th May, 1942.

TIDE (AM 125) — Sunk by mine off Normandy, 7th June, 1944.

PATROL VESSELS

ASHEVILLE (PG 21) — Sunk by Japanese warships south of Java, 3rd March, 1942.

CYTHERA (PY 26) — Torpedoed and sunk by German submarine off North Carolina, 2nd May, 1942.

ERIE (PG 50) — Torpedoed by German submarine *U-163* off Curacao, 12th November, and capsized while in tow off Willemstad, 5th December, 1942.

LUZON (PR 7) — Scuttled off Corregidor, 6th May, 1942 (salvaged and scuttled as Japanese *Karatsu* at Manila, 3rd February, 1945).

MINDANAO (PR 8) — Sunk by Japanese aircraft off Corregidor, 5th May, 1942.

OAHU (PR 6) — Scuttled off Corregidor, 6th May, 1942.

PLYMOUTH (PG. 57) — Torpedoed and sunk by German submarine *U-566* off North Carolina, 5th August, 1943.

ST. AUGUSTINE (PG 54) — Sunk in collision with s.s. *Camas Meadows* off Cape May, N.J., 6th January, 1944.

WAKE (PR 3) — Captured at Shanghai, 7th December, 1941 (served during war as Japanese *Tatara*, recovered during August 1945).

SUBMARINE TENDERS AND RESCUE VESSELS

CANOPUS (AS 9) Scuttled off Mariveles Bay, Bataan, 10th April, 1942.

MACAW (ASR 11) Lost by grounding on reef in Midway Channel, 12th February, 1944.

PIGEON (ASR 6) Sunk by Japanese aircraft off Corregidor, 5th May, 1942.

SALVAGE VESSELS

EXTRACTOR (ARS 15) Torpedoed and sunk in error by U.S. submarine *Guardfish* in Philippine Sea, 24th January, 1945.

REDWING (ARS 4) Sunk by explosion at Bizerte, 27th June, 1943.

RESCUER (ARS 18) Lost by grounding in Aleutian Islands, 1st January, 1943.

SEAPLANE TENDERS

GANNET (AVP 8) Torpedoed and sunk by German submarine *U—653* off Bermuda, 7th June, 1942.

LANGLEY (AV 3) Sunk by aircraft bombs south of Java, 27th February, 1942.

THORNTON (AVD 11) Damaged in collision with oiler Ashtabula off Okinawa and beached 5th April, 1945, and scrapped.

OILERS

KANAWHA (AO 1) Sunk by Japanese aircraft at Tulagi, 7th April, 1943.

MISSISSINEWA (AO 59) Torpedoed and sunk by Japanese midget submarine at Ulithi, 20th November, 1944.

NECHES (AO 5) Torpedoed and sunk by Japanese submarine *I—172* 135 miles west of Honolulu, 23rd January, 1942.

NEOSHO (AO 23) Sunk by Japanese aircraft during Battle of the Coral Sea, 11th April, 1942.

PECOS (AO 6) Sunk by Japanese aircraft south of Christmas Island, 1st March, 1942.

PORCUPINE (IX 126) Sunk by Kamikaze attack off Mindoro, 30th December, 1944.

SHEEPSCOT (AOG 24) Irreparably damaged by grounding off Iwo Jima, 5th June, 1945, and scrapped.

TRANSPORTS

EDWARD RUTLEDGE (AP 52)	Torpedoed and sunk by German submarine *U—130* off Fedala, Morocco, 12th November, 1942.
GEORGE F. ELLIOT (AP 13)	Sunk by Japanese aircraft off Guadalcanal, 8th August, 1942.
HUGH L. SCOTT (AP 43)	Torpedoed and sunk by German submarine *U—130* off Fedala, Morocco, 12th November, 1942.
JOHN PENN (APA 23)	Sunk by Japanese aircraft off Guadalcanal, 13th August, 1943.
JOSEPH HEWES (AP 50)	Torpedoed and sunk by German submarine *U—173* off Fedala, Morocco, 11th November, 1942.
LEEDSTOWN (AP 73)	Torpedoed and sunk by German aircraft off Algiers, 9th November, 1942.
McCAWLEY (APA 4)	Torpedoed by Japanese aircraft off Rendova, and sunk by U.S. m.t.b's, 30th June, 1943.
SUSAN B. ANTHONY (AP 72)	Sunk by mine off Normandy, 7th June, 1944.
TASKER H. BLISS (AP 42)	Torpedoed and sunk by German submarine *U—130* off Fedala, Morocco, 12th November, 1942.
THOMAS STONE (AP 59)	Torpedoed by German aircraft off Cape Palos, Spain, 7th November, and went aground in Algiers Harbor and abandoned, 25th November, 1942.

HIGH SPEED TRANSPORTS

BARRY (APD 29)	Damaged by Kamikaze attack off Okinawa, 25th May, and sunk as decoy, 21st June, 1945.
BATES (APD 47)	Sunk by Kamikaze attack off Okinawa, 25th May, 1945.
BELKNAP (APD 34)	Damaged beyond repair by Kamikaze attack at Lingayen, 11th January, 1945, and scrapped.
BROOKS (APD 10)	Damaged beyond repair by Kamikaze attack in Lingayen Gulf, 6th January, 1945, and scrapped.
COLHOUN (APD 2)	Sunk by Japanese aircraft off Guadalcanal, 30th August, 1942.
DICKERSON (APD 21)	Damaged by Japanese aircraft off Okinawa, 2nd April, and scuttled, 4th April, 1945.
GREGORY (APD 3) LITTLE (APD 4)	Sunk by Japanese destroyers off Lunga Point, Guadalcanal, 5th September, 1942.
McKEAN (APD 5)	Torpedoed and sunk by Japanese aircraft off Bougainville, 17th November, 1943.
NOA (APD 24)	Sunk in collision with destroyer *Fullam* off Palau, 12th September, 1944.
WARD (APD 16)	Sunk by Kamikaze attack off Ormoc, Leyte, 7th December, 1944.

CARGO VESSELS

ALUDRA (AK 72)
DEIMOS (AK 78) } Torpedoed and sunk by Japanese submarine *Ro—103* off San Cristobal Island, 23rd June, 1943.

MOUNT HOOD (AE 11) — Destroyed by explosion at Manus, Admiralty Islands, 10th November, 1944.

POLLUX (AKS 2) — Wrecked in Placentia Bay, Newfoundland, 18th February, 1942.

PONTIAC (AF 20) — Foundered off Halifax, 30th January, 1945; hulk scrapped.

SERPENS (AK 97) — Destroyed by explosion off Guadalcanal, 29th January, 1945.

FLEET TUGS

ATR-15 — Lost by grounding off Normandy, 19th June, 1944.

ATR-98 — Sunk in collision off Azores Islands, 12th April, 1944.

GENESEE (AT 55) — Scuttled off Corregidor, 5th May, 1942 (salvaged and sunk as Japanese *Patrol Boat No. 107* by U.S. aircraft, 5th November, 1944).

GREBE (AT 134) — Wrecked south of Fiji, 5th December, 1942.

NAPA (AT 32) — Scuttled off Bataan, Luzon, 8th April, 1942.

NAUSET (AT 89) — Sunk by German aircraft in Gulf of Salerno, 9th September, 1943.

NAVAJO (AT 64) — Sunk by explosion east of New Hebrides Islands, 11th September, 1943.

PARTRIDGE (ATO 138) — Torpedoed and sunk by German m.t.b. off Normandy, 11th June, 1944.

SEMINOLE (AT 65) — Sunk by Japanese destroyers off Lunga Point, Guadalcanal, 25th October, 1942.

SONOMA (ATO 12) — Sunk by Japanese aircraft off Leyte, 24th October, 1944.

MISCELLANEOUS AUXILIARIES

AILANTHUS (AN 38) — Lost by grounding in Aleutian Islands, 26th February, 1944.

ATIK — Sunk in battle with German submarine *U—123* in North Atlantic, 27th March, 1942.

MUSKEGET (AG 48) — Probably torpedoed and sunk by German submarine *U—755* in North Atlantic, 9th September, 1942.

NIAGARA (AGP 1) — Sunk by Japanese aircraft near San Cristobal Island, 23rd May, 1943.

ROBERT L. BARNES (AG 27) — Captured at Guam, 8th December, 1941.

UTAH (AG 16) — Torpedoed by Japanese aircraft at Pearl Harbor, and capsized, 7th December, 1941.

DCH-1 (IX 44) Scuttled while under tow from San Diego to Pearl Harbor, 28th December, 1941.

Notes:—The hulk of the old discarded cruiser ROCHESTER (ex-CA.2) was scuttled as a blockship in Subic Channel, Luzon, 24/12/41.

COAST GUARD CUTTERS

ACACIA (WAGL 200) Sunk by gunfire of German submarine *U—161* south of Haiti, 15th March, 1942.

ALEXANDER HAMILTON (WPG 34) Torpedoed by German submarine *U—132* off Iceland, and capsized in tow, 29th January, 1942.

BEDLOE (WPC 128) Foundered during hurricane off Cape Hatteras, 14th September, 1944.

BODEGA (WYP 342) Lost by grounding during salvage operations off the Panama Canal, 20th December, 1943.

DOW (WYP 353) Lost by grounding during gale off Mayaguez, Puerto Rico, 14th October, 1943.

ESCANABA (WPG 77) Sunk by explosion of undetermined cause off Ivigtut, Greenland, 13th June, 1943.

JACKSON (WPC 142) Foundered during hurricane off Cape Hatteras, 14th September, 1944.

MAGNOLIA (WAGL 231) Sunk in collision with s.s. *Marguerite LeHand* off Mobile, 24th August, 1945.

NATSEK (WYP 170) Foundered in Strait of Belle Isle, 17th December, 1942.

WILCOX (WYP 333) Foundered in heavy seas off Cape Hatteras, 30th September, 1943.

UNNAMED VESSELS

LST 6	Mine	Seine River	18th Nov. 1944
LST 43	Explosion	Pearl Harbor	21st May, 1944
LST 69	Explosion	Pearl Harbor	21st May, 1944
LST 158	Aircraft	Licata, Sicily	11th July, 1943
LST 167	Aircraft	off Vella Lavella	25th September, 1943
LST 179	Explosion	Pearl Harbor	21st May, 1944
LST 203	Grounded	Nanumea, Ellice Is.	2nd October, 1943
LST 228	Grounded	Azores Is.	20th January, 1944
LST 282	Glider bomb	St. Tropez, France	15th August, 1944
LST 313	Aircraft	Gela, Sicily	10th July, 1943
LST 314	German M.T.B.	off Normandy	9th June, 1944
LST 318	Aircraft	Caronia, Sicily	10th August, 1943
LST 333	*U—593*	off Algeria	22nd June, 1943
LST 342	Jap. s/m *Ro—106*	W. of Guadalcanal	18th July, 1943
LST 348	*U—410*	off Anzio	20th February, 1944
LST 349	Grounded	near Gaeta	26th February, 1944
LST 353	Explosion	Pearl Harbor	21st May, 1944

LST 359	*U—870*	N.E. of Azores Is.	20th December, 1944
LST 376	German M.T.B.	off Normandy	9th June, 1944
LST 396	Explosion	off Vella Lavella	18th August, 1943
LST 447	Kamikaze	Okinawa	6th April, 1945
LST 448	Aircraft	off Bougainville	5th October, 1943
LST 460	Kamikaze	off Mindoro	21st December, 1944
LST 472	Kamikaze	off Mindoro	15th December, 1944
LST 480	Explosion	Pearl Harbor	21st May, 1944
LST 493	Grounded	Plymouth, England	12th April, 1945
LST 496	Mine	Normandy	11th June, 1944
LST 499	Mine	Normandy	8th June, 1944
LST 507	German M.T.B.	Lyme Bay	28th April, 1944
LST 523	Mine	Normandy	19th June, 1944
LST 531	German M.T.B.	Lyme Bay	28th April, 1944
LST 563	Grounded	Clipperton Is.	22nd December, 1944
LST 577	Jap. s/m *Ro—50*	E. of Mindanao	11th February, 1945
LST 738	Kamikaze	off Mindoro	15th December, 1944
LST 749	Kamikaze	off Mindoro	21st December, 1944
LST.750	Aircraft	off Los Negros	28th December, 1944
LST 906	Grounded	Leghorn, Italy	18th October, 1944
LST 921	*U—764*	Bristol Channel	14th August, 1944
LSM 12	Foundered	off Okinawa	4th April, 1945
LSM 20	Kamikaze	off Ormoc, Leyte	5th December, 1944
LSM 59	Kamikaze	off Okinawa	21st June, 1945
LSM 135	Kamikaze	off Okinawa	25th May, 1945
LSM 149	Grounded	Philippine Is.	5th December, 1944
LSM 318	Kamikaze	off Ormoc, Leyte	7th December, 1944
LSM(R) 190	Kamikaze	off Okinawa	4th May, 1945
LSM(R) 194	Kamikaze	off Okinawa	4th May, 1945
LSM(R) 195	Kamikaze	off Okinawa	3rd May, 1945
APc.21	Aircraft	Arawe, New Britain	17th December, 1943
APc 35	Grounded	New Georgia	22nd September, 1943
PC 496	Mine	off Bizerte	4th June, 1943
PC 558	*U—230*	N. of Palermo	9th May, 1944
PC 1129	Suicide boat	off Nasugbu, Luzon	31st January, 1945
PC 1261	Mine	Normandy	6th June, 1944
PC 1603	Kamikaze	Okinawa	21st May, 1945
SC 521	Foundered	Santa Cruz Is.	10th July, 1945
SC 694	Aircraft	Palermo	23rd August, 1943
SC 696	Aircraft	Palermo	23rd August, 1943
SC 700	Burned	off Vella Lavella	10th March, 1944
SC 709	Grounded	Cape Breton	21st January, 1943
SC 740	Grounded	Great Barrier Reef	17th June, 1943
SC 744	Kamikaze	Leyte Gulf	27th November, 1944
SC 751	Grounded	Western Australia	22nd June, 1943
SC 984	Grounded	New Hebrides	9th April, 1944
SC 1019	Grounded		22nd April, 1945
SC 1024	Collision	off North Carolina	2nd March, 1943
SC 1059	Grounded	Bahamas Is.	12th December, 1944
SC 1067	Foundered	off Attu	19th November, 1943

PGM 7	Collision	Bismarck Sea	18th July, 1944
PGM 17	Grounded	off Okinawa	4th May, 1945
PGM 18	Mine	off Okinawa	7th April, 1945
PE 56	Explosion	off Portland, Me.	23rd April, 1945
YMS 14	Collision	Boston harbor	11th January, 1945
YMS 19	Mine	off Palau	24th September, 1944
YMS 21	Mine	off Toulon	1st September, 1944
YMS 24	Mine	off St. Tropez	15th August, 1944
YMS 30	Mine	off Anzio	25th January, 1944
YMS 39	Mine	off Balikpapan	26th June, 1945
YMS 48	Shore batteries	Manila Bay	14th February, 1945
YMS 50	Mine	off Balikpapan	18th June, 1945
YMS 70	Foundered	off Leyte	17th October, 1944
YMS 71	Mine	off Brunei	3rd April, 1945
YMS 84	Mine	off Balikpapan	8th July, 1945
YMS 103	Mine	off Okinawa	8th April, 1945
YMS 133	Foundered	Coos Bay, Oregon	21st February, 1943
YMS 304	Mine	Normandy	30th July, 1944
YMS 350	Mine	Normandy	2nd July, 1944
YMS 365	Mine	off Balikpapan	26th June, 1945
YMS 378	Mine	Normandy	30th July, 1944
YMS 385	Mine	Ulithi	1st October, 1944
YMS 409	Foundered	N. Atlantic	12th September, 1944
YMS 481	Shore batteries	Tarakan, Borneo	2nd May, 1945
CG 83415	Foundered	Normandy	21st June, 1944
CG 83421	Collision	off Florida	30th June, 1943
CG 83471	Foundered	Normandy	21st June, 1944

INDEX

INDEX

NOTE: This index lists all named ships of the Navy and Coast Guard other than district craft, with all assigned names including those cancelled or not used. After each name is found the ship's official number. If any ship was reclassified during the war, both numbers are given. The figures in italics denote the page numbers of illustrations.

411

412

413

414

Bon Homme Richard (CV 10), 42
Bon Homme Richard (CV 31), 42
Bonita (SS 165), 186
Bonneville (WIX 375), 390
Boone (WPC 335), 384
Bootes (AK 99), 332
Booth (DE 170), 166
Bordelon (DD 881), 152
Boreas (AF 8), 329
Borie (DD 215), 109
Borie (DD 704), 146
Borum (DE 790), 163
Bosque (APA 135), 348
Boston (CA 69), 79
Bostwick (DE 103), 164
Botetourt (APA 136), 348
Bottineau (APA 235), 348
Bougainville (CVE 100), 60
Boulder (WPYc 352), 384
Boulder Victory (AK 227), 334
Bountiful (AH 9), 351
Boutwell (WPC 130), 378
Bowditch (AG 30/AGS 4), *316*, 317
Bowers (DE 637/APD 40), 161
Bowfin (SS 287), 199
Bowie (APA 137), 348
Bowstring (WPC 365), 384
Boxer (CV 21), 46
Boxwood (AN 8), 311
Boyd (DD 544), 138
Boyle (DD 600), 129
Bracken (APA 64), 348
Brackett (DE 41), 155
Bradford (DD 545), 138
Braine (DD 630), 141
Bramble (WAGL 392), 388
Brant (AM 24/AT 132/ARS 32), 218 and 308
Braxton (APA 138), 348
Bray (DE 709/APD 139), 164
Brazos (AO 4), *315*, 317
Breakhorn (AM 353), 231
Bream (SS 243), *196*, 197
Breckinridge (DD 148/AG 112), 106
Breeman (DE 104), 164
Breese (DM 18), 212
Bremerton (CA 130), 82
Brennan (DE 13), 155
Breton (CVE 23), 52
Brevard (AK 164), 334
Briareus (AR 12), *291*, 293
Bridge (AF 1), 329
Bridgeport (PF 58), 250
Bridgeport (CA 127), 82
Brier (WAGL 299), 386
Bright (DE 747), 167
Brill (SS 330), 201
Brinkley Bass (DD 887), 152
Briscoe (APA 65), 348
Brisk (PG 89), 244
Brister (DE 327), *169*, 170
Bristol (DD 453), *130*, 132
Bristol (DD 857), 147

Broadbill (AM 58), 221
Broadwater (APA 139), 348
Brock (APD 93), 279
Bronco (WYP 340), 384
Bronstein (DE 189), 166
Brontes (AGP 17), 290
Bronx (APA 236), 348
Brookings (APA 140), 348
Brooklyn (CL 40), 85, *87*
Brooks (DD 232/APD 10), 109
Broome (DD 210/AG 96), 109
Brough (DE 148), 168
Brown (DD 546), 138
Brownson (DD 518), 138
Brownson (DD 868), 152
Brownsville (PF 10), 248
Brule (APA 66), 348
Bruleson (APA 67), 348
Brunswick (PF 68), 250
Brush (DD 745), 147
Brusstar (WYP 312), 384
Bryant (DD 665), 141
Bryce Canyon (AD 36), 285
Buchanan (DD 484), 132
Buck (DD 420), 126
Buck (DD 761), 147
Buckeye (AN 13), 311
Buckingham (APA 141), 348
Buckley (DE 51), 157
Buckthorn (AN 14), *309*, 311
Bucyrus Victory (AK 234), 334
Buffalo (CL 84), 94
Buffalo (CL 99), 94
Buffalo (CL 110), 98
Bugara (SS 331), 201
Bull (DE 693/APD 78), 161
Bullard DD 660), 141
Bullfinch (AM 66), 219
Bullhead (SS 332), 201
Bullock (AK 165), 334
Bulmer (DD 222/AG 86), 109, *368*
Bumper (SS 333), 201
Bunch (DE 694/APD 79), 161
Bunker Hill (CV 17), 42, *43*
Buoyant (AM 153), *224*, 225
Burden R. Hastings (DE 19), 155
Burdo (APD 133), 280
Burias (ARG 13/AG 69), 296
Burke (DE 215/APD 65), 158
Burleigh (APA 95), 347
Burlington (PF 51), 250
Burns (DD 588), 140
Burrfish (SS 312), 199
Burrows (DE 105), 164
Bush (DD 529), 138
Bushnell (AS 15), 287
Butler (DD 636/DMS 29), 135
Butte (APA 68), 348
Butternut (AN 9), 311
Buttonwood (WAGL 306), 388
Buttress (ACM 4), 254
Byron (WIX 344), 390

Centaurus (AKA 17), 334
Cepheus (AKA 18), 334
Cero (SS 225), 195
Cetus (AK 77), 332
C. G. Jackson (WPG 120), 254
Chaffee (DE 230), 163
Chaffinch (AM 81), 219
Chain (ARS 20), 308
Chambers (DE 391), 170
Champion (AM 314), 221
Champlin (DD 601), *127*, 129
Chandeleur (AV 10), 301
Chandler (DMS 9/AG 108), *214*, 215
Change (AM 159), 225
Chanticleer (ASR 7), 289
Chaparral (WAGL 178), 386
Chara (AKA 58), 334
Charger (CVE 30), 52, *53*
Charles Ausburne (DD 570), 140
Charles Carroll (AP 58/APA 28), 342, *345*
Charles E. Brannon (DE 446), 174
Charles F. Hughes (DD 428), 126
Charles H. Roan (DD 853), 152
Charles J. Badger (DD 657), 141
Charles J. Kimmel (DE 584), 163
Charles Lawrence (DE 53/APD 37), 157
Charles P. Cecil (DD 835), 150
Charles R. Greer (DE 23), 155
Charles R. Ware (DE 547), 175
Charles R. Ware (DD 865), 152
Charles S. Sperry (DD 697), 146
Charleston (PG 51), *235*, 238
Charlevoix (AK 168), 334
Charlotte (PF 60), 250
Charlottesville (PF 25), 248
Charr (SS 328), 201
Charrette (DD 581), 140
Chase (DE 158/APD 54), 158
Chateau Thierry (AP 31), 338
Chatelain (DE 149), 168
Chatham (AK 169), 334
Chatot (ATA 167), 355
Chattanooga (PF 65), 250
Chattanooga (CL 118), 98
Chaumont (AP 5), 335
Chauncey (DD 667), 141
Chautaqua (WPG 41), 376
Chauvenet (AGS 11), 231
Chawasha (ATF 151), 354
Chehalis (AOG 48), 325
Cheleb (AK 138), 332
Chemung (AO 30), *318*, 321
Chenango (AO 31/CVE 28), 55, 322
Chepachet (AO 78), 324
Cherokee (ATF 66), 352
Cherry (WAGL 258), 386
Chestatee (AOG 49), 325
Chester (CA 27), 67
Chester T. O'Brien (DE 421), 174
Chestnut (AN 11), 311
Chetco (AT 99), 354
Chetco (ATO 166), 355
Chevalier (DD 451), 135

Chevalier (DD 805), 150
Chew (DD 106), 103
Chewaucan (AOG 50), 325
Chewink (ASR 3), 289
Cheyenne (CL 86), 94
Cheyenne (CL 117), 98
Chicago (CA 29), 67
Chicago (CA 136), 82, *77*
Chickadee (AM 59), 221
Chickasaw (ATF 83), 354
Chickwick (SS 340), 201
Chicopee (AO 34), 324
Chicot (AK 170), 334
Chief (AM 315), 221
Chikaskia (AO 54), 322
Childs (AVD 1), 303
Chilton (APA 38), 347
Chilula (ATF 153), 355
Chimaera (ARL 33), 297
Chimariko (ATF 154), 355
Chimo (ACM 1), 209
Chinaberry (AN 61), 312
Chincoteague (AVP 24), 305
Chinook (WYT 96), 388
Chinquapin (AN 17), 311
Chipola (AO 63), 322
Chippewa (ATF 69), 352
Chiron (AGP 18), 292
Chivo (SS 341), 201
Chiwaukum (AOG 26), 325
Chiwawa (AO 68), 323
Chloris (ARVA 4), 298
Choctaw (ATF 70), 352
Chocura (IX 206), 252
Chopper (SS 342), 201
Chotauk (IX 188) 328
Chourre (ARV 1), 296
Chowanoc (ATF 100), 354
Christiana (IX 80), 362
Christopher (DE 100), 164
Chub (SS 329), 201
Chukawan (AO 100), 322
Chukor (AM 355), 231
Cimarron (AO 22), *319*, 321
Cinchona (AN 12), 311
Cincinnati (CL 6), 85
Cinnamon (AN 50), 312
Circe (AKA 25), 335
Cisco (SS 290), 199
Citrus (WAGL 300), 388
City of Dalhart (IX 156), 362
Claiborne (AK 171), 334
Clamagore (SS 343), 201
Clamour (AM 160), 225
Clamp (ARS 33), 308
Clarence K. Bronson (DD 668), 141
Clarence L. Evans (DE 113), 164
Clarendon (APA 72), 348
Clarion (AK 172), 334
Clark (DD 361), 114
Clash (PG 91), 244
Claxton (DD 571), 140
Clay (APA 39), 347

417

Eisner (DE 28), 155
Eisner (DE 192), 166
Elden (DE 264), 157
Elder (AN 20), 311
Eldorado (AGC 11), 273
Eldridge (DE 173), 166
Electra (AK 21/AKA 4), 331
Elizabeth C. Stanton (AP 69), 340
Elk (IX 115), 327
Elkhart (APA 80), 348
Elkhorn (AOG 7), 325
Ellet (DD 398), 124
Elliot (DMS 4/AG 104), 215
Ellis (DD 154/AG 115), 106
Ellyson (DD 454/DMS 19), 132
Elm (WAGL 260), 386
Elmore (APA 42), 347
Elokomin (AO 55), 322
El Paso (PF 41), 250
Elusive (AM 225), 225
Ely (DE 309), 157
Embattle (AM 226), 225
Embroil (AM 227), 227
Emery (DE 28), 155
Emmons (DD 457/DMS 22), *131*, 132
Emporia (PF 28), 248
Enceladus (AK 80), 332
Endicott (DD 495/DMS 35), *130*, 132, *214*
Endymion (ARL 9), 297
England (DE 635), 161
English (DD 696), 146
Engstrom (DE 50), 155
Enhance (AM 228), 227
Eniwetok (CVE 125), 64
Enoree (AO 69), 323
Enright (DE 216/APD 66), 158
Entemedor (SS 340), 201
Enterprise (CV 6), *37*, 38, *40*
Epperson (DD 719), 148
Epping Forest (LSD 4), 263
Equity (AM 229), 227
Erben (DD 631), 141
Ericsson (DD 440), 129
Eridanus (AK 92), 332
Erie (PG 50), *235*, *236*, 238
Ernest G. Small (DD 838), 150
Escalante (AO 70), 323
Escambia (AO 80), 324
Escanaba (WPG 77), 373
Escanaba (WPG 64), 376
Escape (ARS 6), 308
Escatawpa (AOG 27), 325
Escolar (SS 294), 199
Espada (SS 355), 201
Esselen (ATO 147), 355
Essex (CV 9), *41*, 42
Esteem (AM 230), 227
Estes (AGC 12), 276
Etamin (AK 93/IX 173), 332
Etlah (AN 79), 314
Eucalyptus (AN 16), 311
Eugene (PF 40), 248

Eugene A. Greene (DE 549), 175
Eugene A. Greene (DD 711), 148
Eugene E. Elmore (DE 686), 164
Euphane (WYP 360), 385
Eureka (IX 221), 252
Europa (AP 177), 340
Euryale (AS 22), 288
Evans (DD 552), 140
Evansville (PF 70), 250
Evarts (DE 5), 153
Event (AM 231), 227
Everett (PF 8), 248
Everett F. Larson (DE 554), 175
Everett F. Larson (DD 830), 150
Everglades (AD 24), 285
Evergreen (WAGL 295), *377*, 388
Eversole (DE 404), 174
Eversole (DD 789), 150
Ewing (WPC 137), 380
Execute (AM 232), 227
Extractor (ARS 15), 310
Extricate (ARS 16), 310

Fabius (ARVE 5), 298
Facility (AM 233), 227
Fair (DE 35), 155
Fairfield (AK 178), 334
Falcon (ASR 2), 289
Falgout (DE 324), 168
Fallon (APA 81), 348
Fall River (CA 131), 82
Fancy (AM 234), 227
Fanegal (SS 356), 201
Fanning (DD 385), 118
Fanshaw Bay (CVE 70), 58
Farenholt (DD 491), 129
Fargo (CL 85), 94
Fargo (CL 106), 98
Faribault (AK 179), 334
Farquhar (DE 139), 168
Farragut (DD 348), 112
Faunce (WPC 138), 380
Favorite (IX 45), 362
Fayette (APA 43), 347
Fechteler (DE 157), 158
Fechteler (DD 870), 152
Feland (AP 18/APA 11), 338
Fentress (AK 180), 334
Fergus (APA 82), 348
Fern (WAGL 304), 386
Fessenden (DE 142), 168
Fieberling (DE 640), 161
Fillmore (APA 83), 348
Finback (SS 230), 195
Finch (AM 9), 218
Finch (DE 328), 170
Finnegan (DE 307), 157
Fir (WAGL 212), 386
Firebush (WAGL 393), 388
Firedrake (AE 14), 328
Firm (AM 98), *222*
Fiske (DE 143), 168
Fiske (DD 842), 150

Gen. John Pope (AP 110), *337*, 342
Gen. J. R. Brooke (AP 132), 343
Gen. LeRoy Eltinge (AP 154), 347
Gen. M. B. Stewart (AP 140), 343
Gen. M. C. Meigs (AP 116), 342
Gen. M. L. Hersey (AP 148), 347
Gen. M. M. Patrick (AP 150), 347
Gen. O. H. Ernst (AP 133), 343
Gen. Omar Bundy (AP 152), 347
Gen. R. E. Callan (AP 139), 343
Gen. R. L. Howze (AP 134), 343
Gen. R. M. Blatchford (AP 153), 347
Gen. S. D. Sturgis (AP 137), 343
Gen. Stuart Heintzelman (AP 159), 347
Gen. T. H. Bliss (AP 131), 343
Gen. W. A. Mann (AP 112), 342
Gen. W. C. Langfitt (AP 151), 347
Gen. W. F. Hase (AP 146), 347
Gen. W. G. Haan (AP 158), 347
Gen. W. H. Gordon (AP 117), 342
Gen. W. L. Black (AP 135), 343
Gen. W. P. Richardson (AP 118), 342
Gen. William Mitchell (AP 114), 342
Gen. William Weigel (AP 119), 342
Genesee (ATO 55), 355
Genesee (AOG 8), 325
Geneva (APA 86), 348
Gentian (WAGL 290), 388
Gentry (DE 349), 172
George (DE 697), 161
George A. Johnson (DE 583), *162*, 163
George Clymer (AP 57/APA 27), 341
George E. Badger (DD 196/AVD 3/APD 33), 106
George E. Davis (DE 357), 172
George F. Elliot (AP 13), 335
George F. Elliot ii (AP 105), 342
George K. MacKenzie (DD 836), 150
George M. Campbell (DE 773), 167
George W. Ingram (DE 62/APD 43), 158
Gertrude L. Thebaud (WPYc 386), 385
Gherardi (DD 637/DMS 30), 135
Giansar (AK 111), 332
Gilbert Islands (CVE 107), 62, *63*
Gillespie (DD 609), 129
Gillette (DD 681), *160*, 161
Gilliam (APA 57), 348
Gilligan (DE 508), 175
Gillis (AVD 12), 303
Gilmer (DD 233/APD 11), 109
Gilmore (DE 18), 155
Giraffe (IX 118), 327
Girasol (PY 27), 240
Glacier (AK 183), 334
Gladiator (AM 319), 223
Gladwin (APA 106), 347
Gladwyne (PF 62), 250
Gleaves (DD 423), 126
Glendale (PF 36), 248
Glennon (DD 620), 132
Glennon (DD 840), 150
Globe (WYP 381), 385

Globe VIII (WYP 380), 385
Gloucester (PF 22), 248
Glynn (APA 239), 348
Goff (DD 247), 112
Goldcrest (AM 80), 219
Golden City (AP 169), 340
Golden Gate (WYT 94), 390
Goldenrod (WAGL 213), 386
Goldfinch (AM 77), 219
Goldring (SS 360), 201
Goldsborough (DD 188/AVD 5/APD 32), 106
Gold Star (AG 12), 359
Golet (SS 361), 201
Goodhue (APA 107), 347
Goodrich (DD 831), 150
Gordius (ARL 36), 297
Gordonia (AF 43), 329
Goshawk (AM 79/IX 195), 219
Goshen (APA 108), 347
Gosper (APA 170), 348
Goss (DE 444), 174
Gosselin (APD 126), 280
Grackle (AM 73), 219
Grady (DE 445), 174
Graffias (AF 29), 329
Grafton (APA 109), 347
Grainger (AK 184), 334
Grampus (SS 207), 193
Grampus (SS 523), 204
Grand Canyon (AD 28), 285
Grand Forks (PF 11), 248
Grand Island (PF 14), 248
Grand Rapids (PF 31), 248
Granville (APA 171), 348
Grapple (ARS 7), 308
Grasp (ARS 24), 308
Gratia (AKS 11), 332
Grayback (SS 208), 193
Graylag (AM 364), 231
Grayling (SS 209), 193
Grayling (SS 492), 204
Grayson (DD 435), 129
Great Lakes (AD 30), 285
Great Sitkin (AE 17), 328
Grebe (AM 43/ATO 134), 218
Greenbrier (WAGL 214), 386
Greene (DD 266/AVD 13/APD 36), 112
Greenfish (SS 351), 201
Greenlet (ASR 10), 289
Greenling (SS 213), 195
Greensboro (PF 101), 252
Greenwich Bay (AVP 41), 305
Greenwood (DE 679), 161
Greer (DD 145), 106
Gregory (APD 3), 276
Gregory (DD 802), 143
Greiner (DE 37), 155
Grenadier (SS 210), 193
Grenadier (SS 525), 204
Gresham (WPG 85), 363
Greyhound (IX 106), 362
Gridley (DD 380), 124

Heed (AM 100), 221
Heermann (DD 532), *137*, 138
Helena (CL 50), *72*, 85
Helena (CL 113), 98
Helena (CA 75), 79
Helios (ARB 12), 297
Helm (DD 388), 124
Hemlock (WAGL 217), 386
Hemminger (DE 746), 167
Hempstead (AVP 43), 305
Hempstead (APA 241), 348
Henderson (AP 1), 335
Henderson (DD 785), 148
Hendry (APA 118), 348
Henley (DD 391), 124
Henley (DD 762), 147
Hennepin (AK 187), 334
Henrico (APA 45), 347
Henry A. Wiley (DM 29), 212
Henry R. Kenyon (DE 683), 161
Henry T. Allen (AP 30/APA 15/AG 90), 338
Henry W. Tucker (DE 377), 172
Henry W. Tucker (DD 875), 152
Herald (AM 101), 221
Herald of the Morning (AP 173), 340
Herbert (DD 160/APD 22), 106
Herbert C. Jones (DE 137), 168
Herbert J. Thomas (DD 833), 150
Hercules (AK 41), 331
Herkimer (AK 188), 334
Hermes (WPC 109), 383
Hermitage (AP 54), *339*, 340
Herndon (DD 638), 135
Heron (AVP 2), 303
Herring (SS 233), 195
Herzog (DE 178), 166
Hesperia (AKS 13), 332
Heywood (AP 12/APA 6), 335
Heywood L. Edwards (DD 663), 141
Heyliger (DE 510), 175
Hibiscus (WAGL 218), 386
Hickory (WAGL 219), 386
Hickox (DD 673), 141
Hidalgo (AK 189), 334
Hidatsa (ATF 102), 354
Higbee (DD 806), *149*, 150
Highlands (APA 119), 348
Hilarity (AM 241), 227
Hilary P. Jones (DD 427), 126
Hilbert (DE 742), 166
Hill (DE 141), 168
Hilo (PG 58/AGP 2), 238, 290
Hilton Head (LSD 24), 266
Hingham (PF 30), 248
Hinsdale (APA 120), 348
Hissem (DE 400), 170
Hitchiti (ATF 103), 354
Hiwassee (AOG 29), 325
Hobby (DD 610). 129
Hobe Sound (AV 20), 303
Hobson (DD 464/DMS 26), 132
Hocking (APA 121), 348

Hodges (DE 231), 163
Hoe (SS 258), 197, *198*
Hoel (DD 533), 138
Hoel (DD 768), 148
Hogan (DMS 6/AG 105), *213*, 215
Hoggatt Bay (CVE 75), 58
Hoist (ARS 40), 308
Holder (DE 401), 170
Holder (DD 819), 150
Holland (AS 3/ARG 18), 287
Hollandia (CVE 97), 60, *61*
Hollis (DE 794/APD 86), 163
Hollister (DD 788), 150
Holly (AN 19), 311
Hollyhock (WAGL 220), 386
Holt (DE 706), 164
Holton (DE 703), 163
Honolulu (CL 48), 85, *86*
Hooper Island (ARG 17), 296
Hope (AH 7), 351
Hopewell (DD 681), 143
Hopi (ATF 71), 352
Hopkins (DMS 13), 215
Hopping (DE 155/APD 51), 158
Hop Tree (AN 62), 312, *313*
Hoquiam (PF 5), 248
Horace A. Bass (APD 124), 280
Hornbeam (WAGL 394), 388
Hornet (CV 8), 38, *40*
Hornet (CV 12), 42
Housatonic (AO 35), 324
Houston (CA 30), *69*, 67
Houston (CL 81), *92*, 94
Hovey (DMS 11), 215
Howard (DMS 7/AG 106), 215
Howard D. Crow (DE 252), 168
Howard F. Clark (DE 533), *173*, 175
Howard W. Gilmore (AS 16), 287
Howorth (DD 592), 141
Hudson (DD 475), 135
Hudson (WYT 87), 388
Hugh L. Scott (AP 43), 338
Hugh Purvis (DD 709), 146
Hugh W. Hadley (DD 774), 147
Hughes (DD 410), 126
Hulbert (DD 342/AVD 6), 112
Hull (DD 350), 114
Humboldt (AVP 21), 305
Hummer (AM 367), 231
Humphreys (DD 236/APD 12), 109
Humphreys (WYP 325), 385
Hunt (DD 674), 143
Hunter Liggett (AP 27/APA 14), 338
Hunter Marshall (APD 112), 279
Huntington (CL 77), 94
Huntington (CL 107), *97*, 98
Huron (PF 19), 248
Hurst (DE 250), 168
Huse (DE 145), 168
Hutchins (DD 476), 135
Hutchinson (PF 45), 250
Hyacinth (WAGL 221), 386

Mariposa (WAGL 397), 388
Marita (WPY 175), *375*, 385
Mariveles (IX 197), 328
Markab (AK 31/AD 21), 285
Marlin (SS 205), *192*, 195
Marmora (IX 189), 328
Marquette (AKA 95), 334
Mars (AR 16), 293
Marsh (DE 699), 161
Marshall (DD 676), 143
Martin (DE 30), 155
Martin H. Ray (DE 338), 170
Marts (DE 174), 166
Marvel (AM 262), 227
Marvin H. McIntyre (APA 129), 348
Maryland (BB 46), *6*, *23*, 24
Masbate (ARG 15), 296
Mascoma (AO 83), 324
Mason (DE 529), *156*, 157
Massachusetts (BB 59), 28, *29*
Massey (DD 778), *142*, 147
Mastic (AN 46), 312
Mataco (ATF 86), 354
Matagorda (AVP 22), 305
Matanikau (CVE 101), 60
Matanzas (AVP 46), 305
Matar (AK 119), 332
Mathews (AKA 96), 334
Matinicus (AG 38), 359
Mattabesset (AOG 52), 325
Mattaponi (AO 41), 323
Mattole (AO 17), 321
Maui (ARG 8), 296
Maumee (AO 2/AG 124), 317
Mauna Loa (AE 8), 328
Maurice J. Manuel (DE 351), 172
Maury (DD 401), *123*, 124
Mayfield Victory (AK 232), 334
Mayflower (WPG 183), *375*, 376
Mayo (DD 422), 126
Mayrant (DD 402), 124
Mazama (AE 9), 328
McAnn (DE 179), 166
McCaffery (DD 860), 152
McCall (DD 400), 124
McCalla (DD 488), 132
McCawley (AP 10/APA 4), 335
McClelland (DE 750), 167
McConnel (DE 163), 164
McCook (DD 496/DMS 36), 132
McCord (DD 534), *136*, 138
McCormick (DD 223/AG 118), *107*, 109
McCoy Reynolds (DE 440), 174
McCracken (APA 198), 348
McDermut (DD 677), 143
McDougal (DD 358), 114
McFarland (DD 237/AVD 14), 109
McGinty (DE 365), 172
McGowan (DD 678), 143
McKean (APD 5), 276
McKean (DD 784), 148
McKee (DD 575), 140
McLanahan (DD 615), 129

McLane (WPC 146), 380
McLennan (APA 246), 348
McNair (DD 679), 143
McNulty (DE 581), *162*, 163
Meade (DD 602), 129
Measure (AM 263), 227
Mecklenburg (APA 247), 348
Medea (AKA 31), 335
Medregal (SS 480), 204
Medrick (AM 369), 231
Medusa (AR 1), 292
Megara (ARVA 6), 298
Megrez (AK 126), 332
Mellena (AKA 32), 335
Mellette (APA 156), 348
Melucta (AK 131), 332
Melville (AD 2), *282*, 283
Melvin (DD 680), 143
Melvin R. Nawman (DE 416), 174
Memphis (CL 13), 85
Menard (APA 201), 348
Mendocino (APA 100), 347
Mendota (WPG 69), *374*, 376
Menelaus (ARL 13), 297
Menemsha (AG 39/WAG 274), *358*, 359, 390
Menges (DE 320), 168
Menhaden (SS 377), 202
Menifee (APA 202), 348
Menkar (AK 123), 332
Menominee (ATF 73), 354
Merak (AF 21), 329
Merapi (AF 38), 329
Mercury (AK 42/AKS 20), 331
Mercy (AH 8), 351
Meredith (DD 434), 129
Meredith (DD 726), 146
Meredith (DD 890), 152
Meredosia (IX 193), 328
Merganser (AM 135), 219
Meriwether (APA 203), 348
Mero (SS 378), 202
Merrick (AKA 97), 334
Merrill (DE 392), 170
Merrimack (AO 37), 322
Mertz (DD 691), 143
Mervine (DD 489/DMS 31), 132
Mesquite (WAGL 305), 388
Messick (WYP 358), 385
Metcalfe (DD 595), 141
Method (AM 264), 227
Metivier (DE 582), 163
Metomkin (AVP 47), 305
Mettawee (AOG 17), 325
Miami (CL 89), 94, *97*
Miantonomah (CMc 5/CM 10), *206*, 209
Micawber (WPYc 159), 385
Michigamme (AOG 65), 325
Micka (DE 176), 166
Midas (ARB 5), 297
Midland (AK 195), 334
Midway (AG 41), 359,
Midway (CVE 63), *57*, 58

Midway (CVB 41), 48, *49*
Mifflin (APA 207), 348
Might (PF 94), 244
Migrant (IX 66), 362
Milledgeville (PF 94), 252
Miller (DD 535), 138
Millicoma (AO 73), 323
Mills (DE 383), 170
Milton Lewis (DE 772), 167
Milwaukee (CL 5), 85
Mimosa (AN 26), 311
Minah (AM 370), 231
Mindanao (PR 8), *241*, 243
Mindanao (ARG 3), *294*, 296
Mindoro (CVE 120), 64
Mingo (SS 261), 197
Minidoka (AK 196), 334
Minivet (AM 371), 223
Mink (IX 123), 327
Minneapolis (CA 36), 71
Minnetonka (WPG 67), 376
Minos (ARL 14), 297
Minotaur (ARL 15), 297
Mintaka (AK 94), 332
Mirth (AM 265), 227
Mispillion (AO 105), 322
Mission Bay (CVE 59), 58
Mississinewa (AO 59), 322
Mississippi (BB 41), *19*, 20
Missoula (APA 211), 348
Missouri (BB 63), *30*, *31*, 32
Mistletoe (WAGL 237), 387
Mitchell (DE 43), 155
Mizar (AF 12), 329
Mizpah (PY 29), 240
Moale (DD 693), 146
Moberly (PF 63), 250
Mobile (CL 63), 94
Mobjack (AGP 7), 290
Moctobi (ATF 105), 354
Modoc (WPG 46), *364*, 365
Moffett (DD 362), 114
Mohawk (WPG 78), 373
Mohican (WYT 73), 388
Mojave (WPG 47), 365, *367*
Molala (ATF 106), 354
Monadnock (CMc 4/CM 9/ACM 10), 209
Monaghan (DD 354), 114
Mona Island (ARG 9), 296
Monitor (LSV 5), 261
Monomoy (AG 40/WAG 275), 359, 390
Monongahela (AO 42), 323
Monrovia (AP 64/APA 31), 342
Monssen (DD 436), 129
Monssen (DD 798), 143
Montague (AKA 98), 334
Montana (BB 67), *33*, 34
Montauk (LSV 6), *262*, 263
Montcalm (ATO 39), 352
Monterey (CVL 26), 48
Montgomery (DM 17), *210*, 212
Monticello (AP 61), 340

Montour (APA 101), 347
Montpelier (CL 57), *92*, 9
Montrose (APA 212), 348
Moore (DE 240), 168
Moose (IX 124), 327
Moosehead (IX 98), 360
Moray (SS 300), 199
Moreno (ATF 87), 354
Morris (DD 417), *125*, 126
Morris (WPC 147), 380
Morrison (DD 560), 140
Mosley (DE 321), 168
Mosopelea (ATF 158), 355
Motive (AM 102), 221
Mount Baker (AE 4), 328
Mount Hood (AE 11), 328
Mount Katmai (AE 16), 328
Mount McKinley (AGC 7), 273
Mount Olympus (AGC 8), 273
Mountrail (APA 213), 348
Mount Vernon (AP 22), 338
Mugford (DD 389), 124
Muir (DE 770), 167
Mulberry (AN 27), 311
Muliphen (AKA 61), 334
Mullany (DD 528), 138
Munargo (AP 20), 338
Munda (CVE 104), 60
Munsee (ATF 107), 354
Murphy (DD 603), 129
Murray (DD 576), 140
Murrelet (AM 372), 223
Murzim (AK 95), 332
Muscatine (AK 197), 334
Muskallunge (SS 262), 197
Muskeget (AG 48), 359
Muskegon (PF 24), 248
Muskingum (AK 198), 334
Muskogee (PF 49), 250
Mustang (IX 155), 362
Mustin (DD 413), 126
Myers (APD 105), 279
Myles C. Fox (DE 546), 175
Myles C. Fox (DD 829), 150
Myrmidon (ARL 16), 279
Myrtle (WAGL 263), 387

Nahant (AN 83), 314
Naifeh (DE 352), 172
Namakagon (AOG 53), 325
Nanok (WYP 169), 385
Nantahala (AO 60), 322
Nanticoke (AOG 66), 325
Naos (AK 105), 332
Napa (AT 32), 352
Napa (APA 157), 348
Narcissus (WAGL 238), 387
Narragansett (ATF 88), 354
Narraguagas (AOG 32), 325
Narwhal (SS 167), 186
Nashville (CL 43), 85
Nassau (CVE 16), 52
Natchaug (AOG 54), 325

431

Ogden (PF 39), 248
Ogeechee (AOG 35), 325
Oglala (CM 4/ARG 1), 293
Oglethorpe (AKA 100), 334
O'Hare (DD 889), 152
Ohio (BB 68), 34
Ojanco (SS 381), 202
Ojibway (WYT 97), 388
Okala (ARST 2), 298
Okaloosa (APA 219), 348
Okanogan (APA 220), 348
Okinawa (CVE 127), 64
Oklahoma (BB 37), 16
Oklahoma City (CL 91), *93*, 94
Oleander (WAGL 264), 387
Oliver Mitchell (DE 417), 174
Olmsted (APA 188), 348
Olympia (IX 40), 360
Omaha (CL 4), 85
Ommaney Bay (CVE 79), 58
Oneida (APA 221), 348
O'Neill (DE 188), 166
Oneota (AN 85), 314
Ono (SS 357), 201
Onondaga (WPG 79), 373
Onslow (AVP 48), 307
Ontario (ATO 13), 355
Ontonagon (AOG 36), 325
Opponent (AM 269), 227
Opportune (ARS 41), 308
Oracle (AM 103), 221
Orange (PF 43), 250
Orca (SS 381), 202
Orca (AVP 49), 307
Orchid (WAGL 240), 387
Ordronaux (DD 617), 129
Oregon (IX 22), 360
Oregon City (CA 122), 79, *81*
O'Reilly (DE 330), 170
Orestes (AGP 10), 290
Oriole (AM 7/ATO 136), 218
Orion (AS 18), 287
Oriskany (CV 18), 42
Oriskany (CV 34), 46
Orlando (PF 99), 252
Orizaba (AP 24), 338
Orleck (DD 886), 152
Ormsby (APA 49), 347
Ortolan (ASR 5), 289
Orvetta (IX 157), 363
Osage (LSV 3), 261
Osberg (DE 538), 175
Osmond Ingram (DD 255/AVD 9/APD 35), 112
Osmus (DE 701), 163
Osprey (AM 56), 219, *220*
Ossipee (WPG 50), 365
Ostara (AKA 33), 335
Osterhaus (DE 164), 164
Oswald (DE 767), 167
Oswald A. Powers (DE 542), 175
O'Toole (DE 527), 157
Ottawa (AKA 101), 335

Otter (DE 210), 158
Ottern (WYP 379), 385
Otterstetter (DE 244), 168
Otus (AS 20/ARG 20), 288
Overseer (AM 321), 223
Overton (DD 239/APD 23), 109, *111*
Owasco (WPG 39), *374*, 376
Owen (DD 536), 138
Owl (AM 2/ATO 137), *217*, 218
Oxford (APA 189), 348
Oyster Bay (AGP 6), 290
Ozark (CM 7/LSV 2), 205, 261
Ozbourn (DD 846), 150

Paddle (SS 263), 197
Paducah (PG 18), 233
Paiute (ATF 159), 355
Pakana (ATF 108), 354
Palau (CVE 122), 64
Palawan (ARG 10), 296
Palisade (AM 270), 227
Palisana (AF 39), 329
Palm (AN 28), 311
Palmer (DMS 5), 215
Palmetto (WAGL 265), 387
Palmyra (ARST 3), 298
Palo Blanco (AN 64), 314
Palo Verde (AN 65), 314
Pamina (AKA 34), 335
Pamanset (AO 85), 324
Pampanito (SS 383), 202
Panamint (AGC 13), 276
Panay (PR 5), 243
Panay (AG 41), 359
Panda (IX 125), 327
Pandemus (ARL 18), 297
Pandora (WPC 113), 383
Panther (IX 105), 254
Papago (ATF 160), 355
Papaw (WAGL 308), 388
Papaya (AN 49), 312
Parche (SS 384), 202
Pargo (SS 264), 197
Paricutin (AE 18), 328
Parker (DD 604), 129
Parks (DE 165), 164
Parle (DE 708), 164
Parris Island (AG 72), 254, 360
Parrott (DD 218), 109
Partridge (AM 16/ATO 138), 218
Pasadena (CL 65), 94
Pasco (PF 6), *247*, 248
Pasig (AO 89), 324
Pasig (AO 91/AW 3), 324, *326*
Pasquotank (AOG 18), 325
Passaconaway (AN 86), 314
Passaic (AN 87), 314
Passumpsic (AO 107), 322
Pastores (AF 16), 329
Patapsco (AOG 1), 325
Pathfinder (AGS 1), 317
Patoka (AO 9/AG 125), 317
Patroclus (ARL 19), 297

433

434

Polana (AKA 35), 335
Polaris (AF 11), 329
Pollack (SS 180), 190
Pollux (AKS 2), 332
Pollux (AKS 4), 332
Pomfret (SS 391), 202
Pomodon (SS 486), 204
Pompano (SS 181), 190
Pompano (SS 491), 204
Pompon (SS 267), 197
Ponaganset (AO 86), 324
Ponchatoula (AOG 38), 325
Pondera (APA 191), 348
Pontchartrain (WPG 70), 376
Pontiac (AF 20), 329
Pontotoc (AK 206/AG 94/AVS 7), 307, 334
Pontus (AGP 20), 292
Poole (DE 151), 168
Pope (DD 225), 109
Pope (DE 134), 167
Poplar (WAGL 241), 387
Porcupine (IX 126), 326, 327
Porpoise (SS 172), 189
Portent (AM 106), 221
Porter (DD 356), 114
Porter (DD 800), 143
Porterfield (DD 682), 143
Portland (CA 33), 71, 73
Portsmouth (CL 102), 94
Portunus (AGP 4), 290
Poseidon (ARL 12), 297
Potawatomi (ATF 109), 354
Potomac (AG 25), 359
Poughkeepsie (PF 26), 248
Power (DD 839), 150
Prairie (AD 15), 285
Prairie State (IX 15), 360
Pratt (DE 363), 172
Preble (DM 20/AG 99), 212
Prentiss (AKA 102), 335
Preserver (ARS 8), 308
Pres. Adams (AP 38/APA 19), 341
Pres. Hayes (AP 39/APA 20), 341
Pres. Jackson (AP 37/APA 18), 341
Pres. Monroe (AP 104), 341
Pres. Polk (AP 103), 341
Pres. Warfield (IX 169), 361, 362
Presidio (APA 88), 348
Presley (DE 371), 172
Preston (DD 379), 118
Preston (DD 795), 143
Prevail (AM 107) 221
Price (DE 332), 170
Prichett (DD 561), 140
Pride (DE 323), 168
Prime (AM 279), 228
Primrose (WAGL 316), 387
Prince Georges (AP 165/AK 224) 332
Princeton (CVL 23), 46
Princeton (CV 37), 46
Prince William (CVE 31), 52
Pringle (DD 477), 133, 135

Procyon (AK 19/AKA 2), 331
Project (AM 278), 228
Prometheus (AR 3), 292
Propus (AK 132), 332
Proserpine (ARL 21), 297
Protector (ARS 14), 309, 310
Proteus (AS 19), 287
Providence (CL 82), 94
Provo Victory (AK 228), 334
Prowess (AM 280), 228
Prudent (PG 96), 246
Pruitt (DM 22/AG 101), 212
PT 78, 259
PT 105, 257
PT 139, 257
PT 533, 259
PT 337, 259
Ptarmigan (AM 376), 223
Pudiano (SS 392), 202
Pueblo (PF 13), 248
Puerto Rico (CB 5), 34
Puffer (SS 268), 197
Puget Sound (AV 13), 301
Puget Sound (CVE 113), 62
Pulaski (WPC 149), 380
Purdy (DD 734), 147
Pursuit (AM 108), 221
Putnam (DD 537), 138
Putnam (DD 757), 147
Pyro (AE 1), 328

Quail (AM 15), 218
Quail (AM 377), 223
Quapaw (ATF 110), 354
Quastinet (AOG 39), 325
Queenfish (SS 393), 202
Queens (APA 103), 348
Quest (AM 281), 228
Quick (DD 490/DMS 32), 132
Quillback (SS 424), 203
Quincy (CA 39), 71
Quincy (CA 71), 79
Quinnebaug (AOG 71), 325
Quirinus (ARL 39), 298
Quiros (IX 140), 327

"R" Class submarines, 178, 179
Rabaul (CVE 121), 64
Raby (DE 698), 161
Raccoon (IX 127). 327
Racer (IX 100), 254
Racine (PF 100), 252
Radford (DD 446), 135
Rail (AM 26/ATO 139), 218
Rainier (AE 5), 328
Raleigh (CL 7), 84, 85
Rall (DE 304), 157
Ralph Talbot (DD 390), 116, 124
Ramapo (AO 12), 321
Rambler (WAGL 298), 387
Rampart (AM 282), 228
Ramsay (DM 16/AG 98), 212

437

Sarda (SS 488), 204
Sargent Bay (CVE 83), 58
Sargo (SS 188), *191*, 193
Sarita (AKA 39), 335
Sarpedon (ARB 7), 297
Sarsfield (DD 837), 150
Sarsi (ATF 111), 354
Sassafras (WAGL 401), 388
Satinleaf (AN 43), 312
Satterlee (DD 626), 132
Saturn (AK 49/AF 40), 332
Satyr (ARL 23), 297
Saucy (PG 65), 243
Saufley (DD 465), 135
Saugatuck (AO 75), 323
Saugus (LSV 4), 261
Sauk (WYT 99), 388
Saunter (AM 295), 228
Saury (SS 189), 193
Sausalito (PF 4), 246
Savage (DE 386), 170
Savannah (CL 42), 85, *91*
Savo Island (CVE 78), 58
Sawfish (SS 276), 197
SC 1009, *253*
SC 1472, *253*
SC 1497, *253*
Scabbardfish (SS 397), 202
Scamp (SS 277), 197
Scania (AKA 40), 335
Schenck (DD 159/AG 82), 106
Schley (DD 103/APD 14), 103
Schmitt (DE 676/APD 76), 161
Schroeder (DD 501), 138
Schuyler (AK 209), 334
Schuylkill (AO 76), *320*, 323
Sciota (ATO 30), 352
Scorpion (SS 278), 197
Scoter (AM 381), 223
Scott (DE 214), 158
Scout (AM 296), 228
Scranton (PF 63), 250
Scranton (CA 138), 82
Screven (AK 210), 334
Scribner (APD 122), 280
Scrimmage (AM 297), 228
Scroggins (DE 799), 163
Scuffle (AM 298), 228
Sculpin (SS 191), 193
Sculpin (SS 494), 204
Sculptor (AK 103), 332
Scurry (AM 304), 228
Seabird (WYP 330), *381*, 385
Sea Cat (SS 399), 202
Sea Cloud (WPG 284/IX 99), 362, 376
Sea Devil (SS 400), 202
Sea Dog (SS 401), 202
Seadragon (SS 194), 193
Sea Foam (IX 210), 328
Sea Fox (SS 402), 202
Seagull (AM 30/ATO 141), 218
Seahorse (SS 304), 199
Seal (SS 183), 190

Sea Leopard (SS 483), 204
Sealion (SS 195), 193
Sealion (SS 315), 199
Seaman (DD 791), 150
Sea Otter II (IX 53), 362
Sea Owl (SS 405), 202
Sea Panther (SS 528), 204
Sea Poacher (SS 406), 202
Searaven (SS 196), 193
Sea Robin (SS 407), 202
Seattle (IX 39), 360
Seaward (IX 209), 266
Seawolf (SS 197), 193
Sebago (WPG 42), 376
Sebastian (AK 211), 334
Sebasticook (AOG 72), 325
Sebec (AO 87), 324
Sederstrom (DE 31), 155, *156*
Sedge (WAGL 402), 388
Sedgwick (AKA 110), 334
Seekonk (AOG 20), 325
Seer (AM 112), 221
Seginus (AK 133), 332
Segundo (SS 398), 202
Seid (DE 256), 155
Seize (ARS 26), 308
Selfridge (DD 357), *102*, 114, *117*
Selinur (AKA 41), 335
Sellstrom (DE 255), 168
Seminole (AT 65), 335, 352
Seminole (AKA 104), 335
Semmes (AG 24), 359
Seneca (ATF 91), 354
Sennet (SS 408), 202
Senorita (SS 412), 203
Sentinel (AM 113), 221
Sentry (AM 299), 228
Sepulga (AO 20), 321
Sequatchie (AOG 21), 325
Sequoia (WAGL 243), 387
Sequoia (AG 23), 359
Serapis (IX 213), 328
Serene (AM 300), 228
Serpens (AK 97), 332
Serrano (ATF 112) 354
Severn (AO 61), 322
Sevier (APA 233), 348
Seymour D. Owens (DD 767), 148
Shackle (ARS 9), 308
Shad (SS 235), 195
Shadbush (WAGL 287), 387
Shadwell (LSD 15), 263
Shakamaxon (AN 88), 314
Shakori (ATF 162), 355
Shamrock Bay (CVE 84), 58
Shangri-La (CV 38), 69
Shannon (DM 25), *210*, 212
Shark (SS 174), 190
Shark (SS 314), 199
Shasta (AE 6), 328
Shaula (AK 118), 332
Shaw (DD 373), 118
Shawmut (CM 11), 209

Tang (SS 306), 199
Tangier (AV 8), 301
Tantalus (ARL 27), 297
Tappahannock (AO 43), 323
Tarawa (CV 40), 46
Tarazed (AF 13), 329
Tarbell (DD 142), 106
Tarpon (SS 175), 190
Tarrant (AK 214), 334
Tasker H. Bliss (AP 42), 338
Tate (AKA 70), 335
Tatnuck (ATO 27), 352
Tattnall (DD 125/APD 19), 106
Tatum (DE 789/APD 81), 163
Taurus (AF 25), 329
Taussig (DD 746), 147
Tautog (SS 199), 193
Tawakoni (ATF 114), 354
Tawasa (ATF 92), 354
Taylor (DD 468), 135
Tazewell (APA 209), 348
Teaberry (AN 34), 311
Teak (AN 35), 311
Teal (AVP 5), 303
Tekesta (ATF 93), 354
Telamon (ARB 8), 297
Telfair (APA 210), 348
Tellico (AOG 74), 325
Temptress (PG 62), *242*, 243
Tenacity (PG 71), 244
Tench (SS 417), 203
Tenino (ATF 115), 354
Tennessee (BB 43), *6, 21, 22,* 24, *65*
Tercel (AM 386), 223
Terebinth (AN 59), 312
Tern (AM 31/ATO 142), 218
Terror (CM 5), 205, *206*
Terry (DD 513), 138
Tesota (AN 71), 314
Teton (AGC 14), 276
Tetonkaha (AOG 41), 325
Texas (BB 35), 16
Thaddeus Parker (DE 369), 172
Thalassa (WPYc 348), 385
Thatcher (DD 514), 138
Theenim (AKA 63), *333*, 334
Theodore E. Chandler (DD 717), 148
The Sullivans (DD 537), 138
Thetis (WPC 115), 383
Thetis Bay (CVE 90), 60
Thomas (DE 102), 164
Thomas E. Fraser (DM 24), 212
Thomas F. Nickel (DE 587), 164
Thomas Jefferson (AP 60/APA 30), 341
Thomas J. Gary (DE 326), 168
Thomas Stone (AP 59), 341
Thomason (DE 203), 158
Thompson (DD 627/DMS 38), 132
Thorfinn (WYP 383), 385
Thorfjell (WYP 384), 385
Thorgault (WYP 377), 385
Thoris (WYP 378), 385
Thorn (DD 505), 138

Thorn (DD 647), 135
Thornback (SS 418), 203
Thornhill (DE 195), 166
Thornton (AVD 11), 303
Threadfin (SS 410), 203
Threat (AM 124), 221
Thresher (SS 200), *192*, 193
Thrush (AVP 3), 303
Thuban (AKA 19), 334
Thurston (AP 77), 340
Tiburon (SS 529), 204
Ticonderoga (CV 14), *45*, 46
Tide (AM 125), 221
Tidewater (AD 31), 285
Tiger (WPC 152), 380
Tigrone (SS 419), 203
Tilefish (SS 307), 199
Tillman (DD 641), 135
Tills (DE 748), 167
Timbalier (AVP 54), 307
Timmerman (DD 828), 150
Tingey (DD 539), 138
Tinian (CVE 123), 64
Tinosa (SS 283), 197
Tinsman (DE 589), 164
Tioga (WYT 74), 388
Tippecanoe (AO 21), 321
Tipton (AK 215), 334
Tirante (SS 420), 203
Tiru (SS 416), 203
Tisdale (DE 33), 155
Titania (AK 55/AKA 13), 332
Todd (AKA 71), 335
Toiler (ARS 47), 310
Token (AM 126) 221
Toledo (PF 33), 248
Toledo (CA 133), 82
Tolland (AKA 64), 335
Tollberg (APD 103), 279
Tolman (DM 28), *211*, 212
Tolovana (AO 64), 322
Tolowa (ATF 116), 354
Tomahawk (AO 88), 324
Tomatate (SS 421), 203
Tombigbee (AOG 11), 325
Tomich (DE 242), 168
Tonawanda (AN 89), 314
Topeka (CL 67), 94
Torchwood (AN 55), 312
Toro (SS 422), 203
Torrance (AKA 76), 335
Torsk (SS 423), 203
Tortuga (LSD 26), 266
Toucan (AM 387), *222*, 223
Tourmaline (PY 20), 240
Towaliga (AOG 42), 325
Towhee (AM 388), 223
Towner (AKA 77), 335
Townsend (AV 18), 301
Tracy (DM 19), 212
Tranquility (AH 14), 351
Transfer (IX 46), 360
Trapper (ACM 9), *208*, 209

441

ADDENDA

For later dispositions of ships in service after 1946 see the author's *US WARSHIPS SINCE 1945*.

p.10   July 13; correct spelling, Kolombangara

p.24   BB.47 WASHINGTON; add col 3; : /Westinghouse

p.28   NORTH CAROLINA class; Armor: belt 12 in., turrets 16 in.
SOUTH DAKOTA class; Armor: belt 12 in.

p.32   IOWA class; Armor: belt 12 in., turrets 17 in.

p.34   MONTANA class; add Armor: belt 16 in., turrets 18 in.

p.38   SARATOGA class; note on 3rd line, should read: During late 1941, 8 in. guns were replaced by 5 in. DP.

p.46   Add to notes: REPRISAL launched 1945 to clear slip. INDEPENDENCE sunk 29/1/51.

p.50   CVB.56 & 57; last column should read 28/3/45.

p.52   CVE.18 ALTAMAHA, 4th col; launched 25.5.42.
CVE.25 CROATAN; launched 1.8.42.

p.55   CVE.27 correct spelling: SUWANNEE.

p.62   CVE.106 BLOCK ISLAND; delete *.
CVE.110 SALERNO BAY; add *.
CVE.118 SICILY; add †.

p.64   CVE.121 RABAUL; add *.
CVE.124-139; canceled 12/8/45.
IX.64 WOLVERINE; tonnage 4,152 tons.
IX.81 Sable; tonnage 6,564 tons.

p.85   last col: OMAHA, CINCINNATI, RALEIGH, MARBLEHEAD, scrapped Philadelphia, others scrapped 1947. OMAHA, MILWAUKEE, CINCINNATI; builder should read: Seattle/Westinghouse, completed by Todd (Tacoma).
CL.41 PHILADELPHIA col. 5: add Scrapped 1974.
CL.43 NASHVILLE col. 5: add Scrapped 1982.
CL.46 PHOENIX col. 5: add Lost /4/82.
CL.47 BOISE col. 5: add Scrapped 1981.
CL.49 ST. LOUIS col. 5: add Scrapped 1976.

p.105 Caption to BERNADOU, change date to 1942.

p.112 Notes, line 7 from bottom change 'required' to 'requiring'
line 2 & 3 from bottom change Ix to IX.

p.114 DD.358 McDOUGAL; col. 5 add: Scrapped 8/49.
DD.359 WINSLOW col. 5 add: Scrapped 2/59.

p.138 TURNER; should read DD.506.

p.150 DD.845; should read BAUSELL.

p.155 DE.259; should read WILLIAM C. MILLER.

p.158 DE.205 NEWMAN; cols. 4 & 5 misaligned.

p.166 MARTS; should read DE.174.

p.167 DE.175 GAYNIER; col. 4: 30.1.44.
DE.752 CURTIS W. HOWARD; col. 4: 1.44.
DE.753 JOHN J. VAN BUREN; col. 4: 16.1.44.
DE.772 MILTON LEWIS; col. 4: 6.8.44.

p.190 SS.182 SALMON; col. 1: SS 182.
SS.184 SKIPJACK; amend col. 5: sunk 11/8/48.

p.195 SS.213; should read GREENLING.

p.200 picture: BLACKFIN (SS 322).

p.203 TURBOT, ULUA launched to clear slips.

p.205 col. 3 builder is Willamette.

p.216 picture: HARDING, add (see p.127).

p.223 AM.383 SURFBIRD; add Merc. HELENKA B. (1976).
Add Note: AM.82-99, named ADROIT, ADVENT, ANNOY, CONFLICT,
CONSTANT, DARING, DASH, DESPITE, DIRECT, DYNAMIC, EFFECTIVE,
ENGAGE, EXCEL, EXPLOIT, FIDELITY, FIERCE, FIRM and FORCE, were
built 1942 as minesweeper versions of steel-hulled submarine chasers. They were
reclassified PC.1586-1603 6/44 without names.

p.225 AM.141; lost 12/8/44.
AM.145; lost 12.8.44.
AM.147; lost 24/9/44.
AM.153 BUOYANT; add Chinese FEI HSING (5/46).
AM.214-215; completed at Charleston Navy Yd.

p.227 AM.243-245; builder: Winslow Marine.
AM.250; lost (date unknown).
AM.270; lost 14/8/45.

p.228 AM.290; last column HARCOURT MALCOLM (1947), COTTON BAY (1953) . . .
AM.291 RISK; add: lost 25/6/67.

p.231 AM.366; col. 5: Merc. SEA SCOPE (1964), ATLANTIC COAST (1975).

p.233 PG.17 DUBUQUE; col. 5: Scrapped 1947.
PG.18 PADUCAH; col. 5: Merc. PADUCAH (1947), BEULAH (1948), Scrapped
1949.

p.238 PG.22 TULSA; Scrapped 1946.
PG.59 SAN BERNARDINO; add: Scrapped 1968.

p.240 PY.18; add (ex-PC 459).
PY.31; last col: . . . Israeli MADZ (1948), Merc. SANTA MARIA DEL MARE
(1950).
Add note at bottom: 52 smaller vessels were added as Coastal Yachts (PYc). Of these,
7 were originally acquired as submarine chasers (PC.454-456, 458, 460, 509 & 826). An
8th boat, PC.457, was lost 14/8/41. PYc 4 was acquired as AM.78 and PYc40 as
AM.132.

p.241 CAPTOR; add: (see p.219).

p.276 Conversion of McFARLAND, WILLIAMSON, HULBERT and DECATUR to
APD.26-28, 30 canceled.

p.278 ROPER; add: (see p.105).

p.280 Conversion of the following canceled: ENGLAND (41), SCOTT (64), JENKS (67),
DURIK (68), BORUM (82), MALOY (83), DE LONG (137), COATES (138).

p.285 AD.17-19 originally ordered from Sun Sbdg Co.
AD.26-29 originally ordered from Tampa Sbdg.
AD.33 completed by Long Beach NYd.
AD.28 completed by Lake Washington SY.
Add: Note: AD.32 was to be of a new class, improved DIXIE type.

p.292 add to note at top: Conversion of LST.1152 to AGP.19 canceled.

p.295 SWIVEL; delete 'steel-hulled'.

p.301 PINE ISLAND; col. 1 should read AV.12.

p.303 AV.19-20; builder: Newport News.

p.310 ARS.35; Merc. CAROL ANN (1948).
ARS.36; Scrapped 1970.

p.312 AN.45; Merc. MARIA INES (1947), SEA PEARL (1956), lost 3/6/57.
AN.46; add: lost 27/6/75.
AN.54; Merc. MARILYN (1948).
AN.56; delete lost 12/4/63; add: PUELCHE (1970).
AN.63; irreparable damage 6/12/48.

p.314 AN.65; add: Merc. PORT OF BEAUMONT (1947), ARCTIC SEALER (1948), lost 15/4/63.
AN.80; should read SUNCOOK.

p.321 AO.16; col. 4: 26/11/19.

p.322 AO.33; should read SUWANNEE.

p.324 AO 102-104; completed as merchant ships.

p.327 144 & 145; col. 1 change XI to IX.

p.352 SAGAMORE; col. 1 change to ATO 20.

p.358 WYOMING; add: 30 Apr 1945.

p.359 AG.27; col. 5, add: British M.T.S. No.2 (1945), scrapped 1949.

p.360 Notes, line 3: should read AG.51-65.

p.363 Add note after IX 228: Missing numbers included 13 concrete barges (IX 149-154, 158-164) and a number of small sailing vessels. IRENE FORSYTE (IX 93) served as a Q-ship. Schooner RONAKI (IX 94) lost 18/6/43. IX 205 was a German trawler captured off Greenland 15/10/44..
GRESHAM; col. 4: 12.9.96 add note: Sold 1935 but reacquired 21/1/43.

p.365 UNALGA; col. 5: add: Merc. ULUA (1947).
OSSIPEE; col. 1: WPR 50.

p.373 COMANCHE; col. 1: WPG 76; col. 4: 6.9.34.

p.376 BODKIN (ex-Burke, ex-USS Nokomis); col. 3: 1000/14; col. 5: canceled 15/7/43.
MAYFLOWER; col. 3: 2690/96.

p.383 NIKE; col. 4: 7.7.34.
TRITON; col. 4: 7.7.34.

p.384 WYP.373; col. 2: should read BELLEFONTE.
BELMONT; sold 11/46.
BLANCHARD; decomm 11/43.
BLANCO; decomm 10/45.
BLAZE; 79/17; sold 3/46.
BOONE; 79/17; sold 3/46.
BOULDER; 55/06; decomm 6/43.
BOWSTRING; 79/17; sold 1/45.
BRONCO; sold 11/46.
BRUSSTAR; rtnd 6/43.
CADDO; rtnd 3/44.
CONANT; rtnd 12/43.
COVINGTON; rtnd 7/43.

p.385 EDWARDS; rtnd 3/44.
EUPHANE; rtnd 12/44.
GERTRUDE L. THEBAUD; rtnd 2/44.

GLOBE; acqd 1942; rtnd 7/43.
GLOBE VIII; acqd 12.42; rtnd 7/43.
HUMPHREYS; rtnd 3/44.
JOE; rtnd 3/44.
KODIAK; rtnd 4/44.
MADALAN; rtnd 10/45.
MARGARET; rtnd 6/43.
MARITA; sold 5/45.
MESSICK; rtnd 3/44.
MICAWBER; should read (ex-Nevada); rtnd 2/46.
NELLWOOD; sold 9/47.
NANOK; rtnd 9/44.
NOGAK; rtnd 7/44.
NORTHUMBERLAND; rtnd 3/44.
OTTERN; acqd 1942; rtnd 7/43.
PELICAN; rtnd 3/46.
POCAHONTAS; rtnd 3/45.
POL; rtnd 7/43.
REED; rtnd 3/43.
ROWE; rtnd 7/43.
SEABIRD; rtnd 7/44.
STEPHEN McKEEVER; rtnd 12/43.
THALASSA; sold 6/46.
THORFINN; decomm 7/43.
THORGAUT; rtnd 7/43.
THORFJELL; decomm 7/43.
THORIS; rtnd 7/43.
VERNON McNEAL; rtnd 3/44.
WARREN EDWARDS; rtnd 11/43.
WICOMICO; add: (ex-Catoctin 8/43); decomm 6/45.

p.388 CALUMET; col. 4: 28.9.34.
HUDSON; col. 4: 10/34.
NAVESINK, TUCKAHOE; col. 4: 28.9.34.
APALACHEE, YANKTON; col. 4: 29.4.43.
MOHICAN, CHINOOK; col. 4: 16.6.43.
OJIBWAY, SNOHOMISH, SAUK; col. 4: 10.9.43.

p.390 BEVERLY; add: (ex-Maurice R. Shaw) col. 4: 10.42.
ALEXANDER GRAHAM BELL; col. 4: 10/44 rtnd 12/44.
BISON; add: (ex-Beaufort, ex-President) col. 4: 2/43 sold 3/47.
BONNEVILLE; col. 3: 79/17 rtnd 9/45.
MacNICHOL; col. 3: 98/91.

p.391 STORIS; col. 4: 4.4.42.

p.407 add:
PC.357 collision US East coast 14th August 1941.